Exploring Communication Ethics

Exploring Communication Ethics is a comprehensive textbook on the ethical issues facing communication professionals in today's rapidly changing media environment.

Empowering students to respond to real-world ethical dilemmas by drawing upon philosophical principles, historical background, and the ethical guidelines of major professional organizations, this book is designed to stimulate class discussion through real-world examples, case studies, and discussion problems. Students will learn how to mediate between the best interests of their employers and their responsibilities toward other parties, and to consider how economic, technological, and legal changes in their industries affect these ethical considerations.

It can be used as a core textbook for undergraduate or graduate courses in communication or media ethics, and provides an ideal supplement for specialist classes in public relations, professional communication, advertising, political communication, or journalism and broadcast media.

Dr. Randy Bobbitt is a Florida-based textbook author, freelance writer, and veteran of three decades of teaching courses in journalism, media law and ethics, and public relations.

Exploring Communication Ethics

A Socratic Approach

Randy Bobbitt

Routledge
Taylor & Francis Group

NEW YORK AND LONDON

First published 2020
by Routledge
52 Vanderbilt Avenue, New York, NY 10017

and by Routledge
2 Park Square, Milton Park, Abingdon, Oxon, OX14 4RN

Routledge is an imprint of the Taylor & Francis Group, an informa business

© 2020 Taylor & Francis

Library of Congress Cataloging-in-Publication Data
Names: Bobbitt, Randy, 1955- author.
Title: Exploring communication ethics / Randy Bobbitt.
Description: New York, NY : Routledge, 2020. | Includes bibliographical references and index.
Identifiers: LCCN 2019047130 (print) | LCCN 2019047131 (ebook) |
ISBN 9780367334338 (hardback) | ISBN 9780367342081 (paperback) |
ISBN 9780429324475 (ebook)
Subjects: LCSH: Communication–Moral and ethical aspects. |
Journalistic ethics. | Advertising–Moral and ethical aspects. |
Public relations–Moral and ethical aspects.
Classification: LCC P94 .B635 2020 (print) |
LCC P94 (ebook) | DDC 302.2–dc23
LC record available at https://lccn.loc.gov/2019047130
LC ebook record available at https://lccn.loc.gov/2019047131

ISBN: 978-0-367-33433-8 (hbk)
ISBN: 978-0-367-34208-1 (pbk)
ISBN: 978-0-429-32447-5 (ebk)

Typeset in Baskerville
by Integra Software Services Pvt. Ltd.

Contents

10 Ethical Issues in Political Communication

Preface

Exploring Communication Ethics is the culmination of two decades' worth of work in researching, teaching, and writing about communication ethics.

Communication ethics is often a difficult subject for students to grasp, but it is important for those who plan on careers in journalism, broadcasting, advertising, and public relations. Basic knowledge of decision-making processes will often help you to operate in the best interests of yourself or your employer. Other times it involves respecting the rights and feelings of others.

Nearly all aspects of communication ethics are complex, in part because of the rapidly changing nature of the technology with which professional communicators work. That means encountering many questions for which there are no simple answers. As one of my favorite graduate school professors often told his Constitutional Law classes, sometimes the safest answer to legal and ethical questions is "sometimes ... maybe ... it depends."

Like many textbooks written by college professors, this book would not be possible without the help of many people. The biggest thanks go out to research librarians Britt McGowan and Sherri Johnson at the University of West Florida and my editors at Taylor & Francis, Brian Eschrich, Laura Briskman, and Nicole Salazar. Special thanks also to Mark Neuzil, Brent Kice, and Brian Steffen, who reviewed this book in its early stages.

In addition to those individuals, I also thank Bruce Swain, my former department chair at the University of West Florida, whose 1978 book *Reporters' Ethics* was one of the first on the subject.

About the Author

Dr. Randy Bobbitt is a Florida-based textbook author, freelance writer, and veteran of three decades of teaching courses in journalism, media law and ethics, and public relations. He has taught at the Cape Fear Community College (North Carolina), the University of West Florida, the University of North Carolina Wilmington, Marshall University, and the University of South Florida. He earned a Ph.D. in communication law and policy from Bowling Green State University and is a frequent speaker at student and professional conferences.

He is the author of two other textbooks: *Developing the Public Relations Campaign* (2005, 2009, and 2013, co-authored with Ruth Sullivan) and *Exploring Communication Law* (2017). His nonfiction books include *Controversial Books in America's K-12 Classrooms and Libraries* (2019); *Free Speech on America's K-12 and College Campuses* (2017); *Us Against Them: The Political Culture of Talk Radio* (2010); *Lottery Wars: Case Studies in Bible-Belt Politics* (2008); and *Who Owns What's Inside the Professor's Head?* (2002). He is currently working on his first novel, *I Don't Know What I Want, But I Know It's Not This*, a story about professors entering the latter stages of their careers.

Understanding the Socratic Dialogue

Although sometimes (and understandably) attributed to the Greek philosopher Socrates, the **Socratic dialogue** was actually developed by Plato, one of his star pupils, who dutifully named it in honor of his mentor.

The Socratic dialogue is sometimes confused with the **Socratic method**, which was indeed the creation of Socrates. In the Socratic method, Socrates would force students to jump through a series of intellectual hoops in order to defend what they believed to be the "truth." The objective of this sometimes confrontational method was to engage an individual student in a series of back-and-forth exchanges, repeatedly confronting him with information that contradicted his beliefs. Many times the result was the student's concession that his original idea was incorrect. Today, a formal application of the Socratic method is typically used in law school classes, not to embarrass or humiliate students but rather to sharpen their ability to "think on their feet" and prepare them for the rigors of courtroom debate. An informal application of the Socratic method is found in the format of political talk shows on radio and television, where the moderator attempts to embarrass or intimidate guests and assert his or her own intellectual superiority.

A true Socratic dialogue, however, is less confrontational and more constructive than the Socratic method. Developed by Plato after years of study under Socrates, the Socratic dialogue involves more than just a back-and-forth dialogue between professor and student. Instead, it involves a group of students or other participants discussing a topic in an atmosphere in which participants are encouraged to express their own opinions, agree with or add to the opinions expressed by others, or respectfully disagree with or challenge them. A successful Socratic dialogue requires a skilled moderator or facilitator, as well as sincere and enthusiastic participants. As James M. Lang wrote in his 2005 book *Life on the Tenure Track*, when the professor calls upon a student in a class discussion, it should be framed as "an invitation to participate in an intellectual feast, not as challenging the student to a duel."[1]

Contrary to popular belief, the desired objective of a Socratic dialogue is not consensus. Instead, the objectives are to motivate participants to examine their own beliefs, develop the self-confidence to express them, and encourage them to consider the opinions of others.

If your professor has chosen this textbook, he or she is likely to be an advocate of the Socratic dialogue method of teaching. His or her role will be to choose which questions from this book will be used (class time or student interest may limit the number of questions that can be used), assign the appropriate background reading, and keep the discussion on track. The role of the students is to prepare for the discussion in advance, participate enthusiastically, and answer challenging questions of the professor and classmates. Each class will build on those that came before it in a logical manner, making consistent attendance and punctuality a necessity. Both the professor and students must also be open to and respectful of divergent viewpoints. It is possible to criticize another person's ideas without criticizing the person. In an effective Socratic dialogue, there are no "right" or "wrong" answers.

Your professor will likely use the Socratic dialogue for the "Your Turn" section at the end of each chapter. That section consists of *case studies* (true stories), *discussion problems* (fictional stories), and *discussion questions* (broader, more general questions).

Here are some examples of how discussion problems begin:

> You're the editor of the *Mudville Daily Tribune* and one of your reporters has gotten in trouble because …

> You're the public relations officer at Mudville State University, and university administrators have asked you to …

> You're a videographer for a local television station and one of your sources has asked you to …

Most of the case problems will provide two or more possible courses of action and ask you to choose one and then be prepared to defend it. There are no right or wrong answers for discussion problems. Which side you take will not affect your course grade or how the professor evaluates your level of preparation—what is much more important is how well you are able to support your answer.

For most case studies and discussion problems, you should apply both philosophical principles (from Chapter 2) and the codes of ethics of major professional organizations (summaries are at the beginning of each chapter).

Note

1 James M. Lang, *Life on the Tenure Track: Lessons from the First Year*. Baltimore, MD: Johns Hopkins University Press (2005), p. 28.

1   An Overview of Communication Ethics

Defining Communication Ethics

Edward L. Bernays, one of the founding fathers of the modern public relations industry and an advocate of communicating ethically, once addressed an audience of college students and amused them and their instructors by analogizing unethical behavior to halitosis. "For many people, making unethical decisions is much like bad breath—you notice it on other people before you notice it on yourself," Bernays said.[1]

Bernays' unusual analogy aside, the communications profession has struggled for decades to develop or decide on a functional definition for what constitutes ethical behavior. Another commonly heard analogy comes from a 1964 U.S. Supreme Court case that required the justices to develop a definition for what was obscene and what was not. Justice Potter Stewart, one of the most quotable justices in the history of the Court, told his colleagues, "I cannot give you a definition for obscenity, but I know it when I see it."[2]

Many professional communicators feel the same way about ethics. Most have not looked at the field's ethical codes or even thought about the rights and wrongs of workplace conduct since taking their last exams in college. If someone were to ask them to explain the ethical principles involved in their work, most could not provide formal definitions or even define the parameters involved in making those decisions. But all of them know—or at least claim to know—right and wrong when they see it.

Nearly every textbook about communication ethics begins with a discussion of definitions, and this one is no exception. One accepted definition of ethics (in general) is "the study of what constitutes right or wrong, or good and bad, human behavior."[3]

Another common definition says that "ethics is what you do when no one else is looking."[4] Still another rule simply says that "a clear conscience makes a very soft pillow."[5]

To establish a more appropriate working definition for *communication ethics*, the best starting point is to distinguish the field from its legal counterpart, *communication law*. That comparison is appropriate because within the communication programs found at many universities, courses in ethics and law are taught by the same instructors and are found on the same page of the university catalog. At some institutions, the two topics are even combined into one course.

There are some important differences between ethics and law, however. While communication law deals mostly with formal rules and guidelines that are developed and enforced by federal, state, or local governments, communication ethics deals mostly with voluntary decisions that are made by individual professional communicators or media organizations. Put another way, while the law tells you what you *can and cannot do*, ethics tells you what you *should and should not do*. Justice Stewart and CBS News President Fred W. Friendly are both credited with the definition of media ethics as "knowing the difference between what you have the right to do and what is the right thing to do."[6]

The dean of a journalism department once paraphrased Stewart when he explained his opinion that print and broadcast journalists should not publish or broadcast the names of rape victims, even though the law allows them to do so. "Just because you can," he told student journalists and students taking his ethics class, "doesn't mean that you have to."[7]

Journalism professor Roy L. Moore asserts that ethical quandaries are a common part of a communicator's job and that print and broadcast reporters who are content to simply "do their jobs and avoid controversy" will find themselves with little to report. "It is difficult enough to avoid legal sanctions," Moore wrote in his 1999 textbook *Mass Communication Law and Ethics*. "It is virtually impossible to eschew ethical dilemmas."[8]

Sources of Ethical Guidance

The first step in making in decision is determining whether the issue is one of law or ethics. If it is a legal issue, the decision is clear. Regardless of whether the matter is personal or professional, an individual's first obligation is to make decisions that are consistent with applicable state and federal law. If the situation calls for an ethical decision rather than a legal one, individuals should make decisions based on applicable ethical codes, but in these cases the stakes are lower. Consequences for not making good decisions include being sanctioned by an employer or professional organization, or in some cases merely dealing with one's own conscience.

Professional communicators should constantly focus on earning and then maintaining credibility with their audiences as well as others whom they work with on a daily basis: their superiors, subordinates, peers, and sources. Journalists who lose their jobs because of ethical breaches will find it difficult to find subsequent jobs if the reasons for their dismissal are known.

Most professional communicators have a broad array of sources they can turn to guidance in decision-making. The most commonly referred-to sources are personal standards, employer standards, and the standards of professional and industry associations.

Personal Standards   ↗ room for bias

Some professional communicators make their decisions based solely on their own personal beliefs that are often influenced by their family or religious upbringing. Media ethicist Davis Young says that an individual cannot be forced to lose his or her values; those values are only lost if the individual chooses to relinquish them.[9] For individuals without good family role models, personal standards can be influenced by role models such as teachers, clergy, or youth counselors.

In many cases, an individual's "moral compass" is based on his or her religious beliefs. The term "Judeo-Christian ethics" refers to a set of rules based on biblical principles. The term was coined in the 1940s by British writer George Orwell and referred to the effort by Jews and Christians to find common ground in their views of decision-making.[10] In the eight decades since, the term has been used mostly by social conservatives to refer to a religion-based method of decision-making in personal, professional, and governmental matters, although a number of liberal presidents, including Franklin D. Roosevelt, Lyndon B. Johnson, and Jimmy Carter, have also used the term.

Other religious conservatives contend their "moral compass" is based on the Ten Commandments, including "Though shall not kill" and "Though shall not steal."

interesting because idk many people my age who make professional choices based on religion, even if they are very religious

An even simpler version of the "moral compass" idea is found in the "What Would Jesus Do?" catchphrase that became popular among Christian and Catholics in the 1990s. The phrase, often abbreviated as WWJD, became a popular method of reminding individuals to "act in a manner that would demonstrate the love of Jesus through the actions of the adherents."[11] According to counselors Karen B. Helmeke and Catherine Ford Sori, the phrase is "an attempt to call people to consider how Jesus Christ might respond to personal situations in daily life."[12]

Still another spiritual source of a "moral compass" is the so-called "Golden Rule," which states that you should "do unto others as you would want them to do unto you." Although found in the Bible (Matthew 7:12), similar versions are found in the writings of Greek, Egyptian, and Indian philosophers that pre-date the Christian era. Some of the versions are cast in the negative, such as, "what you do not want to happen to you, do not do it others either."[13] While the concept may sound valid in the abstract, media ethicists say it is unlikely it could be applied in journalism settings. "Much of the hard news in the paper deals with the wrongdoing or tragedy of people, and an editor cannot start leaving it out because he would shrink from seeing his own troubles in print," wrote Gene Gilmore and Robert Root in a media ethics textbook.[14]

Public relations textbook authors Laurie J. Wilson and Joseph D. Ogden even recommend young professionals beginning their careers start putting money in a "freedom fund" that would provide some degree of financial security in case leaving a job over ethical considerations became necessary. "If asked to do something that violates your personal code of ethics, you should first try to reason or negotiate not to do it," Wilson and Ogden wrote. "If you are unable to convince your employer, a freedom fund allows you to quit a job rather than compromise standards and jeopardize your professional reputation."[15]

Over the last thirty years, the fastest-growing concept in theological studies is a concept known as secular humanism, a lifestyle choice that is often in spiritual limbo: depending on whom you ask, it may or may not be a religion. It is based on concepts of living in harmony and caring for other people, but doing so without giving allegiance to or receiving direction from a deity. The term is often used to lump together both atheists (individuals who do not believe in God) and agnostics (individuals who question the existence of God).

Some critics of secular humanism, especially fundamentalist Christians, equate secular humanism with dishonesty and a lack of personal ethics. In a 2002 court case involving the Boy Scouts of America's policy of not allowing atheist students to become scouts, for example, one BSA leader was quoted as saying, "Anybody who doesn't believe in God isn't a good citizen … If an atheist found a wallet on the ground, they would pick it up, plunder the money, and throw the wallet back on the ground."[16]

Researchers, however, have found that secular humanists are just as moral and ethical as Christians. The difference, they have found, is that while Christians find their "moral compass" in the Bible and church beliefs, secular humanists base their decision-making on internal forces, such as their own conscience.

"There can be no doubt that for some people, religion provides grounding for ethical behavior, but it would be a mistake to conclude that religion is necessary for morality, or that without religion there would be moral decay," wrote attorney and secular humanist David Niose in his 2012 book *Nonbeliever Nation*. "For others, experience and reason, not divine revelation, teach us what is right and wrong. We may have a sentimental attachment to the church of our upbringing, and we may even have learned some lessons about right and wrong through the religious teachings of that church, but that does not mean our underlying sense of right and wrong is of divine origins."[17]

Sociology professor and author Phil Zuckerman claims that advocates of Judeo-Christian ethics do not hold a monopoly on the Golden Rule and states that "secular morality depends on little else than not harming others and helping those in need, both of which flow easily and directly from the Golden Rule's basic, simple logic of empathetic reciprocity."[18]

Employer Standards

Most media outlets, as well as advertising and public relations agencies, have employee policy manuals that explain the ethical principles that employees are expected to follow. The degree to which companies enforce those guidelines varies greatly. "NPR is primarily a news organization," begins the introduction to National Public Radio's Code of Ethics and Practices. "We are always testing and questioning the credibility of others. We have to stand that test ourselves."

Many working journalists look at ethical codes with some degree of skepticism. Among the reasons cited for that attitude are the perception that codes are too often written in negative terms; some consist mostly of lists of behaviors that are forbidden rather than lists of positive behaviors to be emulated. Another criticism is that too much adherence to ethical codes results in "wishy-washy journalism." Much like libel litigation has resulted in a "chilling effect" that discourages journalists from aggressively pursuing controversial stories, being overly concerned with ethical rules might result in a reluctance to pursue certain stories for fear of hurting the feelings of news sources or causing them embarrassment.[19]

Many media scholars point out that unfortunately many employer-based codes of ethics are not taken seriously because they are either not enforced by management or ignored by journalists because they were not asked to contribute to their creation. Numerous studies have shown that codes of ethics are rarely discussed in newsrooms.[20]

Code of ethics specific to an organization are common in the journalism business. Some noteworthy examples include *The New York Times'* Code of Ethics or the Gannett Newspaper Division's Principles of Ethical Conduct for Newsrooms. Some large newspaper chains, such as Knight-Ridder and Scripps-Howard, combine their ethical codes with their style manuals.

Inside and outside the media, employer-specific codes are designed to help in training new hires and teach them the "rules of the road." Some employers use adherence to ethical codes as gauges by which they can measure employee performance, and in some cases document reasons for termination.

Industry and Professional Association Standards

When professional communicators find their personal standards and employer policy manuals are either contradictory or simply not helpful, they can turn to the formal ethical guidelines of the profession in which they are employed.

Media historians believe the Society of Professional Journalists (SPJ) was the first professional organization to develop a code of ethics for journalists, doing so in 1923. At the time, the American government was plagued by a series of political scandals—most of them associated with the presidency of Warren G. Harding—and the SPJ announced that if the profession was going to scrutinize the ethical misdeeds of politicians, it must first make sure its own house was in order. The best way to do that, the organization's leaders believed, was to develop and enforce a code of ethics that placed journalists on a higher ethical plane than politicians and individuals employed in other fields.

In terms of print journalism, the Commission on Freedom of the Press concluded in1947 that the better job the media can do in self-regulating—through codes of ethics or other means—the less likely it is that government agencies will step in to do so.[21]

In addition to the SPJ's guidelines for individual journalists, the American Society of Newspaper Editors (ASNE) and the Radio Television Digital News Association (RTDNA) provide guidelines for media organizations as a whole. These codes deal with issues such as conflicts of interest, correcting errors in a timely manner, respect for the privacy of persons in the news, and the use of confidential sources. The Public Relations Society of America, International Association of Business Communicators, and the American Advertising Federation have established similar guidelines for those fields. The PRSA, IABC, and AAF codes deal with issues such as conflicts of interest, confidentiality, truthful communication, fair competition, and respectful treatment of past and present clients.

The six professional associations listed above have one thing in common: If you skim their publications, survey their websites, and look at the agendas from their conferences, you will see that ethics and professional standards is one of the most talked-about topics among those professions in the past three decades—perhaps second only to the impact of technology.

In many fields, codes of ethics have been viewed as too superficial to be of any value. "A code of ethics cannot be effective unless it addresses a profession's important ethical issues," wrote Shelby D. Hunt and Lawrence B. Chonko in an article in *Journal of Advertising*. In one example, the authors found that of the twelve major ethical issues faced by the advertising and marketing industry, only four of them were addressed by any of the professional organizations' codes of ethics.[22]

Joann Byrd, the ombudsman at *The Washington Post* in the 1980s, once analogized journalism ethics to a "stern old woman, sitting in a rocking chair on her verandah, her lips pursed … she says only one thing: No. Journalists don't like her, and they don't invite her to their parties."[23]

In his 1996 book *Ethics in Human Communication*, ethicist Richard Johannesen wrote that meaningful ethical codes must use clear language, address the specific issues faced by the profession, state realistic goals, and be enforceable.[24]

Industry-wide codes are designed to enhance the public perception of the fields, but research produces no empirical evidence that it does.[25]

The Three Sources Sometimes Agree and Sometimes Don't

In some cases, professional communicators may draw upon all three sources for help in decision-making. But what happens when a professional communicator's personal beliefs are in conflict with the standards of their employer or industry? Most communicators would tend to follow their personal beliefs rather than industry standards, especially for the long term. Those who place loyalty to their employer or industry above adherence to their personal standards for conduct would likely do so only in short-term circumstances.

The late Mike Wallace, a veteran reporter for CBS News and one of several featured interviewers on the long-running program *60 Minutes*, wrote in a 2010 book that when the three sources are in conflict, it is up to journalists to "find their own moral compass," which he defined as a friend, family member, or co-worker whose opinion the journalist trusts. Wallace cited the example of former CBS colleague Bernard Kalb, who admired legendary anchor Edward R. Murrow so much that he often asked himself, when faced with an ethical dilemma and conflicting opinions about how to resolve it, "What would Murrow do?"[26]

The Changing Nature of the Media

Libertarianism vs. Social Responsibility

Media historians studying the development of American media over the last two centuries have divided that history into two eras: that of "libertarianism" and "social responsibility."

Libertarianism was the prevailing philosophy guiding the American media through the 1800s and early 1900s. Most journalists of the day felt free to publish anything they pleased, even content that bordered on being defamatory.

The powerful newspaper publishers of the time had considerable influence in molding social and political trends. The development of inexpensive printing methods (the so-called "penny press") allowed newspaper circulation to expand beyond the small circle of intellectual and privileged business leaders and outward to less-educated, lower-income audiences. Publishers became successful and wealthy by lowering production costs, increasing circulation, and expanding their advertising bases. The philosophy of that time was that newspapers could succeed in their role as "watchdogs" on the government and major corporations while still returning a profit to their owners and shareholders.

In the early 1900s, American media shifted away from the libertarian philosophy and toward a newer approach called **social responsibility**, an idea that is theoretically still followed today. The social responsibility model is similar to the libertarian model in that the media are free to disseminate any information they consider important. But instead of stopping there and expecting the audience to interpret the information to judge its truth and value, the media take the additional step of helping the audience to interpret the information and make judgments about its value and importance.

The social responsibility model continues to emphasize the "watchdog" role of the media. In the early 1900s, journalists known as "muckrakers" believed that the accumulation of wealth and economic power was harmful for democracy because it resulted in less choice for consumers. Authors and journalists such as Ida Tarbell, Upton Sinclair, and other muckrakers used the watchdog approach to investigate large corporations they believed to be exploiting their employees, unduly influencing politicians, and misleading or neglecting consumers. Joseph Pulitzer's *New York World* was one of the first newspapers to give the muckrakers a venue to perform that role.

The term "social responsibility" can be traced back to the Hutchins Commission, an academic study launched in 1947 by the University of Chicago and the ownership of *Time* magazine. It was named after Robert M. Hutchins, then president of the university. The purpose of the project was to study the impact of the news media on American culture and determine what role the media should play in society. After several years of work, the commission issued its findings which are used today as theoretical guidelines for journalism schools and media organizations. According to the commission, the news media should (1) place the news of the day in context, (2) provide a realistic picture of society, (3) provide an outlet for diverse viewpoints, and, most importantly, (4) perform their watchdog function on government and big business.

Today, that latter idea has been encapsulated into the journalism buzz-phrase "the people have a right to know." While sometimes erroneously attributed to the First Amendment (which says nothing about the people having the right to know), the phrase is more accurately attributed to the Hutchins Commission findings, as well as to the Society of Professional Journalists' Code of Ethics. The SPJ code cites the "people's right to know" as one of the cornerstones of the journalism business.

As more readers get their national news from online sources, many small and mid-size daily newspapers are hoping that placing more emphasis on local people, businesses, and events will help them survive. While online sources can cover local news as well, daily newspapers claim that their reporting will be more thorough because of the time put into attending government meetings and examining public documents. Using the term "hyper-local," news executives believe that readers will choose daily newspapers (or their online counterparts) instead of purely online sources that have no hard-copy versions. *Pensacola News Journal* Executive Editor Richard Schneider uses the example of his newspaper using wire-service copy to cover the Super Bowl and World Series while using its local reporting staff to cover the games involving local high school football and baseball games, and using wire-service copy to cover the Academy Awards while using its staff to cover performances of the local high school drama club and other sources of local entertainment.[27]

A *Washington Post* columnist used the example of a dollar-store opening in rural Ohio as an example of a news event that would be ignored by national media but would be perfect for a local daily newspaper. "In southern Ohio, the opening of a dollar store is real news because it means that local residents no longer have to drive 30 minutes or more to buy important household and grocery items," wrote Gary Abernathy in a 2017 column about the plight of small-town dailies. "Small-town newspapers report hard news and local political controversies. But they also do stories on dollar-store openings, because sometimes their presence as the only store in town is real news that will affect lives. They also feature stories on school bus route changes, real news to parents who might have to get up an hour earlier or make new childcare arrangements."[28]

Special-audience newspapers are moderately successful in both their print and online editions. Most major cities have weekly publications serving black, Asian, Latino, and LGBT audiences.

One of the fastest-growing category of specialty publications consists of those serving Native American reservations. Research conducted by the Native American Journalists Association (NAJA) reveals that independent weekly publications serving reservations are more successful (both in advertising sales and readership numbers) than the special editions published by nearby daily newspapers.[29]

In terms of the LGBT audience, the so-called "gay press" has reported successful financial times as well. Industry publications such as *Editor & Publisher* report that those publications, mostly weeklies, are far more successful than in the past of attracting mainstream advertisers rather than depending on just gay-oriented businesses for financial support.[30] Successful papers serving the LGBT audience include the *Washington Blade* in the nation's capital, *Bay Windows* in Boston, *Between the Lines* in Detroit, *Out & About* in Nashville, and the *Dallas Voice* in Texas.

One of the primary news organizations dealing with women's issues is the Fuller Project, a non-partisan, nonprofit news organization reporting globally and in the United States. Founded in 2014, some of the organization's primary supporters are *The New York Times*, *Newsweek*, Cable News Network (CNN), National Public Radio (NPR), *The Washington Post*, *USA Today*, and *The Atlantic*. Among the topics the organization researches and monitors are women's rights in developing countries, workplace issues in the United States, and international sex trafficking.

"Women are persistently underrepresented in news. Our reporting addresses this gap in coverage through investigative, explanatory, and solutions-driven reporting. We publish our reporting with the world's leading news outlets, including locally."[31]

The organization is named in honor of Margaret Fuller (1810–1850), the first American war correspondent.

* different sectors of journalism to address diff issues / stories

Ethics and Decision-Making in Journalism Today

Here are some of the most significant trends that have either direct or indirect effects on how journalists, their editors, and other professional communicators make ethical decisions.

Technology

As they have in most areas of society, the Internet and social media have created both opportunities and challenges for professional communicators and the companies that employ them. For newspapers, magazines, and television stations and networks, the Internet—as well as other delivery devices such as smartphones and tablet computers—represents the opportunity to reach larger audiences, including individuals who may not subscribe to the hard copy of the newspaper or watch a traditional television newscast. From an employment standpoint, the Internet creates more opportunity for journalists, as newspaper and television stations need larger and more technology-oriented professionals who are capable of quickly adapting to new methods of gathering and presenting the news. Many college journalism programs are teaching future journalists to prepare news stories in three formats—print, broadcast, and online. One example of the trend is found in college catalogs, where separate listings for courses with titles such as "Newspaper Reporting" and "Broadcast Reporting" have been replaced with more general courses with titles such as "Media Reporting." In professional settings, the two terms that have emerged from this trend are **media convergence** and the **common newsroom**.

While the Internet provides another outlet for established media organizations to reach their audiences, it has also turned out to be a competitor for those same organizations. Upstart news organizations that produce web-only content, as well as individual bloggers who seek the same professional status and privileges as traditional journalists, have a built-in advantage in terms of the speed with which they can get information to their audiences.

As of 2019, many established media organizations still look at media convergence as either "experimental" or a "work in progress." Since the turn of the new century, large media corporations that have found a way to make their print and online products complement each other have survived and will continue to survive, although the era of monopolies and massive profits have been replaced by an era of "just getting by."[32]

Shortly before his death in 2012, CBS news veteran Mike Wallace commented on the trend. Wallace opined that one day in the future, traditional hard-copy newspapers and magazines will be hard to find, and that younger members of the audience will think it's completely normal for such publications to exist only online. But Wallace was not at all pessimistic, commenting that "the transition will take much longer than most people think, but it is inevitable."[33] *Washington Post* editor Marcus Brauchli added that "it doesn't ultimately matter whether newspapers survive or not … what matters is that journalisms survives … that it remains independent and continues to hold the state and the powerful accountable."[34]

Prior to the growth of the Internet in the 1990s, the generalization among media researchers was that consumers with high levels of education and income preferred daily newspapers over television, while those with relatively lower levels of education and income preferred television over newspapers.[35] But for the last two decades, the popularity of the Internet and social media has affected those numbers. The latter category still prefers television, but the former is now dividing its attention between the traditional daily newspaper and online sources. Despite the growing popularity of online news services, research indicates that readers will understand and retain far more information from a printed source than an online source.[36]

tech = ad = positive

The advertising industry has also taken advantage of the new technology in the form of banner and "pop-up" advertising and other forms of direct-response advertising that many Internet users find intrusive. Despite the negative connotation, many advertisers have found the Internet and social media to be effective ways to execute either web-only campaigns or web-based promotions that complement other forms of advertising.

For the public relations industry, the Internet presents both opportunities and challenges. The opportunities include the potential to communicate more effectively with employees, stockholders, potential stockholders, customers, potential customers, and the media. But the technology also presents a number of potential threats, as organizations and their public relations staffs must deal with angry consumers and advocacy groups that launch their criticisms using a variety of non-traditional media such as online review sites, blogs, and social media platforms.

The Internet age has produced a new challenge for employers as they struggle to find a balance between respecting the privacy and free-speech rights of their employees and their own interests in protecting their organizational reputations. The result is an increase in the number of employers who regularly monitor (depending on which survey being considered, the percentage is somewhere between 60 and 85 percent) and sometimes take punitive action. Examples in Chapter 12 will include stories of a school teacher fired over the content of her Facebook page, an employee of a high-tech firm fired for expressing a controversial political opinion on his own blog, and a public official fired for making critical comments on social media regarding a Supreme Court nominee.

Competition, Clutter, and the Need for Speed

In 1481, a letter reporting the death of a Turkish sultan took two years to reach England. In 1841, in took nearly four months for news of the death of President William Henry Harrison to reach California.[37]

Since the 1980s, competition for news and advertising revenue among newspapers, broadcast networks, cable networks, and Internet news services results in more cases of bad decision-making, carelessness, sloppy reporting, and clutter. As many media critics are fond of saying, the competition among media outlets often spins out of control as journalists and their employers place too much importance on being first with a news story and not enough emphasis on being accurate.

An issue closely associated with competition is that of the speed with which journalists gather and report news. For most of the previous century, daily newspapers were faced with only two deadlines per day—late morning for an afternoon newspaper and early evening for the next day's morning newspaper. When television broadcasters established news operations in the 1960s, the deadline structure was similar, as producing only one newscast per day meant having only one deadline per day. But in the 1970s, local television stations began to offer late evening newscasts, and in 1980s they added newscasts at mid-day and again in the late afternoon—in effect increasing the number of daily newscasts from one to as many as four. Another development of the 1980s was the emergence of twenty-four-hour cable news channels. The result of the latter two phenomena is the creation of nearly round-the-clock deadlines. The growth of Internet news services only compounds the deadline problem.

In their 2008 book *No Time to Think: The Menace of Media Speed and the 24-Hour News Cycle*, authors Howard Rosenberg and Charles S. Feldman point out that speed at expense of accuracy is not a problem known only to American media. They quote a British Broadcasting Corporation (BBC) guide for reporters that reads, "Your story must be accurate, impartial, balanced, and uphold the values of BBC News … never publish anything that you do not understand, that is speculation, or inadequately source." And then, the authors point out, with no sense of contradiction the statement adds, "Get the story as fast as you can … we encourage a sense of urgency – we want to be first."[38]

The Radio Television Digital News Association's Code of Ethics states that terms such as "trending," "going viral," and "exploding on social media" may increase urgency, but these phenomena only heighten the need for strict standards of accuracy.[39]

The Debate over the Role of Journalism

The shift toward "public service journalism" that began in the 1990s remains controversial in the new century. Newspapers and television stations of all sizes organize "town hall meetings" to gather public input on local issues, sponsor holiday toy drives and pet adoption programs, help blood banks recruit donors, and assist nonprofit organizations in reaching potential volunteers and donors. Some media historians and other critics believe that such efforts place journalists in roles far outside those of journalistic tradition. But others are not concerned, commenting that the trend is just an interesting development in an ever-evolving field. Some observers believe that public service journalism might represent the only way that traditional print and broadcast media outlets can survive in a media jungle dominated by the Internet.

The Need for Newsroom Diversity

Although media-related industries made great strides in the area of newsroom diversity between the 1970s and 1990s, those efforts have stalled in the new century. Surveys by organizations such the National Association of Black Journalists indicate that many young minority journalists become disillusioned early in their careers and leave the profession to explore other fields where they perceive opportunities to be better. One commentator responded to the grim numbers by predicting even grimmer numbers in the future, as minority journalists feel "disrespected, unappreciated, undercompensated, underdeveloped, and uninspired."[40] The issue is discussed in more detail in Chapter 4.

Shifts in Ownership

One trend growing since the 1980s is that of more newspapers and broadcast outlets being owned by corporations (or wealthy individuals) who run those outlets as profit-making businesses and fewer being owned by families that see their purpose being public service rather than profits.

Newscorp, owned by Australian business mogul Rupert Murdoch, has grown steadily over the last three decades and now includes *The Wall Street Journal* and the cable television channel Fox News. In 2013, Jeff Bezos, founder of Amazon.com, purchased the *The Washington Post* but has said he has no desire to purchase additional media outlets or attempt to compete with Murdoch for influence in the industry.

While the alleged harm from such purchases is difficult to quantify, media critics worry that if the trend continues, the result with be more and more outlets owned by fewer and fewer companies. That lack of competition would limit the diversity of information sources available to the mass audience. Critics also worry that the emphasis on profits over public service will weaken the media's role as "watchdogs" over the government and business. Corporate ownership, combined with the loss of advertising revenue to non-journalistic outlets such as Craigslist, has already resulted in the loss of thousands of newsroom jobs, which media critics have blamed for a decrease in the quality of journalism and increase in editorial workloads.

The Debate over "Who Is a Journalist?"

The growth of social media has reignited the debate over "who is a journalist?" In the 1970s and 1980s, the debate was based on the popularity of desktop-publishing software and the ability of anyone to produce a slick and professional-looking community newsletter containing local news and gossip. While those hard-copy publications still exist, they have been surpassed in popularity by social media platforms. Even though the debate continues over whether or not producers of social media content should be treated as "journalists" in terms of legal protection, the court system has still not provided consistent legal opinions. Producers of social media content have also seen mixed results in their attempts to be treated with the same level of access to governmental news conferences and other news events.[41]

"Bloggers may claim to be journalists, but they are not journalists in the traditional sense," stated a 2019 op-ed in the *Pensacola News Journal*. "The blogger is not going to sit through a four-hour school board meeting or spend an entire day at the courthouse poring over government records. He or she will wait for the real journalists to do that, then write commentary about what the journalists find and call that 'news.'"[42]

Americans' Cynical View of the News Media

Leon Nelson Flint, a journalism professor at the University of Kansas, once conducted a study to measure public perception of American newspapers. He found that the audience's complaints included (1) news is often distorted, (2) newspapers invade individuals' privacy, (3) stories involving sex and scandal are published solely to increase circulation, and (4) newspapers are overly suspicious and critical of government and businesses.

What year would you guess the results of the study were published? Maybe 2019, when President Donald Trump accused the media of peddling "fake news"? Maybe 1995, when many Americans said the media went overboard in its coverage of the scandals surrounding the presidency of Bill Clinton? Or perhaps 1973, when many Americans said they were tired of the constant coverage of the Watergate scandal?

None of the above; in order to find the results of Flint's study you would have to track down the book he wrote—in 1925.[43]

Flint, a veteran journalism educator and author of what is believed to be the first textbook written for high school journalism classes, conducted his research at a time when daily newspapers were the primary source of news for most Americans. Radio was mostly for music, magazines dealt mostly with celebrity news and popular culture, and television didn't yet exist. And the Internet was still seventy years away.

The point being made here is that criticism of the media is not a new phenomenon. For much of the previous century, Americans had a love–hate relationship with the media; they appreciated the spotlight it focused on corruption and wrongdoing, but didn't like it when the news hit too close to home. Politicians, entertainers, and business leaders—whose scandals and failures were often topics of media coverage—were even more critical than the average citizen.[44]

While Americans generally appreciate freedom of speech and press as abstract concepts, many hold cynical views about the state of American media in respect to specific media behaviors. One common complaint is that the media tends to over-report the negative and under-report the positive. "Millions of Social Security checks worth billions of dollars are delivered accurately and on time each month," wrote Gannett News columnist Richard Benedetto. "But let one recipient run into a bureaucratic snafu and the news media stand ready to paint the entire system as a hopeless boondoggle."[45] The media defend themselves against such criticism by claiming that their job is to report the unusual and point out the problems, not to praise government agencies and companies for the routine performance of their jobs. Speaking to a group of college journalists, a newspaper publisher once said that "when we pick up the telephone and get a dial tone, we're not going to celebrate that because it's what we expect ... but when phone service is disrupted city-wide, it's something that we need to write about."

On a similar note, another complaint of consumers is that the media sometimes go beyond simply reporting on conflict, and often create conflict—in effect, creating news stories where no news stories previously existed.

One example of the problem is illustrated in a series of conversations that took place in the newsroom of a mid-size daily newspaper in the Southeast. During a storm that passed over a government office building, a large tree was struck by lightning and its damaged limbs threatened to fall across the parking lot. While waiting for a contractor to come and remove the tree, one of the building's employees posted a hand-made sign to direct pedestrians around the tree and into a side door of the building. The sign featured a caricature of a Native American and the words, "We chopp'em down big tree—paleface go that way."

When word of the sign reached the local newspaper, an editor dispatched a reporter and photographer to the building to ask who created the sign. When no one admitted to the artwork, the reporter was assigned to contact a representative of a local Native American tribe to ask if he had seen the sign and if his people were offended. He visited the site but told the reporter that it was "no big deal." Disappointed with that result, the editor told the reporter to contact the leaders of a different nearby tribe. That group also sent a representative to check out the sign, but he, too, reported back that it was "no big deal" and that his people had more serious issues to worry about.

When the reporter expressed concerns about "pursuing a political correctness agenda" and artificially creating a news story where no news story previously existed, the editor's response was that the newspaper was simply "reporting a conflict between a government entity and an important constituent group within the community and that the conflict would be of interest to the readers ... it was news."

"Yes," the reporter responded. "But it *wasn't* news until we *made it* news."

At the same newspaper a few years later, a sportswriter was on the receiving end of similar criticism while a guest on a radio call-in show. In order to describe how sportswriters worked with their sources, he used an example from a story he had written about the chilly relationship between the coach of the local professional football team and its former quarterback who had left several years earlier to play for another team. On a slow Monday afternoon, he called the quarterback and asked him if he still held hard feelings toward his former coach. He told the sportswriter that he did, and he provided some colorful quotes. Those quotes appeared in Tuesday morning's newspaper. On Tuesday afternoon, the sportswriter called the coach to ask him for his reaction, which generated another story for Wednesday's paper. On Wednesday afternoon, the sportswriter called the quarterback again to tell him what the coach has said, and that conversation generated a story for Thursday's paper. At that point, the sports editor stepped in and put a stop to the sportswriter's "he said/he said" approach to generating news stories.

When a caller to the radio show accused the sportswriter of artificially creating a news story where no news story previously existed, the writer's defense was that he was simply "reporting a conflict between a coach and one of his former players that was of interest to the readers ... it was news."

"Yes," the caller responded. "But it *wasn't* news until you *made it* news."

While some researchers identify the early 2000s as the turning point, others contend that media credibility and public perception were problems as far back as the mid-1980s. Following a decade of post-Watergate euphoria over the role of the press as watchdogs on government and big business, the media fell on hard times and has stayed there for more than three decades. Annual surveys indicated that Americans blamed the media for being too sensational, too rude, too pushy, too uncaring about the people they cover, and driving public controversy rather than covering it.[46]

Even before his election in 2016, President Donald Trump carried out a vendetta against the media, first accusing them of demonstrating bias against him and toward his democratic opponent, former Secretary of State Hillary Clinton. In his first two years in office, he has labeled the media as generators of "fake news" and "the enemy of the people" numerous times, accusing them of downplaying his accomplishments, over-emphasizing his failures in the real estate business, and attempting to generate public and political opposition for his cabinet and Supreme Court nominees. During one campaign event, Trump actually praised a congressional candidate who had been criminally charged with assaulting a journalist. At other events, Trump encouraged his audience to boo and jeer at journalists covering the events, causing many of them to be concerned about their safety.

Partly as a result of Trump's criticisms, public confidence in the media dipped below 50 percent for the first time in 2017, according to a Reuters-Ipsos poll.[47]

Trump's frequent tirades against the media have caught on among public officials at lower levels. In one recent incident in Florida, a re-elected county commissioner used his inaugural address to blast local media about their coverage of his most recent campaign.[48]

Across the country, newspapers and television stations have reported an increase in the frequency of threating phone calls, mail, and email, directed at either specific journalists or the organizations as a whole. Individually, reporters say they have been confronted at grocery stores and other public places by neighbors and acquaintances complaining about their employers' coverage of certain issues.[49]

Even before Trump, some of the anti-media rhetoric had serious consequences. In 2012, a former military contractor whose job it was to spread "disinformation" about America's enemies around the world began a vendetta against *USA Today*, attempting to discredit stories it published about him and personally threatening two of the newspaper's reporters.[50]

Between 2003 and 2016, the percentage of Americans who say that they have a great deal or fair amount of trust in the media fell from 54 to 32 percent. It rebounded slightly in 2017, reaching 41 percent.[51]

Media consultant Clarence Jones blames the loss of trust partially on the shift away from local ownership of newspapers to national ownership. "This is a major cultural shift for the United States," Jones wrote in his 2005 book *Winning with the News Media*. "Until the 1970s, most American newspapers were locally owned, usually by a local family, and very provincial. Today, the locally owned independent newspaper is very rare."[52]

While some Americans are simply predisposed to hold negative attitudes toward the media based on vague or incomprehensible reasons, others cite examples of media mistakes or missteps to support their attitudes. Media researchers provide the following as examples:

- From 1981 through the early part of the new century, a series of scandals jarred the print journalism industry, as reporters from established publications such as *The Washington Post*, *The New York Times*, *Boston Globe*, and *The New Republic* were caught plagiarizing stories from other publications or, in some cases, inventing entire stories using their imagination. While the reporters (and in some cases, the editors who supervised them) were immediately fired and the publications apologized to their readers, the damage to the reputation of those publications was more long-term.[53]

- In 1988, CBS News anchor Dan Rather engaged Vice-President George H. W. Bush in a confrontational interview that was broadcast live on the network's evening news program. Rather's defenders believe that Bush, running for president to succeed Ronald Reagan, may have orchestrated the confrontation in order to address criticisms that he wasn't "tough enough" for the top job, while the majority of Americans (according to polls) believed that Rather came across as a bully and reinforced the stereotype of journalists being overly aggressive and arrogant. Almost two decades later, Rather left the anchor chair after admitting numerous errors in a story he reported about President George W. Bush's service in the National Guard. His admission provided further evidence for critics of the news media to assert that journalists sometimes behave recklessly and often demonstrate a bias against conservatives and republicans holding or seeking public office.

- In the late 1990s, the town of Grand Forks, North Dakota was devastated by weeks of rain that produced record flooding. More than 7,000 families were homeless, and hundreds of businesses closed down. Despite its own building and employees being affected by flood, the town's daily newspaper continued to keep its readers informed, distributing papers for free for several weeks. When an individual donated $15 million to help the town rebuild, the newspaper disregarded her request for anonymity, deciding that her identity was newsworthy and that its readers deserved to know who it was. The donor turned out to be Joan Kroc, widow of McDonald's founder Ray Kroc. Much of the goodwill the newspaper had earned with its readers through its coverage of the tragedy was lost with one story. The paper's own poll indicated that 85 percent of respondents thought Kroc's name should not have been published.

- In the aftermath of Hurricane Katrina, which devastated the city of New Orleans in 2005, local and national media published and broadcast stories about rampant crime affecting the city, including vandalism of downtown businesses and murders and sexual assaults in the Superdome, a multi-purpose downtown facility that served as an evacuation shelter. Rumors that murder victims were being shipped to "secret morgues" at local schools and in the basement of the Superdome and local hospitals were euthanizing patients were being reported as fact. Some media based their reports on erroneous quotes from city officials, while others blamed the false reports on merely repeating dubious accounts they overheard inside the shelters without doing additional fact-checking.[54]

- Two cases involving wrongly accused criminal suspects embarrassed the media who were caught up in the frenzy and forgot about the legal principle of "innocent until proven guilty."
  One such case occurred in 1996, when a security guard at the Summer Olympic Games in Atlanta was accused of planning a bomb in order to put himself in the position of hero. He was eventually cleared as a suspect and later completely vindicated while the actual perpetrator, a well-known anti-abortion activist, was caught. Several media outlets covering

the story avoided libel litigation by reaching out-of-court settlements with the man, but in the process lost credibility with the public, according to surveys.[55]

A decade later, North Carolina and national media were caught up in the frenzy after three members of the lacrosse team at Duke University were accused of allegedly raping an exotic dancer they had hired to entertain at a team party in March 2006. The athletes were white and the complainant was black, which triggered debates about race relations, sexual violence, and allegations of "white privilege" at a prestigious private university. Media coverage included newspapers as far away as London, where a newspaper headline read, "University Rape Highlights Racial Divisions in the South."[56] Much of the erroneous information was provided by an aggressive prosecutor who was in the midst of a tough re-election campaign and called the players "hooligans." He was also criticized for withholding evidence from the defendants' attorneys and publicly discussing details of the case that should have been kept secret until after the investigation was closed. After a lengthy investigation, the prosecutor dropped the charges against the players, citing inconsistencies in the statements of the accuser and witnesses. The prosecutor who provided much of the false information to the media and made other missteps resigned from his office and was later disbarred.

A lack of respect for the journalism profession is nothing new. As far back as the mid-1970s, opinion polls showed that the majority of Americans labeled the press—both individual reporters and media organizations—as arrogant, criticized the media for invading individuals' privacy, and believed that media organizations cover up their mistakes. The chair of the journalism program at a major university recently suggested in a journal article that his friends and colleagues should "feel sorry for him because he was teaching an undergraduate course in media ethics at a time when ethics seems to matter less and less in the conduct of professional journalists."[57]

Despite that skeptical view, enrollment in journalism programs grew exponentially between the mid-1970s (the beginnings of the so-called "Watergate effect") and the early 2000s. At many schools, enrollment has either leveled off or dropped slightly in the last decade. Unrelated to the decline in enrollment, many journalism programs have established course in communication ethics and made them requirements to complete a journalism degree program. That follows a similar trend found in business schools, where the downturn in public perception of American businesses has prompted business educators to offer more courses in business ethics and make them requirements rather than electives.

Journalism historians trace the profession's "watchdog role" back to *The New York Times* and its exposé of the corrupt political organization Tammany Hall and its leader, Boss Tweed, in the 1870s. In the 1970s, journalists in their watchdog role uncovered the Watergate scandal that resulted in the resignation of President Richard Nixon.

More recently, it was traditional journalists using the tools of hard-nosed investigative reporting that:

- uncovered the lack of oversight of the Federal Emergency Management Agency in distribution of money designated for survivors of natural disasters. After four hurricanes crossed the state of Florida in 2004, FEMA was called in to assist with the disaster recovery claims, most of which were legitimate. But the agency was oblivious to the millions of dollars paid to families who fraudulently claimed hurricane damage and used their FEMA checks to purchase luxury items. That fraud would not have been exposed if journalists had not uncovered it.[58]

- uncovered the National Security Agency's unauthorized wiretapping of private American citizens under the administration of President George W. Bush;
- uncovered decades of sexual abuse of young boys by priests in the Boston area (a story told in the 2015 film *Spotlight*);
- uncovered the struggles of retired National Football League players dealing with migraine headaches, depression, and violent behavior caused by the cumulative effect of concussions and other brain injuries;
- uncovered the alarming rates of suicides among veterans of the wars in Iraq and Afghanistan that had gone unnoticed by the Department of Defense and Department of Veterans Affairs;
- uncovered years of sexual harassment claims against movie producer Harvey Weinstein, a phenomenon that gave birth to the "#MeToo" movement;
- uncovered how government incompetence and corruption lead to a health crisis in Flint, Michigan, where an aging pipe system caused the public water supply to be contaminated with lead;
- uncovered the embarrassingly light sentence given to billionaire financier Jeffrey Epstein, who struck a plea deal with U.S. Attorney Alexander Acosta to serve only thirteen months in a minimum-security prison amid charges involving sex with dozens of underage girls.[59]

On the local level, it was reporters from a local television station in Mobile, Alabama that uncovered a funeral home and cemetery that was exhuming bodies—without permission of the families—then re-burying the bodies in unmarked graves and reusing the caskets. "None of these things could have been exposed by Facebook or Reddit," wrote media critics Paul Janensch in a 2019 op-ed piece in newspapers published by the Gannett newspaper chain.[60]

Cynicism Directed at Other Fields

While media industries deserve much of the criticism and cynicism they receive, nearly every other professional field in American society is equally subject to similar contempt.

Despite all of the talk about the importance of ethical behavior in all fields of endeavor, the integrity of nearly every aspect of society continues to be treated much like the weather in the classic Mark Twain quote: "Everyone talks about the weather, but no one does anything about it."

In society in general, business travelers continue to falsify travel reports, employees take home office supplies, politicians make campaign promises they know they will be unable to fulfill, students plagiarize term papers, used car dealers turn back odometers, and welfare recipients and the unemployed lie about their eligibility for government assistance.

Some advertising agencies produce campaigns that are misleading and sometimes false. Some public relations departments distribute news releases that don't include false information, but intentionally leave out information that would give reporters and the general public a more complete understanding of the issues.

Historians and social scientists point to government deception surrounding the Vietnam War in the late 1960s, the Watergate scandal of the early 1970s, and other political scandals of the 1980s as factors contributing to a decline in trust and an increase in cynicism regarding the government. In the 1990s, scandals involving American oil companies and other corporate giants caused Americans to become cynical of the business environment as well, as did the Wall Street scandals of the early 2000s.

What is the result of Americans' growing level of dissatisfaction with government and business institutions? According to William Bennett, a former Secretary of Education and now an author and television commentator, the result is the inability of citizens to be shocked or angered by the behavior of government or business. In his 1998 book *The Death of Outrage*, Bennett claimed that political scandals from Watergate to Iran-Contra (the exchange of weapons for political hostages during the Reagan administration of the 1980s) to President Clinton's affair with a White House intern have created a culture in which people simply accept scandal and misbehavior by public officials as routine.[61]

Another reason for the rise of cynicism in America is the tendency of politicians and celebrities to lie about their personal and professional behavior, even after considerable evidence comes to light to indicate their guilt. "It amazes me that people can do that stuff with a straight face and get away with it," wrote *Miami Herald* columnist Leonard Pitts Jr., in a 2007 column. "I suspect that public figures spew so many lies, alibis, and rationalizations that we become desensitized. When controversy arises, they pretend to apologize or explain, and you and I continue to believe … it's a spin doctors' world, and we're just living in it."[62]

In addition to the problem of cynicism, sociologists and other researchers have found that Americans are simply taking issues such as ethics and decision-making less seriously. Examples:

- Annual surveys of business trends consistently report that prospective employers found that more than 80 percent of résumés they received included inaccuracies ranging from "minor exaggerations" to "outright falsehoods." Management journals reporting the results did not condone the falsehoods, but claimed that sorting through the deceptions has become a routine part of the recruiting process. Since the beginning of the new century, numerous corporate executives, elected and appointed public officials, and even a high-profile college football coach have lost their jobs when their falsified or exaggerated resumes became public. In many cases, one common denominator is the irony that the individuals involved did not need the false credentials in order to qualify for the jobs they held—they appeared to be cases of ego and self-aggrandizement rather than perceived necessity. Examples are discussed in Chapter 11.
- Studies of academic honesty involving several prestigious universities, including military academies (which administer severe punishments compared to civilian institutions) found that more than 75 percent of seniors admitted having committed some form of academic misconduct during their college careers. Examples of that misconduct ranged from cheating on exams to plagiarism on term papers. While the 75 percent figure in itself is alarming, what is even more troubling is that those are *just the ones who admitted it*. In the last decade, several prestigious graduate programs disclosed that they have detected an increase in plagiarism in master's degrees and doctoral dissertations, in many cases resulting in those degrees being revoked.[63]
- Evidence has emerged that the cheating culture in education had trickled down to the K-12 level, but ironically the cheating is done by teachers and administrators rather than students. In 2014, for example, teachers and administrators in the Atlanta public school system allegedly changed answers and artificially inflated student test results. Similar cases were subsequently found in other school districts around the country. Education officials attempted to justify their behavior by claiming it was in response to "high-stakes" testing programs that not only determined student progress but also salary increases for employees and other forms of teacher and administrator recognition.[64]

- Surveys of public relations professionals often find that more than 35 percent admit "exaggerating" when providing information to a boss, client, or journalist; and another 25 percent admit to telling outright falsehoods. While that 60 percent total might cause concern, keep in mind that, like the students in the above-mentioned survey, those are *just the ones who admitted it.*[65]

Your Turn

Case Study 1A: Perception of Honesty and Ethical Standards of Employment Fields

Each year since 1976, the Gallup organization has conducted a survey in which respondents were asked to rate various professions on their honesty and ethical standards. Some professions are included every year, while others are included on a rotating basis.

Among the professions consistently scoring high every year are nurses and medical doctors. In the 2018 survey, nurses scored highest among all of the professions included on the survey (for the seventeenth consecutive year) with 84 percent describing their perception of the field as either "high or very high." Doctors were second at 67 percent, followed by pharmacists (66), high school teachers (60), and police (54).[66]

The lowest scoring occupation was members of congress, with 58 percent of respondents describing their perception as either "low" or "very low." Slightly ahead of them, but still near the bottom of the list, were telemarketers (56) and car sales-persons (44).[67]

Traditionally, professional communicators have ranked near the middle of the list or slightly below the middle. In the 2018 survey, journalists scored 33 percent for "high" and "very high" and 34 percent "low" or "very low." The 33 percent score represented a 10-point bump since the 2016 survey and was its highest ranking since 1977. The 2018 survey lumped together newspaper and television reporters under the blanket term "journalists." The 2017 survey listed them separately, but the results were mediocre for both, with newspaper reporters earning scores of 35 percent for "low" and "very low" while television reporters earned scores of 37 percent for those categories.

Advertising representatives, the only other communications specialty included in the 2018 survey, scored 37 percent for "low" or "very low."[68]

1. Of all of these rankings, which of them surprise you?
2. Which of them merely confirm your previously held beliefs?

Case Study 1B: The National Football League: Concussions, Offensive Nicknames, and the National Anthem Controversy

While baseball has long been considered America's "national pastime," television ratings and ticket sales indicate that professional football is the most popular sport in terms of television audiences and game attendance. That popularity was tested between 2012 and 2018 when three major controversies affected public perception of the sport.

The first controversy began when Native American groups organized protests aimed at persuading the Washington Redskins to change their name, claiming the "redskin" image was offensive to their culture. The protestors became even more vocal when team owner Daniel Snyder vowed he would "never" change the name.[69]

Protestors then turned to a little-known clause in trademark law that prohibits the government from providing trademark protection in cases in which a product name is offensive (that effort was ineffective). Throughout the controversy, some television commentators and print journalists expressed their own view of the controversy by refusing to use the nickname themselves, instead referring to the team as the "Washington NFL team" or similar monikers.

At about the same time, many news outlets, including ESPN, began looking into accusations that many retired players were suffering from brain diseases resulting from the cumulative damage caused by multiple concussions suffered during their careers. Many retired players were suffering from migraine headaches, dementia, and a newly discovered ailment called chronic traumatic encephalopathy (CTE). The latter condition could be detected only during an autopsy, and dozens of such procedures were conducted on players who died in their fifties, many by suicide.

From the beginning, there were criticisms that the NFL had tried to cover up its liability by discouraging media coverage of the issue.[70] When ESPN cancelled an investigative report on the issue, it was accused by media critics of bowing to pressure from the NFL and cancelling its report in order to maintain its relationship with the league (ESPN and the NFL have a long-term contract that allows the network to broadcast *Monday Night Football* as well as Sunday pre-game and post-game highlight programs).[71]

In the end, the league reached a financial agreement with the NFL Players Association to provide money for both ongoing medical care for veteran players and research into ways to prevent long-term brain damage.

The third controversy began in 2016 when Colin Kaepernick, then quarterback of the San Francisco 49ers, refused to stand for the pre-game performance of the national anthem. At first, he merely sat on the bench while his teammates stood, but once asked about it by sportswriters, he began kneeling in a way that was much more visible. By the end of that season, a handful of teammates and players on other teams also knelt. Players claimed their protests were aimed at drawing attention to the treatment of black motorists by white police officers. In the three years leading up to the controversy, numerous unarmed black men had been killed by police, many of them at traffic stops.

At the beginning of the 2017 season, hundreds of players across the league began kneeling during the anthem. After President Trump condemned the protests, many players responded by standing for the anthem but locking arms with each other, their coaches, and team owners. For several weeks, networks covering the games showed the protests, alternating between wide shots showing entire teams and shots of individual players kneeling. That represented a departure from their usual practice of breaking for commercials during the anthem. After several weeks of complaints from viewers who criticized the networks for paying too much attention to the issue, the networks reverted to breaking for commercials.

Critics of the NFL cited a 12 percent decline in television ratings for the first half the 2016 season as evidence the league's prestige was waning, but owners and league executives blamed the decline on Americans being distracted by the presidential election. Some observers were skeptical of that defense, but the owners and executives were vindicated when ratings from the latter half of November and all of December rebounded and were down only 8 percent compared to the same weeks in 2015. Throughout the playoffs and Super Bowl (early January–early February 2018), ratings had fully recovered.[72]

1. In all three of these controversies, should print and broadcast journalists cover them as news stories or sports stories?
2. In the case of the Washington Redskins controversy, what is your opinion of individual print and broadcast journalists refusing to use the name "Redskins," in effect inserting their own opinion into the controversy?
3. In the case of the concussion controversy, what is your opinion of ESPN bowing to the pressure from the league (if it did) in order to preserve its business relationship with the NFL?
4. In the case of the national anthem controversy, how should television networks respond to both forms of criticism—from fans who claim it was focusing too much attention on the issue and "giving the players a platform for protest," and fans who claim that to not show the protests the networks are ignoring an important news story? What it is your opinion of the broadcast networks avoiding the issue by switching to commercials?

Discussion Problem 1: What's Fair?

Marianne Clayton, the owner of a local discount clothing store, has announced that she is running for mayor of your town. Which of the following details of her life and work should be mentioned in a newspaper profile you write about her?

Yes	No	
_____	_____	Clayton is fifty-five years old.
_____	_____	Clayton has no previous experience in politics and, according to public records, is not even registered to vote.

_____ _____ Clayton was diagnosed with breast cancer in her late forties but has made a full recovery.

_____ _____ Clayton's grandfather was convicted of insurance fraud in 1965.

_____ _____ Clayton has been divorced four times.

_____ _____ Her business donates more than $1 million a year to local charities, and Clayton serves on the board of directors of several local nonprofit organizations.

_____ _____ Clayton is a Methodist but has not attended church in more than ten years.

_____ _____ Clayton has diabetes.

_____ _____ When she was in college, Clayton and three sorority sisters stole a goat from a local petting zoo and placed it in the office of a professor they disliked. They were disciplined by the university but faced no criminal charges.

_____ _____ Two of Clayton's siblings were police officers in the town. A brother was killed in the line of duty in 2008. Her sister shot and killed an unarmed black teenager in 2017. She was cleared in the shooting but resigned the following year and is working in another field.

_____ _____ Clayton is a recovered alcoholic and has not had a drink in twenty years.

_____ _____ Her business has been named "Small Business of the Year" by the the local Chamber of Commerce six years in a row.

_____ _____ An old news story indicates her business failed to pay county taxes in 2006 and 2007 and paid them only after the county threatened to seize the business.

_____ _____ Clayton's business has high satisfaction ratings from online review sites, but a competitor has complained that many of the reviews are fake.

_____ _____ When she was in her late twenties and early thirties, Clayton was fired from three jobs due to her drinking.

_____ _____ Clayton was a survivor of domestic violence during her third marriage.

_____ _____ Clayton had two DUIs in 1995.

_____ _____ Clayton had a nephew in another state who died from opioid abuse in 2016. Keaton has told friends privately that the death inspired her to make fighting the city's opioid problem a major part of her campaign.

_____ _____ In 2013, two teenagers were caught breaking into her store when it was closed. Instead of pressing charges, Clayton paid for the two to participate in a "diversion" program for young offenders. Today, both of the young men are employed at the store.

_____ _____ Clayton's campaign flyer and website indicate that she attended the University of Minnesota, but you check and find out that she did not graduate.

Discussion Questions

101. This chapter included some alarming statistics about the phenomenon of job applicants lying on résumés and college students cheating. Do those statistics surprise you? What do those trends say about our society and how we look at honesty and ethics?

102. This chapter discusses the growth of media ethics courses in colleges and universities. Some skeptics of such courses believe that college students preparing for careers as professional communicators should already have a sense of right and wrong before entering college, and that such efforts at "ethics education" come too late. Do you agree or disagree?

Notes

1 Edward L. Bernays, address to public relations students and instructors at the University of South Florida, February 19, 1991.
2 This quote is from Justice Stewart's written opinion in *Jacobellis v. Ohio*, 378 U.S. 184 (1964).
3 Rushworth Kidder, *How Good People Make Tough Choices: Resolving the Dilemmas of Ethical Living*. New York: HarperCollins (2003), p. 63.
4 This quote has been attributed to UCLA basketball coach John Wooden, politician Ross Perot, and an old French proverb.
5 This proverb has been attributed to German, English, and Chinese philosophy, but the actual origin is unknown.
6 Kathleen Parker, "Is Technology Killing Our Decency?" Syndicated newspaper column, October 10, 2010. See also: Conrad C. Fink, *Media Ethics*. Boston: Allyn & Bacon (1995), p. 33.
7 Randy Bobbitt, *Free Speech on America's K-12 and College Campuses: Legal Cases from Barnette to Blaine*. Lanham, MD: Lexington Books (2017), p. 45.
8 Roy L. Moore, *Mass Communication Law and Ethics*. Mahwah, NJ: Lawrence Erlbaum Associates (1999), p. 14.
9 Laurie J. Wilson and Joseph D. Ogden, *Strategic Communications Planning*. Dubuque, IA: Kendall-Hunt (2010), p. 174.
10 Sonia Orwell and Ian Angus. *George Orwell: An Age Like This, 1920–1940*. Boston: D.R. Godine (2000), p. 401.
11 Karen B. Helmeke and Catherine Ford Sori, *The Therapist's Notebook for Integrating Spirituality in Counseling*. New York: Routledge (2012), p. 150.
12 Helmeke and Sori, p. 150
13 Simon Blackburn, *Ethics: A Very Short Introduction*. Oxford: Oxford University Press (2001), p. 101.
14 Gene Gilmore and Robert Root, "Ethics for Newsmen." In *Ethics and the Press*, John C. Merrill and Ralph D. Barney, ed. New York: Hastings House Publishers (1978), pp. 30–31.
15 Wilson and Ogden, p. 176.
16 David Niose, *Nonbeliever Nation: The Rise of Secular Americans*. New York: Palgrave Macmillan (2012), p. 181.
17 Niose, pp. 85–86.
18 Phil Zuckerman, *Living the Secular Life*. New York: Penguin Press (2014), p. 13.
19 Ron F. Smith, *Journalism Ethics*. Malden, MA: Blackwell Publishing (2008), p. 9.
20 Lisa H. Newton, Louis Hodges, and Susan Keith, "Accountability in the Professions: Accountability in Journalism." *Journal of Mass Media Ethics*, Vol. 19, No. 3 and 4 (2004), pp. 166–190.

21 Wilbur Schramm, "Quality in Mass Communications." In *Ethics and the Press*, John C. Merrill and Ralph D. Barney, ed. New York: Hastings House Publishers (1978), pp. 37–47.

22 Shelby D. Hunt and Lawrence B. Chonko, "Ethical Problems of Advertising Agency Executives." *Journal of Advertising*, Vol. 16, No. 4 (1987), pp. 16–24.

23 Brian Richardson, "Four Standards for Teaching Ethics in Journalism." *Journal of Mass Media Ethics*, Vol. 9, No. 2 (1994), pp. 109–117.

24 Richard Johannesen, *Ethics in Human Communication*. Long Grove, IL: Waveland Press (1996), pp. 197–220.

25 Johannesen, "What Should We Teach about Formal Codes of Communication Ethics?" *Journal of Mass Media Ethics*, Vol. 3, No. 1 (1988), pp. 59–64.

26 Mike Wallace and Beth Knobel, *Heat and Light: Advice for the Next Generation of Journalists*. New York: Three Rivers Press (2010), p. 235.

27 Richard Schneider, "Newspapers Still Are the Ones Finding the News." *Pensacola News Journal*, April 11, 2010.

28 Gary Abernathy, "The Vital Job of Small-Town Newspapers." *The Washington Post*, July 25, 2017.

29 "Trail of Truth-Telling." *Editor & Publisher*, June 17, 2002, p. 9.

30 Mark Fitzgerald, "For Gay Press, 'Good Old Days' Are Here Today." *Editor & Publisher*, September 2007, p. 9.

31 The Fuller Project website, http://www.fullerproject.org.

32 Robert J. Samuelson, "Long Live the News Business." *Newsweek*, May 28, 2007, p. 40.

33 Wallace and Knobel, p. 220.

34 Wallace and Knobel, p. 220.

35 Michael Schudson, *The Sociology of News*. New York: W.W. Norton and Company (2003), p. 175.

36 John H. Johnson and Mike Gluck, *Everydata: The Misinformation Hidden in the Little Data You Read Every Day*. Brookline, MA: Bibliomotion (2016), p. 2.

37 Howard Rosenberg and Charles S. Feldman, *No Time to Think: The Menace of Media Speed and the 24-Hour News Cycle*. New York: Continuum Books (2008), p. 13.

38 Rosenberg and Feldman, p. 3.

39 RTDNA Code of Ethics.

40 *Newsday* reporter Herb Lowe, quoted in Ron Smith, *Groping for Ethics in Journalism*. Ames, IA: Wiley-Blackwell (2003), p. 110.

41 "Lines Blur as Journalism Heads Back to the Future." *USA Today*, November 10, 2010, p. 8-A. See also: Gene Policinski, "How Do We Decide Who Is, Or Isn't a Journalist?" *USA Today*, January 3, 2012, p. 5-B.

42 Randy Bobbitt, "Why Journalism Still Matters." *Pensacola News Journal*, July 12, 2019, p. 8-A.

43 Leon Nelson Flint, *The Conscience of the Newspaper*. New York: D. Appleton Century Co. (1925).

44 Sandra Dickson, "The Golden Mean in Journalism." *Journal of Mass Media Ethics*, Vol. 3, No. 1 (1988), pp. 33–37.

45 Richard Benedetto, "What Readers Don't Understand about Daily Newspapers." Syndicated newspaper column, January 5, 1993.

46 Andrew Kohut, "Public Support for the Watchdogs is Fading." *Columbia Journalism Review*, May/June 2001, p. 52.

47 Mark Oppenheimer, "Why Does the Public Hate the Media?" Syndicated newspaper column, October 29, 2017.

48 "Escambia Needs a Watchdog." *Pensacola News Journal*, November 25, 2016, p. 5-B.

49 Jason Wilson, "Doxxing, Assault, and Death Threats: New Dangers Facing U.S. Journalists." *Guardian*, June 14, 2018.

50 Gregory Korte, "Propaganda Firm Owner behind Attack on Media." *USA Today*, May 25, 2012, p. 2-A.

51 "Indicators of News Media Trust." Gallup/Knight Foundation Survey, 2018.

52 Clarence Jones, *Winning with the News Media*. Anna Maria, FL: Winning News Media, Inc. (2005), p. 28.

53 Peter Johnson, "Jayson Blair Uproar Has Yet to Quiet Down." *USA Today*, May 29, 2003.

54 Joe Strupp, "Watchdogs Still Awake?" *Editor & Publisher*, October 2009, pp. 16–20. See also: Brian Thevenot, "Myth-Making in New Orleans." *American Journalism Review*, December 2005/January 2006, pp. 30–37.

55 "Ex-Suspect Sues Newspapers, Networks." *The Washington Post*, January 29, 1997.

56 Rachel Smolkin, "Justice Delayed." *American Journalism Review*, August/September 2007, pp. 20–22.

57 Philip Meyer, *Ethical Journalism: A Guide for Students, Practitioners, and Consumers.* Lanham, MD: University Press of America (1987), p. 12.

58 Mark Tapscott, "Boondoggles Need Exposure." Syndicated newspaper column, December 8, 2004.

59 Paul Janensch, "How Excellent Investigative Journalism Revealed Epstein." *Pensacola News Journal*, July 17, 2019, p. 8-A.

60 Janensch.

61 William Bennett, *The Death of Outrage.* New York: Free Press (1999), pp. 1–5.

62 Leonard Pitts, "Celebrities and Politicos Take the Truth Out for a Spin." Syndicated newspaper column, May 30, 2007.

63 Menachem Wecker, "10 High-Profile People Whose Degrees Were Revoked." *U.S. News and World Report*, May 2, 2012.

64 Richard Fausset and Alan Blinder, "Atlanta School Workers Sentenced in Test Score Cheating Case." *The New York Times*, April 14, 2015.

65 Adam Leyland, "One Out of Four Pros Admits to Lying on the Job." *PR Week*, May 1, 2000, p. 1.

66 Megan Brennan, "Nurses Again Outpace Other Professions for Honesty, Ethics." Gallup.com, December 20, 2018. These are the results of a telephone survey conducted in November 2018 with a sample size of approximately 1,000 individuals aged eighteen and older. The margin for error was plus or minus three points.

67 Brennan.

68 Brennan.

69 Erik Brady, "Daniel Snyder Says Redskins Will Never Change Name." *USA Today*, May 9, 2013. See also: Nancy Armour, "Snyder Needs to Follow Cleveland's Lead." *USA Today*, January 30, 2018, p. 5-C.

70 Matt Vasilogambros, "The NFL's Concussion Cover-Up." *The Atlantic*, May 23, 2016.

71 Marc Tracy, "ESPN Quit Its Concussions Investigation with 'Frontline' Under Curious Circumstances." *The New Republic*, August 22, 2013.

72 Anthony Crupi, "Can Anything Dethrone the NFL?" *Advertising Age*, September 11, 2017, pp. 20–21.

2 Philosophical and Critical Perspectives on Communication Ethics

Absolutism, Pragmatism, and Self-Interest

This chapter describes the work of twenty-four of the most celebrated philosophers (and one organization) in world and American history and explains how their concepts can be applied to the modern-day challenges facing the communications professions. They can be divided into three categories, based on their differing approaches to decision-making. Those who believe in making decisions based on hard-and-fast rules are known as absolutists, and their primary decision-making philosophy is known as **absolutism**. This philosophy is most commonly associated with the work of Immanuel Kant, a German philosopher known for a concept he called the categorical imperative.

In contrast, pragmatists believe that individuals should make decisions based on the merits of the situations immediately in front of them. The idea of pragmatism is best illustrated by the concepts attributed to American philosopher Joseph Fletcher, who coined the term **situational ethics**.

A third category consists of philosophers who either believe that individuals should be free to make decisions based on their self-interests or describe how individuals can be distracted by self-interest as they make critical decisions. The primary philosopher behind the idea is Ayn Rand, a Russian-American author who espoused the concept of **objectivism**.

In addition to those philosophers, the chapter also includes a discussion of the work of several modern and contemporary media critics.

Absolutism

Socrates and Plato

Two of the best-known philosophers in the history of the discipline lived more than two thousand years ago in Greece and provided the foundation for most philosophical thought in the Western world. According to the ancient Greeks, including Socrates and Plato, ethics was one of the fundamental branches of philosophy.

The Greeks also believed that curiosity was an important trait in human development and that it was the responsibility of a society's intellectuals to pursue knowledge and seek wisdom and virtue by reflection, inquiry, argumentation, and (eventually) consensus.

Socrates (470–399 B.C.) believed that right and wrong were concepts that could be, and should be, identified and practiced in both public and private affairs. He exposed ignorance, hypocrisy, and incompetence in governmental matters and was known for bringing out into the open controversial ideas that individuals would otherwise be reluctant to discuss publicly.

He believed that society was best served when its citizens put aside their fear of ridicule and were instead willing to openly debate and evaluate controversial issues.

Plato (427–347 B.C.) was a student of Socrates. Many modern-day philosophers believe that Plato may have been the most influential of the Greek philosophers, and perhaps the most influential of all time, claiming that nearly all the important ideas in the field were either the direct work of Plato or the result of someone applying his work.

Plato's writings and teachings dealt mainly with political persuasion. He was critical of politicians who spoke in superficial terms and over-relied on euphemisms and misleading comparisons—what modern-day critics would call *spin*. More than 2,000 years after his death, Plato's principles are standard part of undergraduate and graduate classes in rhetoric, debate, and argumentation.

Plato encouraged moral conduct even when it might be inconsistent with current social norms. He believed that one should avoid wrongdoing regardless of the consequences. Even though the expressions did not exist in his time, it is likely that Plato would agree with the principles that "two wrongs do not make a right" and that "the ends do not justify the means."

Plato contended that the goal of political communication should be to enhance the well-being of the audience, not to advance the agenda of the person or organization speaking. The essence of many of his writings was that people should always seek, rather than fear, new knowledge. In one essay, he wrote that, "We can easily forgive a child who is afraid of the dark; the real tragedy of life is when men are afraid of the light."[1]

Critics of modern-day political or advertising campaigns say those efforts are aimed clearly at promoting the agendas of the speakers rather than the audience, while idealists such as Plato would likely say that, in a perfect world, a communication campaign or other persuasive effort could be aimed at producing benefits for both. Today, leaders of the public relations industry claim just that, contending that "mutually beneficial outcomes" are always the goal of any persuasive campaign.

Aquinas, the Natural Law Doctrine, and "Jocose Lies" [handwritten: human nature → customs and laws]

St. Thomas Aquinas (1225–1274) was an Italian monk who wrote more than forty volumes about philosophy, and more than seven centuries after his death, his theories are still taught in Catholic schools around the world. He is most famous for his Natural Law Doctrine, which states that universal laws of human nature are determined by reason and take priority over artificial created customs and laws created by governments. Aquinas taught that natural law is derived from divine law, and should therefore serve as the basis for people's moral decision-making.[2]

Aquinas advocated a Christian view of ethics and advocate intellectual virtue as being more important than material things. Aquinas believed the best source of guidance for moral decisions is a combination of divine guidance and rational argument. He argued that in order to lead a good life, it is necessary to focus more on our exemplars than on ourselves, imitating their behavior as much as possible.[3]

Some of Aquinas' more interesting writings—and rare departure from his absolutist ideals—dealt with the issue of deception. His philosophy allowed for **jocose lies** (the Latin term for "joking") and lies that do no harm, what in modern times we would refer to as "white lies." In other words, Aquinas said, there are degrees of falsehood—on one extreme are those that are potentially harmful and based on illegitimate motives of the speaker; and on the other extreme are those minor falsehoods that serve some valid short-term purpose. But in the latter case, Aquinas said, the perpetrator of a falsehood must be prepared to justify the falsehood once it is exposed.

[handwritten: socrates: outside normal thinking/discussion ↓ plato: politics, moral conduct]

One example of applying Aquinas' philosophy of deception to the newsgathering process is the decision to use deception to uncover wrongdoing on the part of businesses or government agencies. In such cases, followers of Aquinas would claim, a journalist could justify deception because (1) it serves a greater purpose, and (2) the media organization participating in the deception would be prepared to explain it once it is detected.

Bacon and Rational Decision-Making

Bacon = scientific method → no one liked science

Sir Francis Bacon (1561–1626) was an English philosopher and politician who believed in scientific inquiry and was an advocate and defender of a process of fact-finding known as the scientific method. His work came at a time when political leaders considered science to be unimportant, and scientists were generally distrusted. *→ FACTS!*

One of Bacon's philosophies on decision-making was that no decision should be made in haste, and that decisions are best made after a careful review of the facts and seeking of input from all interested parties. He believed that individuals were constantly subject to internal and external pressures and that it was the responsibility of the individual to keep his or her passions under control and to make decisions in a rational manner.

An example of applying Bacon's philosophies in the journalism business includes the function of newspaper editorial boards, which gather information from interested parties prior to determining the newspaper's editorial policy, and reporters' consultation with social service agencies when developing stories about issues such as hunger, poverty, and homelessness.

Blackstone and the Blackstonian Doctrine

free speech but can be punished if harmful

William Blackstone (1723–1780) was an English legal scholar best known for being an advocate of free speech while warning that those taking advantage of the privilege were also required to accept the consequences of such speech. Blackstone believed that expression should never be suppressed (such as in the case of government censorship), but that the government had the right to punish the source of harmful speech after it takes place under the appropriate laws such as those involving copyrights, libel, or obscenity. Writing in 1769, Blackstone stated that, "Every free man has an undoubted right to lay what sentiments he pleases before the public; to forbid this is to destroy the freedom of the press, but if he published what is improper, mischievous, or illegal, he must take the consequences of his own temerity."[4] Today, the principle of not allowing for government censorship, but allowing instead for punishment after the fact, is known as the **Blackstonian Doctrine.**

Kant and the Categorical Imperative

Immanuel Kant (1724–1804) was a German philosopher who wrote and taught that individuals and organizations should make decisions based on moral duty rather than self-interest.

Kant is best known for a rule known he called the **Categorical Imperative**, which states that, once created, a society's rules and laws must be followed to the letter and are not subject to interpretation or exception. Put simply, the Categorical Imperative is based on Kant's belief that the process of making a decision was more important than the results. If one uses the correct procedure or process in making a decision (i.e., following established rules or guidelines), what happens as a result of that decision is not important.

follow established rules + guidelines = best decision

He further stated that unlike other philosophical concepts of the time period, the categorical imperative had no connection to God, as right and wrong should not be limited to religious connotations. Loosely interpreted, the Categorical Imperative has been interpreted with expressions such as "rules are rules" and "rules are set in concrete." Under the Categorical Imperative, rules cannot be set aside or bent, even when some short-term benefit may result. According to Kant, the long-term benefit of following the rules outweighs any short-term benefit that may result from breaking or bending them. Other interpretations of the Categorical Imperative include rules such as "always tell the truth and always keep promises" and "do your duty whether you want to or not."

Another aspect of the Categorical Imperative is that one should not make any decision or take any action in one case unless he or she were prepared to make a similar decision or take a similar action in all other similar cases—either that day or at any point in the future. Today, many people in a position of authority decline to help others based on their contention that "if I do it for one person, I will have to do it for everyone else."

An example of applying the Categorical Imperative in journalism is the decision to identify rape victims by name in published or broadcast news stories. While most media organizations have a policy of not identifying victims, the few that do claim that part of their rationale was the need for consistency—because they identify the victims of other types of crimes, they believe they are obligated to also identify rape victims.

Bentham, Mill, and Utilitarianism

Philosophers Jeremy Bentham (1748–1832) and John Stuart Mill (1806–1873) were known as reformers—social activists who wanted to improve the condition of British citizens and workers, many of whom lived and worked in appalling economic conditions, similar to those portrayed in the novels of Charles Dickens. Bentham was a friend of James Mill, father of John Stuart Mill, and Bentham became the younger Mill's teacher and mentor. Bentham and Mill developed the concept of **utilitarianism**, which has been loosely translated as "the greatest good for the greatest number of people."

According to utilitarianism, the consequences of actions are the most important factor in deciding whether those actions are ethical, and the more people who benefit from a decision, the more likely it is to be the appropriate choice. Utilitarianism is one of several philosophies based on the assumption that one's ethical behavior should be based on the outcome of the behavior rather than the person's intent (i.e., the ends justify the means). Under utilitarianism, one's actions are always judged by the results, and ends often justify the means because the utility of the ends outweighs the disutility of the means.

Outliving his mentor by more than forty years, Mill refined the principle of utilitarianism to put more emphasis on long-term results than on the short-term results. For example, a person might receive greater pleasure in spending an evening eating a fine meal than in reading great literature, but the literature will be of a higher quality and the benefit will be more for the long term.

In his 1859 essay *On Liberty*, Mill wrote that he supported free expression because he believed people should always be open to new ideas instead of being inclined to reject them without a fair hearing. He added that people need to be exposed to false ideas in order to value those that are true. Mill was not as optimistic as John Milton (discussed later in this chapter) concerning the ability of truth to win out over falsity, pointing out that history was littered with "instances of truth put down by persecution," such as the tendency of European governments to imprison scientists who espoused ideas that were inconsistent with religious doctrine. But he also believed that the only way truth could win in its battle against falsity was through true freedom of speech and press.

A modern-day example of utilitarianism in journalism is found in decisions regarding investigative reporting. While a few people may be hurt by the publication or broadcast of a news story, in most cases it is the proper thing to do because far more people will benefit from the story than will be harmed by it.

Skeptics of applying the concept of utilitarianism to decision-making in journalism point to the fact that journalists are unlikely to predict the long-term consequences of their decisions. "A reporter may believe a story about teen suicide will cause schools and the public to understand and help depressed youths," wrote Ron F. Smith, professor of journalism at the University of Central Florida, in a 2008 textbook. "But the story may have the unintended effect of touching off a wave of 'copycat' suicides."[5]

Dewey and Societal Roles   *everyone sticks to known roles/duties*

John Dewey (1859–1952) was an American philosopher and educator who is best known for his belief in strict society roles and called for every profession or government agency to stay within its traditional or assigned function: police investigate crime, teachers teach children, and the military protects the country. One example was his admonition to school administrators that it was not appropriate for schools to attempt to teach values, as those were better learned in the home.

Applying the concept to the field of journalism, one could contend that it is not appropriate for the media to advocate for or against public issues, but instead concentrate on reporting on those issues in a neutral fashion. America's newspaper publishers, however, counter with their belief that a competent newspaper can "walk and chew gum at the same time"—having reporters cover the news without taking sides while also employing editorial writers whose job it is to advocate only one side of an issue. Nevertheless, Dewey would likely express concern over public journalism (discussed in more detail in Chapter 3), a trend in which media organizations step outside of their traditional roles in order to take the lead in the development of their communities.

Meiklejohn and Free-Speech Absolutism

Alexander Meiklejohn (1872–1964) was a legal scholar who identified himself as an absolutist, meaning that there should be absolutely no limitations of personal expression. Those views were in line with Kant's categorical imperative, and he often took positions that would inflame co-workers, superiors, and subordinates.

Meiklejohn said that the purpose of the First Amendment was to aid citizens in understanding the "issues which bear upon our common life" and there must be no constraints on the free flow of information and ideas.[6]

Rawls and the Veil of Ignorance

John Rawls (1921–2002), a Harvard University professor and author of dozens of books on ethics, decision-making, and political philosophy, is one of the few American philosophers to achieve international recognition and in some circles is considered the American equivalent of John Stuart Mill.

Rawls is best known for his theory of decision-making he called the **veil of ignorance**. He contended that a person faced with making a difficult decision should do so without considering his own interests in the outcome or the identity of the persons affected. Some decision-makers believe it is easier to make difficult decisions if the people affected by those decisions "don't have names or faces."

When applied to journalism decisions, the veil of ignorance is more practical when the veil is not used to conceal the identity of the decision-maker, but instead the identity of those individuals or groups affected by those decisions. One example involves the decision over how far a news story should go in revealing potentially embarrassing details regarding the life of a crime victim or suspect. A reporter or editor applying the veil of ignorance would reach the decision without regard to the identity of the person; that is, giving no consideration to how the decision might be different if the person in question was his or her spouse, child, parent, or friend. A few years ago, a newspaper publisher addressing the privacy issue while speaking to a group of college journalists said that he instructs his reporters and editors to "remember that everyone we write about in the newspaper has a mother"—an attitude clearly inconsistent with the veil of ignorance.

Rotary International

One of the simplest guidelines for decision-making in American society does not come from the code of ethics of a professional organization, but rather a fraternal one. In 1932, Rotarian Herbert J. Taylor was the owner of an aluminum supplier in Chicago on the edge of bankruptcy. Concerned over the potential for misconduct on the part of well-meaning employees attempting to save the company from financial ruin, he issued a list of four simple rules to guide their decision-making. Those four rules have since been incorporated into the Rotary Club's formal operating policy.[7] Instead of do's and don'ts, the rules take the form of questions:

1. Is it the *Truth*?
2. Is it *Fair* to all concerned?
3. Will it build *Goodwill* and better *Friendships*?
4. Will it be *Beneficial* to all concerned?

Pragmatism

Aristotle and the Golden Mean

Unlike his predecessors Socrates and Plato, Aristotle (384–322 B.C.) did not believe that everything in the world could be explained in precise and finite terms. In politics and government, for example, there could be no concrete laws or rules, such as those governing the sciences.

Aristotle spoke and wrote of three rules for ethical decision-making. First, the decision-maker must understand the facts and conditions surrounding the decision, rather than taking action based on accident, chance, or assumptions. Second, the decision-maker must be free to choose without being coerced or inappropriately influenced by others. And third, the decision made must be consistent with the character of the person making the decision.

He also believed that mediation was a virtue, and his primary contribution to modern philosophical thought was a principle he called the **Golden Mean**, which referred to making decisions by finding the "just right" mid-point between two extremes, which he claimed would be the ideal place to find virtue and wisdom.

Aristotle did not, however, intend for individuals to determine where the extremes were in a situation and then determine what position would fall at the mathematical center mark. Instead of such an artificial position, Aristotle suggested that a virtuous person would

1) understand scenario
2) no bias / coersion
3) character

naturally be drawn to the mid-point without considering where the extremes would be found. He further stated that the mid-way point was not a fixed point that would be the same for each individual. Instead, that point could be any one of a number of points that fit the perspectives of individuals while still avoiding the extremes.

For Aristotle and his followers, there are cases in which the middle ground doesn't exist, such as murder or other violent crimes. In the case of a journalist working on a story that is important to do but would harm a great deal of people, he or she would present the story in a way that adequately told the story while minimizing harm to innocent persons.

Today, professors introducing the Golden Mean to journalism ethics classes use the following example to illustrate its applications to decision-making in newsrooms: A newspaper editor must decide whether or not to publish one or more photographs showing a badly burnt victim being removed from a collapsed building by paramedics. The two extremes would be clear: (1) choose a photograph or photographs that illustrate the drama of the situation, without taking into consideration the privacy of the individual or the feelings of the family, or (2) do not use any of the photographs in any form. A logical middle point between the two extremes (i.e., a compromise) would be to choose a photograph that illustrates the drama of the rescue without showing the victim's face.

Abelard: Focus on Intent Rather than Consequences

Peter Abelard (1079–1142), one of the earliest of the French philosophers to achieve international recognition, believed that it was man's nature to constantly question and challenge authority, but one should do so not to serve one's self-interest, but rather to serve and improve society.

Abelard's philosophy centered largely on the notion of intention, with little regard for the consequences. A media application of that decision-making philosophy is found in the case of a newspaper editor who must decide how much of a criminal suspect's background should be included in a reporter's accounts of the investigation. An editor following the journalism axiom of "the people have a right to know" might decide to publish details of the suspect's life and facts uncovered in the investigation, without regard to the effect such revelations might have on the family of the defendant or the pool of perspective jurors for a criminal trial.

Machiavelli: Results More Important than the Process

Niccolò Machiavelli (1469–1527) was an Italian philosopher who believed that the results of an action are far more important than the action itself, and it was acceptable to break or bend the rules in order to achieve a result that is a greater positive than the negative value assigned to the behavior. Today, that belief is paraphrased by the expression "the ends justify the means."

A common media application of this principle is found in the case of a television news producer who must decide whether to authorize a team of reporters to use hidden cameras while investigating alleged wrongdoing at a local business. If he or she decided to allow the reporters to use that newsgathering technique, he or she is going along with Machiavelli's belief that the results of an activity are more important than the process of conducting that activity.

Milton, Jefferson, Libertarianism, and the Marketplace of Ideas

John Milton (1608–1674) was an English poet and essayist who argued that government censorship deprives citizens of knowledge and ideas that could improve their lives. He further argued that efforts at limiting the individual's access to information were futile because the most important information would always find its way to the audience. In addition, Milton feared that individuals carrying out the task of censorship would likely be the least qualified to do so because those most qualified would not want such a boring task. And lastly, Milton wrote, there was considerable value in the intellectual exercise of processing large quantities of information and deciding what was valuable and what was not.

Milton was the first true libertarian[8] and believed that everyone should be free to openly discuss controversial social and political issues, even if it meant challenging the views of authority figures or anyone else. In the battle between truth and falsity, Milton believed, truth would always win if the audience carefully evaluated the competing ideas. Milton called the search for truth a "self-righting process" in which truth would survive and falsity would be vanquished. Three centuries later, the U.S. Supreme Court para-phrased the idea when it coined the term "marketplace of ideas."[9] In a 1967 Supreme Court case, Justice William Brennan cited the "marketplace" metaphor in writing that "the nation's future depends upon leaders trained through wide exposure to that robust exchange of ideas which discovers truth out of a multitude of tongues rather than through any kind of authoritative selection."[10]

Milton and other libertarians of the day believed that individuals should have absolute rights of free expression, and that it was the responsibility of the populace to determine what was true and what was false, and what was important and what was trivial. That belief ran counter to the prevailing authoritarian philosophy of the time, which held that only the English monarchy and other government officials were qualified to determine the value of ideas and who would be allowed to express them.

In the early 1800s, the libertarian philosophy of free expression was advocated by Thomas Jefferson (1743–1826), the third president of the United States, who believed that education and journalism went hand-in-hand. Journalism was necessary to inform people about important issues, Jefferson believed, but in order to read the newspaper and make sense of the information they process, individuals needed a broad, liberal arts education. Toward that end, Jefferson spent much of his later years advocating the interrelated topics of education, literacy, and free speech and press. Jefferson said that the "art of printing secures us against the retrogradation of reason and information."[11] In a letter to Charles Yancey, a Virginia farmer and politician, Jefferson wrote that "where the press is free and every man able to read, all is safe."[12]

Today, the "marketplace of ideas" principle first espoused by Milton and John Stuart Mill is often cited by critics of mergers among media companies. Such mergers, the critics contend, is inconsistent with the spirit of the marketplace principle because it limits the number of voices that can reach prospective audiences.

In contrast, many social commentators contend that libertarianism is alive and well on the Internet, as bloggers and other non-traditional journalists are free to express whatever outrageous opinions and falsehoods they choose, but are not responsible for how the information is processed or interpreted.

How would Milton feel about today's methods of political discourse, such as Internet discussion groups, blogs, and various forms of social media? It's likely he would go along with the Supreme Court's "marketplace of ideas" principle, saying that while much of the information one finds in such venues is inaccurate (and often distasteful and objectionable), it would be inappropriate to prohibit it or legally punish the individuals who post it. Instead, Milton might say, it is more appropriate to offer competing information and let the audience make decisions as to its accuracy and value.

"The best way to discover truth is through robust competition of a multitude of voices," wrote media scholar W. Wat Hopkins in a 1996 article in *Journalism and Mass Communication Quarterly*.[13]

Rousseau and Compassionate Decision-Making

Jean-Jacques Rousseau (1712–1778) was a French philosopher who believed that both individuals and governments should use conscience and compassion to make ethical decisions that promote harmony among all concerned.

Many of Rousseau's ideas were espoused more than a thousand years earlier in the teachings of St. Augustine (A.D. 354–430), who taught that Christian principles (the "Judeo-Christian ethic") such as respect for others and concern for those impacted by your actions should guide all decision-making. The same concept was found in the African word *ubuntu*. The word is found in the Zulu, Xhosa, and other African languages and translates approximately as "humanity toward others." Another term associated with the idea of compassion is *communitarianism*, which refers to the interdependence of all constituent groups within a culture (i.e., "we're all in this together").

Applied to the world of journalism, Rousseau's philosophy would require that newspaper editors and television news directors to make the extra effort to protect the privacy and dignity of individuals in the news, without sacrificing their news judgments.

"As human beings, editors and reporters ought to be terribly burdened, haunted, by the very real consequences of our decisions to publish," said Arnold Rosenfield, former editor of the *Dayton Daily News*. "We ought to live uncomfortably with the fact that our journalism does damage. It can only be redeemed by the knowledge that, on balance, it helped more than it hurt."[14]

A photojournalist taking pictures at the scene of a driving crash might be faced with a decision as to whether to take pictures showing a victim trapped in one of the vehicles. Using the Rousseau approach, he or she could show compassion for the family of the victim and not take the picture, or the Mill approach, deciding that taking the picture might serve the utilitarian goal of warning others about the consequences of drunk driving. If he or she were to take one or more photos and then submit them to an editor, he or she is making a third choice—passing along the decision to someone else.

Kierkegaard, Multiple Motives, and Avoiding Procrastination

Soren Kierkegaard (1813–1855) was a Danish philosopher who believed that most problems facing society or individuals might be addressed in different but equally effective ways. Using the example of man's desire to help the poor, Kierkegaard wrote that while two individuals might have honorable intentions in wanting to help the poor, they might choose to do so in different ways, with neither method necessarily better than the other.

Kierkegaard also believed that the most effective way to make decisions is to consider all the possible options or choices, then consider the motives connected to each. While motives should not the sole basis for choosing one option over another and the decision-maker should not feel compelled to always choose the course of action associated with the most honorable motive, he believed that motives should be given considerable weight in the decision-making process. Unlike Francis Bacon and other philosophers who spoke and wrote about the value of seeking consensus in decision-making, Kierkegaard believed in making decisions quickly and independently. Much like Machiavelli, Kierkegaard believed that excessive consultation and assigning too much value to the opinions of others was a form of procrastination and simply a way to avoid taking responsibility for one's own decisions.

Durkheim and Cultural Relativism

Emile Durkheim (1858–1917) was a French sociologist and an advocate of **relativism**—a philosophical concept that says that many ideas cannot be identified as universally right or wrong, as what is right for one person may be wrong for another, and vice-versa. Relativism is often described in terms of clichés such as "one man's meat is another man's poison," "what is pornography to some is art to others," and "one man's vulgarity is another man's lyric."[15]

One example is found in the working relationships between the public relations representatives and journalists. American public relations professionals representing their companies in foreign countries are often aghast to find the bribing of journalists is commonplace in those cultures, while in the United States both the public relations and journalism professions would find such conduct unethical. While communication researchers might also label it as such, anthropologists and other social scientists, applying the concept of relativism, would avoid using labels such as "right and wrong," preferring instead to refer to them as "different."

Fletcher and Situational Ethics

Joseph Fletcher (1905–1991) was an American professor, sociologist, and bioethicist who was best known for coining the term **situational ethics** (sometimes shortened to "situation ethics") to refer to the concept of making decisions based on the merits of individual cases and not according to rigid or inflexible sets of rules. That idea was the opposite of Immanuel Kant's Categorical Imperative. In short, while Kant believed that following the correct process in decision-making was more important than the results, Fletcher believed that results were more important than the process.

His view of ethics and decision-making was grounded in his Christian beliefs, one of which was the premise that important decisions should always be made based on the merits of the situation at hand, and not on some inflexible set of rules or standards. In 1966, he published these ideas in his controversial book *Situation Ethics: The New Morality*.

Many readers may consider this as another way of saying that the "ends justify the means," but that might be a bit too extreme, as Fletcher would not agree with the principle that *any* behavior is acceptable if it produces a good result. Instead, Fletcher is simply claiming that instead of following rigid sets of rules (the means), a decision-maker should be flexible and consider both the ends and the means.

Nearly all of the professional codes, such as those of the Society of Professional Journalists, National Association of Broadcasters, Public Relations Society of America, and American Advertising Federation, are based on situational ethics. While purists in those professions may claim to base their decisions on Kant's Categorical Imperative (rules are rules; they're carved in stone), a more practical view is that the ethical codes can only provide a framework; decisions made in the real world must always be based on the merits of specific cases.

Examples of situational ethics applied to journalism include reporters misrepresenting themselves or using hidden cameras and microphones; that could easily be justified by claiming that the ends (of uncovering illegal or ethical business practices) made it acceptable to use those means (of newsgathering).

Applying situational ethics to journalism is problematic for several reasons, argued journalism researcher Sandra Dickson in a 1988 article in the *Journal of Mass Media Ethics*.

"A policy is a guideline, not a rule," said the policy manual of the *Longview Daily News* in Washington. "A guideline is not an undeviating course that must be followed invariably. This is not to say that deviation from all policies is permissible, but rather to allow the flexibility that is necessary oftentimes to deal sensibly with unusual or unexpected situations."[16]

Bok and the Principle of Veracity

Sissela Bok (1934–) is a Swedish-American philosopher who has spent much of her academic career studying various forms of deception in human communication—from the "white lies" individuals tell each other to the more harmful types of deception found in corporate advertising and public relations campaigns and information released by government agencies and officials. Her 1978 book *Lying: Moral Choice in Public and Private Life* is considered the starting point for any serious study of deception.

Bok explains her philosophy about deception with a concept she calls the **principle of veracity**. The principle refers to telling falsehoods only under the following conditions: (1) it is done as a last resort after all other alternatives have been considered; (2) the person speaking must be prepared to justify the need for the deception once it is exposed; and (3) before entering into the deception, the individual must carefully weigh the potential benefits from the deception against the potential for harm. The first condition requires that any time a practical and truthful alternative action is available to the potential liar, the more truthful alternative must be given priority. The second condition places the burden of justifying the lie solely on the liar to justify the reason for the lie, as opposed to the potential victim of a lie having to explain why it is harmful. Regarding the third condition, Bok rejects the ends-justify-the-means justification for lying and believes that liars tend to *underestimate* the potential harm of their lies and *overestimate* the possible benefits.

Bok summarized her concept by stating that, "In any situation where a lie is a possible choice, one must first seek truthful alternatives."[17] In the specific area of journalistic decision-making, media ethicist and Edmund B. Lambeth adds that "patience, imagination, determination, and craftsmanship will usually uncover stories that truly need to be made public without resorting to deceptive means."[18]

Self-Interest

Sartre and Individual Responsibility

Jean-Paul Sartre (1905–1980) was a French philosopher who advocated the principle of individual responsibility. Instead of uniform rules to determine right and wrong, Sartre believed that nearly any decision made or action taken by an individual was acceptable as long as he or she was prepared to accept the consequences for it. There were only a few concrete limits to human behavior, among those being the prohibition against intentionally harming another person or squandering one's personal wealth while not taking the opportunity to use one's resources to help others.

Rand and Objectivism

Ayn Rand (1905–1982) was a Russian-American novelist whose work is studied in both literature and philosophy classes around the world. Her first work, *The Fountainhead*, was published in 1943, and her most famous, *Atlas Shrugged*, followed in 1957. Each has sold more than six million copies and has been translated into more than twenty languages.

Her novels espoused her belief in the virtues of capitalism and the importance of individual freedom and self-determination, a philosophy she later called **objectivism**. At the core of objectivism was the notion of self-interest, which allowed individuals to disregard service to or concern for others and make decisions that benefited their own interests without regard to the impact on society. According to Rand, humans were predisposed to make decisions based on what was best for them, and they should not feel guilty or be criticized for doing so. "The pursuit of his own rational self-interest and of his own happiness is the highest moral purpose of his life," she wrote in "Introducing Objectivism," one of her few works of non-fiction.[19] While some observers believe that objectivism is at the root of Robert Ringer's self-help manual *Looking Out for #1*, a better match is the adage of "to thine own self be true," from Shakespeare's *Hamlet*.

Although it's unlikely that Rand would approve of the following behaviors, there are examples of objectivism or acting in one's self-interest all around us. Employment counselors report an increase in the number of job-seekers exaggerating on their résumés and justifying it by saying "everyone fudges on their résumé; if I don't do it, that puts me at a disadvantage." An individual caught stealing cable television service justifies in by saying the cable company's customer service representatives are rude, and therefore it's acceptable to steal cable service. An artist or musician who supplements his income by offering private lessons may not report that money on his income tax but rationalizes it by saying "the federal government doesn't do enough to support the arts."

As bizarre as those rationalizations may sound, even more excuses are found in the stories of journalists caught plagiarizing or fabricating stories (discussed in more detail in Chapter 4). Stephen Glass, a reporter who fabricated dozens of stories for *The New Republic*, said he fed off the adrenaline of attending story meetings and the "buzz" of hearing co-workers getting excited about his stories.

Jayson Blair, who fabricated or plagiarized stories while at *The New York Times*, said as an African American journalist hired under the newspaper's diversity initiative, he felt additional pressure to do well. Mike Barnicle, a columnist for the *Boston Globe*, may have had the weakest excuse, claiming that he fabricated stories because he simply "ran out of ideas."

Some modern-day political philosophers believe that Rand's work is misunderstood and has been treated unfairly. At the core of her objectivism philosophy was not that individuals should *always* make decisions based on self-interest, but only that it was *acceptable* to do so.[20]

Modern and Contemporary Media Criticism

Many outside of the academic world confuse the terms "modern" and "contemporary," believing those terms are synonymous. But for academic discussions, as well as the text of this chapter, they are quite different. "Modern" is a term used to describe the lives and work of scholars and artists of the twentieth century, most of whom are no longer living; while "contemporary" refers to those scholars and artists who are still alive and working today.

Modern Media Criticism

Individuals considered part of the "modern" era of media criticism include Jean Baudrillard, Noam Chomsky, Neil Postman, Walter Lippmann, Marshall McLuhan, and Daniel Boorstin.

Baudrillard (1929–2007) was born in France but spent most of his adult life in the United States, where he became both fascinated and repulsed by American culture. His criticism of American entertainment and mass media was based on a theory he called **hyper-reality**. In short, the theory stated that people were more interested in spectacle than substance and were so absorbed in popular culture that they are incapable of seeing it for what it is—a distraction from what was important.

In several books, he claimed that individuals were so absorbed in technology, entertainment, and retail consumption that they no longer enjoyed the simple things in life, and in some cases could no longer distinguish between the real world and the artificial world that corporations and the mass media had created for them. Baudrillard believed that the media —especially those found in America—had the potential to be both intrusive and manipulative. He also claimed that modern technology had "turned society into a video game." In 1991, for example, Baudrillard published a book titled *The Gulf War Did Not Happen*. In it, he claimed that the first Gulf War (1990–1991) did not actually take place, but was instead a fictional event created entirely by the federal government in cooperation with the television networks. That premise was illustrated in the 1997 movie *Wag the Dog*, in which the U.S. government hired a Hollywood film director to create a fictional war to district the population from a political sex scandal.

His hyper-reality theory was spoofed in a scene in the 1999 film *The Matrix*, which told the story of a futuristic world in which most people had lost the ability to distinguish reality from hallucinations. In the scene, the main character opens a copy of a Baudrillard book to reveal a collection of pirated computer disks. Baudrillard claimed the film misinterpreted his theories, but it nonetheless motivated moviegoers to learn more about him and his work.

While supposedly repulsed by popular culture, Baudrillard was also absorbed in it. He reportedly subscribed to hundreds of American newspapers and magazines and in his home had more than fifty televisions simultaneously tuned to different cable channels.

When Baudrillard died on March 6, 2007, his followers paid tribute to him by posting messages on the Internet that "Jean Baudrillard's death did not actually take place."[21]

Baudriallard's beliefs have plenty of support among other critics of American popular culture. Researcher David Niose often quotes a recent study reporting that fewer 30 percent of Americans can name the U.S. vice president, but nearly all can recognize photographs of Lady Gaga and other figures from popular culture.[22]

Chomsky added that "Americans can memorize sports statistics, relay details of the personal lives of celebrities, and recall television episodes from a generation ago ... but ask them to intelligently assess the actions of their government, the influence of corporate interests, or the details of any legislative proposal, and you will often be met with either blank stares or cynical dismissals." Chomsky called Americans' vulnerability to being lulled into powerlessness "the manufacture of consent."[23]

When *Newsweek* columnist Andrew Romano wanted to test Chomsky's criticisms in 2011, he orchestrated the magazine's "citizenship test" that involved 1,000 randomly selected American adults. Twenty-nine percent couldn't name the vice president. Seventy-three percent couldn't correctly say why we fought the Cold War. Forty-four percent didn't know that the first ten amendments to the Constitution were also known as the Bill of Rights, and far fewer could name any of them. Six percent couldn't even circle Independence Day on a calendar.[24]

Parodying the work of Baudrillard and Chomsky while commenting on the tendency of celebrities to remain in the spotlight a short period of time, pop artist Andy Warhol once commented that "in the future, everyone will be famous for fifteen minutes." Long before popular culture icons such as Paris Hilton and Kim Kardashian became famous based on having little or no talent, Daniel Boorstin commented that some celebrities become "well-known for their "well-knownness."[25]

Postman (1931–2003), referred to by some as Baudrillard's American counterpart, was a media critic and author who was best known by for his 1985 book about the history of television, titled *Amusing Ourselves to Death*. Postman described himself as a "humanist" and often claimed that "new technology can never substitute for human values." Much like Baudrillard, Postman was highly critical of American media and popular culture, especially television. In his book, Postman admonished the television industry for over-simplifying complex ideas and placing more emphasis on image than on substance. Postman believed that when everything is presented as entertainment, the role of the news for self-government is damaged, because "we are losing our sense of what it means to be well-informed."[26]

Lippmann (1889–1974) spent much of his career as a working journalist and was co-founder and editor of *The New Republic*. He did not become famous, however, until becoming a university professor and lecturer in his later years.

He did his most important work in the early 1900s, as American businesses began to embrace the persuasion business on a large scale, and the advertising and public relations industries began to apply new and sometimes manipulative persuasive techniques while simultaneously mastering new communications technologies capable of spreading their messages to larger and larger audiences. Lippmann was concerned about the vulnerability of unsuspecting audiences to such messages, and while he urged the media to play a bigger role in consumer protection, he was skeptical as to whether they were capable of doing so. In his 1922 book *Public Opinion*, he described journalism as "a searchlight, moving here and there across the night sky, illuminating one small section and then the other, but never providing the broad, even light needed to conduct the public's business."[27]

Lippmann believed that, at best, American media operate in an "imperfect system" and that despite their skill and desire for accuracy and objectivity, they will always present a picture of reality that is a bit misleading in one direction or another. In crime stories, for example, newspapers and television news programs may both cover trends in local crime working from the same set of facts gleaned from police reports and other government sources. Because they choose different words and approaches to presenting the story, television stories might make the crime problem seem worse than it actually is, while newspapers might make it appear less serious. He stopped short of claiming that such differing results cancel each out or combine to give the audience an accurate picture. Instead, he emphasized the need for audience members to be skeptical of the information they receive from the media and make decisions based on information from a diversity of news sources.

Lippmann added that even with their best efforts, journalists could never reach the same level of high performance of academic researchers, whose work is submitted for peer review prior to publication, or physicians, who rely on an entire profession's body of knowledge in performing their work. Journalists, by comparison, have no authoritative way of examining, testing, and evaluating their information because of the speed and competitive pressures involved in their work.[28]

McLuhan (1911–1980) was a Canadian sociologist who lived much of his adult life in the United States. He is most famous for his 1967 book *The Medium Is the Message*. Much like Baudrillard, McLuhan wrote about the influence of the mass media, the vulnerability of the public to be manipulated by media messages, and the need for them to be skeptical about the information they received. Observing the effect of media coverage of the Vietnam War on public opinion regarding the war, McLuhan stated that America's next war "will be fought not with bullets, but with images."[29] McLuhan was proven to be right in 1991, when the U.S. government employed a New York public relations firm to "sell" the first Gulf War to the American people.

Boorstin (1914–2004) was a professor, historian, and attorney who was best known for his criticism of the public relations and advertising industries. He coined the term **pseudo-events** to refer to activities that appeared to be important news events but were really just thinly disguised efforts at free publicity. Boorstin applied the term to any planned news event, implying that only spontaneous or unforeseen events could be truly newsworthy, and anything else was either propaganda or other form of "fake news."

Boorstin may have been the first to use the term *photo op* (short for "photo opportunity") to refer to the artificial photography sessions that political strategists arrange. While a standard part of a modern political campaign, such events were considered innovative during the early-to-mid-1900s. Boorstin criticized both the campaign strategists for arranging such photographs—typically the candidate kissing babies, walking through a flag factory, or greeting foreign dignitaries—as well as the media for publishing them under the guise of legitimate news. "We (Americans) are the most illusioned people on earth," Boorstin wrote. "Yet we dare not become disillusioned, because our illusions are the very house in which we live."[30]

Contemporary Media Criticism

Contemporary media critics whose ideas are worth noting include Ben Bagdikian, Howard Kurtz, David Horowitz, John Stauber, Nicholas Negroponte, and Jeff Jarvis.

Bagdikian was born in Turkey but has spent much of his adult life in the U.S. He is a retired journalist, political commentator, and editor. His most famous work is *The Media Monopoly* (1983), in which he expressed his concern that mergers and consolidation in the news business created the potential for too much of the news to be controlled by too few media companies.

Bagdikian disputes the claim of media owners that they don't exercise influence over how their reporters cover issues that directly affect the media organization or the industry in which it operates. "Many media corporations claim to permit great freedom to the journalists, producers, and writers they employ," Bagdikian wrote. "Some do grant great freedom. But when their sensitive economic interests are at stake, the parent corporations seldom refrain from using their power over public information."[31]

In *Media Circus* (1994), Kurtz provided dozens of examples in which the media focused attention on political scandals and other tawdry stories while failing to report on government waste, fraud, and other "boring" (but more significant) stories. The financial scandals involved bad judgment and billions of dollars in taxpayer money, while the sex scandals involved only bad judgment. In *The Fortune Tellers* (2000), Kurtz claimed that erroneous reporting of business news is more dangerous than erroneous reporting of political news because, in the former, the work of individual reporters can affect the stock market and the economic health of the nation, whereas in politics, the work of individual journalists would not have such an effect.

Horowitz is a social and media critic, but is not employed by any specific publication. His views, which he expresses in books, articles, media interviews, and on the Internet, focus mostly on what he perceives as the liberal bias of American media. He is also an outspoken critic of affirmative action, speech codes on college campuses, and political correctness.

On the opposite end of the political spectrum from Horowitz is Stauber, who identifies himself as a consumer advocate but is best known for his liberal views on government, politics, and the media. He first became known for his 1995 book *Toxic Sludge Is Good for You*, which took a critical look at the world of corporate advertising and public relations. Using a number of examples from contemporary advertising and public relations campaigns, Stauber criticized corporations and governmental agencies for their use of euphemisms in news releases and other communications materials intended to soften or mask the true impact of their actions. The title of the book is derived from a case he cited in which a company specializing in the disposal of solid waste uses such euphemisms to make the industry and its products to appear to be less harmful than they actually are.

In *Weapons of Mass Deception* (2003), Stauber and co-author Sheldon Rampton criticized the administration of President George W. Bush for what they called a "highly successful public relations campaign that sold the Iraqi war to the American public."[32]

Today, Stauber runs a nonprofit think-tank called the Center for Media and Democracy. One of its publications, which appears in both print and electronic form, is *PR Watch*, a newsletter that scrutinizes the work of the American public relations industry.

Negroponte is an author, futurist, media critic, and professor at the Massachusetts Institute of Technology. Much like McLuhan, he contrasts the older idea of a source "pushing" information to the receiver with the newer idea of the receiver "pulling" information from the source. That will change not only the nature of the publishing business, Negroponte points out, but also the nature of libraries. Libraries of the future will handle more information electronically and less in hard-copy form. The book publishing industry, which Negroponte describes as "squeezing ink onto dead trees," will survive only if it is able to adapt to the public's new preferences for receiving information.[33]

Jarvis is a journalist, college professor, and media critic; in many ways he is a modern-day version of Marshall McLuhan. He is a proponent of citizen journalism (discussed in more detail in Chapter 3), once saying that "not everyone can be a journalist, but anyone can perform an act of journalism."[34] Through his blog and podcast, Jarvis advocates the "open Internet" and "Internet entrepreneurship." He argues against any proposal involving government regulation of the Internet, even those designed to protect privacy.[35]

Your Turn

Case Study 2A: Football Stories Too Good to Be True (Because They Weren't)

For a few days in the spring of 2008, Kevin Hart—the high school football player, not the comedian—was a celebrity in his small town of Fernley, Nevada. The 6-5, 290-pound offensive lineman was clearly the best player on his high school football team and, with the help of school administrators and local sports journalists, staged a hoax that eventually embarrassed him, his school, and the media.

The beginning of the end was a news conference in the school gymnasium, where he placed caps from the University of Oregon and University of California on the table in front of him. After a few minutes of artificial suspense, he announced that he had chosen to attend California over Oregon.

For months before the event and several days afterward, Hart told his parents, friends, classmates, coaches, school administrators, and local sports journalists that Oregon and California had offered him full scholarships and emerged from a long list of potential college football programs competing for his services.

Hart's first mistake was to tell reporters at the news conference that Jeff Tedford, the head coach at California, recruited him personally and that the two spoke on the phone "many, many times." The story then fell apart when online sports journalists contacted Tedford, who said he had never heard of Hart and he had no scholarship offer. Reporters then contacted the University of Oregon, but officials there said Hart attended a football camp there but was evaluated him as "average at best" and unlikely to compete at the Division I level. Those online journalists then learned that in addition to his mediocre football skills, Hart's grade-point average was too low for him to be admitted to a university and was barely high enough for him to remain eligible to play in high school.

"I wanted to play Division I ball more than anything," Hart said in an apologetic public statement. "When I realized that wasn't going to happen, I made up what I wanted to be reality."[36]

While local reporters were angry at being victims of Hart's deception, their editors were angry at the reporters for not being more vigilant in covering the story. All had swallowed the deception in its entirety; if they had called the college coaches for comment, they would have known about the falsity of the story immediately. They missed several red flags associated with the story, including the fact that no college coaches had visited Hart's home, met his parents, or contacted his high school coach—all standard steps in the recruiting process.

When the story unraveled, Hart attempted to explain it with another lie—that a man claiming to be a talent scout working on behalf of several universities had duped him into believing the recruitment offers were real. In order to make that story sound plausible, he reported the fictional man to local police. When that part of the story was also exposed as a lie, Hart found himself facing charges of filing a false police report. The county school system also considered holding him responsible for the expenses associated with the meaningless news conference in the school gymnasium.

Meanwhile, national sports journalists used the story to illustrate their contention that the business of recruiting high school athletes to play at the college level was largely "hype," and that the problem was not the original lie told by Hart, but the willingness of local journalists to ignore inconsistencies in the situation and other "red flags" in order to write a good story.

Five years later, sports journalists were again the victims of an athlete's hoax—this time on a national scale. Manti T'eo was a star player at Notre Dame, a candidate for the Heisman Trophy, and a project first-round pick in the National Football League draft. The national media covered wanted to know more about his life, and they learned that his girlfriend, a Stanford University student named Lennay Kekua, had just died of leukemia. The media, as well as Notre Dame football fans and sports fans in general, learned about how they met when his team played a game at Stanford four years earlier, how their relationship grew from a distance, how he consoled her by telephone during her chemotherapy treatments, how he played in a game just hours after learning that she had died, and that she requested that he not attend her funeral but instead send white flowers. Then the media learned there was a good reason for the story sounding too good to be true: it wasn't.

The Internet news service Deadspin.com learned it was a hoax: Kekua was actually the creation of a T'eo family friend. According to Deadspin reporters, they first became suspicious about the relationship when they couldn't locate any of Kekua's friends, family members, classmates, or doctors; and no death certificate or newspaper obituary could be found. Then Stanford officials confirmed that no student by that name had ever enrolled at the school.

Even though T'eo claimed to have met Kekua in person and the two vacationed together in Hawaii, when the story unraveled, he claimed no knowledge of the hoax and that he had been the victim of someone's "sick joke."[37]

Since the T'eo scandal, many other Division I schools have implemented new social media policies for their student-athletes, and the University of Michigan even hires an outside consulting firm to contact their athletes with dubious offers of friendship or romance in order to test the athletes' gullibility.[38]

1. In the Hart case, do you agree with the opinion of the national sports journalists, who used the story to illustrate their contention that the business of athletic recruiting is largely "hype"?
2. While Hart had little justification for his deception, how much responsibility for the hoax lies with the media who covered the event (for not being more thorough in their fact-checking)? If you were the sports editor of one of the local newspapers involved, what punishment would you apply to your reporters who wrote the inaccurate stories?
3. In both cases, it took online journalists to uncover the deceptions. What does this say about print and broadcast journalists? Are these examples of online journalists being more thorough (or skeptical) in the fact-checking? Or examples of print and broadcast journalists getting so wrapped up in a "too good to be true" story that they ignored red flags?
4. Which philosophers or philosophies discussed in this chapter would help you with deal with these hoaxes?

Case Study 2B: The Reporter and the Hit Man

It started with a murder-for-hire plan in Hattiesburg, Mississippi, and ended with a debate over the role of journalism appearing on the editorial pages of newspapers across the country and in several media ethics textbooks, including this one.

Local police heard that an unknown man was hoping to hire a hit man to kill a witness in a grand jury proceeding and was willing to pay $35,000 to have it done. There were two unusual conditions: the murder had to be carried out by that weekend, and the payment would be made only after the death was reported in the media. Police investigators contacted the local U.S. attorney, who then called in representatives of the local daily newspaper, the *Hattiesburg American*, and a local television station, WDAM. The police and U.S. attorney pitched a plan to stage the murder of the man, Oscar Black III, and have the newspaper and television station report it as though it actually happened. After the alleged perpetrator was caught, the police would publicly admit the hoax.

The television station went along with the plan, while the newspaper agreed only to report that police were "seeking information suspected foul play directed toward Oscar Black III."

The suspect figured out it was a hoax and refused to pay the money. Seven months later, the police identified the suspect through more conventional methods, and the man was eventually convicted of soliciting a murder-for-hire.

A television station executive told other media that he went along with the hoax because the "life ethic" should take priority over the media ethics.[39]

The station's own non-scientific polling indicated that 80 percent of its audience agreed with its decision to participate in the deception. The reaction among the national media was not as kind; station executives found themselves under fire from both other daily newspapers as well as commentators on television and radio talk shows. "To all of the critics of my decision, it is far easier to advocate purism than to be a purist," wrote General Manager Cliff Brown in a commentary in the *Journal of Mass Media Ethics*. "There are cases such as this one where judgment calls for a break with journalistic ethics."[40]

The publisher of the *Hattiesburg American* also defended his position. He told other media outlets that he was faced with a decision among three bad options: (1) refuse and publish nothing; (2) expose the hoax as a news story in itself; or (3) go along with hoax, as the television station did. He briefly considered issuing a vague statement similar to that broadcast by the television station, but eventually decided to do nothing. He cited three reasons: participating in the deception would be a violation of journalism ethics, it would establish a dangerous precedent to become part of the law-enforcement process, and there were too many possible negative outcomes that could be not anticipated."[41]

1. Which position do you agree with in this case—that of the television station to cooperate, or that of the newspaper to refuse?
2. Did the fact that the suspect was eventually apprehended using more conventional investigative techniques vindicate the position of the newspaper not to cooperate?
3. While the television station did not cooperate to the extent the police wanted it to —broadcasting only a vague statement instead of a detailed story—is there a significant difference between the two?
4. Which philosophers or concepts from earlier in this chapter would be helpful in deciding this case?

Case Study 2C: Naming Names in Nashville and Norfolk

In 1989, the *Nashville Tennessean* followed its usual policy of naming those arrested for crimes—no matter how embarrassing the offense—when a police sting resulted in the arrests of 125 persons charged with hiring prostitutes. Those arrested included business leaders, a minister, and a popular high school basketball coach. The editor of the paper said the goal was to "publish bad news no matter who is involved … our readers have to believe that we do not play favorites. Our credibility is on the line here."[42]

At least one reporter said she had second thoughts about publishing the names after the paper was published, telling a researcher that she questioned if "the social value (of publishing the names) outweighed the potential tragedy this publication would cause in these people's lives."[43]

At about the same time as the prostitution sting in Nashville, an increase in the number of drunk-driving crashes in Norfolk, Virginia and the surrounding resort towns prompted local law enforcement to place more emphasize on stopping suspected drunk drivers. Two local newspapers did their part by publishing the names of those arrested, even after some in the newsroom disagreed with the practice. "We are going to publish all of the names all of the time," said one local newspaper executive.[44]

1. Without meaning to do so, three individuals quoted in this case study alluded to philosophical concepts mentioned earlier in this chapter. In the editor's claim that he would "publish bad news no matter who is involved ... our readers have to believe that we do not play favorites," he might have been citing John Rawls' "veil of ignorance." When a reporter for that paper questioned if "the social value (of publishing the names) outweighed the potential tragedy this publication would cause in these people's lives," there is a case to be made that Rousseau's concept of "showing compassion for those affected by your decisions" could be applied. When the news executive in the drunk-driving case said the paper would "publish all of the names all of the time," a case could be made that she was citing Immanuel Kant's Categorical Imperative. Which of these three philosophies have the most merit when applied to these cases?
2. Are there any other concepts in this chapter that could be applied?

Case Study 2D: Witnessing the Final Act: Should Executions Be Televised?

On June 11, 2001, domestic terrorist Timothy McVeigh was executed by legal injection at the U.S. Penitentiary in Terre Haute, Indiana. While many states have their own death penalty statutes, McVeigh was the first prisoner to be executed under the federal death penalty law since 1963. McVeigh was sentenced to death for his part in the 1995 bombing of the Alfred P. Murrah Federal Building in Oklahoma City, which killed 168 people.

As with state executions, there were a limited number of individuals allowed to witness the execution in person: McVeigh's attorney, members of the legal team that prosecuted him, and members of a media pool. In an unusual move, the federal government allowed the execution to be shown by closed-circuit television to a gathering of 232 family members of the victims at a secure location in Oklahoma City.[45]

Before the execution, national media organizations sought approval from federal officials to televise the execution. Among the individual journalists seeking permission to do so was talk-show host Phil Donahue. All of the requests were denied.

It wasn't the first time such a request was made and rejected. In 1994, Donahue failed in his quest to televise the execution of a convicted murderer in North Carolina; the condemned man also requested that the execution be recorded for later airing on television.[46]

Prior to the McVeigh execution, the last time a camera was in a death chamber was in 1928, when a reporter from *The New York Daily News* hid one in his pants leg and came out with an exclusive photograph of the prisoner strapped into the electric chair. He was unable to capture the actual execution.[47]

In 2002, a California court ruled that the media have a First Amendment right of access to attend executions, but not to photograph or televise them. In the nearly two decades that have passed since that decision, several other courts have issued similar rulings.[48]

The slim chances that an execution could ever be televised were reduced to almost zero in 2014. Following the "botched" execution of an inmate in Oklahoma, reporters described how the condemned man suffered convulsions and other signs of distress for nearly two hours. Within days, the Oklahoma Department of Corrections issued new policies that would reduce the number of media witnesses for future executions from twelve to five and allow for the curtains on the death chamber to be closed if the execution did not proceed as planned.[49]

The rules also reinforced the previous ban on photography and videography. The *Oklahoma Observer*, joined by the American Civil Liberties Union, sued the ODOC, claiming the new rules were a form of prior restraint. The court ruled in favor of the state, determining that the new rules did not violate the journalists' First Amendment right to gather news.[50]

Despite the persistent requests by some networks and individual journalists, many important voices in the journalism business are still against it. "Lots of people might want to watch a television execution," wrote Deborah Potter, director of the journalism think-tank NewsLab, in a 2001 opinion piece in *American Journalism Review*. "It could draw big numbers. But that's not a sufficient reason for a station or network news division to put it on the air. There are plenty of other things viewers want to see, too, and piles of reasons not to broadcast them."[51]

Adds Martin Kaplan of the Annenberg School for Communication at the University of Southern California: "I think it's pornographic. I think it caters to the lowest appetite that we have."[52]

1. Do you agree with the court rulings that specify that the media has the right to witness executions, but not photograph or televise them. Agree or disagree?
2. Is the idea of prohibiting television coverage of executions but allowing closed-circuit broadcasts for family member of victims (such as in the McVeigh case) an example of Aristotle's Golden Mean, i.e., finding the "just-right mid-point between the two extremes"?
3. What philosophers or concepts from Chapter 2 can be applied here?

Discussion Problem 2: One More for the Road

You're the publicist for a trio of country recording artists called The Renegades, who have taken their act from small clubs in Nashville to national prominence in less than a year. The group's live concerts are well attended and financially successful, their television appearances have received high ratings, and their music is selling well across numerous platforms.

Their most recent song, titled "One More for the Road," has created controversy, however. The song's lyrics describe a man's night of drinking at several different bars and then his attempt to drive home while intoxicated.

The song has been criticized by Mothers Against Drunk Driving, national politicians, and even other recording artists, many of whom have lost family members to drunk-driving crashes. They contend that the song "trivializes" the serious issue of impaired driving.

The song is being defended by music critics and politicians who dismiss the criticism as "another example of political correctness" and "a non-story." They also cite the First Amendment right of freedom of expression to defend the group's artistic license. They also point out that the song is not much different from Jimmy Buffett and Toby Keith's song, "It's Five O'Clock Somewhere."

One radio talk-show host and political commentator, well known for promoting bizarre conspiracy theories, even accused the group of intentionally creating the controversy in order to promote their concerts and music.

1. The group's manager comes up with several options for responding to the criticism and wants your recommendation. Which of the following has the most merit, and why?

    a. Stop using the song altogether and issue an apology to anyone who was offended.
    b. Revise the lyrics of the song to eliminate any alleged glorifying of drunk driving and issue an apology to anyone who was offended.
    c. Keep the song exactly as it is and clarify that it does not glorify drunk driving,
    d. Keep the song exactly as it is but don't do anything else. Decline all requests to discuss the song publicly, either in media interviews of otherwise. Adopt the policy that "there's no such thing as bad publicity" and "the only thing worse than being talked about is not being talked about."

2. This scenario is fictional, but can you think of any true stories involving music, movies, or television programs that are similar? What do you think should be done (or should have been done) in those cases?
3. What philosophies and concepts from this chapter can be applied here?

Discussion Questions

201. What have you learned from reading about the philosophers discussed in this chapter that you can apply to decision-making in your own life, either inside or outside of the workplace?

202. Baudrillard was highly critical of American media of the 1950s and 1960s, and Postman was equally critical of media of the 1970s and 1980s. Do those criticisms have more or less application today than during those decades?

203. In the section about St. Thomas Aquinas is a hypothetical scenario about ugly clothing. How do you believe Aquinas would have approached that dilemma? How would you have approached that dilemma and which other philosophers from this chapter do you believe would have the best advice for handling that scenario?

204. Do you agree with the media critics and historians who claim that John Milton's libertarian philosophy of media regulation (or lack of it) applies to cyberspace?

205. Working either individually or in groups, describe a scenario—either recalling one from your working experience or creating one that is entirely fictional—in which you believe it is either acceptable (or possibly acceptable) to lie. The audience for the lie should be an individual in one of the following categories:

(a) your boss or other superior;
(b) a co-worker;
(c) a subordinate;
(d) a client or customer;
(e) a vendor, supplier, or other business contact.

Summarize the scenario in a paragraph of five to ten sentences, and be prepared to discuss with the class.

Notes

1 The original source of this quote is unknown, but it appears in nearly every list of quotations attributed to Plato.
2 Today, many religious leaders and other persons claiming to make decisions based on religious principles believe that acts such as abortion, contraception to prevent pregnancy, or homosexuality are immoral simply because they are unnatural. More recently, the same argument has been made against cloning and stem-cell research; while not condemning all science, many religious leaders claim that advances in science that are inconsistent with the natural life cycle should not be allowed.
3 John C. Merrill, "Ethics and Journalism." In *Ethics and the Press*, John C. Merrill and Ralph D. Barney, ed. New York: Hastings House Publishers (1978), p. 8. See also: David Brooks, *The Road to Character*. New York: Random House (2015), p. 107.
4 Robert Trager, Joseph Russomanno, and Susan Dente Ross, *The Law of Journalism and Mass Communication*. Boston: McGraw-Hill, 2007, p. 99.
5 Ron F. Smith, *Ethics in Journalism*. Malden, MA: Blackwell Publishing (2008), p. 29.
6 Alexander Meiklejohn, *Political Freedom, the Constitutional Powers of the People*. Oxford: Oxford University Press (1965), p. 189.
7 Rotary Club operating policy: Rotary International website, http://www.rotary.org.
8 In contemporary political discussions, the term "libertarian" is used to refer to a political philosophy that rejects the Democrat–Republican and liberal–conservative dichotomies and instead offers an alternative political philosophy that at times resembles one end of the spectrum and at other times resembles the other end. In the modern-day interpretation of libertarianism, the emphasis is on personal freedom and individual responsibility in decision-making.
9 The first Supreme Court case in which this phrase was used was the 1919 case of *Abrams v. United States*, in which Justice Oliver Wendell Holmes wrote that "the best test of truth is the power of a thought to get itself accepted in the competition of the market."
10 *Keyishian v. Board of Regents*, 385 U.S. 589 (1967). See also: W. Wat Hopkins, "The Supreme Court Defines the Marketplace of Ideas." *Journalism & Mass Communication Quarterly*, Vol. 73, No. 1 (Spring 1996), pp. 40–52.
11 Al Gore, *The Assault on Reason: Our Information Ecosystem, From the Age of Print to the Age of Trump*. New York: Penguin Books (2017), p. 250.
12 Gore, p. 252.
13 W. Wat Hopkins, "The Supreme Court Defines the Marketplace of Ideas." *Journalism and Mass Communication Quarterly*, Vol. 73, No. 1 (Spring 1996), pp. 40–45.

14 Conrad C. Fink, *Media Ethics*. Boston: Allyn & Bacon (1995), p. 37.
15 This quote comes from the Supreme Court case of *Cohen v. California*, 403 U.S. 15 (1971).
16 Conrad Fink, *Media Ethics*. Boston: Allyn & Bacon (1995), p. 127.
17 Warren G. Bovee, "The End Can Justify the Means—But Rarely." *Journal of Mass Media Ethics*, Vol. 6, No. 3 (1991), pp. 135–145. See also: Sissela Bok, *Lying: Moral Choice in Public and Private Life*. New York: Vintage (1979), p. 33.
18 Edmund B. Lambeth, *Committed Journalism: An Ethic for the Profession*. Bloomington, IN: Indiana University Press (1986), p. 130.
19 Ayn Rand, "Introducing Objectivism," *The Objectivist Newsletter*, Vol. 1, No. 8 (August 1962), p. 35.
20 Mark Sanford, "Atlas Hugged." *Newsweek*, November 2, 2009, pp. 54–55.
21 Elaine Woo, "Baudrillard Kept a Sharp Eye on Reality." *Los Angeles Times*, March 11, 2007, p. 15-B.
22 David Niose, *Nonbeliever Nation: The Rise of Secular Americans*. New York: Palgrave Macmillan (2012), p. 211.
23 Noam Chomsky, "Sports and Spectacle." *Nation*, August 15, 2011.
24 Andrew Romano, "How Dumb Are We?" *Newsweek*, March 20, 2011.
25 Jacob Silverman, *Terms of Service: Social Media and the Price of Constant Connection*. New York: HarperCollins (2015), p. 67.
26 Gore, p. xii.
27 Walter Lippmann, *Public Opinion*. New York: Simon & Schuster (1922), p. 358.
28 Lippmann, p. 204.
29 Philip Marchand, *Marshall McLuhan: The Medium and the Messenger*. New York: Tichnor & Fields (1989), p. 24.
30 Daniel Boorstin, *The Image: A Guide to Pseudo-Events in America*. New York: Atheneum (1961), p. 241.
31 Ben Bagdikian, *The Media Monopoly*. Boston: Beacon Press (1992), p. xxxi.
32 John Stauber and Sheldon Rampton, *Weapons of Mass Deception*. New York: Penguin Group (2003), pp. 65–112.
33 Randy Bobbitt and Ruth Sullivan, *Developing the Public Relations Campaign*. Boston: Pearson (2014), p. 119. See also: Nicholas Negroponte, *Being Digital*. New York: Alfred A. Knopf (1995), p. 7.
34 Tania Ralli, "A Journalist and Blogger Tries Teaching." *The New York Times*, September 12, 2005.
35 Evgeny Morozov, "The Internet Intellectual." *The New Republic*, November 3, 2011.
36 Gene Wojciechowski, "College Recruit's Lie a Tale Gone Horribly Wrong." ESPN.com, February 8, 2008.
37 Paul Myerberg, "Inspirational Girlfriend a Hoax." *USA Today*, January 17, 2013, p. 1-A. See also: Dan Wolken, "T'eo Mystery Has Complicated Plot." *USA Today*, January 17, 2001, p. 2-C.
38 George Schroeder, "Schools Try to Keep Athletes Off 'Catfish' Hook." *USA Today*, March 7, 2013, p. 7-C.
39 "Cases and Commentaries: The Oscar Black Case." *Journal of Mass Media Ethics*, Vol. 1, No. 2 (Spring/Summer 1986), pp. 88–96.
40 "Cases and Commentaries: The Oscar Black Case."
41 "Cases and Commentaries: The Oscar Black Case."
42 "Cases and Commentaries: Police Sting in Nashville." *Journal of Mass Media Ethics*, Vol. 4, No. 2 (1989), pp. 281–289.
43 "Cases and Commentaries: Police Sting in Nashville."
44 "Cases and Commentaries: Police Sting in Nashville."
45 Deborah Potter, "Witnessing the Final Act." *American Journalism Review*, July/August 2001, p. 76. See also: Jim Yardley, "The McVeigh Execution on TV Brings Little Solace." *The New York Times*, June 12, 2001.
46 "Killer Executed After Losing Videotape Request." *The New York Times*, June 16, 1994.
47 Potter.
48 *California First Amendment Coalition v. Woodford*, 299 F. 3d 868 (2002).
49 *Oklahoma Observer v. Patton*, Case 5:14-cv-00905-HE (2014). See also: Tom Isler, "New Oklahoma Policies Restrict Media Access to Executions." *RCFP News*, October 6, 2014.
50 Isler.
51 Potter.
52 Potter.

3   Journalism and Broadcasting
Content Issues

Background

Many issues related to media content have their origins in academic studies on the impact of the mass media on society, the formation of government regulatory agencies, and the ethical codes of major professional organizations. In the mid-1900s, as politicians and media researchers began to consider the potential impact that news and entertainment media might have on the public, they studied those issues and developed theories to explain them. In addition, the federal government addressed the potential impact of the media by establishing a regulatory agency (the Federal Radio Commission, later to become the Federal Communications Commission), and professional associations did so by developing voluntary codes of ethics.

Academic Studies

In the previous century, researchers developed a variety of theories concerning the impact of the media, and those theories fell into two categories. The category that would later be known as **powerful effects theories** was based on the potential danger of the media influencing and manipulating their audiences. One of those theories, known as the **magic bullet theory**, contended that the media were so powerful that society might one day be at the mercy of the individuals or companies that controlled the media. The magic bullet theory and most other powerful effects theories have since been discounted, but were credible enough at the time that the federal government established rules to limit the size of media conglomerates and encourage competition.

In response to the powerful effects theories, researchers who believed the media had considerably less impact on their audiences developed a group of alternative theories known as **minimal effects theories**. Among these was the **cumulative effects theory**, which stated that while the media had some potential to affect public opinion and consumer behavior, that effect was realized only after the audience's repeated exposure to those messages over long periods of time.

The Role of Government

In the 1920s, with radio expanding in popularity for both news and entertainment, Congress saw the need to regulate the rapidly growing industry. The result was the Radio Act of 1927, which created the Federal Radio Commission and charged it with overseeing the industry, including the establishment of a licensing process. The FRC was the first federal government agency to have any responsibility for media regulation (the Federal Trade Commission already existed, but it did not assume responsibility for regulation of advertising until much later).

As for the role of the FRC, there was little concern for content. Instead, the major concern was ensuring that radio frequencies were assigned fairly and entertainment programming did not overshadow more important applications of radio, such as communication during emergencies. With the invention of television, Congress expanded the scope of the FRC and renamed it the Federal Communications Commission.

Today, the FCC remains the main source of media regulation within the federal government. It is charged with ensuring that broadcasters operate with regard to the "public interest, convenience, and necessity." The vague term "in the public interest" is often used to justify the FCC's regulatory and licensing procedures, which are often sources of controversy and debate.

Professional Organizations and Their Codes of Ethics

The first professional organization dealing with the media was the National Association of Broadcasters, which established a "Code of Good Practice" in 1929. The rationale behind the code was to avoid excessive governmental regulation in the industry and the NAB's "desire to do our own housecleaning without waiting for regulation by the government."

Approaching the end of the century, the NAB became more concerned with overall regulation of the industry than day-to-day issues involving broadcast outlets, and it no longer publishes a code of ethics.

Today, the major professional organizations serving the broadcasting industry are the Radio Television Digital News Association (formerly the Radio Television News Directors Association) and the Public Media Journalists Association (formerly the Public Radio News Directors Inc.). The Society of Professional Journalists serves mostly print journalists, but its membership includes some broadcast journalists as well.

While the SPJ Code of Ethics deals mainly with issues of policy—mostly the methods by which the reporters gather information—it also addresses a number of issues related to content. The most significant items are found within the first section titled "Seek Truth and Report It." According to the code, journalists should:

- avoid stereotyping by race, gender, age, religion, ethnicity, geography, sexual orientation, disability, physical appearance, or social status;
- support the open exchange of views, even views they find repugnant;
- give voice to the voiceless; official and unofficial sources of information can be equally valid;
- distinguish between advocacy and news reporting; analysis and commentary should be labeled and not misrepresent fact or context;
- distinguish news from advertising and shun hybrids that blur the lines between the two.

In the section titled "Minimize Harm," the code requires that journalists:

- be sensitive when seeking or using interviews or photographs of those affected by tragedy or grief;
- recognize that gathering and reporting information may cause harm or discomfort; pursuit of the news is not a license for arrogance;
- show good taste; avoid pandering to lurid curiosity.

The Radio Television Digital News Association Code of Broadcast News Ethics requires that broadcasters:

- strive to present the source or nature of broadcast news materials in a way that is balanced, accurate, and fair;
- evaluate information solely on its merits as news, rejecting sensationalism or misleading emphasis in any form;
- clearly label opinion and commentary.

Issues and Controversies

Public Service Journalism

The concept of "public service journalism" or "civic journalism" began in the early 1990s when local newspapers and television stations began going beyond reporting the news and took leadership roles in community improvement projects. Working either together or independently, newspapers and television stations began taking on a number of community projects. Examples:

- In many communities, media organizations sponsor holiday toy drives during which they invite their audiences to bring toys to the newspaper or TV station. Employees dress for the events as Santa Claus, elves, or other holiday characters. In other communities, media organizations sponsor litter-pickups, for which they supply volunteers with garbage bags, gloves, and refreshments. In both cases, the newspapers and television stations that organized the events then cover them as new stories.
- In other communities, television stations work with the American Red Cross or other nonprofit blood banks to promote blood donation drives and often host the events in their studios. During live newscasts, reporters interview blood donors and blood bank personnel.
- In Charlotte, North Carolina, in the 1990s, the *Charlotte Observer* and a local television station organized a number of community projects, including having their employees work as volunteers for various nonprofit organizations.At the same time in Huntington, West Virginia, the daily newspaper worked with a television station to organize a series of "town hall" meetings at which citizens could express opinions on the city's most pressing needs. Employees of the two media outlets organized volunteers into committees to address issues such as health care, education, law enforcement, and the environment. The newspaper and television station then covered the committee meetings as news stories.
- In a nationwide example of public service journalism, NBC developed "To Catch a Predator," a concept it incorporated into its popular *Dateline* series. Working with police and a nonprofit group called Perverted Justice, NBC personnel set up a sting operation that lured suspects, believing they would be meeting underage children for sex, to a home equipped with hidden cameras (this series is addressed in more detail in Chapter 5).

Advocates of public service journalism claim it produces win–win results: the communities receive much-needed help in a variety of areas, and the newspapers and television stations, while they deny that ratings and economics play a role, draw larger audiences and sell more advertising. Proponents dispute the theoretical concepts of "objectivity" and "detachment" and contend that journalists cannot function as "social hermits" and retreat from all involvement in the communities. Instead, they believe that both media outlets and individual reporters should be more involved in their communities because doing so makes them more aware of problems and opportunities that might otherwise be missed.

Critics of public service journalism, however, have two main concerns. The first, typically expressed by those who believe in the traditional values of journalism, is that when media organizations "adopt" nonprofit organizations and get involved in addressing community problems that are ordinarily the responsibility of local government, they are going beyond their traditional roles. The job of the media, they say, is to report on such projects, not organize them. Some use the metaphor of "marching in the parade rather than just reporting on the parade." One journalist phrased it this way: "If I'm a journalist responsible for covering the parade, I need to ask a lot of questions: Who is paying for the parade? Was that money well spent? Was the parade conducted safely and efficiently? Because of my newspaper's interest in diversity, I want to know if anyone was left out of the parade. Those are all important questions to ask, but I can't ask the questions about the parade and march in the parade at the same time."[1]

Another concert is that a newspaper or television station cannot simultaneously organize an event and then cover it as a news story without the potential for conflicts of interest. What happens when something goes wrong? Will journalists responsible for reporting on the success or failure of other community projects apply the same scrutiny to problems with an event that was organized by their own employer?

In a 2013 case, for example, a television station in Alabama took on the "special project" of advocating for a proposed animal cruelty law that was making its way through the state legislature. The station was criticized by media ethicists for taking part in a news story instead of merely covering it, and the criticism got stronger when the bill passed and the station actively boasted on the airwaves and on its website about the part it played in the political victory.[2]

Sponsored News, Advertorials, Partnerships, and "News Look-Alikes"

Another trend at local newspapers and television stations is to negotiate special rates for major advertisers who pay to sponsor and provide content for special pages (and sometimes entire sections) in the newspaper or segments on evening news broadcasts. Advocates call them **sponsored news** or advertorials, while television and newspaper advertising managers and senior executives use the term "partnerships." Critics use the derogatory term "news look-alikes." Regardless of what they are called, late in the twentieth century these pages, sections, and television segments are popular and effective communication vehicles for high-dollar advertisers who want to do more than just purchase traditional advertising space and time.

One example involves hospitals, which sponsor and provide content for newspaper features and television segments about health topics while indirectly promoting their services. For other sponsors, newspapers produce "special sections" to promote community events and offer major advertisers the opportunity to sponsor the sections and generate community goodwill by associating themselves with the event. Other newspaper advertisers are invited to sponsor weekly "theme pages" such as those targeted at children or seniors. Traditionalists in the newsroom or newspaper management often criticize this form of promotion because it blurs the lines between news and advertising.

There is less concern at television stations, however. Many local television stations have morning talk shows that some media ethicists describe as "paid advertising, poorly disguised as news," during which representatives of hospitals and other local companies answer "soft-ball" questions from interviewers while subliminally promoting their employer's products or services. Depending on the size of the market, those companies may be paying up to $3,000 for their spokespersons to be "interviewed."[3]

The newspaper version of sponsored news often involves "special sections" that promote upcoming events such as home shows. The *Des Moines Register*, for example, offers "custom publishing" for such events, producing publications that include feature articles, written by a combination of freelancers and the paper's regular news staff, appearing next to advertisements for the products and services mentioned in the stories.[4]

As confusing as sponsored ads might be for readers of printed news products, it is even worse in the case of online publications. In a 2015 study, four out of six focus groups said with near consensus they could not distinguish between "sponsored" and traditional news stories in online newspapers. The study also found that "native ads" (a slang term for sponsored news on the Internet) were effective in raising awareness for newly introduced brands. "Sponsored content is fundamentally designed to blend in with the look and feel of the other articles on a site, and actual written disclosures such as 'sponsored' or 'advertisement' are often so hard to see even if you're looking for them," wrote Ginny Marvin, author of the study, on the website MarketingLand.com. "So is it any wonder that consumers can't tell the difference between content that brands pay for and regular articles?"[5] The following year, a study at the University of Georgia reported that more than 60 percent of subjects did not notice the sponsor disclosure label at the top of sponsored articles.[6]

In 2016, the Federal Trade Commission introduced its first rules regarding sponsored ads, announcing they were aimed at preventing "unfair or deceptive practices."[7]

A study in *Columbia Journalism Review* found that hospitals and pharmaceutical companies are the major providers of sponsored news, resulting in an epidemic of "unhealthy deals" involving television newsrooms and local hospitals.[8]

The study found that one of the major culprits in the trend was the Cleveland Clinic, a major health-care provider in Ohio. Each week, the "Cleveland Clinic News Service," which is actually the hospital's in-house public relations department, produces dozens of "news stories" that it provides free to news stations across the country. The video packages include interviews with Cleveland Clinics doctors, researchers, and patients and made to look like legitimate television news spots.

But the Cleveland Clinic is hardly the only hospital engaged in such a marketing program. Other hospitals produce their own news stories and pay local stations to get them on the air. While many traditional journalists at those stations express concerns about the relationships, advertising directors and other executives get around the station's ethical codes by using the term "partnership" instead of "sponsored news."[9]

One concerned television newsroom employee said such programs are "more like a Billy Graham television special" than a true news program, and a spokesperson for the Radio Television News Directors Association (now the Radio Television Digital News Association) said that "once viewers and listeners start to think your news content is for sale, you'll lose credibility and the value that advertisers want will be damaged." An article in *Columbia Journalism Review* called sponsored news an attempt to "substitute lazy journalism and gee-whiz technology stories for the real thing."[10]

Critics invoke two sections of the SPJ Code in explaining their concerns. In the section titled "Seek the Truth and Report It," the code requires that journalists "distinguish news from advertising and shun hybrids that blur the lines between the two." In the section titled "Act Independently," the code requires journalists to "deny favored treatment to advertisers and special interests and resist their pressure to influence news coverage."

Does the News Media Show a Bias Toward Liberal Views?

Accusations of an alleged "liberal bias of the press" go back to the 1960s and the work of Edith Efron, a journalist and media critic. Writing a series of columns for *TV Guide* and a 1971 book titled *The News Twisters*, Efron based her theories largely on anecdotal evidence from the 1968 presidential election campaign, in which the news media, according to her, conspired to support liberal Democrat Hubert H. Humphrey and oppose conservative Republican Richard Nixon, the eventual winner. Much of her methodology was later found to be flawed, but the book was popular among Republicans and conservatives. In order to artificially create "buzz" for the book, a member of President Nixon's White House staff allegedly bought $8,000 worth of books in order to vault it into the *New York Times* best-seller list.

In the 1960s, many conservative politicians accused media organizations of being anti-American because they opposed against the Vietnam War on their editorial pages and because individual reporters appeared to second-guess military leaders on the execution of the war.

One of the earliest academic studies of alleged media bias took place in 1986, when researchers Robert Lichter and Stanley Rothman concluded that journalists were "predominately liberal" in their own political beliefs and that bias offered showed in their reporting. According to their survey, 54 percent of print and broadcast journalists admitted to being liberal, with most being registered Democrats. Only 17 percent identified themselves as conservative, but slightly more were registered Republicans. About 30 percent identified themselves as independent or "middle of the road."[11]

Two more recent books by former network news reporter Bernard Goldberg have explored the issue of alleged media bias. The first, simply titled *Bias*, was a 2003 work that documented dozens of examples of media allegedly showing favoritism toward Democratic politicians and bias against their Republican opponents. In his follow-up book, titled *Arrogance: Rescuing America from the Media Elite*, Goldberg claimed that the traditional media's liberal bias and concern for political correctness are at least partially responsible for the industry's decline. If they continue down that path, Goldberg wrote, "they will cease to be serious players in the national conversation and will become the journalistic equivalent of the leisure suit—harmless enough, but hopelessly out of date."[12]

Despite persistent criticisms of bias, media executives continue to claim that while journalists may have a variety of political leanings, those leanings seldom show up in their work. "At our paper, we don't ask reporters to take a political litmus test," wrote Pat Rice, editor of the *Northwest Florida Daily News*, in a 2007 column. "But we do insist that they leave their own political slant out of their stories."[13]

While accusations of liberal bias have focused mostly on privately owned media, those that are publicly owned have been the targets of similar criticism. The two national media outlets— Public Broadcasting Service (PBS) and National Public Radio (NPR)—have been criticized for decades as being biased against large corporations and Republican officeholders. In 2005, the chairman of the Corporation for Public Broadcasting (CPB), the federal government agency that operates PBS and NPR, hired consultants to monitor those broadcast outlets for signs of anti-Republican, anti-conservative, anti-business, and anti-military bias in their reporting. As a result of the consultants' report, CPB established two news and business programs with a conservative slant and hired two ombudsmen—one conservative and one liberal—to "bring balance" to PBS and NPR programming, despite public opinion surveys that indicated that the audience did not believe the programming was biased in one direction or the other.

Today, conservative groups such as Accuracy in Media (AIM) and the Media Research Center have taken up where Efron left off. While media bias remains a popular belief among many political conservatives, it is not fully supported by those groups. Some political observers claiming to be "moderate conservatives" believe the issue is largely overstated and accuses more conservative politicians of using the "liberal bias of the press" allegation as an excuse for the failings of the Republican Party and other conservative groups.

Political commentator Mark R. Levin claims that one result of media bias is "group-think"—the tendency of all members of a group to think and act alike. The results of not participating, he wrote in a 2019 book on media bias, is that reporters who do not "go along to get along" will find themselves ostracized. "When a journalist breaks from the rest of the media pack, which is quite rare, their careers are typically threatened or reviled by the rest of the press," Levin wrote. He points to the example of Lara Logan, a former *60 Minutes* correspondent who was critical of the media's liberal slant in a 2019 podcast, who was subsequently shunned by her former colleagues at CBS as well as reporters at other networks she once considered friends.[14]

While Americans often complain that the media demonstrate a bias against conservative politicians and their positions, in Europe many citizens have the opposite complaint: that media blindly support conservative politicians and government programs.[15]

Levin quotes George Mason University Professor Tim Groseclose, who believes that the progressive political views of journalists "distort the natural views of Americans and prevent us from seeing the world as it actually is … instead we see only a distorted version of it. It is as if we see the world through a glass—a glass than magnifies the facts that liberals want us to see and shrinks the facts that conservative wants us to see."[16]

In a 2014 study conducted at Indiana University, more than 1,000 journalists were questioned about their political affiliations. About 50 percent indicated they were registered as independents, 28 percent as Democrats, 7 percent as Republicans, and 15 percent as "other."[17] A 2018 study conducted by Arizona State University and Texas A & M revealed even more lopsided statistics involving business journalists. According to that study, 68 percent of business journalists self-identified as "liberal," 37 percent as "moderate," and less than 5 percent as "conservative."[18]

While the results of surveys based on journalists' self-perception is telling, a more trouble-some statistic involves how the public perceives them. According to a 2017 Gallup Poll, 62 percent of those surveyed believed that journalists favor Democratic political candidates."[19]

In the 1960s, British journalist Claud Cockburn said that "news stories are often written backwards … they are supposed to begin with facts and develop from there, but in reality, they begin with a journalist's point of view and it is that point of view from which facts are subsequently gathered."[20]

As far back as the 1940s, the Hutchins Commission pointed out in its final report that the media should pay special attention to the difference between fact and opinion.[21]

Although criticisms of liberal bias are common, some conservative media outlets are occasionally accused of doing just the opposite. When movie producer Harvey Weinstein was accused in 2017 of decades of sexual misconduct, Fox News spent more than twelve hours covering the case in a three-week span. Nearly all the stories emphasized that Weinstein was a financial supporter of numerous Democratic political candidates. During that same time, however, the network dedicated less than twenty minutes to coverage of similar allegations against one of its own staffers, commentator Bill O'Reilly.[22]

In a 2017 study, researchers found that the degree of mistrust ran according to party lines, with slightly more than half of Democrats and 90 percent of Republicans having lost trust in the media. Members of both parties said their attitude toward the media was based on problems with accuracy and bias as well as "partisan and ideological leaning."[23]

In his 2001 book *Coloring the News: How Crusading for Diversity Has Corrupted American Journalism*, author and media critic William McGowan accuses large media organizations of carrying out a liberal agenda, including advocacy for affirmative action, abortion rights, gun control, and support of liberal politicians and political candidates. As examples, McGowan points to a series of stories published in *The New York Times* and *Washington Post* about the career of a New York physician who grew up in poverty but became one of the country's leading obstetricians in the mid-1970s, serving mostly low-income women. They emphasized the doctor had achieved admission to a medical school under its affirmative-action admissions policy that would later be ruled unconstitutional in a 1978 Supreme Court case. The stories praised the physician, the medical school he attended, and affirmative action in general as being responsible for the "American success story."[24]

But when it was learned in the 1990s that the physician had opened a plastic-surgery clinic as a side business and performed high-risk procedures without adequate training—causing one death and dozens of permanent disfigurements—the *Times* and *Post* covered the legal proceedings against him but failed to mention their earlier praise for him. McGowan claims that ignoring that aspect of the story illustrates the media's bias toward the cause of affirmative action as part of a larger liberal agenda.[25]

In 2000, when a child attending the first grade in Flint, Michigan was killed by a classmate who brought a gun to school, McGowan noted that most media organizations gave extraordinary coverage of President Bill Clinton's comments that blamed the tragedy on the availability of guns—a popular Democratic and liberal talking point—instead of looking at the larger issue of failed government programs aimed at addressing poverty and family dysfunction. McGowan also asserted that race played a role: the victim was white, the suspect was black. Ignoring race, McGowan claimed, was more evidence of the media's fear of appearing to cast the story in racial terms.[26]

In another example, McGowan called out *The Washington Post* for avoiding the racial aspect to a story about black teenagers harassing white passengers on the city's subway system, passing it off as "youthful rowdiness."[27] McGowan contends that in addition to avoiding stories that make racial minorities "look bad," the media also play down stories that might offend gays (such as those about the military's "don't ask, don't tell" policy),[28] women,[29] and immigrants.[30]

In 2017, the "liberal bias" label was attached to ESPN. The sports network drew criticism from *The New York Times* for its coverage of the national anthem controversy affecting the National Football League, professional sports teams declining President Trump's invitations to visit the White House, the unequal-pay conflicts involving the men's and women's U.S. soccer teams, and the network's selection of transgender Caitlyn Jenner for its Arthur Ashe Courage Award. ESPN President John Skipper responded to criticism by pointing out that the network's parent company, The Walt Disney Company, was "committed to diversity and inclusion" and that it treats issues "not as a political stance but as a human stance."[31]

Many journalism scholars believe that complaints about the so-called liberal bias of the press are overstated. CNN, MSNBC, and large daily newspapers such as *The Washington Post* and *The New York Times* may appear to be liberal simply because they point out the failures of conservative politicians, but they point out the failures of the liberal politicians, too. And audience members who still believe that the mainstream media are too liberal have alternatives such as *The Wall Street Journal*, *The Washington Times*, and Fox News. Add conservative radio talk-show hosts such as Sean Hannity, Rush Limbaugh, and Glenn Beck and the options for conservative audience members expands exponentially.[32]

In April 2019, Senators Ted Cruz of Texas and Marsha Blackburn of Tennessee joined the chorus of conservative voices accusing social media platforms of demonstrating bias against them and their causes. At a senate hearing, Cruz threatened social media companies with potential regulation, while Blackburn has called on social media companies to "embrace the spirit of the First Amendment." Media Matters for America, a liberal media watchdog groups, disputed the criticisms, releasing a study that found that on Facebook right-leaning and left-leaning pages were approximately equal in number and traffic.[33]

In July 2019, President Trump convened a "Social Media Summit" at the White House in order to discuss his accusations that platforms such as Facebook, Twitter, and Google exhibited a "terrible bias" against his administration and conservative causes in general. Trump accused the first two platforms of giving his critics a platform for promoting liberal causes while denying access to conservative causes. He accused Google of "rigging" its algorithms so that anti-Trump stories would be ranked higher than pro-Trump stories in search results. Ironically, the three organizations of which Trump was most critical were not invited to the summit. Instead, he was merely "preaching to the choir," as invitees included conservative social media platforms and Republican lawmakers already on his side.[34]

Parody and Ridicule

While public figures often file lawsuits based on alleged damage to their reputations, others complain—sometimes in court and sometimes by other means—over matters of taste.

In 1902, the *Philadelphia North American* portrayed Pennsylvania Governor Samuel Pennypacker as an obese parrot in an editorial cartoon. Pennypacker and his supporters responded by pushing a bill through the legislature making it illegal to depict men "as birds or other animals." The newspaper complied, and instead began depicting politicians as vegetables.[35]

Throughout his career, the late evangelist Jerry Falwell was often the target of newspaper editorial cartoonists and other forms of parody. In the late 1980s he accused *Hustler* magazine and flamboyant publisher Larry Flynt of crossing the line from satire into bad taste. At first glance, the full-page item appeared to be part of a series of advertisements in which celebrities talked about their first time drinking Campari Liqueur. But the Falwell piece was actually a parody that suggested that the reverend had sex (i.e., his "first time") with his mother and addressed his congregation while drunk. At the bottom of the page, in tiny print, was a disclaimer that read, "ad parody—not to be taken seriously." Falwell sued Flynt for both libel and emotional distress. A court ruled that Falwell had no grounds for a libel case because it determined that the ad was "so outrageous that no reasonable person would have believed it," but the court ruled in his favor on the emotional distress claim. The Supreme Court eventually overturned that ruling, however, determining that the item was protected as free speech because it was a parody of a public figure and was analogous to a political cartoon or caricature.[36]

In 2006, American astronaut Lisa Nowak was caught in a love triangle with two other astronauts and was accused of stalking her female rival. As the case unfolded, print and broadcast media labeled the story "Lust in Space" and focused on the more bizarre details of the story. Among those details were reports that during a long drive from Houston to Orlando to confront the other woman, Nowak wore an adult diaper in order to avoid having to make bathroom stops. For weeks that followed, the news media repeated that detail and late-night television comedians focused on it. Nowak's attorney denied that aspect of the news reports and pleaded with the media to stop reporting it, but most continued.

In 2007, a contestant in the Miss Teenage America Pageant was the victim of not only an embarrassing moment on stage, but also months of ridicule that followed. Seventeen-year-old Lauren Caitlin Upton, representing South Carolina in the pageant, was asked by a judge on the panel for her opinion on weaknesses of the American education system. She responded with a rambling, forty-five-second answer that not only failed to address the question, but made little sense at all. The following day, radio talk shows across the country used the sound bite to ridicule the young woman based on the stereotype of blonde women being inarticulate. Others used the sound bite as part of their tirade against the quality of public schools and what they believed was the superficial nature of beauty pageants.

One of the most famous cases of a private person being exposed to public ridicule as a result of media exposure began with a March 6, 1995 taping of an episode of *The Jenny Jones Show* to be titled "Same-Sex Secret Crushes." Jones' production staff invited automobile mechanic Jonathan Schmitz to be part of the program and told him he would be meeting his "secret crush"—but did not tell him the title of the episode. When he finally met his crush in front of a studio audience, it turned out to be one of his customers, Scott Amedure. Schmitz reacted with laughter while on the show, but became disturbed by the incident later. Unknown to the show's producers, Schmitz had a history of mental illness and drug and alcohol abuse. Three days after the show's taping, after enduring ridicule by family members and friends, Schmitz shot and killed Amedure. Schmitz was later convicted of second-degree murder and was sentenced to prison for twenty-five to fifty years, and the episode was never aired.

While media personnel are often responsible for providing the background material on which much parody and ridicule are based, at other times they find themselves on the other side of the issue—as targets of ridicule. In 2003, for example, a popular sports director for a television station in Tampa, Florida, was arrested for drunk driving (see Case Study 4E). Compounding his legal problems were the public comments generated by the fact that the offense took place in a part of town known for drug-dealing and prostitution. Local radio disc jockeys, while admiring the man for his humility in admitting and apologizing for his offense, couldn't resist the opportunity to poke fun. "Everyone knows that if you go into that part of town late at night, you're looking for one of two things," one early-morning disc jockey said.

A decade earlier, a news anchor for a competing station in Tampa was arrested after being caught soliciting sex from a fifteen-year-old prostitute. One radio disc jockey joked that a local sandwich shop that was well known for naming its sandwiches after local celebrities should offer a new hot dog named after the newscaster; it would consist of a "tiny little wiener on fifteen-year-old buns."

Political columnist Kathleen Parker sites the reluctance of newspapers to publish cartoons that "push the envelope" as evidence that mainstream newspapers have lost their edge. "Heaven forbid we should allow anything as controversial and evocative as a political cartoon," she was quoted as saying in a 2004 story in *Editor & Publisher*. "People might get excited, start talking, laugh out loud and tell their friends. We should be allowed to be irreverent, even at the risk of hurting someone's feelings. Chances are pretty good that if no one is offended, no one is reading."[37]

School Shootings and Other Tragedies: How Much Coverage Is Too Much?

For much of the twentieth century, the news media covered mass murders and other tragedies involving the loss of human life very much after the fact. Limitations in technology meant that the details of those stories, and the photographs and video used to illustrate them, were at best presented to the audience on the following day.

Beginning in the 1980s, however, advances in technology such as smaller, lighter cameras and mobile news vans and helicopters meant that news crews could provide same-day coverage of tragedies and in some cases even provide live coverage of events as they unfolded.

Many such tragedies took place on or near high school and college campuses. The first of such cases happened at the University of Florida in 1990. During the first week of fall semester, five students were murdered in their off-campus apartments over a span of three days. The crimes attracted media from all over the country, and the media struggled with issues such as (1) balancing the public's right to know with the potential for creating unnecessary panic, (2) sorting through rumors and unsubstantiated information from questionable sources, (3) avoiding the release of information that might harm the law-enforcement investigation, and (4) showing concern for the privacy of the families affected. While there was some criticism of print and broadcast journalists in the aftermath, most critics gave the media high marks for covering the tragedy in a thoughtful and sensitive manner.

The media was challenged again in 1999, when two students at Columbine High School in Littleton, Colorado killed twelve of their classmates, a teacher, and themselves. Television stations in nearby Denver broke into their morning programming to cover the tragedy live, and one station stayed on the air to provide non-stop and commercial-free coverage for thirteen hours. Two daily newspapers serving the area published late-afternoon special editions. The following day, newspapers across the state each provided more than twenty pages of coverage that included gruesome details of how the students died and photographs showing bodies as they were removed from the building.

In the weeks that followed the killings, media critics scrutinized the coverage. While none objected to the amount of coverage, many found problems with the degree to which the images of the dead and wounded were shown. More importantly, both print and broadcast media were criticized for numerous factual errors that resulted from their desire to upstage their competitors. For example, early media reports indicated that more than twenty-five students had been killed—almost twice the number who actually died. One television station attempting to show photographs of the killers showed the yearbook photograph of the wrong student, and that photograph also appeared briefly on the station's website.

On April 16, 2007, a student at Virginia Polytechnic Institute (Virginia Tech) carried out a similar massacre on that campus, resulting in the deaths of thirty-two students and faculty members and eventually the killer himself. The reviews of the media coverage were mixed. In the first two days after the tragedy, the media were praised for demonstrating restraint, good taste, and sensitivity. But much of that goodwill was lost two days later when television networks aired excerpts from a video prepared by the killer and mailed to NBC News (see Case Study 3D).

The Debate over Video News Releases

As the term indicates, video news releases are electronic versions of the more commonly used news releases issued (on paper) by individuals and organizations as part of the public relations process. The idea was born in the mid-1980s, when advances in technology allowed public relations professionals to produce video products quickly and inexpensively. Today, video news releases can either be provided on digital video disks or through the organization's website or other digital delivery method. The most common applications of video news releases are to introduce new products, respond to crises, or address other news stories that have a substantial need for video content.

Most public relations professionals who produce VNRs, as well as the reporters who accept them, see the issue as one of convenience. Some television news directors and other policy makers, however, object to the use of VNRs because they consider them a shortcut to accept any materials directly from the source. Many news directors believe that "if it's important enough for us to do a news story on the topic, it's important enough for us to shoot our own video." Some news directors are also concerned over the authenticity of the video. In an age of video manipulation and computer-generated images, some news executives worry that accepting video from outside sources leaves them vulnerable to hoaxes. Still other news directors see them as superficial attempts at free publicity presented in the form of what many media ethicists refer to video news releases as the "original fake news."[38]

The Radio Television Digital News Association (RTDNA) includes in its code of ethics a set of guidelines that broadcasters should use in determining the appropriateness of using video provided by public relations representatives or any other party. Referring to such materials as "non-editorial video and audio," the guidelines suggest that such material is acceptable if (1) similar material cannot be recorded by the station's own reporters and is not available from other sources, (2) the source of the material is disclosed to the audience, (3) news directors have evaluated the motives of the organization providing the material, and (4) news directors have made sure that the producers of the material adhered to standard journalistic principles, such as those regarding truth, objectivity, and conflicts of interest.

Labeling VNRs with a simple subtitle reading "video courtesy of X" or "video provided by Y" is usually enough to prevent readers from confusing VNR content with station-produced or network-produced video. That step was missed in one incident in 2004, when television stations around the country aired a ninety-second VNR, produced by the federal government, promoting its new prescription drug benefit for Medicare recipients. The segment showed an elderly couple discussing the plan with their pharmacist, and all three agreed that it was a good idea. At the end of the segment, a voice-over artist is heard saying, "In Washington, this is Karen Ryan reporting." Failing to delete that portion of the audio led audiences to believe the segment was part of an objective news story rather than a partisan promotional video.[39]

The following year, "Karen Ryan" made yet another appearance in a "news story" produced by the Bush administration, this time narrating a piece promoting the Department of Education's "No Child Left Behind" initiative. Many local stations used brief clips of the video but substituted the narration of their own reporters instead of Ryan's. But a few ran it in its entirety, in many cases confusing viewers who thought it was an actual news story and that Karen Ryan was one of the station's reporters.

"In the process (of the two spots), the complicit press took the process one step farther than Karen Ryan had," wrote Thomas Lang and Zachary Roth in a 2004 article in *Columbia Journalism Review*. "It's one thing for a PR operative to pose as a reporter; it's another for a reporter to act as a cog in the PR wheel of a government agency."[40]

Citizen Journalism and User-Generated Content

One of the fastest-growing trends on the Internet is that of **citizen journalism, open-source journalism, or user-generated content**. It takes two forms: (1) the contribution of video to traditional media outlets and (2) the distribution of that material through personal web pages or Internet services such as YouTube. Advances in technology such as small, hand-held video recorders (many of them built into cellular telephones) caused both forms of citizen journalism to expand exponentially in the early 2000s.

The concept of citizen journalism, however, can be traced back to the latter half of the previous century. Throughout the last half of the twentieth century, individuals who were at the "right place at the right time" could take their photographs or video to the nearest newspaper or television station and negotiate a price. The most famous example is that of Abraham Zapruder, a Dallas clothing manufacturer who recorded the 1963 assassination of President John F. Kennedy using a hand-held 8mm movie camera. He later turned the camera over to the U.S. Secret Service so the film could be processed, after which agents returned the camera along with a copy of the film. While the original became part of the law-enforcement investigative materials, Zapruder sold his copy to *Life* magazine for $150,000, a portion of which he donated to the widow of a Dallas police officer who was killed attempting to question the assassin on the day of the crime.

In 1991, an amateur videographer captured the beating of motorist Rodney King by Los Angeles police officers. He gave (not sold) the tape to a local television station. The tape was later part of the key evidence in the police officers' trial and became part of worldwide television coverage of the case.

Today, television networks and local stations eagerly accept such videos, with most even providing links on their websites to make the process of submitting them easier. Few are as dramatic as the Zapruder film or King video, and networks and stations seldom pay for them. The most common examples are videos showing a tornado moving through a neighborhood or the results of a plane crash or traffic accident.

While newspapers employ freelance contributors who are paid and agree to follow accepted principles of journalism, most citizen journalists have no training and are not compensated for their contributions—they offer their photographs or video simply believing they are performing a public service or for the notoriety of seeing their names on television. Individuals not wishing to work through television stations or networks (or having their contributions rejected) can post their work products directly on the Internet.

A 2017 study published in *Newspaper Research Journal* indicated that readers exposed to citizen journalism have a more positive attitude toward civic participation, including volunteering, donating to nonprofit organizations, voting, and support for youth activities.[41]

"With the massification of digital and interactive technologies, the news industry has gradually opened its 'gates' and warmed to audience participation and engagement in the production of news," found researchers at the University of Kentucky in another 2017 study. "Recognizing the need to create a culture of sharing and participation by partnering with news audiences, media organizations are now presenting multiple opportunities for users to comment, share, and create content to varying degrees."[42]

For the last decade, the researchers reported, the idea of citizen journalism or "user-generated content" was the second-most mentioned topic in a study asking media managers to identify the most pressing issues they face on the job (employee training was the first).[43]

Media ethicist Andrew Keen describes citizen journalism as "journalism by non-journalists" and "not a dictatorship of experts but a dictatorship of idiots," claiming the practice "slaughters our culture by drooling over media novices instead of professionals." He adds the analogy that "owning a computer and Internet connection doesn't transform one into a serious journalist any more than having access to a kitchen makes one a serious cook."[44]

Your Turn

Case Study 3A: Public Service Journalism: *The Los Angeles Times* and the Staples Center

In 1999, *The Los Angeles Times* created controversy when it published a special section to celebrate the opening of the Staples Center, an arena built partially by taxpayer money as the new home of the Los Angeles Clippers of the National Basketball Association and Los Angeles Kings of the National Hockey League. While presented as news, the section was actually an advertisement paid for by Staples, a leading office supply retailer, which had also paid for the naming rights to the facility. Criticism came from both traditionalists working in the newsroom as well as media critics working for other publications. The management and ownership of the newspaper later acknowledged it was a "lapse in judgment," but nearly two decades later, the case remains a popular one for discussion in media ethics classes and at journalism conferences.

What troubled media ethicists was not just the blurring of the lines between advertising and news, but the fact that money was flowing in both directions. While Staples was paying for the production of the newspaper supplement, the *Times* had agreed to pay the company $1.6 million over five years for the rights to be a "founding partner" of the new facility. After the financial arrangements were uncovered by the newspaper's own media critic, the publisher claimed that while she did not see any ethical conflicts in the situation, it was a mistake not to disclose the arrangement to all concerned, including newsroom personnel. The idea of keeping the relationship secret, she claimed, was to avoid influencing how the newsroom covered the opening of the facility.

1. Re-read the description in the section on "Sponsored News" of the two sections of the SPJ Code of Ethics: "Seek the Truth and Report It" and "Act Independently." How can those sections be applied here?
2. Do you believe the newspaper management's decision to keep the financial arrangement secret was a valid attempt to make sure the coverage of the arena opening would be more objective? Or was it an effort to avoid criticism?

Case Study 3B: Parody and Ridicule: Amtrak Derails and a Fertilizer Plant Explodes

Two cases of ridicule based on news stories of tragedies resulting in the loss of life caused grief for a television network and a popular cartoonist.

In the early 1990s, executives at Amtrak complained to NBC about the late-night host Jay Leno's repeated jokes about the safety record of Amtrak, the government-subsidized train service serving mostly routes in the Southeast and Northeast. In a series of accidents—some of them blamed on Amtrak, others on bad weather or faulty tracks and bridges—dozens of passengers were killed and hundreds injured.

In one *Tonight Show* monologue, Leno ridiculed an Amtrak television ad showing a traveling couple falling asleep in each other's arms. "Of course," Leno said, "a near-death experience always bring you closer together." After the company announced plans to lay off more than 600 managers, Leno speculated that it "wouldn't fire them, it would just put them on one of its trains."[45]

Few viewers complained about the jokes, but the company didn't think the jabs were funny. It announced plans to cancel $2 million in advertising on NBC, a threat it eventually carried out. It announced that it would spend more money in other forms of advertising in order to compensate for the negative image of the company that it claimed Leno perpetuated. In a letter to NBC President Robert C. Wright, Amtrak Chairman Thomas M. Downs wrote that "NBC can write Amtrak jokes faster than we can spend advertising dollars on your network, so I am directing our advertising agency to withdraw all of our ads from NBC as soon as possible."[46]

In his response to Downs, Wright responded that he would "bring the issue to Jay's attention," but stopped short of indicating that any change of monologue content would result. He also indicated that the network would have preferred to have learned about Amtrak's concerns without the accompanying threat.

In a later letter to NBC, Downs indicated that his decision to cancel advertising was not a "threat," but rather a recognition of NBC's relationship with its talent. "We are sensitive to any appearance of an attempt to infringe upon a First Amendment right," Downs wrote. "As an advertiser, we have no right to expect any ability to control what is said on your network."[47]

More than two decades later, an editorial cartoonist at the *Sacramento Bee* came under fire for his depiction of the explosion at a fertilizer plant in Texas that killed four workers and ten firefighters in April 2013. With the support of his paper, Jack Ohman used the tragedy as an opportunity to point out that the failure of Texas to effectively regulate the state's manufacturing industries. The cartoon showed the plant exploding in the background while in the foreground Governor Rick Perry was declaring that "business is booming in Texas."

Perry demanded an apology from the paper, which never came. "While I will always welcome healthy policy debate, I won't stand for someone mocking the tragic deaths of my fellow Texans and our fellow Americans," Perry wrote in a letter to the newspaper's editor. "Additionally, publishing this on the very day our state and nation paused to honor and mourn those who died only compounds the pain and suffering of the many Texans who lost family and friends in this disaster."[48]

Lieutenant Governor David Newhurst called for Ohman to be fired and added that it was "reprehensible for a member of the media to sit in safety and mock such a profound tragedy regardless of any 'point' he was trying to make."[49]

Editorial page editor Stuart Leavenworth defended the cartoon, explaining that it "made a strong statement about the governor's disregard for worker safety, and his attempts to market Texas as a place where industries can thrive with fewer regulations."[50]

1. Late-night comedians such as Jimmy Fallon, Seth Myers, Jimmy Kimmel, and Stephen Colbert often claim they have a First Amendment right to ridicule political candidates and other public figures. But what about companies such as Amtrak? (Keep in mind that in libel law, large companies are considered the equivalent of public figures).
2. Because some passengers died in these tragedies, does that make the subject off-limits for ridicule?
3. Do you agree with Amtrak's strategy of cancelling its advertising on NBC? Would it have been more appropriate to first ask the network to stop making such jokes and use its advertising contract as leverage? (Before deciding, read the section on "Biting the Hands That Feed" in Chapter 7).

Case Study 3C: Parody and Ridicule: Did a Sportswriter Cross the Line in Ridiculing Pro Golfer?

Throughout the world of golf journalism, a popular topic of debate centers on identifying the professional golfer considered to be the best player to not have won any of the sport's major championships: the Masters, U.S. Open, British Open, or PGA Championship. The ongoing debate is so popular that it has earned its own acronym: BPNWM (Best Player to Never Win a Major).

In the August 2017 edition of *Golf* magazine, columnist Alan Shipnuck turned the topic around and wrote a satirical piece in which he chose the "Worst Player Ever to Win a Major." As recipient of the "award," Shipnuck chose Shaun Micheel, a forty-eight-year-old tour veteran whose moderately successful career included winning the 2003 PGA Championship—but no other tournaments before or since.

"So many strong candidates [for this award]," Shipnuck wrote. "But we have to go with Shaun Micheel, whose out-of-nowhere win at the 2003 PGA Championship remains his only Tour victory, and for the rest of his career he finished better than 22nd in a major only once."[51]

Micheel confronted Shipnuck at the following week's tournament, questioning why he would write such a hurtful column and calling the writer what Shipnuck described as "a few unprintable things."[52]

"I told him that I was just trying to educate and entertain the *Golf* magazine readership," Shipnuck recalls telling him. "I wasn't calling him a bad husband or father, or intimating that he kicks puppies for a hobby. I was merely critiquing his playing record, which comes with the territory of being a celebrated, well-paid professional athlete."[53]

Shipnuck said the confrontation ended when he gently placed his hand on Micheel's chest and asked him to step back. A few days later, Micheel sought out Shipnuck and apologized for the harsh tone of their previous conversation, but the apology ended up going both ways. Shipnuck described the twenty-minute conversation as "heartfelt."[54]

Shipnuck learned during the conversation that in the three years prior to publication of the column, Micheel had undergone major heart surgery and lost both parents. As a result, he faced physical, emotional, and scheduling challenges.

"I accepted his apology and offered my own," Shipnuck wrote in a subsequent column. "I am deeply aware of the power of words, but in this case, I honestly never even considered how my column might affect Micheel personally. There were a lot of other ways I could have filled that paragraph, and it was unkind of me to pile on. I told Micheel that I truly appreciated him reminding me of the human toll that can come with the barbs I type."[55]

After the two parted, Micheel followed-up on Twitter, describing the conversation as one that enlarged his perspective and vowing not to let future criticism bother him that much.

"Getting yelled at is occasionally part of a reporter's job, if he or she is doing it well," wrote Shipnuck, a twenty-five-year-veteran of golf journalism, frequent contributor to *Golf* magazine and *Sports Illustrated*, and author or co-author of five golf-themed books. "I can't make 1.4 million copies of *Golf* disappear, but there is another story to be told, too. I'll certainly be rooting for Micheel going forward. After I told him his journey would make a compelling feature story, he gave me his cell number so we could keep in touch. We've become text buddies."[56]

Shipnuck's feature story on Micheel, which was far more complimentary than critical, was published in the online version of *Golf* in August 2018.[57]

1. Was Shipnuck correct in his initial view that Micheel's position as a "celebrated, well-paid professional athlete" means that he is fair game for scrutiny? Or do you believe that the column crossed the line from scrutiny into ridicule?
2. Shipnuck wrote in a subsequent column that the situation reminded him "of the human toll that can come with the barbs I type." Do you agree or disagree?

Case Study 3D: How Much Coverage Is Too Much: Tragedy at Virginia Tech

On the morning of April 16, 2007, a mentally disturbed twenty-three-year-old student at Virginia Polytechnic Institute killed two students in a campus dorm. Less than an hour later, he entered a building on the opposite side of campus, where he killed twenty-nine other students and faculty members and eventually himself. In the days following the tragedy, the national news media were praised for their tasteful and restrained coverage. University officials, law-enforcement personnel, and media critics commended journalists and their employers for respecting the privacy of the families affected. Many critics commented that the media appeared to have learned from the mistakes they made in covering previous tragedies.

Two days after the massacre, the offices of NBC News in New York received a package that investigators believed the gunman mailed during the time that elapsed between the dormitory murders and the classroom killings. The package contained what investigators called a "multi-media manifesto"—a lengthy, rambling video in which the killer criticized the university and his classmates. Before turning over the package to law-enforcement agencies, NBC made a copy that it aired in its entirety on the evening news. Other networks copied it from NBC's broadcast and aired either parts or all of it on their own news programs.

NBC was criticized by many of the same individuals and organizations that had praised it a few days earlier. Viewers wrote letters, called the network switchboard, and used the company's website to register complaints. Media critics also blasted the network for its "reckless and irresponsible" decision to air the tapes, and family members of those killed protested by canceling scheduled appearances on NBC's *Today Show*. Other television networks, as well as national newspapers, were criticized for showing the video photographs taken from the video that showed the suspect in various threatening poses. The criticism was based on their belief that such photos glorified the perpetrator. In contrast, national magazines such as *Time* and *Newsweek* chose their cover illustrations and inside text more tastefully—emphasizing the suffering by the victims' families and alleged failures of the mental health-care system.

The university was closed for a week following the tragedy, and when students returned, the media became more aggressive in attempting to interview students who would have preferred to put the matter behind them and concentrate on resuming their education. A few days after their return to campus, many students posted signs on campus that read "media go away."

1. Do you agree or disagree with NBC's decision to air the video? Does the news-worthiness of the video outweigh the family member's privacy concerns? Should the network have also considered the possibility that airing of the video might inspire copycat crimes at other universities?

2. In cases such as this, is it practical to have a predetermined policy about the airing of controversial videos such as the one involved in this case? Or is each incident so unique that a fixed policy would be ineffective? Is it more practical to make such decisions based on the merits and circumstances of each case?

3. Are there any provisions of the Hutchins Commission findings that are applicable to this issue? What about professional codes of ethics? Which philosophers or philosophies (from Chapter 2) are applicable here?

Discussion Problem 3: Public Service Journalism: Tell Me More

You've recently moved to a new town and subscribed to the local daily newspaper. The first week in town, two stories caught your eye. One was a story about a local family that lost its home in a fire. No one was hurt, but the house was destroyed, and the family's insurance was insufficient to rebuild it. The other story was about a local charity that was in financial trouble and was in danger of closing if it could not pay its office rent and utility bills that were past due.

The newspaper is conducting an experiment called "Tell Me More." At the bottom of each story is a web address and a note reading, "For more information on this story, visit our website at …" In the online edition, there is a link at the bottom of each story that reads, "Tell Me More."

You click on a few of the links, but before you can find out more, the site requires that you register as a "member." It does not cost anything, but you did have to provide your name and email address. In addition to reading a more detailed version of each story, the site offers you the option of signing up for email alerts providing future updates for stories you select.

A few weeks later, you begin getting email updates that provide new information about the family that lost its home and then asks, "Would you like to help the family?" It offers you the opportunity to make a donation by entering your credit card information. The next day, you get an email update on the story about the charity about to lose its lease. At the bottom of the item, it asks, "Would you like to make a donation to the charity?" Again, it asks you to donate money by entering your credit card information.

a. Are these two scenarios examples of an "innovative role" for a daily newspaper (as the newspaper management claims), or an example of public service journalism gone too far?

b. If the link had read, "Here's How You Can Help" instead of "Tell Me More," would you be more accepting of the newspaper's project?

c. Are there any provisions of the Hutchins Commission findings that are applicable to this issue? What about professional codes of ethics? Which philosophers or philosophies (from Chapter 2) are applicable here?

Discussion Questions

301. Re-read the excerpts from professional codes of ethics provided earlier in this chapter. In your opinion, do today's journalists and the media organizations they work for do a good job or poor job of living up to these ideals?

302. Between now and the next class, watch at least one national television newscast (NBC, CBS, ABC, CNN, Fox, or MSNBC) or listen to either the morning or evening news on National Public Radio. Make mental (or written) notes concerning your perceptions of the news being slanted to reflect either a "liberal" or "conservative" viewpoint and be prepared to discuss your opinion with the class.

303. Were local radio stations justified in ridiculing the sports director arrested for drunk driving and the news anchor caught soliciting a fifteen-year-old prostitute? Libel law says that public figures must accept a certain level of public criticism and ridicule as part of their roles, but did the disc jockeys mentioned cross the line?

304. Find stereotyped characters in drama or comedy television programming. What do you believe are the root causes of such stereotypes? What is the harm?

305. Working either individually or in teams, assume the role of an individual or group chosen to select ten current television programs to be compiled onto a DVD and included in a time capsule to be buried and then uncovered and opened in a hundred years. Aim for a combination of drama, comedy, sports, news, and reality formats. What ten programs would you choose? If a cultural anthropologist working a hundred years from now viewed those programs, what conclusions (positive or negative) about American culture might they draw from watching them?

Notes

1   *Headlines & Soundbites: Is That the Way It Is?* Cronkite-Ward Videos, 1995.
2   Paige Malone, "Animal Cruelty Bill Promoted by Local Television Station Passes." Alabama Newspapers Syndicate, February 27, 2013.
3   Joe Strupp, "New Advertorials Raise Old Ethical Questions." *Editor & Publisher*, November 17, 2003, pp. 6–7.
4   Strupp.
5   Ginny Marvin, "Consumers Can't Tell the Difference Between Sponsored Content and Editorial." MarketingLand.com, September 9, 2015.
6   Will Heilpern, "How 'Deceptive' Sponsored News Articles Could be Tricking Readers—Even with a Disclosure Message." BusinessInsider.com, March 17, 2016.
7   Heilpern.
8   Trudy Lieberman, "Epidemic: Phony Medical News is on the Rise, Thanks to Dozens of Unhealthy Deals Between TV Newsrooms and Hospitals." *Columbia Journalism Review*, March/April 2007, pp. 38–43.
9   Lieberman.
10 Lieberman.
11 Robert Lichter and Stanley Rothman, *The Media Elite.* Chevy Chase, MD: Adler & Adler Publishing (1986), p. 28.
12 Bernard Goldberg, *Arrogance: Rescuing America from the Media Elite.* New York: Warner Books (2003), p. 1.
13 Pat Rice, "The Internet is Making Newspapers Better." *Northwest Florida Daily News*, June 10, 2007, p. 8-F.
14 Mark R. Levin, *Unfreedom of the Press.* New York: Threshold Editions (2019), p. 11.
15 Matthew Kieran, *Media Ethics.* New York: Routledge (1998), p. 57.
16 Levin, p. 18.
17 Levin, pp. 19–20.
18 Levin, p. 20.
19 Levin, p. 3.
20 Deborah Lipstadt, *Beyond Belief: The American Press and the Coming of the Holocaust.* New York: Free Press (1986), p. 10.

21 Levin, p. 11.

22 David Bauder, "12 Hours vs. 20 Minutes: Fox's Uneven Coverage." Associated Press report, October 27, 2017.

23 "Indicators of News Media Trust." Gallup/Knight Foundation Survey, 2018.

24 William McGowan, *Coloring the News: How Crusading for Diversity Has Corrupted American Journalism*. San Francisco: Encounter Books (2001), pp. 1–5.

25 McGowan, pp. 1–5.

26 McGowan, pp. 49–50.

27 McGowan, pp. 59–60.

28 McGowan, pp. 105–113.

29 McGowan, pp. 123–143.

30 McGowan, pp. 179–217.

31 Marc Tracy, "Claims of Liberal Bias Hit ESPN, Too." *The New York Times*, May 2, 2017, p. 8-B.

32 John Dausener, "The Myth of the Liberal Media." UWire, February 27, 2019.

33 Jessica Guynn, "Cruz Threatens to Regulate Facebook, Google, and Twitter Over Charges of Anti-Conservative Bias." *USA Today*, April 10, 2019.

34 Tony Romm, "Trump Accuses Social Media Companies of 'Terrible Bias' at White House Summit." *The Washington Post*, July 11, 2019.

35 Stephen Bates, *If No News, Send Rumors*. New York: St. Martin's Press (1989), p. 42.

36 *Hustler v. Falwell*, 485 U.S. 46(1988). See also: Randy Bobbitt, *Exploring Communication Law*. New York: Taylor & Francis (2018), p. 212. A more detailed version of the *Hustler v. Falwell* case can be found in Rodney Smolla's book *Jerry Falwell v. Larry Flynt: The First Amendment on Trial* Urbana, IL: University of Illinois Press (1988).

37 David Astor, "Newspapers are Sooo Lame, Says Columnist." *Editor & Publisher*, August 2004, p. 8.

38 Thomas Lang and Zachary Roth, "Video News Releases—They're Everywhere." *Columbia Journalism Review*, October 13, 2004.

39 Gene Foreman, *The Ethical Journalist*. Malden, MA: Wiley-Blackwell Publishing (2011), p. 170.

40 Lang and Roth.

41 Seungahn Nah, Kang Namkoong, Rachael Record, and Stephanie K. Van Stee, "Citizen Journalism Practice Increases Civic Participation." *Newspaper Research Journal*, Vol. 38, No. 1 (2017), pp. 62–78.

42 Chung, Nah, and Yamamoto.

43 Chung, Nah, and Yamamoto.

44 Howard Rosenberg and Charles S. Feldman, *No Time to Think: The Menace of Media Speed and the 24-Hour News Cycle*. New York: Continuum Books (2008), p. 92.

45 Paul Farhi, "Amtrak Derails NBC Over Leno's Jokes." *The Washington Post*, October 14, 1994.

46 These comments were taken from correspondence provided by the Amtrak media relations office (provided to the author).

47 These comments were taken from correspondence provided by the Amtrak media relations office (provided to the author).

48 "Perry Disgusted by California Newspaper Cartoon Depicting Explosion." *The Washington Post*, April 26, 2013.

49 "Perry Disgusted by California Newspaper Cartoon Depicting Explosion."

50 "Perry Disgusted by California Newspaper Cartoon Depicting Explosion."

51 Alan Shipnuck, "Best Player Never to Win a Major? Here's a New Class of Major 'Winners' to Debate." Golf.com, August 8, 2017.

52 Shipnuck, "An Inconvenient Truth." *Golf*, November 2017, pp. 24–25.

53 Shipnuck, "An Inconvenient Truth."

54 Shipnuck, "An Inconvenient Truth."

55 Shipnuck, "An Inconvenient Truth."

56 Shipnuck, "An Inconvenient Truth."

57 Shipnuck, "How Shaun Micheel's PGA Championship Became a Burden on His Career." Golf.com, August 6, 2018.

4 Journalism and Broadcasting

Personnel Issues

Background

The Society of Professional Journalists' Code of Ethics, in its section titled "Act Independently," requires journalists to:

- avoid conflicts of interest, real or perceived;
- remain free of associations and activities that may compromise integrity or damage credibility;
- refuse gifts, favors, fees, free travel and special treatment, and shun secondary employment, political involvement, public office, and service in community organizations if they compromise journalistic integrity.

The American Society of Newspaper Editors' Statement of Principles states that journalists "who abuse the power of their professional roles for selfish motives or unworthy purposes are faithless to the public trust."

The Radio Television Digital News Association Code of Broadcast News Ethics requires that broadcasters "strive to conduct themselves in a manner that protects them from conflicts of interest, real or perceived."

Issues and Controversies

Conflicts of Interest

Much like governmental officials, journalists hold positions of trust in American society. Even though they have not been elected by the people they serve, they are still accountable to the public and must avoid situations in which that trust is compromised—or appears to be. Most professional codes of ethics use terms such as "conflicts of interest, real or perceived" to emphasize that journalists should avoid not only those situations that present an *overt* conflict, but also those that may create the *appearance* of impropriety.

"Although business executives of news organizations should be as concerned about profits as those who sell cars or soap, journalists should be indifferent to whether their daily work—reporting and editing—directly enhances profitability or otherwise affects an employer's interests," stated Stephen Klaidman and Tom L. Beauchamp in the 1987 book *The Virtuous Journalist*. "Otherwise, journalists would regularly entangle themselves in conflicts of interest."[1]

Commenting on the problem of conflicts of interest in the journalism business, media critic Howard Kurtz admonishes print and broadcast journalists for employing a double standard in reporting on the ethical shortcomings of other people while failing to recognize them in their own work. "It's striking how often we in the news business fail to live up to the high-minded standards that we prescribe for everyone else," Kurtz wrote in his 1994 book *Media Circus*.[2]

Here are some common problem areas related to conflicts of interest, both real and potential.

Personal Friendships, Family Relationships, and Romantic Relationships

Journalists should never be in a position in which they are reporting a story that involves a friend or family member, or one in which a friend or family member will be affected by the outcome.

In the early 1990s, an art critic for *The New York Times* wrote a review of an art museum in Sarasota, Florida that was so positive that it caused his co-workers and editors to be skeptical about his objectivity. They later learned that the critic's wife, an art historian, accompanied him on the visit and was paid $8,000 for presenting a brief lecture to museum patrons. Although the critic denied the financial compensation influenced his review, the fact that the museum had no history of paying other guest speakers cast doubt over the couple's claim that the husband's positive review and the wife's acceptance of the speaking fee was an "unfortunate coincidence."[3]

There have been several cases in the latter half of the twentieth century in which high-profile journalists have been romantically involved with or married to high-profile political figures. Today, before the relationships become public knowledge, journalists are admonished to meet with their editors to discuss the potential conflict before beginning work on that story. In a short-term situation, an editor will likely reassign the story to a different reporter. In long-term situations, some editors may assign a different reporter to cover those stories, while others may allow the reporter to continue on that beat but will monitor his or her stories to check for signs of possible bias.

That didn't happen in the 1970s, when the *Philadelphia Inquirer* was unaware of a romance between political reporter Laura Foreman and State Senator Henry Cianfrani, who she often wrote about. The relationship was not exposed until after Foreman had moved on to *The New York Times*. Even though she was no longer covering Cianfrani, the *Times* requested Foreman's resignation.

Between 1984 and 1987, NBC News reporter Andrea Mitchell dated economist Alan Greenspan while he worked in a number of low-profile private-sector jobs. But when Greenspan was named Chairman of the Federal Reserve by President Ronald Reagan in 1987, Mitchell reported the potential conflict to management at NBC News. They agreed that Mitchell could continue to cover the White House and Congress but would not report on any issues involving economic policy. That agreement remained in place through the presidencies of George H.W. Bush, Bill Clinton, and George W. Bush. Greenspan left the job in 2006.

In 1989, New York City television news anchor Donna Hanover Giuliani was allowed to remain on the air as her husband, U.S. Attorney Rudy Giuliani, ran for mayor of New York City. She occasionally did field reporting in addition to her anchor job, but she was not allowed to work on stories in which her husband was mentioned. In her anchor role, she was not allowed to write or narrate segues in or out of other reporters' stories that mentioned her husband. She was also required to disclose to viewers that she was married to the mayoral candidate every time she mentioned him on the air.

Business Relationships and Organizational Memberships

One common example of a conflict of interest is when a journalist is assigned to cover a story involving an organization of which he or she is a member or a person with whom he has a business or personal relationship. Memberships in political organizations or other groups involved in controversial public issues also have the potential to reflect poorly on the credibility of both journalists and their employers. Even memberships in non-controversial organizations such as the Rotary Club, chamber of commerce, or parent–teacher association may be problematic.

While all media organizations address such potential conflicts in their personnel policies, they vary greatly in the degree to which those relationships are scrutinized. In the 1980s and 1990s, for example, a daily newspaper in Florida failed to monitor the relationship between its sports editor, who co-owned a travel agency, and professional sports teams that did business with that agency (see Case Study 4B).

The most lenient conflict-of-interest policy would not forbid journalists from joining community organizations, but might caution them to avoid accepting reporting assignments on the organization itself or any issue in which the organization is involved. On the opposite extreme are those policies that prohibit all organizational memberships, regardless of how non-controversial they may be and how far removed their work might be from the reporter's area of expertise. Some other media employers might take a middle ground, allowing reporters to belong to organizations but prohibiting them from serving in leadership positions in which their public statements might be the subject of media coverage.

To avoid conflicts, media organizations often require more detailed information (compared to other types of employers) on employment applications regarding past and current organizational memberships and places of employment. Employers may also inquire about the organizational memberships and places of employment of a reporter's parents and spouse. A reporter whose parent or spouse is a member of the school board or other governmental body, for example, would obviously not be allowed to report on the activities of that body.

Political Involvement

Journalism history is full of examples of journalists becoming public officials and attempting to serve in both roles. In the 1870s, long before he became a newspaper publisher, Joseph Pulitzer was a reporter for a German-language newspaper while also serving in the Missouri state legislature.[4] For months after being inaugurated as president in 1921, Warren G. Harding still held the title of publisher of the *Marion Star* in his hometown in Ohio. Ironically, Harding had won the 1920 election over James Cox, who served three terms as governor of Ohio while still publisher of another newspaper in the state. In the early 1970s, William P. Hobby Jr. served as lieutenant governor of Texas while still the president of the *Houston Post* newspaper chain.

Today, nearly every media organization has a conflict-of-interest policy that prohibits its employees from seeking or holding public office. Running for office would be especially problematic for those working in television news because of their advantage in name recognition. In the 1980s, for example, a television reporter in Kansas City, Missouri refused to resign prior to running for the city council, and after being suspended by the station, he unsuccessfully sued. In 1999, television news anchor Bob Young resigned his position at a station in Augusta, Georgia, in order to run for mayor of the city, an election he won easily.

In order to take pressure off their employers, it is common for print and broadcast journalists to take voluntary leaves of absence prior to running for office. In the case of television journalists, the majority of states have election laws that require television stations to provide equal time to all candidates running for office, meaning that television anchors and reporters who remained on the job would create substantial legal problems for their employers.

Conversely, some journalists have claimed that because of the value that society places on public service, to not allow them to seek public office is a violation of their basic rights as citizens. Their employers and the courts disagree, however, and respond with a simple policy: "You have the right to run for public office. You have the right to work as a journalist. But you don't have the right to do both at the same time."

Another problematic aspect of political involvement is making financial contributions to candidates or supporting their campaigns in other ways. During the 2000 presidential election campaign, for example, CBS anchor Dan Rather embarrassed his network after making a paid appearance at a Democratic Party fund-raiser in his home state of Texas. Rather later apologized to his CBS colleagues and viewers, calling his decision a "serious lapse in ethical judgment."[5]

In the 2002 election for governor of Massachusetts, former Secretary of Labor Robert Reich received more than $2,500 in donations from fifteen Boston-area journalists, including *The Boston Globe* and WGBH, a public television station. That total comprised less than 1 percent of all the donations Reich received, but it was enough to raise ethical concerns among the reporters' employers. Ironically, the first media outlet to report the story was the *Globe*, admonishing its own employees. The worst transgression of the campaign may have been committed by a columnist for *The Newton Tab*, a Boston-area weekly. Not only did she contribute $85 to the campaign, but she served as a Reich delegate at the Democratic Party Convention—all while continuing to cover the Reich campaign for the newspaper.[6]

Following the 2010 mid-term elections, MSNBC commentator Keith Olbermann was suspended for two days after network executives learned that he contributed money to several Democratic candidates, which violated the policy of the network's parent company, NBC Universal. That policy, which is similar to that of other print and broadcast news organizations, prohibits journalists from "doing anything that might call into question their impartiality, such as putting up a candidate's yard sign, making a political donation, or marching at a rally."[7]

In 2015, ABC News anchor George Stephanopoulos was criticized—but allowed to stay on the air—after it was learned that he donated $75,000 to the Clinton Global Initiative, an international foundation headed by former President Bill Clinton, for whom Stephanopoulos worked as a White House aide in the 1990s. Stephanopoulos defended the donation by emphasizing it was to the foundation and not to the 2016 presidential campaign of former First Lady Hillary Clinton, but critics said the close relationship between the foundation and presidential campaign made that point of little significance.[8]

Ironically, the three donations of $25,000 each came to light after Stephanopoulos interviewed the author of *Clinton Cash*, a 2015 book that alleged that some of Hillary Clinton's actions as secretary of state were influenced by donations to the CGI. Stephanopoulos defended the donation by claiming that donations did not affect his coverage of the Clinton family and were simply prompted by his dedication to causes such as AIDS and the environment, both of which are within the CGI's scope of work. He added that he didn't believe he had an obligation to disclose the donations because they were "already a matter of public record."[9]

Stock-Market Considerations

Business journalists, especially those who write stories that may affect a company's stock prices, are prohibited from investing in the stock market. Not only would writing stories that affect the stocks they owned present an obvious conflict of interest, but doing so might also result in charges of insider trading, a violation of a federal law called the Securities and Exchange Act of 1934. "News moves market prices for everything bought and sold in this world, and the temptations for misusing that news are extraordinary," wrote Conrad Fink in his 1995 textbook *Media Ethics.*[10]

Speaking and Consulting Fees

Another issue in the conflict-of-interest arena also involves financial matters. In the 1990s and early 2000s, a series of well-publicized cases surfaced in which television commentators and nationally known newspaper columnists were paid to speak to national organizations they also covered in their role as journalists. Employers and media critics took notice of the problem and criticized it as one that compromises the integrity of the journalism profession and caused perceptual problems for a profession already in trouble. While most employers claimed they were confident that accepting speaking fees would not influence the reporters' news judgment, they were more concerned about public perception that journalists were for sale. In essence, the issue was not what the situation *was*, but what it might *look like.*

ABC News reporter and weekend anchor Cokie Roberts was criticized in 1995 for accepting a $30,000 speaker fee from a little-known nonprofit organization—an arrangement that was approved by network executives because it involved speaking to a nonprofit organization whose work was unlikely to be the subject of any future ABC News reports. That same year, the network was also criticized for not scrutinizing the work of Sam Donaldson, who was allowed to research and produce stories about waste and fraud in the government's system of agricultural subsidies without disclosing the fact that he owned a sheep farm that received subsidies under that system.

A similar conflict occurs when journalists are paid to advise business owners on the operation of their businesses. One example involves restaurant critics who receive consulting fees from restaurant owners seeking advice on the operation of their businesses, a practice that would be prohibited by most daily newspapers.

Reporters who appear on television and radio talk shows are not allowed to accept compensation for their appearances, although in most cases they may accept reimbursement for expenses related to travel to and from the studios. They are also cautioned not to reveal any information on the shows that may compromise ongoing investigations that the newspaper or television station is pursuing.

"NPR journalists must get approval before speaking to groups that may have a relationship to a subject that NPR may cover," reads a paragraph in the National Public Radio Code of Ethics. "NPR journalists may not speak at corporation or industry functions. NPR journalists also may not appear in settings where their appearance is being used to by an organization to promote its services or products. NPR journalists may not speak to groups where the appearance might put in jeopardy NPR's impartiality."[11]

Abuse of Position or Name Recognition

One form of conflict of interest that is seldom addressed in policy manuals is the problem of journalists who exploit their positions at a newspaper or television station or the name recognition of their employers. Although documented cases are rare, they are not unheard of; especially with younger, less experienced reporters who believe they are justified in using their positions for personal gain.

Examples include food critics who visit restaurants without intending to write reviews, but identify themselves in order to secure a preferred table, free meal, or other considerations; sportswriters who use their positions to secure free or discounted memberships at athletic clubs by implying they may write articles about the facilities; or consumer affairs reporters who visit retail stores and use their name recognition to solicit discounts or a higher level of customer service not available to other shoppers.

In 2005, a reporter for the *New York Post* went beyond simply benefitting financially from his relationship with a source—he allegedly generated extra income by blackmailing those he reported on. In exchange for $220,000 a year, reporter Jared Paul Stern promised billionaire and Democratic Party fund-raiser Ronald Burkle he would write only positive stories about him and could keep him off the paper's notorious "Page Six," a gossip column over which he actually had little control. When caught, Stern denied accepting the direct payment but admitted reaching an agreement with Stern to write positive stories in exchange for Burkle investing in his side business, a start-up clothing line. Stern was fired from the *Post*.[12]

"Journalists seldom get into trouble trafficking in the same temptations they write about, such as the greed for money or power," wrote James O'Shea in *The Deal From Hell*, his 2011 exposé of the business side of journalism. "The mistakes that embarrass journalists and their craft usually involve ego—a quest for fame or status."[13]

Moonlighting and Double-Dipping

Few newspapers and magazines allow their reporters to write articles for other publications. Editors may grant their reporters permission to do so, however, in cases in which the second publication is not a competitor and the author is identified as a staff writer for the first publication.

Examples include a sportswriter who is invited to write a "season preview" article for a college or professional sports team's media guide, or a travel writer invited to submit an article for the chamber of commerce's visitor guide. In both cases, the publications are not in direct competition with the writers' primary employers, and having the authors identified by their primary jobs is an opportunity to promote those publications. In some cases, articles that previously appeared in a daily newspaper may be reprinted in non-competing publications. If compensation is offered, however, it would go to the newspaper and not the individual journalists or photographers because they have already been paid for producing the articles or photos. Reporters and photographers would not be allowed to accept direct compensation, because in doing so they would be compensated twice for the same work, a practice known as **double-dipping**.

Cases in which journalists use their employers' resources may also be problematic. In 1996, for example, a daily newspaper in New Jersey fired one of its reporters after learning that he was using the newspaper's access to motor vehicle records to track down individuals as part of his side job as a private detective.

In the early 2000s, Fox News contributor Steven Milloy broadcast a number of stories dismissing the dangers of second-hand smoke and global climate change as "junk science" without revealing that in one of his other jobs he was a lobbyist for tobacco giant Philip Morris and several oil companies.[14]

"NPR journalists must obtain permission for all outside freelance and journalistic work, including written articles and self-publishing in blogs or other electronic media, whether or not compensated," reads the NPR code. "Approval will not be unreasonably denied if the proposed work will not discredit NPR, conflict with NPR's interests, create a conflict of interest for the employee or interfere with the employee's ability to perform NPR duties."[15]

In his 1981 book on newspaper ethics, media historian John L. Hulteng related the story of a business-page editor planning to leave journalism who spent two years writing glowing stories about one particular local company, then resigned from the paper and went to work for that company.[16]

Journalism historian claim that up until the mid-1970s, it was common for reporters at low-paying newspapers—most of them in rural communities—to have side jobs. Regardless of whether those jobs represented a conflict, most bosses were unaware of the practice, while readers were not. The most egregious example may have been that of reporters for daily newspapers in rural Mississippi who were also employed by the local court system as part-time investigators to augment the work of county prosecutors.[17]

Many reporters who are caught moonlighting reluctantly agree to give up their outside jobs, but some have pointed out a double standard. At the *Herald-News* in Passaic-Clifton, New Jersey, for example, reporters were required to give up their outside jobs at the same time the newspaper was publishing the weekly "business review" page, which consisted solely of pseudo-news stories that were published in the same editions the subjects of those glowing stories (all of advertisers are "the greatest" complained the managing editor) had purchased extensive advertising space.[18]

Too Close to the Subject, or Becoming Part of the Story

Closely related to the issue of conflicts of interest is that tendency of some journalists to either get "too close" to their sources or, in some cases, either intentionally or unintentionally, becoming entangled in news stories they are covering.

One example occurred in 1989, when more than 300,000 activists representing both sides of the abortion debate gathered in Washington, D.C. to await the U.S. Supreme Court's ruling in an abortion rights case. Among them was Linda Greenhouse, who covered the case and the abortion issue as a reporter for *The New York Times*. She wasn't the only journalist in the crowd. Dozens of others later admitted they had also taken part—some claiming to be acting as journalists simply seeking to cover the events close-up and others claiming to be acting as private citizens with no intent of writing about their experiences. But Greenhouse insisted she was capable of doing both at the same time, a claim which with her editors did not agree. Greenhouse was given a formal reprimand but was allowed to continue covering the abortion issue and other cases reaching the Supreme Court. Her editors said the matter was closed, but that didn't spare Greenhouse from criticism by her peers.[19]

A similar example was a 2004 case of two female reporters who had written a series of stories on gay issues for the *San Francisco Chronicle*. When the reporters announced their plans to legalize their relationship under California's new domestic partnership law, the newspaper's management prohibited them from covering gay issues in the future.

In 1987, a reporter for the *St. Paul Pioneer-Press* wrote a series of stories about an AIDS patient facing his final months. Jacqui Banaszynski frequently visited the man in his home and interviewed his partner, family, friends, and doctors. When she realized she had become friends with the man and the relationship had gone beyond reporter–source, she asked her editors to pay close attention to her stories and to be "extra diligent" in editing her copy. After the man died, her work received both a Pulitzer Prize and Distinguished Service Award from the Society of Professional Journalists. While co-workers celebrated her notoriety, among media ethicists it raised concerns about whether Banaszynski had gotten too close to her subject.[20]

The don't-get-involved-in-the-story rule would not apply in cases in which reporters witnessed crimes being committed or encountered persons in dangerous situations. In those cases, reporters often close their notebooks and turn off their television cameras and take steps to report the crime or save people from tragedy. When serious crimes or a possible loss of human life is involved, even the strictest media ethicists agree that an individual's obligations as a human being outweigh his or her obligations to the journalism profession.

In 1998, for example, two reporters for a major daily newspaper prepared a multi-part series of stories about families living in poverty, emphasizing the effect the conditions had on children. The reporters observed bruises and other injuries on several children that led them to believe they were being abused by their parents or other family members. The reporters consulted their editor, who at first forbade them to report their suspicions to government agencies that investigated allegations of child abuse, saying their job was to "hold up a reflective mirror to society, not to function as social workers." When a local child welfare agency learned about the reporters' suspicions, she rejected the "reflective mirror" rationale and said the reporters were responsible for whatever harm came to the children in the future. The editor eventually changed his mind and allowed the journalists to report their suspicions.

In other cases, journalists get involved in news stories that do not involve life-and-death situations, but create awkward situations and questions about the proper role of journalists. The philosophy of most newspaper publishers is that, "It is our job to witness and publish the news, not to participate in it." One example of a reporter becoming part of the story is the case of *Sports Illustrated* writer Michael Bamberger, which is detailed in Case Study 4D.

Some of the more famous cases of journalists getting too close to their sources involve political leaders. Through American history, for example, presidents have customarily had a love–hate relationship with reporters who covered them. Some chief executives, including Theodore Roosevelt (1901–1909) and Harry Truman (1945–1953) often socialized with reporters and invited them to accompany them on their daily walks around the White House grounds.

Ben Bradlee, who served as *Washington Post* executive editor from the 1960s through the 1990s, was previously a White House correspondent for *Newsweek*, where he covered the presidency of a good friend, President John F. Kennedy. According to Bradlee biographer Jeff Himmelman, Bradlee and his wife frequently dined with the president and first lady, both in private dinners in the White House residence and formal dinners in the state dining room. On other occasions, the Bradlees and Kennedys were seen socializing outside of the White House.[21] Another faux pas in the relationship occurred when Bradlee frequently showed the president copies of stories before they ran in *Newsweek*.[22]

"Most editors today would never allow a friend to cover a friend the way Ben covered Kennedy," Himmelman wrote.[23]

Another troubling aspect of the Bradlee–Kennedy relationship actually began in the late 1950s, when Bradlee had just begun working at *Newsweek* reporter and Kennedy was a young senator representing Massachusetts. The two were already friends when Bradlee was assigned to cover candidates competing for the 1960 Democratic presidential nomination. After attending a speech by Texas Senator Lyndon B. Johnson, the front-runner for the nomination, Bradlee filed a story for *Newsweek* but then wrote a secret memo for Kennedy summarizing Johnson's speech and outlining its flaws.[24]

In 1980, political columnist George F. Will agreed to help Republican presidential nominee Ronald Reagan for his televised debate against incumbent Jimmy Carter, a job he later regretted because of criticism from his peers. Eight newspapers temporarily discontinued his column when they learned of Will's transgression.[25]

In the late 1990s, National Public Radio reporter Nina Totenberg was criticized for her friendship with Supreme Court Justice Ruth Bader Ginsburg, whom she frequently interviewed while covering court proceedings. After Ginsburg officiated at Totenberg's wedding in 2000, the reporter responded to the criticism by pointing out she had known the justice for years before she was elevated to the Supreme Court and she did not consider it a conflict of interest.[26]

Public Broadcasting Service anchor Gwen Ifill was criticized for accepting the role as moderator for the 2008 vice-presidential debate between Democrat Joe Biden and Republican Sarah Palin. Ifill was known to be working on a book about the election campaign scheduled for release on January 21, 2009—the day after the new president's inauguration—regardless of which candidate won. Although described as a book about the campaign itself that would not focus on either candidate to the exclusion of the other, its title, *Breakthrough: Politics and Race in the Age of Obama*, prompted conservatives to challenge Ifill's ability to be objective in her role as moderator.

Diversity as a Personnel Issue

The value of diversity in the American workplace has become an important issue for American businesses of all types. While just about any business would benefit to some degree by having a workforce that is diverse in terms of age, gender, race, and national origin, the idea is especially important for media organizations. If a newspaper, magazine, online news service, or television or radio station seeks to properly serve a wide variety of audiences, it should employ reporters and editors who can identify with those audiences and can be identified by them.

For example, media organizations with female, African American, Hispanic, or Asian reporters can do a better job of reporting on issues important to those groups than organizations staffed with reporters and editors who are mostly male and white. While valuable for the print media, it is even more important in television, as audience members like to get their news from reporters and anchors "who look like them."

Although many journalists and members of their audiences may see "diversity" as a new concept, it is not. As far back as the 1940s, the Hutchins Commission (see Chapter 1) listed as one of the ideals the media should aspire to the need to "provide a representative picture of the constituent groups in society." Although the terms "diversity" and "multiculturalism" were not applied to this concept until a half century later, it was the Hutchins Commission that first suggested the idea.

During the presidency of Franklin D. Roosevelt, his wife did her part to promote opportunities for women journalists by requiring that only reporters of that gender could attend her news conferences. As a result, every national newspaper with a Washington bureau hired at least one woman.[27]

In 1968, a government-sponsored investigation called the Kerner Commission was charged with determining the root causes for racial strife in America. Although it concluded that the racial divide in the country was too complex to be blamed on one factor, the commission did assign part of the responsibility to the news media, which it accused of over-covering negative stories about racial minorities and under-reporting positive stories. The study also found that the journalism business was running way behind other professional fields in recruiting, hiring, training, and promoting minority employees.

Al Neuharth, founder and first publisher of *USA Today*, once said that "promoting and practicing equal opportunity is not only the right thing to do it's the smart thing to do...No newspaper can cover all of the community unless it employs all of the community."[28]

Beyond simply hiring more minority journalists, media organizations also need to do a better job of retaining them.

A 2008 survey by the National Association of Black Journalists found that 68 percent of African American journalists become disillusioned early in their careers and begin to consider other employment fields, and there's little evidence that attitudes have changed since that survey was taken.[29] The most common reason given for that opinion was the lack of advancement opportunities with their current employers. *Newsday* reporter Herbert Lowe, commenting on the findings of the survey, wrote that "every day, black journalists are leaving the industry because they feel disrespected, unappreciated, undercompensated, underdeveloped, and uninspired."[30]

Despite the obvious benefits of a diverse workforce to media organizations, the idea is not totally without resistance. Some television station managers object to affirmative action and other diversity programs, claiming that reporters and editors should be hired based on their job skills rather than demographic factors, and placing too much emphasis on the latter results in having to work with employees with marginal skills.

Media critic and author William McGowan is so skeptical about diversity initiatives that he wrote an entire book questioning their value. In *Coloring the News: How Crusading for Diversity Has Corrupted American Journalism*, McGowan describes such programs as politically correct efforts to address crises that don't exist.[31]

"To increase the racial and ethnic diversity of their staffs, almost every major news organization has mounted a 'pluralism plan' with aggressive hiring and promotion goals and created a "diversity steering committee," McGowan wrote in his 2001 book. "In some cases, editors have openly admitted to relying on quotas, favoring less qualified minority candidates in filling positions, and violating hiring freezes when minority journalists have been in short supply."[32]

In a 2003 journal article, writing coach Linda Wallace responded to criticism that diversity initiatives might result in the hiring of journalists with weaker skills. "Managing diversity well means seeking ways to reward reporters and editors who achieve cultural competency, meaning they understand how cultures differ and can report and edit across cultural lines," Wallace wrote. "That doesn't mean lowering journalistic standards."[33]

To address the problem of management skepticism, many journalism schools and national media organizations are developing college scholarships and other programs aimed at interesting more high school and college students from diverse backgrounds in pursuing careers in journalism and broadcasting.

While black journalists would likely be more effective than their white counterparts at covering stories affecting the black community, some black journalists complain about "racial pigeonholing"—the tendency of white editors to assign them only those stories. Black reporters understand those as assignments early in their careers, says E.R. Shipp, a former columnist for the New York *Daily News* and *The Washington Post*, but eventually want to move beyond stories about gangs, school violence involving black students, and stories about racially segregated neighborhoods.[34]

In 2002, the Scripps Howard Foundation, affiliated with the Scripps Howard newspaper chain, richly endowed a new journalism program at Hampton University, a historically black institution in Virginia. One of the goals of the Scripps Howard School of Journalism and Communications is to increase not only the number of journalists of color in print and broadcast journalism, but also the number in media management positions.[35] "There is an understanding on the part of the newspaper industry that long-term survival depends on the media workforce reflecting America," said Judith Clabes, president of the Scripps Howard Foundation, in announcing the endowment.[36]

Plagiarism, Fabrication, and the Origins of Fake News

The word **plagiarism** comes from the Latin term *plagiarius*, which in turn was derived from the term *plaga*, which was a net used in ancient times to capture runaway children. Plagiarism has been an issue ever since humans began communicating in writing thousands of years ago. Many of the great writers in world history have been accused of plagiarism, including Homer, author of *The Iliad* and *The Odyssey*; and English writer William Shakespeare, author of dozens of plays and poems.[37]

Long before the well-publicized cases of fabricated stories affecting American newspapers that were perpetrated by individual reporters without the knowledge of their editors, newspaper "hoaxes" were common parts of the journalism industry.

In the 1800s, for example, newspaper staffs created hoaxes in order to embarrass their rivals, boost circulation, or relieve boredom, while individual reporters created hoaxes in order to advance their careers. In 1874, for example, *The New York Herald* published a story that reported that wild animals had escaped from the Central Park Zoo and were on a rampage, attacking citizens throughout the city. While some readers were entertained, others were angry because they hid inside their homes for several days.

In August 1835, the *New York Sun* published a series of articles claiming the famous British astronomer Sir John Herschel had peered through his telescope and observed life on the moon, including a variety of plants and animals that included bat–human hybrids and beavers walking upright.[38] In 1944, the *Sun* was at it again, publishing a story by Edgar Allan Poe that a team of Americans had constructed a balloon that took them on a three-day trip across the Atlantic Ocean—a feat that would not happen in reality for another sixty years.[39]

April Fool's Day was once a popular occasion for newspaper hoaxes. In Kankakee, Illinois, the *Daily Journal* published an April 1, 1965 story that claimed that drillers had struck oil on the grounds of the county courthouse. The story was accompanied by a doctored photograph showing bystanders drenched in oil. A Venezuelan engineer named Loof Lirpa (April Fool backwards) was in charge of the project. Two years later, the paper reported on April 1 that alien spaceships had landed outside the city, and the story was accompanied by photographs of the vessels and an interview with the chief witness, a man named Isa Lyar. On April 1, 1984, shortly before the nation was about to switch to Daylight Savings Time, a California newspaper ran a story claiming to be sponsoring a contest in which its readers would compete to see who could save the most daylight. The daylight could be brought to the newspaper's offices in either in cardboard boxes or glass jars.

Since the 1980s, most reputable daily newspapers have banned the practice of April Fool's Day stories, concerned that if readers did not trust the stories published on that day, they might eventually become suspicious of stories published on other days. More recently, the credibility problems created by reporters fictionalizing news stories have provided more evidence to support the ban. Newspaper editors also worry that the technology of digital photography makes visual hoaxes too easy to create and that doing so puts those newspapers in the same category with tabloid publications.

While the problem of journalists and their employers creating outlandish news stories or "hoaxes" was once widespread, a more recent problem has been individual print reporters writing stories that are grounded in truth but sprinkled with fake sources, events, and quotes. In a 1989 journal article, journalism historian Marie Dunne White noted that journalists are morally bound to tell the truth and when they plagiarize or participate in any other form of dishonesty, they are violating their obligations to both their editors and their readers.[40]

The three biggest scandals involving wholly or partially fabricated stories involved *The Washington Post*, *The New Republic*, and *The New York Times*.

The *Washington Post* story took involved reporter Janet Cooke, who won a Pulitzer Prize in 1981 for her emotionally gripping story about Jimmy, an eight-year-old heroin addict growing up in an economically depressed neighborhood near downtown Washington, D.C. Cooke's story shocked many of the newspaper's readers as well as city officials. The city's mayor ordered the police department to locate the child, and when that failed, the police chief threatened to have Cooke and her editors subpoenaed if they did not help locate him. The *Post* refused to cooperate, but eventually the editors became suspicious themselves and began their own investigation. Cooke simply blamed the inability to locate Jimmy on the likelihood that he and his mother had moved.

Despite their concern for the validity of the story, editors allowed it to be entered in the annual Pulitzer Prize competition, in which it won first place for investigative journalism. That turned out to be Cooke's undoing, as the biographical sketch that accompanied the entry also turned out to be largely fictional. Based on information taken from Cooke's own employment application, the sketch claimed that Cooke had a degree from Vassar (when she had actually attended a less prestigious university), had won six journalism awards at her previous newspaper (false), and was fluent in several foreign languages (she wasn't). When the exaggerations in the sketch were exposed, Cooke also admitted the "creativity" she used in the "Jimmy" story, but insisted he was a composite character of several children she had met and that her descriptions of his life were common for children living in that setting. Unconvinced, the *Post* fired Cooke, returned the Pulitzer, and apologized to its readers. In her memoirs, Cooke admitted that when she learned of her Pulitzer Prize nomination, she feared the deception would be revealed and "prayed that she wouldn't win."[41]

In 1998, *The New Republic* fired associate editor Stephen Glass after an internal investigation revealed he had fabricated all or parts of twenty-seven stories he had written for the magazine over a three-year period. Glass's career unraveled when a reporter for *Forbes* magazine attempted to follow up on one of his stories. When he was unable to locate any of Glass's sources or confirm any of the details in the story, he informed his editor, who in turn alerted the *New Republic* editor of the discrepancies.

In 2003, *The New York Times* fired reporter Jayson Blair for similar practices, but the firings did not end there. The newspaper's parent company also fired two senior editors who supervised Blair for not being more suspicious of his work even after several of his stories raised suspicions. In its public apology, the *Times* called the Blair scandal "a low point in the history of the newspaper."[42] In addition to the fabricated and plagiarized stories, editors found more than fifty errors in Blair stories he wrote over a four-year period.

When Blair wrote a profile of American soldier Jessica Lynch following her service in Iraq, he described the view from her parents' home in West Virginia in a way that neither her family nor her neighbors recognized. In turned out Blair had never been to her hometown and had just guessed what those images would look like. But since the parents never complained, the fabrication went unnoticed.[43]

Here are some lesser-known scandals:

- In 1981, *The New York Times* published a series of stories by freelance writer Christopher Jones, who claimed he had spent several days visiting the training camps of the Khmer Rouge, a violent band of terrorists creating postwar havoc in Thailand, Cambodia, and Vietnam. His deception was eventually uncovered when government officials in those countries reported to *Times* editors that Jones was describing places that did not exist and was quoting government officials whom no one could remember. It was later discovered that Jones had never been to Southeast Asia and that much of the material for the stories was taken from a little-known novel published in 1930.
- In 1984, journalist Alastair Reed admitted to a *Wall Street Journal* reporter that, while working for *The New Yorker* earlier in his career, he often used composite characters and made up fictional settings and invented quotes in what were presented as nonfiction articles.
- In 1998, the *Boston Globe* fired columnists Patricia Smith and Mike Barnicle after they admitted making up people, quotes, and events in their columns. Editors admitted to partial responsibility for not detecting the fabrications earlier because they ignored the newspaper's longstanding policy of verifying confidential sources before allowing stories to be published.[44]
- In 2006, the *Bloomsburg Press-Enterprise* in Pennsylvania fired a reporter assigned to do "man on the street" interviews after checking five months' worth of her work and finding forty-six sources whose names could not be found in the telephone directory, voter registration rolls, county property records, or the newspaper's own archives.[45]
- That same year, the Associated Press fired a reporter who submitted a story about drag-racers in California who reached speeds up to 200 mph on the state's freeway system. The reporter claimed first-hand knowledge of the practice because the dragsters allowed her to ride along with them. The stories quoted California Highway Patrol officers who said they had given up on trying to stop the dragsters because their vehicles could not keep up with them, but those officers later denied having spoken to her. The reporter was fired after her editors discovered that not only had she not been directly involved in the races, she did not have direct knowledge of them and had not interviewed anyone who did—she merely lifted the details from a local tourism magazine.
- The case of journalists losing Pulitzer Prizes (as in the Janet Cooke case) or having nominations withdrawn is not without precedent. In 1988, *Philadelphia Inquirer* reporter Tom Weiner saw his nomination cancelled after he was discovered to have plagiarized much of his series on the Pentagon's "top secret budget," which was was mostly an updated version of a series published a year earlier by the *National Journal*.[46]

Jack Kelley, a foreign correspondent for *USA Today* who was one of the newspaper's first hires when it was founded in 1982, was nominated for a Pulitzer Prize in 2002. But less than two years later, his career unraveled when it was learned he had fabricated many of the quotes he included in his stories and claimed to have witnessed terrorist bombings and other acts of war violence when he was actually safe in his hotel room. In at least one instance, Kelley compounded his falsification by describing events in a telephone interview with CNN anchor Wolf Blitzer.[47] When inconsistencies in his stories generated an internal investigation at *USA Today* head-quarters, he attempted to circumvent the process by generating fake travel receipts and interview notes and hired people he had never met to pretend to have been his sources when investigators called. Investigators reviewed more than 700 stories filed over a ten-year period and found that more than 100 included some quotes or other details that had been falsified. After Kelley resigned under pressure, the newspaper withdrew stories it had nominated for industry prizes and either deleted or flagged problematic stories on the newspaper's website.[48]

- Shortly after the 2000 presidential election campaign, *The Sacramento Bee* fired political reporter Dennis Love after it determined that in his coverage of Al Gore's unsuccessful campaign, he stole material from stories published in *U.S. News & World Report, USA Today, The Boston Globe,* and the *Dallas Morning News.*[49]

- In 2004, reporter Khalil Abdullah was fired from the *Macon Telegraph* in Georgia after editors found that one out of every five stories he wrote were plagiarized from other sources. The editors were unaware that Abdullah had been fired from his previous newspaper, the *Fort Worth Star-Telegram,* where he plagiarized one story out of every nine.

- In 2005, the *Worcester Telegram & Gazette* in Massachusetts fired sportswriter Ken Powers for including in his stories quotes he lifted from *Sports Illustrated* as well as other daily newspapers. The timing of the newspaper's decision was awkward, as Powers learned of his termination (and called home) while he was in Jacksonville, Florida covering the New England Patriots' preparation for the Super Bowl.[50]

- In 2005, the associate managing editor of a daily newspaper in Georgia was fired after plagiarizing eight pieces from nationally syndicated columnist Leonard Pitts Jr. Chris Cecil, who had written personal and political commentary for *The Daily Tribune News* in Cartersville, Georgia for less than a year, was let go after a brief investigation prompted by complaints from the *Miami Herald,* Pitts's full-time employer, and Tribune Media Services, the syndicator that distributed Pitts's column.

  After Cecil's termination, Pitts blasted him in his own column. "I've been in this business for twenty-nine years, Mr. Cecil, and I've been plagiarized before," Pitts wrote. "But I've never seen a plagiarist as industrious and brazen as you…the dictionary is a big book. Get your own damn words. Leave mine alone."[51]

  While Pitts has won several Pulitzer Prizes for political commentary, what irked him the most was Cecil's theft of his words in a column Pitts wrote about learning of his mother's terminal illness. In the original column, Pitts wrote that he was moved to tears about hearing the news while driving on a freeway in southern California. In Cecil's column, he repeated the anecdote nearly verbatim, only changing the location to rural Kentucky.[52]

- In 2018, the *Raleigh News & Observer* fired veteran reporter Anne Blythe after an internal investigation found that she had used information from other sources without permission or acknowledgment. The paper reviewed more than 600 articles that Blythe had written over an eighteen-month period and found more than a dozen cases of phrases, sentences, or entire paragraphs taken from other newspapers.[53]

At the *Fort Worth Star-Telegram* in Texas, a process called "post-publication fact checking" involves the newspaper's "reader advocate" randomly choosing articles for scrutiny, including verification of details as well as application of a plagiarism-detection software program. The percentage of articles chosen is small, but it's enough to deter would-be plagiarists and sloppy reporters.[54]

Immersion Journalism

As the term indicates, **immersion journalism** is a form of newsgathering in which the journalist operates within an organization or among the individuals being researched; much like an undercover law-enforcement officer would do to investigate possible crime.

Such cases go beyond the simple acts of "misrepresentation" (described in Chapter 5). While those are short-term operations, the research in immersion journalism often takes place over the course of weeks or months. Another significant difference is that while acts of misrepresentation are carried out by print and broadcast journalism, the end products of immersion journalism are often books.

Advocates of immersion journalism claim this research methodology allows authors to present a realistic picture of the organization or group being studied without their work being compromised by what social science researchers call the **Hawthorne Effect**—the tendency of research subjects to act differently if they know their behavior is being observed and/or recorded. Critics of the technique, who sometimes call it "stunt journalism," contend that by using such methods, researchers are just "playing tourist" in the lives (and sometimes tragedies) of other people.

The technique of immersion journalism can be traced back to Upton Sinclair, who in 1904 spent seven weeks working in a meat-packing plant to research his exposé of the industry's labor practices. His award-winning book *The Jungle* was published in 1906, and resulted in massive changes to federal labor laws and food safety rules.

In 1963, sportswriter George Plimpton pretended to be a professional quarterback and participated in summer training camp and part of the regular season with the Detroit Lions in order to research his book *Paper Lion*, which focused on the behind-the-scenes lives of professional football players. The book was made into a 1968 movie of the same title, with Alan Alda portraying Plimpton. Later in his career, Plimpton played goalie for the Boston Bruins while researching a book about professional hockey and spent several weeks attempting to play professional golf while researching a book about that sport.

A more recent example of immersion journalism is the work of Thomas French, a police-beat reporter for the *St. Petersburg Times* and author of several true crime books. He is best known for his book *South of Heaven: High School at the End of the Twentieth Century*. His research began in the late 1980s when he obtained permission of school administrators and spent a year blending in with a class of high school seniors. While not pretending to be one of them, he gained their confidence and was able to attend classes, club meetings, sporting events, and social activities. While writing a series of weekly columns based on his experiences, he changed or omitted names and created composite characters while documenting issues such as teenage sex, drug and alcohol abuse, peer pressure, violence, and suicide. When the school year was complete, his newspaper gave him additional time off to expand his newspaper stories into the book, which was published in 1993.

Other recent practitioners of immersion journalism include H.G. Bissinger, author of *Friday Night Lights*, a story of high school football in Texas; and Barbara Ehrenreich, author of *Nickel and Dimed* and *Bait and Switch*.

To research *Friday Night Lights*, Bissinger, at the time a sportswriter for the *Philadelphia Inquirer*, spent the entire 1988 high school football season traveling with and observing the practices and private lives of the Permian High School team in Odessa, Texas. In 2002, the book was named the fourth-best nonfiction sports book of all time by *Sports Illustrated*.

To research *Nickel and Dimed*, Ehrenreich spent three months working in a number of low-wage jobs in the retail and food-service businesses to document the long hours, low pay, and lack of respect that she and her peers received from supervisors and customers. Many literary critics praised her work and referred to her as a "modern-day Nellie Bly." (the story of Nellie Bly is discussed in Chapter 5). To research *Bait and Switch*, Ehrenreich moved up a few notches on the economic ladder and spent almost a year pretending to be an out-of-work female executive and touring the country meeting with employment counselors and attending job fairs and other networking events. Her point was to not only document the frustrations that the unemployed face during an economic downturn, but also the issue of employment discrimination affecting older women. The book was published in 2005.

Perhaps the most unusual example of immersion journalism is Norah Vincent, a lesbian journalist who spent eighteen months disguised as a man. She wore men's clothes, cropped her hair short, and each day applied make-up to her face intended to create the appearance of razor stubble. She even wore a tight-fitting bra to flatten her chest and a jock strap with what she called a "generous amount of padding." She also underwent months of training with a professional voice coach in order to change the pitch of her voice.

Calling herself "Ned Vincent," she worked in a number of occupations customarily male-dominated, such as construction and home repair. She joined her male co-workers in after-work socializing at bars and strip clubs, and even joined an all-male bowling league. "Many of the guys thought I was gay, but none of them suspected I was a woman," she said in media interviews. Her goal, as she explained in her 2006 book *Self-Made Man*, was not to undercover any discriminatory behavior or other wrongdoing, but just "to see what life was like on the other side of the gender divide."[55]

Your Turn

Case Study 4A: Conflicts of Interest: Moonlighting at the Catholic Church

Moonlighting may be problematic even in cases in which journalists are not paid for their secondary roles. In 2002, a reporter for the *St. Petersburg Times* served as a volunteer "media relations consultant" for one of the community's largest Catholic churches. At first, the job consisted mostly of publicizing the church's fund-raisers and other non-controversial activities. But when several female members of the church accused one of the priests of making sexual advances, the story became front-page news, and the reporter found herself in a conflict between her paying and non-paying jobs.

In her role as a journalist, she did not cover the investigation itself, but worked near the reporters who did, and as a consultant for the church, her duties included writing news releases about the case and preparing church officials for media interviews. Eventually, her editors became uncomfortable when the reporter found herself shifting back and forth between the two roles while "on company time." In hindsight, they determined that what she did had not violated the newspaper's conflict-of-interest policy, but she was admonished for not disclosing the potential conflict earlier, as well as for listing her work phone number at the *Times* as the "media contact" number for the church.

1. Does the fact that the journalist's work was voluntary (unpaid) make a difference in how you view her role? If you were her editor, would you consider the case differently if it had been a paid position?
2. If other reporters entered into similar volunteer positions, would you approve it as long as they disclosed the relationship to you before accepting it?
3. What philosophers or concepts from Chapter 2 can be applied here?

Case Study 4B: Conflict of Interest: Skating on Thin Ice

When long-time *Tampa Tribune* Sports Editor Tom McEwen died in 2011, he was eulogized by local political and business leaders, his peers across the country, and administrators of the sports leagues he covered for more than three decades. What was unspoken was that McEwen, a member of numerous halls of fame and nineteen-time Florida Sportswriter of the Year, also left behind a lengthy track record of skirting the ethical guidelines of the both the *Tribune* and the journalism profession.[56]

While McEwen's ethical breaches were "open secrets" among sports department staffers and other low-level newsroom employees, his superiors claimed they did not know about them until he approached retirement.

McEwen's transgressions centered on the travel agency he co-founded with his wife and New York Yankees owner George Steinbrenner, a McEwen family friend and part-time Tampa resident. Steinbrenner, who McEwen often lavished with praise in his columns, funded the agency in 1978 and reportedly sold it to the McEwens for one dollar.[57]

For the next twenty-three years, McEwen wrote extensively—nearly always in glowing terms—about the town's two professional sports franchises, the Tampa Bay Buccaneers of the National Football League and Tampa Bay Lightning of the National Hockey League. In none of his columns did he disclose to readers that his travel agency coordinated all of the team travel for the Lightning. While it did not handle team travel for the Buccaneers, it did reportedly handle travel for individual team executives.[58]

In addition to the conflict of interest involving the travel agency, McEwen failed to report that Lightning's Japan-based ownership group was in financial trouble in its home country and had lied to local government leaders about its solvency while pushing for taxpayer funding to build the Ice Palace, the team's home arena.[59]

McEwen's transgressions first became public outside of the *Tribune* building as McEwen entered the twilight of his career in the late 1990s. It began with stories in two weekly alternative newspapers in Tampa, most of them written by freelancer John Sugg, a former *Tribune* staffer. While denying prior knowledge of the situation, *Tribune* managers defended McEwen, lavishing praise on him as a "tireless community supporter" and accusing Sugg of carrying out a vendetta against his former employer.[60]

Meanwhile, the story was picked up by the paper's regional competitor, the *St. Petersburg Times*, as well as *The New York Times*, *Sports Illustrated*, and industry publications such as *American Journalism Review* and *Editor & Publisher*.

While publicly downplaying the situation, inside the *Tribune* building executives insisted McEwen sever business ties with the Lightning and Buccaneers, put in place new ethical guidelines, and made sure McEwen was the first to sign a document indicating he had read them.[61]

"Tom's career was in a different era when there was another set of rules," said Publisher Reid Ashe. "He is a much-beloved figure in town, and he writes a very popular column."[62] Echoed Managing Editor Donna Reed: "It was a different time. The rules changed."[63] Former *Tribune* staffer Skip Perez added, "That could never happen today in this environment, and it's probably a good thing that it couldn't happen."[64]

1. Many of McEwen's superiors at the Tribune appeared to downplay the serious of the situation and instead asked readers to focus on the good that McEwen did for the community. Is that an acceptable way of justifying having "looked the other way" on his ethical transgressions?
2. Are there any philosophers or concepts from Chapter 2 that might help in this situation?

Case Study 4C: Becoming Part of the Story: The Journalist, the Murderer, and the Author (He Said, He Said, She Said)

On February 16, 1970, a mother, her two young daughters, and her unborn son were stabbed to death in a military housing unit at Fort Bragg, North Carolina. The woman's husband, Army surgeon Jeffrey MacDonald, became the primary suspect. He denied being involved in the murders—claiming that he was asleep in another room —and blamed the killings on a pack of drug-induced home invaders that he described to police. After a five-month investigation, the Army's Article 32 hearing supported MacDonald's claim of innocence, even though no other specific suspects were ever identified.

Four years later, prompted by complaints from the woman's stepfather and MacDonald's appearance on television talk shows, federal investigators re-opened the case and indicted MacDonald for first-degree murder. Within a year a civilian court had convicted him, and a federal appeals court upheld the conviction.

MacDonald began a life sentence in a federal prison in California and almost immediately began searching for an author to tell his side of the story in which he continued to claim his innocence. With advice from his lawyers, MacDonald chose Joe McGinness, a newspaper journalist and author of a controversial and best-selling book on the 1968 presidential election. McGinniss had little experience in crime writing, but he won the job over bigger names in the field, including Edward Keyes and Joseph Wambaugh.

The contract the two men signed gave McGinnis exclusive access to MacDonald and members of the defense team and established that MacDonald would receive 26.5 percent of McGinniss's advance and 33 percent of the royalties. The clause in the contract that would later be problematic for MacDonald was a waiver of potential libel claims should he be unhappy with the finished product.

During the three-year research and writing process, McGinniss did what many criminal biographers do: get as close as possible to his subject, even if it meant feigning belief in the person's innocence. When *Fatal Vision* was released in 1983, MacDonald felt betrayed, claiming that McGinniss deceived him about the story-telling approach he was taking and what tone the finished product would strike. Describing his subject as a "narcissistic sociopath," McGinniss implied in his writing that he knew MacDonald was guilty from the onset. According to *New Yorker* writer Janet Malcolm, McGinniss "treacherously deceived his primary source, then abandoned him once he had the information he needed to complete his book."[65]

The rest of the journalism profession, while siding with McGinniss, nevertheless questioned whether this was a case of a journalist getting too close to a subject.

The story of the MacDonald–McGinniss legal drama was the subject of Malcolm's 1990 book *The Journalist and the Murderer*, which was an expansion of her lengthy 1989 article by the same title in *The New Yorker*. At times appearing to show sympathy for MacDonald's complaint and at other times defending McGinniss's work, Malcolm's book became a popular text for journalism ethics class across the country.[66]

McGinniss was almost as critical of Malcolm's book as MacDonald was of his. In his defense, McGinniss wrote that her book was full of "numerous and egregious omissions, distortions, and outright misstatements" and that he needed to "set the record straight."[67]

He admitted to using some degree of "misdirection" while meeting with MacDonald but claimed it went both ways. In their initial meetings, MacDonald and his lawyers implied that McGinnis was their first choice, not admitting they had already discussed the project with Keyes and Wambaugh. McGinniss also accused MacDonald of lying, both in court and in media interviews, about conversations the two men had.[68]

In 1994, McGinniss avoided a potentially controversial assignment when he turned down the lawyers of accused murderer O.J. Simpson, who wanted him to sit at the defense table and then write a book about the trial in the same manner he did when he wrote *Fatal Vision*.

1. Are you concerned that MacDonald's fraud case was allowed to go forward despite having waived the right to sue? Is the difference between suing for libel and suing for fraud an important legal distinction? Is the matter of fraud so serious that such a waiver would not apply?
2. McGinniss was a former newspaper journalist, but does the fact that his work took the form of a book rather than a newspaper article change you view this case?

Case Study 4D: Becoming Part of the Story: Bamberger Blows the Whistle

In October 2005, *Sports Illustrated* writer Michael Bamberger went beyond just getting "too close" to a story he was covering—he actually affected the outcome of an event he was covering.

Bamberger was covering a women's professional golf tournament in Palm Desert, California, where the star attraction was Michelle Wie, a talented sixteen-year-old playing in her first professional event after an impressive amateur career. Bamberger was on the course and following Wie's group during Saturday's third round when he witnessed what he thought was a rules violation. During Wie's post-round news conference, Bamberger asked her about the incident, but she provided what reporters described as a "vague" answer.

On Sunday afternoon—the final day of the event and after what Bamberger described as a "sleepless night"—he approached a tournament administrator and described the incident from the day before. Rules officials then questioned Wie and reviewed a videotape of the incident, then determined that Wie had indeed violated the rules and disqualified her from the tournament, which cost her a fourth-place check for $53,126.

For decades, golf has been heralded as a "game of honor" in which the players police themselves. At the professional level, one of the guiding principles is that golfers, who typically play in groups of two or three, are responsible for monitoring each other and ensuring a fair competition for the entire field. There are rules officials at every event, but not enough to assign one to each group, so golfers often consult with other players in their group if there is a rules question. In recent years, however, advances in technology allowed television coverage of professional tournaments to become more "close up," and fans watching a telecast from home would often call the tournament office to report alleged violations. In several cases, players were either penalized or disqualified from tournaments as a result of fans reporting rules violations, raising the issue of the role of the television networks and fans in the administration of a competition.

In the Bamberger case, many sports journalists, media ethicists, and golf fans complained that a reporter covering the event should be limited to just that—writing about the event—and should not become involved in the administration of the rules. Tournament officials and fans defending Bamberger contended "rules are rules" and that anyone—fan, journalist, or other individual—who witnessed a possible violation should bring it to the attention of tournament officials. Others questioned why Bamberger waited for more than more than twenty-four hours after witnessing the incident to report it to tournament officials. Still others questioned his motives and accused him of reporting the incident simply to earn notoriety as the person who cost Wie her first professional paycheck.

As a result of the incident, Internet bulletin boards and sports talk shows on television and radio featured lengthy discussions of the topic, with commentator and audience opinions equally divided. While many fans were supportive of Bamberger—a respected golf journalist and author of several books on the sport—many others wrote letters of complaint to *Sports Illustrated*, with some readers even canceling their subscriptions.

1. As an abstract concept, do you agree with the general ethical principle that says that journalists should cover the story and not become part of the story (i.e., covering the parade, not marching in the parade)?
2. Regarding the specifics of this case, which side do you take on the incident above— that Bamberger did the right thing by reporting the incident, or that his actions were too much a departure from his assigned role?
3. When a journalist puts away his or her notebook or television camera in order to help a person in danger—such as cases in which reporters rescue people from a burning building, prevent them from drowning in a river, or talk a person out of suicide—even the strictest journalism ethicists would agree they are acting properly. But the Bamberger–Wie scenario is on the opposite extreme, as no lives were in danger. How does that affect your interpretation of the "don't-get-involved-in-the-story" rule?
4. If you were responsible for drafting a formal policy on such matters for the employees of your newspaper or television station, where would your policy draw the line?

Case Study 4E: Becoming Part of the Story: Reporters Behaving Badly

In 1999, a reporter for *The Salt Lake City Tribune* was arrested for soliciting a prostitute and disorderly conduct. Shawn Foster, who covered police and the court system, was caught in a police prostitution sting and tried to escape the situation by driving away, but instead he struck a police car. He told police he was researching a story on the city's prostitution problem, which was untrue. He paid a $100 fine for two misdemeanors and paid for the damage to the police car.

Faced with the decision on whether or not to cover the arrest, *Tribune* editors consulted the newspaper's policy manual, which specified that individuals arrested for misdemeanors would not be identified unless he or she was a public figure, the offense involved hypocrisy, or the alleged crime endangered public safety. The editors concluded that the Foster story met none of those criteria, and the decision was to not publish the story. Meanwhile, a competing newspaper, the *Deseret News*, covered the story mostly because of Foster lying about being on assignment. "In an era when readers believe our ethical standards are slipping, editors should not sweep under the rug lapses by practitioners of their own profession," said John Higgins, editor of *The Deseret News*.[69]

The story was eventually published in other newspapers and became a case study in journalism textbooks. *Tribune* editors continued to defend their decision, but added a caveat: if the charge had been drunk driving, it would be in the paper.

Ironically, four years later, the editors' off-the-cuff comment about drunk driving became prophetic for news executives at WFLA-TV in Tampa, Florida.

Chris Thomas, the station's popular and easily recognized sports director was arrested for drunk driving, and even before his courtroom appearance, he admitted to station management that he was guilty and apologized on the air for embarrassing the station and "letting down his fans." Letters and phone calls supporting Thomas poured into the station, yet a few days later an executive with the station's parent company in Richmond, Virginia ordered that Thomas be fired. The company claimed that as a public figure and representative of the station, Thomas had an obligation to conduct himself in an appropriate manner and not engage in such risky behavior. Local radio stations jumped on the story and ridiculed Thomas, not only because of the seriousness of the drunk driving charge, but because the incident took place in a part of town known for drug-dealing and prostitution. "Everyone knows that if you go into that part of town late at night, you're looking for one of two things," one early morning disc jockey said.

In 2006, editors at the *Santa Barbara News-Press* deleted a story about the drunk-driving arrest of its editorial page editor, Travis Armstrong, shortly before the presses were scheduled to roll.

The order to kill the story came from the publisher, one of Armstrong's closest friends at the paper. Lower-level editors objected to the decision, stating that they were also friends of Armstrong but believed the newsworthy of the story should have taken priority over personal relationships.[70]

1. In the case of the *Salt Lake City Tribune* reporter lying to police, do you believe that was an offense that merited the reporter being fired?
2. In the Chris Thomas case, do you agree with the company's decision and how it justified firing him? Is a television personality entitled to make mistakes and learn from them like everyone else?
3. Does that fact that it was Thomas' first offense (as opposed to being a habitual drunk driver) change your opinion?
4. Were local radio stations justified in ridiculing Thomas? (See the section titled "Parody and Ridicule" in Chapter 3.) According to libel law, public figures must accept a certain level of public criticism and ridicule as an aspect of their fame, but did the disc jockey cross the line with the comments above?
5. Do you agree with the editors of the *Santa Barbara News-Press* stating the news-worthiness of the arrest (of the editorial-page editor for drunk driving) should have taken priority over his personal relationship with his co-workers at the paper? How do you feel about the editors being overruled by the publisher, who ordered that the story be killed?

Case Study 4F: Immersion Journalism: The Unlikely Disciple

In 2007, a Brown University English major and student journalist employed the immersion technique as he spent an entire semester as a transfer student at Liberty University, a Christian institution founded by evangelist Jerry Falwell. Kevin Roose had never written anything longer than a traditional college term paper or his weekly column in Brown's student newspaper, but his semester at Liberty gave him enough material for a 324-page book that took nearly two years to write.

Titled *The Unlikely Disciple: A Sinner's Semester at America's Holiest University*, the 2009 work chronicles Roose's attempt to "blend in" at the ultra-conservative university, despite his own upbringing in a liberal, non-religious family. Roose's experience at Liberty included taking classes, attending church, singing in the school choir, and living in an on-campus dormitory with Christian roommates who never questioned why he was there and never suspected that he was working undercover. But his hardest adjustment was adherence to the university's forty-six-page code of student conduct, which barred alcohol, tobacco, dancing, cursing, R-rated movies, and hugging other students for more than three seconds. Ironically, Roose pointed out, it was his God-fearing roommates who broke the rules far more often than he did.

In order to prepare for the semester, Roose spent three days with a childhood friend who had since moved to another state but agreed to "coach" him on the Christian life, including a crash course in biblical characters and important verses from scripture. "My goal was to see the real, unfiltered picture of life at Liberty University," Roose said in a National Public Radio interview, admitting that he bent some rules of journalism ethics by misrepresenting himself. "It [the deception] did allow me to get a more accurate—and actually a fairer picture of—what life at Liberty was like."[71]

He admits that he may have taken the acting job a bit too far, walking around campus his first week saying "Glory be" and "Mercy" whenever he had the opportunity. "I found out that Liberty students don't talk like that," he said in the radio interview.[72]

1. Did Roose violate any important journalistic principles in carrying out his deception?
2. Did the fact that Roose was a student journalist affect how you evaluated this case? Or the fact that he was writing a book instead of a newspaper or magazine article?
3. How do you evaluate Roose's deception in light of the three-part test described in Chapter 5?
4. If you had been Roose's roommate that semester, how would you react to his deception after you learned about it?

Discussion Problem 4A: Conflicts of Interest: Plugging the Zoo

You've watched the same television news program for several years, and for most of that time the station has employed the same meteorologist. During almost every weather segment, he makes comments such as "tomorrow will be a nice day to visit the Willoughby Zoo" or "tomorrow afternoon it looks like rain, so if you were planning to go to the Willoughby Zoo, you should plan to go in the morning."

You send an email to the station manager to indicate your annoyance at the constant references to the zoo. The station manager responds by explaining that the meteorologist sits on the board of trustees at the zoo and is simply trying to help out.

1. Because the zoo is a nonprofit organization and the meteorologist does not profit from its success or failure, is there a conflict of interest in this matter?
2. Should the meteorologist be obligated to disclose his relationship with the zoo in order to continue to make such comments?
3. Are there any philosophical concepts (from Chapter 2) or provisions in organizational codes of ethics that apply here?

Discussion Problem 4B: Conflicts of Interest: The Award-Winning Environmental Reporter

You're editor of a mid-size daily newspaper, and your star environmental reporter covers a number of local and national environmental issues, including the work of local advocacy groups. Recently, without your knowledge, the reporter attended the annual awards banquet of one of the groups and was presented an award for his "outstanding reporting on environmental issues." The award included a plaque and check for $1,000.

As a lifelong hard news journalist, you're not comfortable with the situation. You check the newspaper's policy manual and find nothing regarding such conflicts. So you check with your boss, the newspaper's publisher, who is also not comfortable with the situation but leaves it up to you to decide how to handle it.

1. Which of the following actions do you take?

   a. Allow the reporter to keep both the plaque and cash award and continue reporting on the work of that organization.
   b. Require him to return both the plaque and the cash award.
   c. Require him to return the cash prize but allow him to keep the plaque.
   d. Require that he no longer cover the group's activities as part of his work.
   e. Some combination of b, c, and d.

2. To prevent such dilemmas in the future, the publisher asks you to draft a policy regarding such dilemmas. Do so in two or three sentences.

Discussion Problem 4C: Becoming Part of the Story: The Reporter and the Prostitute

You're the editor of a daily newspaper in a mid-size city. One of your reporters is working on a series of stories about the lifestyle of prostitutes working in the downtown area of the city. One of the prostitutes interviewed says she wants out of the business and asks the reporter for transportation to a homeless shelter sponsored by a nonprofit organization running a program to help prostitutes make the transition to a better life. When the reporter and prostitute arrive at the shelter, they find that it has been closed for renovations and there is no one there to direct them to an alternative shelter. The woman is afraid that if she goes back to her street corner, her pimp may hurt or kill her, so the reporter allows the prostitute to stay in her home overnight.

1. What ethical concerns do you have about this situation?
2. Are there any philosophical concepts (from Chapter 2) or provisions in organizational codes of ethics that apply here?

Discussion Questions

401. After reading the highlights of the SPJ, ASNE, and RTDNA Codes of Ethics at the beginning of this chapter, find provisions within those codes could easily be applied, and find at least one provision of the codes that you believe would be difficult to apply.

402. Re-read the section titled "Conflicts of Interest" under "Current Issues and Controversies." Considering the examples provided (such as personal or business relationships, organizational memberships, and running for public office), do you think it is unfair to expect journalists to forgo some of the same social and business opportunities enjoyed by individuals not working in the media? Or do you believe that journalists should be held to a higher standard and should therefore accept such limitations as "part of the job"?

Notes

1 Stephen Klaidman and Tom L. Beauchamp, *The Virtuous Journalist*. New York: Oxford University Press (1987), p. 217.
2 Howard Kurtz, *The Media Circus: The Trouble with America's Newspapers*. New York: Random House (1994), p. 126.
3 Kurtz, p. 127.
4 Stephen Bates, *If No News, Send Rumors*. New York: St. Martin's Press (1989), p. 4.
5 Ron Smith, *Groping for Ethics in Journalism*. Ames, IA: Wiley-Blackwell (2003), p. 371.
6 Allan Wolper, "The Credibility Gap." *Editor & Publisher*, August 12, 2002.
7 "Lines Blur as Journalism Heads Back to the Future." *USA Today*, November 10, 2010, p. 8-A.
8 Roger Yu, "Anchor Blasted for Clinton Donation." *USA Today*, May 15, 2015, p. 2-B.

9 Dylan Byers, "George Stephanopoulos Discloses Contribution to Clinton Foundation." ABC News, May 14, 2015.

10 Conrad Fink, *Media Ethics*. Boston: Allyn & Bacon (1995), p. 128.

11 National Public Radio News Code of Ethics and Practices." www.npr.org/about/ethics (accessed July 7, 2019).

12 Robert Love, "Shakedown: The Unfortunate History of Reporters Who Trade Power for Cash." *Columbia Journalism Review*, July/August 2006, pp. 47–51.

13 James O'Shea, *The Deal from Hell: How Moguls and Wall Street Plundered Great American Newspapers*. New York: Public Affairs (2011), p. 146.

14 Love, "Before Jon Stewart: The Truth about Fake News." *Columbia Journalism Review*, March/April 2007, pp. 33–37.

15 National Public Radio News Code of Ethics and Practices." www.npr.org/about/ethics (accessed July 7, 2019).

16 John L. Hulteng, *Playing it Straight: A Practical Discussion of the Ethical Principles of the American Society of Newspaper Editors*. Chester, CT: The Globe Pequot Press (1981), pp. 6–7.

17 John C. Merrill and Ralph D. Barney, ed., *Ethics and the Press*. New York: Hastings House Publishing (1978), pp. 152–153.

18 Merrill and Barney, pp. 152–153.

19 Smith, *Groping for Ethics in Journalism*, p. 366.

20 Smith, *Journalism Ethics*. Malden, MA: Blackwell Publishing (2008), p. 216.

21 Jeff Himmelman, *Yours in Truth: A Personal Portrait of Ben Bradlee, Legendary Editor of the Washington Post*. New York: Random House (2012), p. 78.

22 Himmelman, p. 87.

23 Himmelman, p. 78.

24 Himmelman, pp. 83–84.

25 Stephen Bates, *If No News, Send Rumors*. New York: St. Martin's Press (1989), p. 188–189.

26 Anthony Violanti, "Nina Totenberg's High-Level Insider's View." *The Buffalo News*, May 14, 2002.

27 Bates, p. 98.

28 Conrad Fink, *Media Ethics*. Boston: Allyn & Bacon (1995), p. 185.

29 Smith, *Groping for Ethics in Journalism*. Ames, IA: Wiley-Blackwell (2003), p. 110.

30 Smith, *Groping for Ethics in Journalism*, p. 110.

31 William McGowan, *Coloring the News: How Crusading for Diversity Has Corrupted American Journalism*. San Francisco: Encounter Books (2001), pp. 10–15.

32 McGowan, p. 10.

33 Linda Wallace, "Diversity: The Operating Manual." *Columbia Journalism Review*, July/August 2003, p. 18.

34 Pamela T. Newkirk, "Guess Who's Leaving the Newsroom." *Columbia Journalism Review*, September/October 2000, pp. 36–39.

35 Travis Loop, "A Boost for Minority Workforce." *Presstime*, November 2002, p. 43.

36 Loop.

37 "Norton Guide to Avoiding Plagiarism." Online resource from Cape Fear Community College website. See also: Marie Dunne White, "Plagiarism and the News Media." *Journal of Mass Media Ethics*, Vol. 4, No. 2 (1989), pp. 265–280.

38 "The Great Moon Hoax of 1835 Claimed Astronomer Had Discovered Life on the Moon." *Pensacola News Journal*, July 2, 2019. See also: Craig Silverman, *Regret the Error*. New York: Sterling Publishing (2007), pp. 30–38.

39 Love, "Before Jon Stewart: The Truth about Fake News."

40 "Plagiarism and the News Media." *Journal of Mass Media Ethics*, Vol. 4, No. 2 (1989), pp. 265–280.

41 "The Big Lie." *Columbia Journalism Review*, November/December 2001, p. 91.

42 Adeel Hassen, "Blair's Victims: That Helpless Feeling." *Columbia Journalism Review*, July/August 2003, pp. 19–21.

43 Hassen.

44 Lori Robertson, "Ethically Challenged." *American Journalism Review*, March 2001, pp. 21–29.

45 Craig Silverman, *Regret the Error*. New York: Sterling Publishing (2007), p. 153.

46 Marie Dunne White, "Plagiarism and the News Media." *Journal of Mass Media Ethics*, Vol. 4, No. 2 (1989), pp. 265–280.

47 Allan Wolper, "How King Con Kelley Got Away with It." *Editor & Publisher*, May 2004, p. 30.

48 Blake Morrison, "Ex-USA Today Reporter Faked Major News Stories." *USA Today*, March 18, 2004. See also: Jacques Steinberg, "USA Today Finds Top Writer Lied." *The New York Times*, March 20, 2014.

49 Robertson.

50 "Worchester Paper Isn't Done Examining Fired Sportswriters' Work." *Editor & Publisher*, February 4, 2005.

51 Leonard Pitts Jr., "Chris Cecil, Plagiarism Gets You Fired." Syndicated newspaper column, June 3, 2005.

52 David Astor, "Plagiarizing Pitts' Column Gets a Georgia Newspaper Editor Fired." *Editor & Publisher*, June 3, 2005.

53 "Veteran Reporter Loses in Job in Plagiarism Probe." Associated Press report, July 21, 2018.

54 Silverman, p. 321.

55 "Self-Made Man." ABCNews.com, January 20, 2006.

56 John F. Sugg, "Tampa Bay's Most Censored Stories: Tom McEwen's Retirement from the Tribune." *Creative Loafing*, May 3, 2001.

57 Sugg, "Skating on Thin Ice in Tampa." *Editor & Publisher*, February 7, 2000, p. 23.

58 Sugg, "Skating on Thin Ice in Tampa."

59 Sugg, "Tampa Bay's Most Censored Stories."

60 Sugg, "Skating on Thin Ice in Tampa." See also: Sugg, "Tampa Bay's Most Censored Stories."

61 Gil Thelen, "Tribune Questioned on McEwen's Business Ties." *The Tampa Tribune*, December 12, 1999.

62 Brent Cunningham, "In the Lab." *Columbia Journalism Review*, May/June 2000, pp. 29–31.

63 Jason Garcia, "Changing Rules." *American Journalism Review*, March 2001. https://ajrarchive.org/Article.asp?id=940

64 Andrew Meacham, "Former Tampa Tribune Sports Editor Tom McEwen Shaped Bay Area Landscape." *Tampa Bay Times*, June 6, 2011.

65 Albert Scardino, "Ethics, Reporters, and *The New Yorker*." *New York Times*, March 21, 1989.

66 Scardino, "Ethics, Reporters, and *The New Yorker*." See also: "Reflections: The Journalist and the Murderer." *The New Yorker*, March 13–20, 1989. Janet Malcolm, *The Journalist and the Murderer*. New York: Alfred A. Knopf (1995).

67 Joe McGinniss, epilogue to second edition of *Fatal Vision*. New York: New American Library, 1989.

68 McGinniss.

69 "Cases and Commentaries: Rival Dailies Clash over Reporter's Arrest." *Journal of Mass Media Ethics*, Vol. 15, No. 2 (2000), pp. 127–138.

70 Susan Paterno, "Santa Barbara Smackdown." *American Journalism Review*, December 2006/January 2007, pp. 44–51.

71 Kevin Roose, *The Unlikely Disciple: A Sinner's Semester at America's Holiest University*. New York: Grand Central Publishing (2009), p. 11.

72 "Undercover at an Evangelical University." NPR.org, accessed May 30, 2009.

5 Journalism and Broadcasting
Policy Issues

Background

Of all the codes of ethics developed by the major professional organizations—many of which are mentioned in this book—the code of the Radio Television Digital News Association (RTDNA) is the most up-to-date and may be the most specific. Last updated in 2015, the code addresses policy issues such as deception and staging of news. More details from the code are found later in this chapter. The RTDNA Code of Broadcast News Ethics requires that broadcasters:

- guard against using audio or video material in a way that deceives the audience;
- respect the dignity, privacy, and well-being of people with whom they deal;
- strive to conduct themselves in a manner that protects them from conflicts of interest, real or perceived, and decline gifts or favors which would influence or appear to influence their judgments.

The code also makes specific references to deception and hidden recording devices (both issues are covered in detail later in this chapter). The code states that "Deception in newsgathering, including surreptitious recording, conflicts with journalism's commitment to truth."

Issues and Controversies

Dealing with Suicide

How to deal with the issue of suicide has been a subject of reflection and debate within the journalism profession for several decades. Questions include whether or not to report suicides (and the level of detail that should be included if the cause of death is mentioned), whether or not photographs or video should be published or aired, and the media's responsibility in covering the issue in a way that does not glamorize suicide or portray it as an appropriate way to deal with personal hardship. In addition, the media often struggles with how to proceed when a person who is the subject of a news story commits suicide, or threatens to.

Should Suicides Be Reported?

Many newspapers have policies of not reporting suicides unless one or more of the following conditions exist: (a) the deceased is a well-known person; (b) there is some doubt as to whether the death was the result of suicide, homicide, or an accident; or (c) the suicide (or threat) takes place in public and creates a public spectacle.[1] Other newspapers add a fourth condition, reporting on murder-suicides.

One example of the "public spectacle" concept took place in the Orlando suburb of Deland, Florida, in the 1990s, when a man threatened to jump from a high floor of a retirement home. Two local newspapers covered the story, partly because it had a happy ending (police talked the man out of jumping) and partly because it had tied up traffic for hours and residents outside of the building at the time were not allowed to re-enter until the situation had been resolved.[2]

Like most daily newspapers, *The Tampa Tribune*[3] had a policy of not covering suicides unless one of the three conditions mentioned earlier was met. That policy was tested in 1991 when a local marketing executive killed his wife and then himself. Because the couple was well known in business and social circles, the *Tribune* and other area media believed they were justified in covering the deaths as a news story, but out of consideration for family members on both sides, they did so tastefully.

Ten months later, however, the *Tribune* published a lengthy article about the couple, focusing on how their financial problems spiraled out of control in the year prior to their deaths. The *Tribune* defended the article as "tastefully presented" and pointed to the fact that it did not glamorize suicide, but instead suggested that other people in similar circumstances need not resort to such drastic measures. The article even posed the question, "Why didn't they do what millions of other Americans do ... declare bankruptcy or seek financial counseling?"[4]

The *Austin American-Statesman* in Texas found its long-standing policy of not reporting suicides (unless it met one of those conditions) put to the test in 2005 when one of its own reporters, Kevin Carmody, took his own life. After much deliberation, editors decided to report it because his award-winning work as an environmental reporter made him a public figure in the community. The newspaper specified the cause of death as suicide in an obituary over the objections of the reporter's family and even his former co-workers in the newsroom.[5]

During one week in 2017, the *Chicago Tribune* was criticized for its coverage of two suicides in the Chicago area but justified both in explanations to readers. The first involved a Northwestern University basketball player, and the second involved a woman who killed her two children before killing herself. The newspaper's editors explained to upset readers that the first case was covered because it involved a prominent person, and the second because it provided an opportunity to explore the issue of economic hardship and its effect on family life. Columnist John Puterbaugh explained to readers that neither decision came easy. "It is important that we always remember that the decisions we make have the potential to cause emotional pain," Puterbaugh wrote. "Some of us [newspaper staffers] have experienced our own pain from losing a family member to suicide ... that helps me think about how I'd talk to the mom or brother of someone whose suicide we reported if they called me after reading a story we published. I'd want to know I was thoughtful about the actions we took that potentially added to someone's pain."[6]

Framing the Issue

Newspapers and television stations and networks that deal with suicide-related stories insist that they do so in good taste and are careful not to glamorize it nor present it as an appropriate way to deal with personal problems. The history of the issue goes back to the 1962 suicide of actress Marilyn Monroe. In the month that followed, suicides jumped 12 percent nationwide, with an even larger increase seen in women in their twenties and thirties. Following the 1977 suicide of comedian Freddie Prinze Sr. and the 1994 suicide of rock musician Kurt Cobain, suicides among young men also increased dramatically.

Following the 2014 suicide of comedian Robin Williams, a different trend was observed. Crisis hotlines across the country reported that the number of calls they received doubled, and for months afterward remained "well above average."[7] Similar trends were spotted after the 2017 suicide of musician Chris Cornell and the 2018 deaths of fashion designer Kate Spade and television personality Anthony Bourdain. Suicide researchers believed that such publicity, when coupled with proper framing of the issue and the publication of suicide hotline numbers and reminders about other resources available, are more likely to save lives than cause copycats.[8]

Child psychologists and other experts worry that media coverage of suicides may have an adverse effect on teenagers, for which suicide is the third leading cause of death. The potential for copycat suicides is known as the **Werther Effect**, named for Johann Wolfgang von Goethe's eighteenth-century novel *The Sorrows of Young Werther*, in which the protagonist commits suicide over the loss of his girlfriend to another man. The novel was believed to have inspired a rash of male suicides in the decade that followed its publication.[9]

Youth counselors fear the coverage of celebrity suicides is especially dangerous, as many teens dealing with romantic and academic setbacks see suicide as a "permanent solution to a temporary problem." When it happens at their schools, they see their peers "have achieved a fame in death they never could in life, and that has some dangerous ramifications for other youths who are trying to get through their lives."[10]

Experts say that one of the worst things a reporter covering a suicide can do is to quote a friend or family member saying the person "has gone to a better place," "his pain is finally gone," or any other comments that idealize death. Instead, suicide counselors prefer that reporters quote experts making comments such as the person "could have gotten help if he/she had asked for it."[11]

Experts suggest that when explaining the cause of an individual's death, reporters should be careful not to over-generalize or draw conclusions in a way that gives readers an incomplete or misleading picture of the person's reasons for taking their own lives. Mental health counselors contend that suicide is rarely based on one event or cause, but more often is due to a combination of factors, with one factor being underlying mental health issues. The media, they warn, should not publish or broadcast stories indicating that a teenager or young adult committed suicide simply over bad grades or the end of a romantic relationship. The American Foundation for Suicide Prevention adds that in covering specific cases, the media should also avoid describing the scene of a suicide or the method. When publishing or broadcasting stories about the larger issue, AFSP requests that media organizations avoid using terms such as "growing problem," an "epidemic," or "skyrocketing." The AFSP and mental health organizations also praise the media for providing the telephone numbers of suicide hotlines each time they cover a specific case or address the overall issue. Each time a celebrity is in the news for committing suicide, for example, publications such as *People* and *Entertainment Weekly* publish those phone numbers on their front pages.

The Poynter Institute for Media Studies recommends that stories about suicide not go into detail about the method used so as to not provide a "how-to manual," and to not use only "neutral" photographs. "Images of a person who appears peaceful, calm, and serene send a message that suicide will get you to that peaceful place," the Poynter guidelines say.[12]

In 2001, the Annenberg Public Policy Center and Office of the U.S. Surgeon General issued a joint report in which they asked the media to be more thoughtful in how they reported on suicides—both individual cases and overall trends.[13]

The report provided examples of bad newspaper headlines, including "Eight-Grade Sweethearts in Suicide Pact" (because it glamorized the idea of teen suicide) and "Bullet Ends Cancer Fight" (because it suggested suicide as an appropriate way to deal with a terminal illness).[14]

A similar study was conducted at the University of Toronto in 2018. The report was issued shortly after the suicides of Spade and Bourdain, and while praising the media for its tasteful coverage and inclusion of hotline numbers, it reminded journalists to exercise caution. "We're not saying reporting on suicide is bad," said Dr. Ayal Schaffer, a University of Toronto psychology professor and co-author of the study. "Our goal is not to blame journalists or tell journalists how to do their jobs. But it is to provide a pretty strong research base to support specific guidelines about how reporting on suicide should be done."[15] One of the report's suggestions is that celebrity suicides be framed as part of a larger public health problem, not just a show business or popular culture story.

Andrew Seaman, chair of the Society of Professional Journalists Ethics Committee and a health reporter, was one of the journalists quoted in the study. Seaman said his philosophy on suicide reporting is grounded in one of the SPJ's guiding principles: "Minimize harm."[16]

On the issue of teen suicides, both the Annenberg and University of Toronto studies encourage media organizations to consult with local mental health agencies when doing stories on teenage suicides in order to discourage "copycats." When publishing or broadcasting stories in communities in which several teenagers have taken their own lives, media organizations typically include warning signs that parents should look for in their own children, as well as the phone numbers of suicide hotlines that teenagers (or adults) can call in times of crisis. While many critics believe the media should stay out of the business of reporting teenage suicides altogether, mental health experts agree that the value of providing the warning signs and hotline numbers outweighs the risk involved in suicide copycats.

Using Video and Photographs

Whether or not to show photographs or video of individuals committing suicide is a topic of ongoing discussion. When individuals commit suicide in front of television cameras, it is unlikely that any television station would show the act if they knew ahead of time what was going to happen. But in recent years, television stations and networks who captured suicides on videotape debated whether or not to replay them on subsequent newscasts. That question arose in cases in which a public official in Pennsylvania killed himself at a news conference (1987), a Louisiana deputy sheriff killed himself in public after killing his wife earlier in the day (1994), and a California man who killed himself on a busy freeway to protest the lack of insurance coverage for AIDS patients (1998). In all three cases, the suicides were inadvertently broadcast live on television. While no stations were criticized for *not* re-showing the video, those that did so it were strongly criticized by parents who complained that their children were watching. Even though many television stations and networks warned viewers in advance, they nevertheless continued to receive complaints for several weeks.

Responding to Suicide Threats

How media organizations should respond when a person involved in a negative news story threatens suicide is a more difficult issue. Newspaper editors and television news directors report that the problem of news subjects threatening to commit suicide in an attempt to dissuade them from publishing embarrassing stories happens more often than the public is aware of. The immediate reaction might be to treat such threats or desperate attempts to prevent the publication or broadcast of a negative news story, but there are reported cases in which the subjects of news stories carry them out, leaving family members angry and media decision-makers plagued with guilt.

One example took place in 1976 when an oil company executive who traveled back and forth to the Soviet Union was found to be a double agent, selling American secrets to the Russian government and Russian secrets to the American government. When he learned that the *Dallas Times-Herald* was about to expose his secret, he threatened to commit suicide. The newspaper ignored his threat, prompting the man to kill himself the day the story was published.

Interviewing and Quotations

Interviewing news sources can be a tricky endeavor for beginning journalists. Here are some of the most common issues with which journalists who are new to the field may struggle:

Promising Confidentiality

Reporters sometimes promise their sources that they can remain confidential, but once the story is complete, the reporter no longer has control over it. An editor who knows the identity of a source may decide to insert the source's name without telling the reporter, which leads the source to believe the journalist was at fault. Promising confidentiality to sources without first getting permission from an editor is discouraged. Reporters should also warn sources that the promise of confidentiality could be overruled by an editor.

During a 1982 election campaign in Minnesota, an advertising agency executive employed by the Republican candidate for lieutenant governor told four reporters that he had "dirt" on the Democratic opponent but would reveal it only if promised confidentiality. Three of the journalists complied, apparently without approval from the news organizations that employed them. Dan Cohen's "dirt" was rather trivial: the opponent in question had been convicted of shoplifting six dollars' worth of merchandise twelve years earlier. Two of the three media outlets—both newspapers—published the story, but editors overruled their reporters' promise and attributed the information to Cohen by name. Cohen lost his job with the advertising agency and sued the two newspapers for breach of contract, even though nothing was ever put in writing. A jury awarded Cohen $700,000 (reduced on appeal to $200,000) and the two newspapers immediately adopted a new policy prohibiting promises of confidentiality.[17]

Promising to Provide a Copy of Story Before It Is Published

Based on either newspaper policy or simply personal experience, most reporters would say "no" to a source's request to see a copy of a story before it is published.

The request usually comes from individuals with little or no experience being interviewed, as those with experience dealing with journalists know that few journalists would agree. Those few journalists who do go along with the request believe it to be helpful because a source may point out errors, but the potential drawbacks are complex and time-consuming. Sources seeing a story in advance may deny having made a specific comment, agree that he or she said it but still ask that it be deleted, may want to respond to another source's quotes, or in some cases may want to argue about semantics.

Showing a source the story in advance may not be addressed by a newspaper's policy manual, but most editors consider it *permissible but strongly discouraged*. If the source is concerned about possibly being misquoted, a better alternative is to contact the source once the story is complete and discuss over the phone only those quotes, facts, or statistics that may be controversial. The practice of **readbacks** allows the source to modify or retract controversial quotes. While most editors allow reporters to make their own decisions regarding readbacks, at some magazines—*Time*, *National Geographic*, and *The New Yorker*—it is standard procedure.

In addition to readbacks, another alternative to showing stories to sources (in cases in which reporters deal with sources who routinely claim they are misquoted) is to either tape record in-person interviews or ask questions by electronic mail so an electronic record of the interview will be created.

Lying to Sources

Some journalists may tell Source A that he or she has already interviewed Source B (often a competitor) in order to coax Source A into agreeing to an interview, even though no such Source B interview has taken place. *Never acceptable under any circumstances.*

Threats and Ultimatums

A reporter frustrated with a source's refusal to be interviewed might say to that individual, "If you don't speak to me, I will get the information from somewhere else, publish the story anyway, and it will make you look bad." Or worse: "If you don't speak to me, I will publish the story anyway and if anything in the story is inaccurate, it will be your fault." *Neither of these tactics is acceptable.* A better alternative: "Everyone else involved in this situation has agreed to talk with me, and if you don't, you will lose your chance to tell your side of the story."

The Ambush Interview

Reporters who believe that a source is attempting to avoid being interviewed might resort to showing up unannounced at the potential source's home or place of business. Television journalists often do this, usually claiming it is either because of a tight deadline or a source's refusal to return phone calls; more often they do it for dramatic effect. Print journalists, however, should give the potential source adequate opportunity to return phone calls or otherwise agree to the interview.

Bait and Switch

An inexperienced reporter might tell a potential source that the story being researched is about one topic, when it's really about another. In the 1980s, for example, *The New York Times* had to establish a policy prohibiting the bait-and-switch interview method when editors learned that reporters preparing "advance obituaries" were telling older celebrities they were interviewing them for a regular feature story and not a post-death feature. The practice came to light when actress Bette Davis, shortly before her death in 1989, suspected that was the case when she agreed to be interviewed by a *Times* reporter and asked, "Are you already writing my obituary?"[18]

Condensing, Paraphrasing, and Altering Quotes

The issue of how much "literary license" a print journalist may use in "improving" quotes by condensing, paraphrasing, or otherwise altering them is not consistently addressed in newspaper stylebooks and policy manuals. The *Associated Press Stylebook* states that reporters should "never alter quotations, even to correct minor grammatical errors or word usage."[19]

Many newspapers have policies that allow such alterations only in cases of paraphrasing. "If the words are surrounded by quote marks, we're telling the readers that those are the speaker's exact words," says one newspaper policy manual. No one expects reporters to be as accurate as professional stenographers or court reporters who are capable of producing verbatim transcripts, but the closer they can get to that ideal, the more accurate the reporting will be.

University of Arizona linguistics professor Adrienne Lehrer contends that newspaper articles that quoted sources verbatim would be excruciating to read. "Most people who do not work with actual conversation are amazed when they read verbatim transcripts," she wrote in a 1989 article in *Journalism Quarterly*. "They are surprised by the [grammatical] errors, fragments, unfinished sentences, and hesitation expressions such as um's and ah's ... Little is to be gained by quoting this kind of material verbatim."[20]

Individual editors will often authorize reporters to clean up quotes in order to avoid embarrassing an individual or portraying him or her as uneducated or inarticulate. In these cases, reporters should call the source once the preliminary draft of the story is completed and read what the altered version of the quote says.

Sometimes altering a quote is done in the interest of conciseness, such as those cases in which a source may provide a valid answer to a question but takes too long to get to the point. Should the journalist condense what the individual said? In the interest of clarity, what if a scientist interviewed for a story can only speak in technical jargon? Should the journalist paraphrase what the scientist said so that the readers will understand it? Those questions can only be answered in consultation with an editor.

Profanity and slang are also problematic for many newspapers. Profanity has long been prohibited by the publishers of most daily newspapers. In some cases, however, editors may allow journalists to use slang terms or profanity in stories if they decide that only a verbatim quotation can properly illustrate a person's character or attitude. In those cases, the newspaper may put a warning at the top of the story that it "includes language that some readers may find offensive."

When the *Los Angeles Times* published a story in which it quoted police officers making offensive comments about women, editors instructed reporters to use paraphrasing instead of verbatim quotes, describing the term they deleted as a "four-letter term used to refer to a woman's vagina." The reporters later complained that the original language should have been used because it better illustrated the officers' demeaning attitudes toward women.

In the 1970s, a case involving *The New York Times* and President Jimmy Carter illustrated how some newspapers might be over-sensitive to the profanity issue. Editors decided that a quotation in which Carter used the term "screw" might be too offensive for their readership, so they paraphrased Carter's comments to indicate that he used "a vulgarism for sexual relations." Once the story was published, they realized that some readers might assume Carter used the word "fuck," so they ran a clarification the next day indicating Carter had used "a common but mild vulgarism for sexual relations." Media critic David Shaw pointed out the absurdity of the incident by writing that the *Times* had "used eight words to clear up the confusion caused by having used five words to replace one word."[21]

When Vice President Dick Cheney told Senator Patrick Leahy to "go fuck yourself" during a 2006 session of the U.S. Senate, the expletive was heard live on C-Span but was deleted or paraphrased in the next day's newspapers. The only exception was *The Washington Post*, which has a policy of not using profanity but bent the rule in this case because to delete it would result in "losing the power and the news value of the exchange," according to Liz Spayd, assistant national editor.[22]

While few mainstream daily newspapers allow profanity in quotes, that's not the case with weeklies and monthlies, especially those calling themselves "alternative" publications. During the 2004 presidential election campaign, for example, daily newspapers cleaned up Democratic candidate John Kerry's quote regarding his opponent, incumbent George W. Bush. Those papers reported that Kerry said that he "never expected Bush to mess up [some papers wrote "screw up"] the Iraq War so much." *But Rolling Stone* used the original quote, in which Kerry used the term "fuck up."[23]

Even attempts to avoid less controversial terms have produced awkward newsroom debates. In an interview with a colorful southern business owner, a reporter at a daily newspaper quoted him about how he viewed his competition. "If we're going to run with the big dogs, we have to know how to piss in the tall grass," the man said. The reporter checked the newspaper's style manual and found that "piss" was listed as a substandard term for "urinate." After convincing his editor that "urinate in the tall grass" did not have the same impact, the quote was allowed to run in its original form.

"Cleaning up" poor grammar is yet another issue. What if the source uses incorrect grammar? Should the journalist change "the company is proud of their employees" to "the company is proud of its employees" in order to be grammatically correct? What about changing "between the three labor unions" to "among the three labor unions"? Most editors would approve of reporters making such grammatical changes.

The issue of condensing quotes and cleaning up language became a court issue in 1991 when a psychiatrist sued *New Yorker* journalist Janet Malcolm. The man claimed that in her book on psychoanalyst Sigmund Freud, Malcolm condensed lengthy comments into shorter quotations and attempted to translate psychiatric terminology into laymen's language, and in the process changed the context of what he said. The case eventually reached the U.S. Supreme Court, where the majority of justices decided that "the practical demands of reporting gave journalists 'breathing room' in their use of quotations" and that reporters often had to "make intelligible a speaker's perhaps rambling comments." One dissenting justice commented that the decision would allow journalists to "lie a little, but not too much."[24]

Deception, Misrepresentation, and Hidden Recording Devices

Many journalism historians trace the "undercover" reporting technique can be traced back to the work of Nellie Bly, a nineteenth-century journalist whose real name was Elizabeth Jane Cochrane. Working for the *New York World* in 1887, she adopted the persona of a mentally disturbed woman and was checked into a mental hospital in New York, where she stayed for ten days. In her published article, "Ten Days in a Mad House," she described the unsanitary conditions and patient neglect she observed, as well as the physical, psychological, and sexual abuse she experienced or witnessed. Her article was later incorporated into a book, *The Complete Works of Nellie Bly*. Today, leaders in the mental health business say that her work laid the groundwork for decades of reforms, and her legacy is celebrated in her hometown of Cochran's Mills, Pennsylvania.

When the press was barred from the New York City pier where the Titanic survivors landed in 1912, many reporters got through the barricades by dressing as doctors or priests.[25]

In 1965, a reporter for the *Cleveland Plain Dealer* attempted to replicate Bly's work, but this time as an attendant, rather than a patient, at a state mental hospital. He did so for seven weeks. He applied for the job using his real social security number and his middle name as his first name, but his work history was falsified. After his stories were published, the governor of Ohio ordered a series of reforms that improved conditions at that facility as well as others in the state.

Later in the twentieth century, reporter Ben Bagdikian published a series of articles in *The Washington Post* that described problems within a state prison in Pennsylvania. In cooperation with the state attorney general's office, Bagdikian researched the article by posing as an inmate. After the series was published and the ruse admitted, the response to Bagdikian's tactics was mixed. Many observers of the journalism profession praised his initiative and courage in taking on such a risky assignment, while others, including *Washington Post* editor Ben Bradlee, were not comfortable with the tactic. Even though he had originally approved Bagdikian's approach, Bradlee later admitted to having second thoughts, contending that if journalists were to do an effective job of exposing government officials who lied and tricked other people, they must not lie and trick people in their own work. "In a day when we are spending thousands of man-hours uncovering deception, we simply cannot deceive," Bradlee said.[26]

In 1977, the *Milwaukee Journal* sent five reporters to the offices of local doctors as part of an investigation of Medicare fraud. The "patients" faked symptoms but had no actual maladies. Nonetheless, many of the doctors prescribed unnecessary medications, performed unnecessary tests, and billed (sometimes over-billed) the costs to Medicare. When exposed by the published story, one doctor fled the country and four others were sanctioned by the State Medical Board.[27]

Veteran *Chicago Tribune* journalist Mike Royko admitted having used dozens of false identities during his lengthy career. Royko claimed that a fake police badge gave him access to crime scenes that his media credentials would not have, and that his ability to disguise his voice in phone conversations allowed him to impersonate a county coroner, a female high school principal, and other officials.

A famous case of misrepresentation and hidden cameras began in 1992 when reporters for ABC's *Prime Time Live* posed as employees and used hidden cameras to document unsanitary conditions in Food Lion grocery stores. Food Lion sued ABC for trespassing and fraud and won a financial settlement, and while the findings in favor of the company remained intact, an appeals court later negated the financial award. The partial reversal was considered a short-term victory for the media, but a long-term setback because it was seen as reflecting an anti-media bias on the part of the court system and the public.

In 2004, a reporter for the *Corpus Christi Caller-Times* got a front-row seat for a police sting operation targeting the customers of local prostitutes—by agreeing to join the local police department's team of undercover officers posing as prostitutes. Venessa Santos-Garza's work resulted in the arrest of four customers, but she ended up in more trouble than the men who were arrested. Santos-Garza did not have permission of her editor prior to entering the agreement, even though she told the police chief she did. Not only was she reprimanded by her employer, but her case became the subject of discussion in national journalism publications. The story she wrote was killed by editor Libby Averyt, who told *Editor & Publisher* that "it was not the kind of journalism I want to practice here."[28] Averyt then called a staff meeting to reminder reporters that their job is to cover the news, not create it. A local defense attorney agreed, telling *Editor & Publisher* that "police would arrest anyone else posing as a prostitute ... she wasn't reporting on a crime, she was creating one."[29]

In early 2011, online journalist Ian Murphy was investigating the political supporters of Wisconsin Governor Scott Walker and misrepresented himself as a wealthy political contributor in a phone call to the governor. The reporter said he was hoping to point out how the governor seemed unsympathetic to the plight of the state's public employees in their attempt to save their union from decertification. In addition, he wanted to document the governor's tendency to return phone calls to Republican lawmakers and political allies while refusing to return phone calls from Democratic legislators or journalists. Knowing the name and some basic facts about one of Walker's big donors, Murphy engaged the governor in a recorded phone call and lured him into a conversation in which he joked about "hitting Democrats over their heads with baseball bats" and admitted that he considered planting "troublemakers" among the union members in order to disrupt their protests.

When transcripts of the conversation appeared on Murphy's website, media ethicists were stunned. "The tactic and deception used to gain this information violates the highest levels of journalism ethics," said Kevin Smith, chairman of the Society of Professional Journalist's Ethics Committee. "To lie to a source about your identity and then to bait that source into making comments that are inflammatory is inexcusable and has no place in journalism."[30] One journalist defended Murphy's tactics by claiming that "a journalist not only has the right to misrepresent himself, but sometimes, as Murphy demonstrated, it is a journalist's only option."[31]

Today, nearly every media organization has one or more policies dealing with deception, misrepresentation, and hidden recording devices such as cameras and microphones. Common examples of misrepresentation include a print or broadcast journalist pretending to be a job applicant in order to expose a business's alleged discriminatory employment practices or pretending to be a potential apartment renter in order to expose a landlord's exclusion of minority tenants.

In most cases, such policies (which also apply to cases of hidden cameras and microphones) include a three-part test:

1. The news story being pursued must be a substantial one for which the reporter has determined the need for further investigation (the search for the so-called "smoking gun"). The policy does not allow for "fishing expeditions."
2. The journalist must have exhausted all other possible reporting methods to obtain the desired information before resorting to hidden cameras and/or misrepresentation.
3. The journalist must have approval in advance from either an editor (in the case of a newspaper or magazine) or news director (in the case of television or radio).

In cases in which the main issue is deception or misrepresentation, some media outlets have codes of ethics that include one or both of two other conditions.

The first additional condition is that the deception must not place the reporter or innocent people in danger. A journalist posing as a law-enforcement officer, firefighter, or paramedic would fail that part of the test because his or her lack of training would likely present a danger for co-workers as well as civilians depending on emergency services.

The second additional condition is that before a story based on such deception is published or broadcast, the reporter must contact the subject of the story, admit to the deception, and offer him or her opportunity to tell his or her side of the story.

Closely related to the issue of hidden cameras is the matter of recording telephone conversations with news sources without their knowledge. The main value of an audiotape or videotape is that it can be used later to contradict the claims of an individual that he or she was misquoted.

In addition to applying the ethical policy explained above, journalists should also be aware of state laws regarding telephone privacy. Some state laws allow telephone conversations to be recorded as long as one party is aware of it, but some state laws require that both parties (or all parties) consent to the recording.

One of the concerns involved in misrepresentation is the potential for entrapment, which is actually a legal term that means that law-enforcement personnel may not take any steps to induce a person to commit a crime; they must wait for the suspect to initiate the illegal behavior.

While most media organizations address such issues in their codes of ethics, National Public Radio may do so with the most specificity and the most prohibitive terms. "Journalism should be conducted in the open," the code specifies. "NPR journalists do not misrepresent themselves. NPR journalists disclose who they are and don't pose as cops, investigators, or other such officials. NPR journalists do not use hidden microphones, recorders, or cameras except where information that serves an important journalistic purpose, such as in reporting on illegal, antisocial, or fraudulent activities, and cannot be obtained by more open means." The code adds that approval for any undercover reporting techniques must be approved in advance by a supervisor as well as NPR's general counsel.[32]

The code does provide one clarification on the rule prohibiting misrepresentation. It allows journalists the option of not identifying themselves when gathering information, but only when observing situations or events in places where any member of the general public has access, such as stores and public buildings.[33]

Britt Hume, a reporter with ABC News and later Fox News, said that "any type of deception carried out by reporters will be seen by the audience as 'dirty pool' and will lead many viewers to feel sympathy with the victims of deception and the journalists as villains."[34]

Much like Sissela Bok's principle of not resorting to deception when there are non-deceptive means of uncovering the same information, media ethicist Louis W. Hodges believes that "deception is never justifiable when the story can be had through honorable means, no matter how much money and time the honorable means take."[35]

In at least two known cases, the board of directors that eventually approves all Pulitzer Prizes has overruled the organization's nominating committee because of the nominee's newsgathering tactics. The first occasion was in 1974, when the *Chicago Sun-Times* ran a sting operation that involved a phony bar it called The Mirage. For four months, reporters pretending to be the bar's owners met with city inspectors, who overtly solicited bribes in exchange for overlooking building code violations and speeding up the permitting process. As a result, dozens of city employees were fired and/or arrested, and the newspaper's multi-part series was nominated for a Pulitzer Prize, but the board overruled the committee.[36]

In the second case, a *Los Angeles Herald Examiner* reporter impersonated an undocumented immigrant and obtained a factory job in order to observe first-hand alleged unsafe working conditions. Linda Wollin's 1981 series was also nominated for a Pulitzer Prize, but the nomination was overruled by the board.[37]

Closely related to the issue of hidden recording devices is the unauthorized acquisition of recordings. One famous example took place in 1998, when the *Cincinnati Enquirer* published a package of ten stories accusing Chiquita, one of the community's largest employers, of a variety of white-collar and environmental crimes. During the year-long investigation, an *Enquirer* reporter obtained from a former Chiquita employee usernames and passwords that allowed him to break into the company's internal voicemail system and make copies of more than 3,000 messages. That material made up the bulk of the documentation used to construct the story, but after the company proved that much of the information was taken out of context, Chiquita sued the newspaper's parent company, Gannett. As a result, Gannett settled out of court with Chiquita for $10 million, published a retraction and apology, and fired the reporter who obtained the messages.[38]

Checkbook Journalism

"Checkbook journalism" refers to the act of paying news sources for interviews or other forms of access. One of the earlier known cases occurred in 1909, when *The New York Times* footed the bill for Robert Perry's expedition to the North Pole in exchange for the exclusive rights to his story. Two decades later, the *Times* paid aviator Charles Lindbergh $5,000 for the rights to the story of his historic New York-to-Paris flight.[39]

In the 1920s, the legendary police beat reporter Hildy Johnson once paid a convicted murderer awaiting execution $200 for the exclusive rights to his life story, then reportedly won the money back from him in a poker game.[40] In the 1970s, CBS News reportedly paid Watergate conspirators H.R. Haldeman and G. Gordon Liddy $100,000 and $15,000, respectively, for the rights to their stories.[41] Later the network paid $10,000 to a man who promised to escort a *60 Minutes* crew to a secret location where they would find the body of missing labor leader Jimmy Hoffa, but the man absconded with the money and was never found.[42]

Today, most media outlets and professional organizations have strict policies prohibiting the payment of sources for interviews or appearances on radio or television news programs. One media ethicist claims that journalism should be based on "the voluntary sharing of information, not their willingness to be the highest bidder."[43]

Tabloid publications have looser policies, however. As a result, individuals are often able to sell their stories. Examples included the neighbor of White House intern Monica Lewinsky, witnesses testifying in the trial of Tonya Harding on charges that she conspired to injure rival skater Nancy Kerrigan, friends of the two high school students accused of carrying out the 1999 massacre at Columbine High School, and jurors in the trial of Los Angeles police officers accused of beating motorist Rodney King.

While media in other countries have similarly loose policies, in extreme cases public criticism can be severe. In 2002, for example, the *News of the World*, a British-based tabloid owned by media mogul Rupert Murdoch, wanted an advantage over its competitors as it followed the investigation into a missing thirteen-year-old girl. In addition to hacking into the girl's voicemail, its employees were caught paying police sources for non-public information. When those ethical transgressions were exposed (along with many others) in 2011, the damage to the reputation of the 168-year-old publication was so severe that Murdoch shut it down.[44]

On September 11, New York businessman Edward Fine survived the collapse of the World Trade Center during the terrorist attacks that day and by the next morning had become an international celebrity, having his photograph—showing him walking away covering his mouth and with his suit covered in ashes—displayed in newspapers around the world. As the first-year anniversary of the tragedy approached the following summer, Fine sought to capitalize on his fame, announcing that he would do media interviews for $500 per hour or $911 for two hours. Few American journalists agreed to pay him, but some international media outlets did, claiming that such practice was common in their home countries. The *New York Post* wrote a story about his enterprise, quoting him as justifying the charges because "giving interviews takes time away from [his] business."[45]

The *Post* emphasized in its story that it did not pay the man for the interview about his policy of charging for interviews.

One of most unusual yet clear-cut case of checkbook journalism involved *New York Times* reporter Kurt Eichenwald. After more than a decade of uncovering corporate scandals as one of the *Times'* chief business reporters, Eichenwald attempted to take on the grim topic of child pornography and sexual abuse affecting teenagers and young adults.

While researching a series of stories that ran in the newspaper in 2005, Eichenwald interviewed Justin Berry, a young adult and amateur musician who claimed that as a child, he frequently sold pornographic images of himself and other children and had briefly worked as a male escort. Eichenwald's first ethical misstep was to contact Berry through social media and introduce himself as a songwriter wishing to collaborate with him. Once Berry began to confide in him, Eichenwald paid him $2,000 in cash to tell his story, and the arrangement was eventually exposed.

Both the misrepresentation and cash payment violated *Times'* ethical standards, but after Berry's family repaid most of the money, Eichenwald received only a written reprimand and moved onto a new job at the newsmagazine, *Portfolio*. Editors at the *Times* later learned that after the initial payment of $2,000, Eichenwald paid Berry an additional $1,100. That revelation led to his resignation at *Portfolio*. Eichenwald never accepted full responsibility for either the misrepresentation or the payments, instead claiming that the medication he took for depression and epilepsy caused him to make "poor judgments."[46]

In 2010, basketball superstar Lebron James decided to leave the Cleveland Cavaliers and entertain offers from other teams. Rather than simply cover the process as a news story, ESPN decided to become a player in the artificially created melodrama. In exchange for exclusivity as James revealed the identity of his new team, ESPN would turn the announcement into an hour-long live program. The Bristol, Connecticut-based network covered all the production costs, allowed James to choose his own announcer, and promised James all of the advertising revenue. Media ethicists had issues with all aspects of the arrangement but found the revenue promise especially problematic. James' pledge to donate all of the money to charity did little to alleviate the criticism. "The most troubling aspect of the whole ill-conceived mess was ESPN's willingness to hand over an hour of prime-time television to an egomaniacal athlete the network should be covering as a news story," wrote Leonard Shapiro of *The Washington Post*. "Does this not-so-subtle form of checkbook journalism pass the smell test anywhere but in Bristol, Connecticut?"[47]

Recently, some media outlets have circumvented ethical policies by paying interview sources "consulting fees" for access to otherwise unavailable documentation, compensating them for travel and hotel costs at a rate several times higher than the expenses actually incurred, or paying sources for photos or video, with the understanding that the sellers will also consent to interviews. Other journalism ethicists advocate policies that prohibit paying sources directly, but are flexible on the idea of paying for photographs or video (as long as it is not done to circumvent the rules, as described above). "Some of the greatest photographs in history were taken by passersby or participants," says Tom Goldstein, former dean of Columbia University's Graduate School of Journalism. "It makes me uneasy that somebody is profiting from the misfortune of others, but that's what a lot of journalism is about."[48]

ABC News denied rumors that it had paid for an interview with the butler of Princess Diana following her 1997 death, but later admitted that it paid him $300,000 for his "video diary."

In 2008, ABC News was criticized when it was revealed it had paid Florida mother Casey Anthony for pictures of her daughter, Caley, who she was accused (and later acquitted) of having murdered. In 2011, the same network offered to pay a mother accused of injecting her eight-year-old daughter with Botox for sharing her story on *Good Morning America*, but after the story aired, the woman admitted it was a hoax and doctors examining the girl confirmed that she had not been injected.[49]

In 2009, NBC's *Today Show* was found to have chartered a private jet to bring American David Goldman and his son home from Brazil. The New Jersey man had just won a lengthy custody battle with his son's stepfather, a Brazilian citizen who had married Goldman's ex-wife. The network was criticized by the Society of Professional Journalists and other industry groups, not only for paying for the jet (in exchange for a promise from Goldman that he would share his story only with the *Today Show*), but the fact that the arrangement was not disclosed to viewers. "By making itself part of the breaking news story on which it was reporting—apparently to cash in on the exclusivity assured by its expensive gesture—NBC jeopardized its journalistic independence and credibility in its initial and subsequent reports," a SPJ statement read. "NBC's ability to report the story fairly has been compromised by its financial involvement."[50]

Freebies and Junkets

The codes of ethics of professional organizations, as well as the policy manuals of individual newspapers, include provisions that prohibit employees from accepting from news sources "freebies" such as gifts and meals or travel opportunities often referred to as "media junkets."

Most such policies have been in place for only a few decades. In prior years, reporters often received meals and small gifts from the individuals, companies, and government agencies on which they reported. While few media critics equated that phenomenon with the overt bribing of journalists that still takes place in other countries, media organizations today claim that journalists must be "above suspicion" and are expected to politely decline such offers.

In determining what constitutes a "gift," many policies use terms such as "more than nominal value," meaning that souvenir items such as pens, T-shirts, or coffee mugs would be allowed, while watches, briefcases, or desk accessories would not be.

Even though there may not be any agreement to alter the content of a news story in exchange for the gift (the Latin term is *quid pro quo*), what media organizations seek to avoid is the *appearance* of any impropriety. The executive editor of one North Carolina newspaper has a simple rule about his reporters accepting such gifts. "It is easy to sell your integrity, but impossible to buy it back," he says.[51] The business editor of the same newspaper recalls a previous publisher's rule that accepting food from a news source was permissible provided the quantity was small enough to be consumed in one day. That policy presented a dilemma for the newspaper staff when one news source provided a quart of whiskey.

Prior to the 1970s, journalists frequently accepted gifts and free meals from sources, prompting one professional baseball team manager to claim that "you can buy a sportswriter with a good steak."[52]

Allan Wolper, author of an ethics column in *Editor & Publisher*, writes that it is inappropriate for travel writers and their editors to employ a "don't ask, don't tell" policy when it comes to allowing resorts and other travel-related entities to provide free hotel rooms, food, and other amenities to journalists who then lavish praise on them. Wolper also points out the hypocrisy involved when a newspaper's political writers criticize public officials for going on "junkets" paid for by lobbyists while the same paper's travel writers are committing similar ethical offenses.[53] In a subsequent column, Wolper chastised student journalists from more than a dozen major journalism schools for attending an all-expenses-paid junket in Detroit, hosted by General Motors, despite having learned in the journalism classes (hopefully) that such behavior raised serious ethical questions.[54]

One example of a strict gift and freebie policy is that of the New York Times Company; the policy applies not only to the flagship paper but also all of the local newspapers the company owns. The policy acknowledges that, while courtesies such as gifts and meals have an important place in American business, the role of the journalist requires a higher standard. "Gifts accepted from or given to anyone with whom the company does business should be promotional in nature and nominal in value," the policy states. "A business courtesy should not be accepted if it does not fall within the guidelines described above or if the donor expects something in return, may be attempting to gain an unfair advantage, may be attempting to influence the employee's judgment, or if acceptance creates the appearance of any of the foregoing. Employees should also avoid a pattern of accepting frequent gifts or business courtesies from the same persons or companies."[55] To define the terms "promotional" and "nominal," the policy states that "a ballpoint pen with a company logo would satisfy the test of being promotional in nature and of nominal value. An inscribed gold wristwatch may be promotional in nature but would unlikely be nominal in value and, therefore, would not be acceptable." In defending the policy, *Times* officials attempt to differentiate its journalistic products from other publications with lesser standards. Accepting freebies, the policy states, "debases the profession and creates the impression that the entire press is on the take."[56]

Mitchell Stephens, in his broadcast news textbook, adds that journalists should be especially wary of accepting even the most modest gift, writing, "Reporters shouldn't accept any gifts from the people they may have to write about—no bottles of Scotch, vacations, fountain pens, or dinners. Reporters don't even want to be in a position of having to distinguish between a gift and a bribe. Return them all with a polite thank-you."[57]

Many ethical codes allow some acceptance of free travel and meals, using terms such as "reasonable" and "legitimate news interest." Among examples of acceptable items would be samples of consumer products which the journalist or freelancer has a firm assignment to write about or free admission to a concert or play for which a critic intends to write a review.

Resorts and theme parks are often criticized by competitors, journalism critics, and media watchdog groups for paying for airline tickets and hotel accommodations for travel writers in an attempt to secure favorable stories. The marketing departments at Disneyland in California and Walt Disney World in Florida, for example, are frequent targets for such criticism because the lavish nature of their media gatherings.

Editors of travel magazines and newspaper travel sections who make such policy decisions are evenly divided on the issue. Those who follow more traditional journalistic values believe that if an event or location is important enough to cover, it is important enough for the publication to pay its own reporters' expenses. Other editors, especially those working for small magazines or newspapers with meager travel budgets, simply contend they could not publish a quality travel magazine or newspaper travel section without allowing reporters to accept free travel.

Prominent travel magazines such as *Conde Naste Traveler* and *Travel & Leisure* employ full-time staff writers and experienced freelancers who are not allowed to accept subsidies in any form. Other travel publications may allow their staff writers to accept free travel and purchase stories from freelancers without asking how much of their travel was subsidized. In between the two extremes are those publications that allow staff writers and freelancers to accept free transportation and accommodations, but only under certain conditions, such as accepting only those arrangements that are available to all media representatives attending the same event, and agreements that no promises as to the content or tone of resulting stories are expected or implied.

The Associated Press provides specific guidelines for newspaper sportswriters who travel to cover college and professional sports teams. Those rules include a requirement that newspapers pay all expenses up front for writers' transportation, accommodations, and food; or if that is not practical, that the newspaper reimburse the home team for such expenses after the fact.

While most American media organizations have strict policies about such issues, international media (as well as businesses in other countries) do not, which causes problems and misunderstandings for American journalists working overseas, as well as for international journalists working in the U.S. When a Moscow cellphone company opened a new retail store, for example, it invited Russian journalists as well as visiting journalists from the U.S., and all were offered the company's most expensive product, a model costing the equivalent of $500 in American money. Beth Knobel, a reporter for CBS News, claimed that her staffers were the only ones attending the event that did not accept the phones. "We probably could have gotten away with it," Knobel explained in a journalism book she co-authored with CBS veteran Mike Wallace. "But it didn't seem worth it to risk our careers over a $500 phone."[58]

Some journalists have compounded their ethical lapses by using online auction sites such as eBay to sell promotional items such as advance copies of books or DVDs of upcoming movies.

Withholding the News

Throughout the history of journalism, print and broadcast journalists have struggled with decisions concerning the publication of controversial information. In many cases, newspaper and magazine publishers, television news directors, and network executives must weigh competing interests such as news value and public interest (in favor of reporting the story) with factors such as national security and the safety of individuals (in favor of not reporting).

One of the first such cases occurred in 1961, when reporters at *The New York Times* learned in advance that American forces were planning the Bay of Pigs invasion in an attempt to liberate Cuba from the dictatorship of Fidel Castro. When President John F. Kennedy and Pentagon officials learned of the newspaper's plans to publish the information, they persuaded the newspaper not to jeopardize the operation by publicizing it in advance.

Other cases are legal in nature rather than ethical. In a famous 1971 case, *The New York Times* obtained a copy of "The Pentagon Papers," a confidential report, commissioned by the Department of Defense, about the history of the Vietnam War. Concerned that release of the report would undermine public support for the war (which was already low), the federal government attempted to block the publication, but the Supreme Court would not allow it to do so. In 1979, the government was unsuccessful in preventing a national political magazine from publishing an article describing how to assemble an atomic bomb.

A more recent case of the media struggling with the report-or-not-report question occurred when Ted Kaczynski, a domestic terrorist nicknamed the Unabomber, submitted a "manifesto" for publication in two national newspapers. Kaczynski was a former mathematics professor who had become a recluse, living in a remote cabin in Montana. For nearly two decades, he mailed package bombs to university professors and airlines, killing three people and injuring more than twenty others. In his 1995 letter to *The New York Times*, he promised to stop the bombing if either the *Times* or *The Washington Post* published his "manifesto"—a rambling, 35,000-word essay about the evils of technology.

The publishers of the two newspapers considered the idea for several days, debating between the news value of publishing the document and the danger of giving Kaczynski publicity and encouraging copycats. Assisting the law-enforcement investigation may not have been a factor, but after both papers published the material, Kaczynski's brother and sister-in-law recognized the writing style and tipped off federal investigators as to the location of Kaczynski's hideout, which led to a successful apprehension.

Although the Kaczynski story had a positive ending, not everyone in the journalism business agreed that the ends justified the means. Rem Rieder, editor of *American Journalism Review*, wrote that agreeing to the Unabomber's terms was "analogous to negotiating with those who take hostages ... Law enforcement experts have long advised against doing so, because it only encourages the taking of yet more hostages. It says that if you desperate enough and irresponsible enough and violent enough, we will turn our news columns over to you."[59]

Following the 2018 killing of seventeen students at Marjory Stoneman Douglas High School in Parkland, Florida and the 2019 killing of thirteen people at a government building in Virginia Beach, Virginia, many media outlets decided to put more emphasis on the victims than on the life stories of the shooters. Anderson Cooper of Cable News Network (CNN) and Lawrence O'Donnell of MSNBC led the way, mentioning the names of the shooters only sparingly, referring to them in most cases as simply "the suspect." More than 140 criminologists signed an open letter to the media urging them to go a step further and impose a "news blackout" on the names of future shooters.

Even before the 2018 and 2019 shootings, police and youth counselors police worried that stories that appeared to make shooters into mythical figures might result in copycat shootings. That fear was proven viable in 2007, when the killer of thirty-two students and professors at Virginia Polytechnic University cited in his suicide manifesto his admiration for two high school students responsible for the Columbine massacre eight years earlier.[60]

On a related note, one of the newest issues in the area of "to report or not report" is the decisions made by local media—especially broadcasters—concerning alleged threats of violence against schools. In the aftermath of the Parkland tragedy, television stations across the country heard dozens of reports of students posting threats on social media to "shoot up" their schools. School officials and law-enforcement agencies were obligated to investigate them, but that didn't mean that local media were obligated to report them. Aware that media coverage would likely encourage more threats, many media outlets decided not to report them until someone was charged.

"As journalists, our goal is to minimize harm," stated a news story posted on the website of a North Carolina television station. "While we won't know all the reasons for some of the threats, we're sure some of it is to seek attention. So, we want to avoid giving that attention unless absolutely necessary. When we learn of a credible threat, we will pass that information along in the name of concern and safety, but we won't give publicity, in terms of news coverage, to those whose sole purpose is only to create chaos in our community."[61]

Staging Photographs and Video

Few newspaper editors or television news directors would approve the staging of photographs and video, but in some cases such material is published or broadcast without their knowledge because of decisions made by reporters.

During the Vietnam War, a CBS News cameraman persuaded an American soldier to cut off the ear of a dead North Vietnamese soldier. The gruesome footage aired on CBS Evening News on October 11, 1967.[62]

Other examples include a 1991 case in which television reporters staged a dog fight while producing a story about animal cruelty and a 1993 case involving television reporter pretending to buy alcohol for teenagers while producing a story about underage drinking. In both cases, the offending reporters were fired and also faced legal charges. A less serious case, which resulted in only a reprimand, was a 2002 incident in which a newspaper photographer asked a public health nurse to pretend to give a child a vaccination because no "real" patients were available.

Perhaps the best-known case of staged new occurred in 1992, when NBC's *Dateline* program aired a story about certain models of General Motors trucks that caught fire as a result of a design flaw that left gas tanks unprotected in cases of side-impact crashes. The report included several cases of children who died in those crashes.

In order to demonstrate the danger, *Dateline* staged a crash in which a GM truck was struck on its side by a car, and as expected, it burst into flames. What the report left out, however, was that officials of the independent testing agency were afraid that the truck might not explode as expected, and because it would be too expensive to try the demonstration a second time, they rigged the truck with remote-controlled ignition devices. Whether the explosion was caused by the design of the gas tank (without the artificial assist) or by the supplementary ignition devices was never determined. But after the incident became public knowledge, the network retracted the story and reprimanded several news producers who approved the deception.

The Radio Television Digital News Association Code of Ethics states that "staging, dramatization, and other alterations—even when labeled as such—can confuse or fool viewers, listeners, and readers. These tactics are justified only when stories of great significance cannot be adequately told without distortion, and when any creative liberties taken are clearly explained."

Digital Alteration of Photographs

One of the more controversial issues in newspaper and magazine journalism today is the availability of computer programs that allow users to manipulate the content of digital photographs. Even though such programs have made such deception easier, the general idea is not new. As far back as 1862, President Abraham Lincoln arranged for one of his official presidential photographs to show his head on the body of another politician with a better physique. Throughout the 1900s, dictators such as Josef Stalin, Mao Tse-Tung, Adolf Hitler, Benito Mussolini, and Fidel Castro routinely employed technicians to air-brush out of photographs the images of other politicians who had fallen out of their favor.

When computer programs replaced air-brushing as the dominant methodology in the 1980s, deception required expensive technology and highly skilled technicians. The most common example was the use of the technology to remove dimples, freckles, or other minor imperfections in photographs of fashion models before those images appeared in magazines or on billboards. For the most part, such deception raised few ethical concerns.

The nature of the issue changed again in the late 1990s, when the Adobe Corporation introduced Photoshop, an inexpensive program that anyone with average computer skills could use. Since that product's introduction, the technology has been applied to a variety of purposes, some controversial and some not. The use of Photoshop software has become so popular that the brand name is often used as a verb to refer to the alteration of any photograph by electronic means, such as when someone suggests that a certain person or object could be "photoshopped" out of an image.

The National Press Photographers Association Code of Ethics includes a paragraph strongly discouraging the use of digitally altered photographs, and the code of ethics of the American Society of Media Photographers (ASMP) states that it is never appropriate for a photographer, journalist, or editor to "alter the content or meaning of a news photograph" or condone such manipulation by other parties. The codes do not, however, prohibit the alteration of photographs for the purpose of color balancing, contrast adjustment, and cropping or enlarging elements of a photograph, provided that such alteration does not change or distort the context of the photo. The guidelines also allow for the masking or blurring of photographs or video to conceal the identity of individuals such as military intelligence officers or law-enforcement personnel working undercover.

The code specifically prohibits the manipulation of photographs in order to change spatial relationships (moving persons or objects closer together or further apart), adding or removing elements not in the original photograph, or merging two or more photographs to create a composite.

Despite the admonitions of ASMP, photomanipulation is common today, although few publications admit having done it until the alterations are detected. The most common rationales used to defend instances of photomanipulation are (1) improving photographic content, (2) dramatic effect, and (3) intentional deception.

Improving Photographic Content

Examples of non-controversial uses include the case of *National Geographic*, which altered a photograph of Egyptian pyramids in order to move the structures closer together and produce a more balanced photograph for the magazine's cover. Another magazine once altered a photo that originally showed a woman standing on a fishing pier with a pelican perched about ten feet away. The altered photograph simply moved the two subjects in the photograph to be about five feet apart. The magazine defended the alteration by claiming it was simply avoiding "wasting space" in between. In another case, a daily newspaper electronically removed a soda can from a person's desk in a news photograph because it distracted from the content of the image and the editors wanted to avoid giving the company free publicity.

"We might extend the sky [in a photograph], but we would never add stars," said a staffer for *Newsweek* magazine.[63]

Dramatic Effect

In 1994, Olympic skaters Tonya Harding and Nancy Kerrigan were shown appearing to skate together on the cover of *Newsday*. A few weeks earlier, friends of Harding had allegedly arranged for Kerrigan to be injured prior to the Olympic trials, so the editorial staff believed the composite photograph (which was identified as such in small print) would be more dramatic than showing them skating separately.

In the same week in 1994, the covers of both *Time* and *Newsweek* featured a photograph of accused murderer O.J. Simpson that had been provided by the Los Angeles Police Department. But there was a striking difference between the two magazine covers. *Time* had used its technology to darken Simpson's skin and add facial stubble, while the *Newsweek* cover showed a more natural-looking Simpson. While looking at the covers separately, many readers would not have noticed a difference, but when looking at the magazine covers side-by-side, the difference was obvious. *Time* editors admitted the idea was to make Simpson look "more sinister" and pointed to its labeling of the cover art as a "photo illustration" rather than a "photograph." But few critics accepted that explanation, and many civil rights groups complained that the deception was based on racial stereotypes of black men as dark-skinned and angry.

In March 2007, the image of former President Ronald Reagan appeared on the cover of *Time*, accompanied by the headline, "How the Right Went Wrong." The image was doctored to include a tear on the face of Reagan, who had died three years earlier. The magazine defended the image by calling it a "conceptual cover."

Intentional Deception

For its 2001–02 student recruiting booklet, the University of Wisconsin wanted a cover photograph showing a diverse student body. Unable to find a suitable photograph in their archives, university officials instructed the publication staff to insert the face of a male African American student into the crowd scene at a football game. Ironically, the African American man had served on a committee to promote campus diversity and said he had never attended a football game in his four years at UW. After the deception was detected by the student newspaper, the university recalled the booklets and had them reprinted with an authentic photograph showing a diverse group of students in the student union.

In some cases, the deception is done simply to show subjects in a more flattering light. One example took place in 1989, when the cover of *TV Guide* showed the head of talk-show host Oprah Winfrey on the body of a much slimmer Ann-Margret, without permission of either woman. The deception was detected when Margret's fashion designer recognized the dress in the photograph. In 1997, the photograph of an Iowa mother who made news by delivering quintuplets was doctored to make her teeth look straighter and whiter. Ironically, the photo had been altered for the cover of *Newsweek*, the same publication that publicly admonished its competitor, *Time*, over the Simpson incident.

In 2002, a newspaper in Los Angeles doctored the photo of a man involved in a freeway car crash to avoid showing that he had wet the front of his pants as a result of the head trauma he suffered in the accident. That same year, a daily newspaper altered a photograph taken at a local zoo, fearing that some readers might have been offended by the sight of a male lion's genitals. In 2006, as CBS News prepared to introduce Katie Couric in her new role as anchor of the evening news, a publicity photograph was altered to give her a trimmer waistline and thinner face.

Your Turn

Case Study 5A: Dealing with Suicide: The Melinda Duckett Story

In September 2006, television talk-show host Nancy Grace was accused of contributing to the suicide of an unstable young mother whose two-year-old son was missing. When twenty-one-year-old Melinda Duckett agreed to be interviewed by telephone, she knew nothing about Grace's aggressive and confrontational style. Grace asked questions in an accusatory manner that did not suggest Duckett was guilty in the disappearance, only that she was not as forthcoming as she could have been in interviews with the media and police. By the end of the interview, Grace was pounding her desk and demanding, "Where were you? Why aren't you telling us where you were that day?"

The interview was on tape, and less than twenty-four hours later, shortly before it was scheduled to be aired on Cable News Network (CNN), Duckett drove to her grandparents' home in Leesburg, Florida, and killed herself with her father's shotgun. CNN learned about the woman's death, but decided to go forward with the broadcast, a decision that angered Duckett's friends and family as well as many in the general public. Grace defended her interviewing style and denied that it influenced Duckett to kill herself. "If anything, I would suggest that guilt made her commit suicide," Grace said in an ABC News interview. "To suggest that a fifteen- or twenty-minute interview can cause someone to commit suicide is focusing on the wrong thing."[64]

Duckett's family disputed any suggestion that the woman hurt her son. They said that the strain of her son's disappearance pushed her to the brink, and the media sent her over the edge. "Nancy Grace and the others, they just bashed her to the end," Duckett's grandfather, Bill Eubank, told the Associated Press.[65]

Some media analysts agree, saying Grace's interview simply went too far. "How is that questioning doing anything but making a person in a desperate situation feeling even more desperate?" asked Hub Brown, a professor at Syracuse University's Newhouse School of Communications.

1. When individuals in the news commit suicide, how much responsibility should be assigned to the aggressive nature of the media, and how much lies with the person, whose mental instability may not be known?
2. Are there any philosophers or concepts from Chapter 2 that could be applied here?

Case Study 5B: Deception and Misrepresentation: How Far Can You Go to "Test the System"?

On March 31, 1997, reporters at a television station in Tampa, Florida resorted to an unusual reporting method to test the vulnerability of a federal office building to a terrorist attack. Renting a Ryder truck from a local dealer, the reporters left it in front of the federal courthouse in downtown Tampa, then watched and waited inside the truck to see how long it would take for courthouse security or law-enforcement personnel to notice it.

Nothing happened while the reporters remained inside the truck, but when one exited and began walking down the sidewalk, he was questioned by building security and the truck was searched. Once the stunt was exposed, law-enforcement personnel criticized the reporters' tactics but did not file any formal charges. Their criticism was based on concerns that the incident unnecessarily distracted security personnel and law enforcement from their other duties and placed the safety of the reporters and bystanders in jeopardy, as private citizens acting on their own might have attacked the truck or its occupants.

Media ethicists were quick to point out that the journalists violated the second and third parts of the three-part test commonly used in making such decisions regarding misrepresentation and deception (the test is described earlier in this chapter). While the station might base its defense on the significance of the story (the life-and-death nature of terrorist attacks), the reporters involved had not exhausted other reporting methods and did not have the permission of an editor or news director.

Even though he claimed to have no advance knowledge of what the reporters were planning, the station's news director defended their actions and claimed that the significance of the story outweighed any ethical concerns. He analogized the incident to a hypothetical case of an individual who pulls a fire alarm (in the absence of an actual fire) to draw attention to the fact that the fire alarm did not work.

The date of the incident was not a coincidence. That morning, in a courthouse in Denver, domestic terrorist Timothy McVeigh was facing the first day of his murder trial. Two years earlier, McVeigh had loaded a Ryder rental truck with homemade explosives and destroyed the Murrah Federal Building in Oklahoma City, killing 168 people.

Five years later, as the nation approached the one-year anniversary of the September 11 terrorist attacks and subsequent creation of the Transportation Security Administration, journalists representing the New York *Daily News* and CBS News, working separately, wanted to test the effectiveness of the agency's screening techniques. *Daily News* reporters tested security at eleven airports and found it easy to sneak through prohibited items such as knives, razor blades, and pepper spray. At other airports, CBS staffers sent through lead-lined film bags through X-ray machines without prompting any additional security.

When those stories became public, government officials were livid. A TSA spokesperson reportedly accused the media of exploiting the story in order to sell papers and boost ratings while aiding terrorists by exposing security gaps. A non-governmental organization, the Air Transport Association, called for the *Daily News* reporters to be charged with violating federal laws prohibiting the circumvention of security procedures. Because there were no prohibited items in the CBS film bags, those reporters could not be charged.

Even though the *Daily News* reporters technically broke the law, their editor analogized their actions to the types of "civil disobedience" seen during the civil rights era of the 1950s and 1960s. Despite his apparent belief that "the ends justified the means," he told other media outlets that the reporters were prepared to accept the consequences.

The phenomenon of reporters "testing the system" is not without precedent. Following the bombing of a Pan American World Airways flight over Scotland in 1988, French journalists were caught attempting to take fake bombs through security screening at John F. Kennedy International Airport in New York. In a separate incident, ABC News reporters were charged with trespassing while testing the security in restricted areas at the same airport. In both cases, charges were eventually dropped.[66]

1. In the Ryder truck case, do you agree with viewpoint of law-enforcement personnel and media ethicists, who claim there was too much potential for this incident to take a wrong turn? Or do you agree with the position of the news director, who claimed that the significance of the story outweighed any ethical concerns over their newsgathering methods (i.e. the ends justified the means)?
2. To what degree, if any, is your view influenced by the date chosen for the Ryder truck stunt (the first day of the McVeigh trial)?
3. In the case of the New York *Daily News* incident, do you agree or disagree with the editor who compared the reporters' behaviors to "civil disobedience"?
4. Are there any philosophers or concepts from Chapter 2 that can be applied here?

Case Study 5C: Deception and Misrepresentation: Dateline's "To Catch a Predator"

One example of investigative tactics that critics say bordered on entrapment was NBC's popular "To Catch a Predator" series that it incorporated into its news program *Dateline*. Working with law-enforcement agencies and a nonprofit organization dealing with the issue of sexually abused children, the project involved equipping a house with hidden cameras and recording equipment. Volunteer "decoys"—many of them actresses in their twenties pretending to be teenage girls—communicated online with potential sexual predators and many times agreed to have the suspects visit them at the house for sexual encounters. After arriving at the house, suspects were videotaped as they were interviewed by host Chris Hansen and were then arrested as they attempted to leave.

Attorneys for the network and law-enforcement agencies were careful not to cross the line into entrapment, having lawyers coach the decoys on what they could and could not say and making sure the suspects initiated the contact.

Although re-runs of the program continued to air on NBC's sister network MSNBC, the original program was cancelled in 2007—partly because of declining ratings and partly because of a $100 million lawsuit filed by the family of one of the men caught in the sting.

The beginning of the end for the series happened when the crew executed a sting in which the target was Louis Conradt Jr., a district attorney thought to be an upstanding member of the community in Murphy, Texas. He was caught exchanging sexually explicit email messages with a volunteer from Perverted Justice pretending to be a thirteen-year-old boy and eventually arranged to meet the decoy in person. Conradt did not show up at the house, but local police believed they had enough evidence against him (based on the transcripts from his online chats with the decoy) to execute a search of his home.

As a team of police officers entered the home with the television crew waiting outside, the man shot and killed himself. In the aftermath of the man's death, the show was put on hold for several weeks as the network began to re-examine the entrapment issue. In media interviews, however, Hansen defended the project and said the he "sleeps well at night."[67]

Conradt's sister filed a lawsuit against NBC and the police department involved, claiming they failed to take reasonable precautions to prevent the suicide and caused her emotional distress. "I will never consider my brother's death a suicide," Patricia Conradt said in media interviews. "It was an act precipitated by the rush to grab headlines where there was no evidence that there was any emergency other than to line the pockets of an out-of-control group and a TV show pressed for ratings and a deadline."[68] The case was eventually settled out of court.

In the years since the Conradt death, *Dateline* had produced no new episodes of *To Catch a Predator*, but the series continues in syndication. Nonprofit organizations working in the area of child sexual abuse and trafficking continue to praise the work of the *Dateline* team and Perverted Justice, and Hansen has continued to speak to parents' groups about the dangers of online predators. Within the journalism business, however, the show is still heavily criticized. Robert Steele, an ethicist with the Poynter Institute for Media Studies, drew a distinction between the role of Perverted Justice being actively involved in the story and "a retired general who is no longer involved in a policy-making role," commenting that while the latter was customary journalism practice, the former was problematic. Steele was also concerned that the law-enforcement agencies involved in the project had in effect "deputized" Hansen and other NBC employees to assist them in their work.[69]

A 2007 article in *Columbia Journalism Review* went a step further and accused NBC of "entrapment" and "crossing the line from reporting the news to creating the news."[70]

Discussion Problem 5A: Deception and Misrepresentation: Helping the Homeless

Assume the position of editor of a daily newspaper or news director of a television station. A reporter comes to you with the idea to dress up as a homeless person and beg for money on a downtown street corner with the intention of writing a story about his experiences. A photographer will be concealed nearby to take photographs (or in the case of a television reporter, a videographer will record the conversations on both video and audio).

1. What are your ethical concerns about allowing this? What conditions or ground rules would you give the reporter and photographer (or videographer)? What happens to the money collected?

2. Assume that you approved the newsgathering technique described above and the story is successful. Now the same reporter comes to you with the idea of pretending to be homeless person seeking admission to one of the city's homeless shelters.In version A of the scenario, there is no suspicion of wrongdoing; the reporter simply wants to use the deception to research a story about homelessness and shelter conditions in the city. What are your ethical concerns? What conditions or ground rules would you give the reporter?In version B of the scenario, suppose there had already been some accusations that the shelter was unsanitary, served substandard food, and that its employees often verbally abused those seeking services. In giving the reporter permission to carry out the deception, do the ends justify the means?

3. Which philosophers discussed in Chapter 2 might help you make this decision? Which ethical codes and provisions might apply?

Discussion Problem 5B: Freebies and Junkets: Fires and Fam Tours

After a summer of devastating wildfires affecting your region, the state government has received a $32 million grant from the federal government to help it recover, with no "strings attached" or limitations as to how the money can be spent. The state government decides that the first priority will be to help property owners who were uninsured or whose insurance policies were insufficient to cover their losses.

After those reimbursement checks were issued, there was $5 million left over, which the state wants to use on a publicity campaign to demonstrate to the country that the tourism industry in the state is "alive and well" and the locales popular among visitors are still open to the public and safe. National environmental advocacy organizations contribute another $2 million, and the local tourism councils—funded by hotels and airlines—contribute another $3 million, bringing the total to $10 million.

The state government agency responsible for economic development tourism, working with the tourism councils and a public relations firm, has organized a series of "familiarization tours" or "fam tours" and invites journalists representing all types of media organizations—daily and weekly newspapers, online news organizations, broadcasters, and travel publications to attend, with airline travel, hotel, and meals fully paid for out of the $10 million fund. Experience freelancers and bloggers are also invited.

1. If you were a newspaper editor or television news director, would you allow a journalist on your staff to attend such an event? If so, what kind of restrictions would you place on the type of stories he or she produced? If a freelance travel writer approached you to pitch the story, knowing that his or her trip was paid for, what questions would you ask before accepting or rejecting the proposed story?

2. If you were the editor of a travel magazine (instead of a daily newspaper), would you look at this differently? If it could be justified in your budget, would you consider sending a reporter at the magazine's expense, or instead allow the reporter to accept the funding from the company in order to save money?
3. Regardless of how you decide the issue, would part of your coverage of the event be questioning whether funding the tours using federal government grants is an appropriate use of taxpayer money?

Discussion Questions

501. Re-read the highlights of the ethical codes provided earlier in this chapter. Which of those provisions do you believe are realistic and easy to enforce, and which do you believe would be unrealistic and difficult to enforce if journalists are to do an effective job of reporting on public affairs and functioning as the "government watchdog"?

502. Suppose you're the managing editor of a daily newspaper or weekly news magazine. What type of policy would you put in place to deal with the issue of photo-manipulation? How would you encourage employees to abide by the policy? Are there any circumstances under which you believe the digital manipulation of news photographs is acceptable?

Notes

1 Tampa Tribune policy manual (approximate date 1981).
2 Ron F. Smith, *Ethics in Journalism*. Malden, MA: Blackwell Publishing (2008), p. 351.
3 In 2011, the Tribune merged with its major rival, the *St. Petersburg Times*. The new name of the newspaper is *The Tampa Bay Times*.
4 Patty Ryan, "Buried Secrets." *The Tampa Tribune*, September 30, 1991, p. 1-D.
5 Joe Strupp, "Deadly Secrets." *Editor & Publisher*, June 2005, pp. 30–52.
6 John Puterbaugh, "Why We Report Some Suicides and Not Others." *Chicago Tribune*, January 23, 2017. See also: "Why Newspapers Don't Report Suicides." *Burlington Times-News* (Burlington, NC), July 9, 2017.
7 Zach Schonfeld, "Two Months After Robin Williams' Death, Suicide Hotlines Still See a Spike in Calls." *Newsweek*, October 12, 2014.
8 Puterbaugh. See also: Michael R. Sisak and Jim Mustian, "Police Confront Suicide Epidemic." Associated Press report, August 17, 2019.
9 Elizabeth B. Ziesenis, "Suicide Coverage in Newspapers: An Ethical Consideration." *Journal of Mass Media Ethics*, Vol. 6, No. 4 (1991), pp. 234–244.
10 Ziesenis.
11 Ziesenis.
12 David Bauder, "Celebrity Deaths Force Media to Examine Suicide Reporting." Associated Press report, June 14, 2018.
13 "Guidelines Given for Suicide Coverage." Associated Press report, August 9, 2001.
14 "Guidelines Given for Suicide Coverage."
15 Jamie Durcharme, "How Should the Media Cover Suicides? A New Study Has Some Answers." *Time*, July 20, 2018.

16   Durcharme.

17   Dan Oberdorfer, "Is 'Burning a Source' a Breach of Contract?" *National Law Journal*, August 1, 1988, p. 8. See also: Stephen Bates, *If No News, Send Rumors*. New York: St. Martin's Press (1989), p. 164.

18   Strupp, "Obits Find New Life." *Editor & Publisher*, January 2006, pp. 44–48.

19   "The Associated Press Statement on News Values and Principles." *Associated Press Stylebook and Briefing on Media Law*. New York: Associated Press (2012), pp. 307–320.

20   Adrienne Lehrer, "Between Quotation Marks." *Journalism Quarterly*, Vol. 66 (1989), pp. 902–941.

21   Smith, *Ethics in Journalism*, p. 143.

22   Allan Wolper, "Truth to Be Found in Dirty Language?" *Editor & Publisher*, March 2006, p. 22.

23   Helen Dewar and Dana Milbank, "Cheney Dismisses Critic with Obscenity." *The Washington Post*, June 25, 2004.

24   G. Michael Killenberg and Rob Anderson, "What is a Quote? Practical, Rhetorical, and Ethical Concerns for Journalists." *Journal of Mass Media Ethics*, Vol. 8, No. 1 (1993), pp. 37–54. See also: *Masson v. New Yorker Magazine*, 18 Media Law Reporter 2241 (1991).

25   Stephen Bates, *If No News, Send Rumors*. New York: St. Martin's Press (1989), p. 170.

26   Bates, p. 171.

27   Paul Braun, "Deception in Journalism." *Journal of Mass Media Ethics*, Vol. 3, No. 1 (1988), pp. 77-83.

28   Allan Wolper, "Undercover Angel Grounded in Texas." *Editor & Publisher*, February 2005, p. 19.

29   Wolper, "Undercover Angel Grounded in Texas."

30   "Remember Ethics in Wake of Fake Phone Call to Wisconsin Governor." *SPJ News*, February 23, 2011.

31   Paul Smith, "Prank Call to Governor Was Good Journalism." *The Voyager* (University of West Florida), March 2, 2011, p. 3.

32   National Public Radio News Code of Ethics and Practices. www.npr.org/about/ethics (accessed July 7, 2019).

33   National Public Radio News Code of Ethics and Practices.

34   Braun.

35   Louis W. Hodges, "To Deceive or Not Deceive." *The Quill*, December 1981, p. 9. See also Braun.

36   Bates, p. 171.

37   Bates, p. 171.

38   Don R. Pember and Clay Calvert, *Mass Media Law*. New York: McGraw-Hill (2008), pp. 368–370.

39   Bates, p. 183.

40   Bates, p. 6.

41   Bates, p. 183.

42   Bates, pp. 183–184.

43   Bridget Harrison, "Blood Money." *New York Post*, September 9, 2002.

44   Leonard Pitts, "Murdoch's Scandal Just the Latest Low Blow." Syndicated newspaper column, July 23, 2011.

45   Smith, *Ethics in Journalism*, p. 134.

46   Kurt Eichenwald, "A Reporter's Essay: Making a Connection with Justin." *The New York Times*, December 19, 2005. See also: Jack Shafer, "Eichenwald's Weird Checkbook Journalism." *Slate*, March 8, 2007.

47   James White, "Big, Bigger, Biggest." *Newsweek*, January 23, 2012, pp. 36–41.

48   "Critics Say ABC Opened its Checkbook for a News Source." *The New York Times*, May 31, 1999, p. 1-C.

49   Adam Clark Estes, "The Botox Mom and Checkbook Journalism." *The Atlantic*, May 20, 2011.

50   "NBC News' 'Checkbook Journalism' Crossed Ethical Line." Society of Professional Journalists' news release, December 28, 2009.

51   Randy Bobbitt and Ruth Sullivan, *Developing the Public Relations Campaign*. Boston: Allyn & Bacon (2009), p. 217.

52   Bobbitt and Sullivan, p. 217.

53   Wolper, "Are Travel Writers Spoiling the Trip?" *Editor & Publisher*, July 2005, p. 28.

54   Wolper, "Student Journos Study Junkets 101."

55 New York Times Company Code of Ethics.

56 New York Times Company Code of Ethics.

57 Mitchell Stephens, *Broadcast News*. New York: Holt, Rinehart and Winston (1986), p. 177.

58 Mike Wallace and Beth Knobel, *Heat and Light: Advice for the Next Generation of Journalists*. New York: Three Rivers Press (2010), p. 176.

59 Rem Rieder, quoted in "Cases and Commentaries," *Journal of Mass Media Ethics*, Vol. 10, No. 4 (1995), pp. 248–256.

60 James Alan Fox, "Cover Shooters But Not Their Lives: Future Copycats Don't Need Role Models." *USA Today*, June 3, 2019.

61 "Here's Why We May Not be Covering a Threat in Your Child's School." WECT News, February 18, 2018.

62 Verne Gay, "CBS Staged Vietnam Atrocity." *Variety*, July 19, 1989, p. 1–2. See also: Marilyn J. Matelski, *TV News Ethics*. Boston: Focal Press (1991), p. 9.

63 Shiela Reaves, "Digital Alteration of Photographs in Consumer Magazines." *Journal of Mass Media Ethics*, Vol. 6, No. 3 (1991), pp. 175–181.

64 Bob Jamieson, "Nancy Grace Ripped After Missing Boy's Mom Kills Herself." ABCNews.com, September 14, 2006.

65 Jamieson.

66 Jane Kirtley, "Testing the System." *American Journalism Review*, November 2002, p. 70.

67 Douglas McCollam, "The Shame Game." *Columbia Journalism Review*, January/February 2007, pp. 28–33.

68 McCollam.

69 McCollam.

70 McCollam.

6 Journalism and Broadcasting
Privacy Issues

Background

The Society of Professional Journalists' Code of Ethics addresses a number of issues related to privacy.

In the section titled "Minimize Harm," the code requires that journalists:

- show compassion for those who may be affected adversely by news coverage and use special sensitivity when dealing with children and inexperienced sources or subjects;
- be sensitive when seeking or using interviews or photographs of those affected by tragedy or grief;
- recognize that gathering and reporting information may cause harm or discomfort; pursuit of the news is not a license for arrogance;
- show good taste; avoid pandering to lurid curiosity;
- be cautious about identifying juvenile suspects or victims of sex crimes.

Issues and Controversies

The Private Lives of Public People

The tension between the media's newsgathering function and the desire of government agencies, businesses, nonprofit organizations, and individuals to keep secrets has created a number of ethical challenges for the print and broadcast media. But the erosion of privacy is a fact of life in modern America, where the media—both mainstream and tabloid—are becoming increasingly more aggressive in their pursuit of news.

Today, advances in technology and citizens' heightened awareness and interest in public affairs means that government agencies can no longer keep secrets from the public (or at least not for very long), while businesses and nonprofit organizations have their financial affairs and operating procedures scrutinized. But what is most concerning for media ethicists is that private individuals, once thought to live in nearly impenetrable zones of privacy, find those protections no longer effective. Personal privacy has become more difficult to maintain in all aspects of American life.

Since the early days of the profession, journalists and editors have faced the challenge of balancing the privacy rights of people in the news with the public's right to know what is happening in their communities and around the nation.

Privacy, as it relates to media coverage of private individuals, has both legal and ethical aspects. As a matter of law, individuals who are considered "private persons" have a greater expectation of privacy than "public figures." When the legal system first got involved in matters of privacy, it recognized only "public officials"—individuals elected or appointed to policy-making positions. But in the latter half of the twentieth century, court decisions expanded the term to include "public figures," which still included public officials but also added to the category entertainers and professional athletes (because of Americans' growing interest in college sports and the media attention paid to college athletes, the phrase commonly used now is "professional and well-known college or amateur athletes").

Some individuals become "limited public figures" as a result of being in the public spotlight on a short-term or limited basis. The label of "private person" is applied to everyone else. While these labels are used mainly in legal cases such as those involving libel and invasions of privacy, journalists often use those same categories in making ethical decisions about what aspects of a person's life should and should not be part of news stories. The same principles apply to photographs and video, which are potentially as embarrassing to individuals as the text of a printed news story.

While legal determinations are often based on state laws that may be decades old, ethical decisions are often based on good or bad taste (how will our audience react to this), fairness (is this the right thing to do?), and empathy (how would I want to be treated if I was the person being discussed?).

Such decisions are seldom easy to make, and the size and diversity of the audience results in a variety of opinions and reactions—what one member of the audience considers a dramatic presentation of the news may be seen by another as unnecessary sensationalism. Photographers and videographers, as well as the editors they report to, must balance the privacy of individuals in the news with the journalistic need to provide the audience with images that illustrate news stories in a meaningful way.

In the case of public officials and other public figures, one of the major privacy considerations is to what extent are their family lives (including marital indiscretions) should be open for public discussion. Journalists often learn about accusations of off-the-job misconduct—sometimes based on rumor and other times on credible information—and must decide on a case-by-case basis. Whether such matters should be subject of news stories is a popular topic for debate within the journalism profession and society in general.

"In theory, most of us agree: on the one hand, the media should never cover consensual and private adult behavior, even when it might seem unsavory," stated a 2005 article in *Columbia Journalism Review*. "On the other, the media should always cover coercive or criminal behavior, especially when it abuses public power or reveals official hypocrisy."[1]

In his 1994 book *Media Circus*, media critic Howard Kurtz wrote that "People who run for office give up their expectation of privacy. If they don't want their dirty laundry aired, they should probably choose a different profession. Besides, readers are more sophisticated than some editors believe. Most people can judge for themselves whether salacious allegations are germane or garbage."[2]

Pursuing such stories often leaves journalists open to charges of political favoritism, whether deserved or not. If the journalist pursues embarrassing stories about the behavior of politicians in one party but not the other, it will be noticed.

Recent revelations have found that the issue of American presidents and other public officials having extramarital affairs is nearly as old the country itself. Prior to the late twentieth century, the media seldom learned about such behavior, and even if they did, they did not report it.

Although verifiable accounts of their motives do not exist, media historians believe their decisions not to report were based on (1) belief that the public did not care, (2) belief that a president's personal conduct did not affect his performance in office, or (3) a reluctance to alienate the president and members of his administration and thereby lose access in the future.

Earlier in the nation's history, journalists ignored rumors—later found out to be true—that Treasury Secretary Alexander Hamilton had an affair with a married woman, that President Thomas Jefferson had fathered a child with one of his slaves, and President Grover Cleveland had fathered a child out of wedlock. Other presidents known for their extramarital affairs—but never exposed by the press—included Warren G. Harding, Franklin D. Roosevelt, and Dwight Eisenhower.

President John F. Kennedy, whose multiple extramarital affairs had been rumored since his days as a young congressman, was the last president to be spared from media scrutiny in terms of his private life. With previous presidents, reporters and editors decided that such behavior had no effect on his performance in office, but with Kennedy there was an additional factor: he was likeable and treated reporters as friends. During his thirty-four months in office, rumors of his extramarital affairs circulated throughout Washington social circles, but reporters either dismissed them as politically motivated or simply unsubstantiated gossip. Decades after Kennedy's death, however, news reports and accounts written by members of Kennedy's inner circle confirmed that much of Kennedy's "bad boy" reputation was deserved.

In 1976, the *Detroit News* revealed that Donald Riegle, a candidate for U.S. Senate representing Michigan, had a "torrid" extramarital affair seven years earlier. Reporter Seth Kantor justified the story by saying that a person's sexual behavior outside of marriage "tells you a lot about his judgment and stability."[3] Michigan voters apparently disagreed, as Riegle's one-point lead in the poll grew into a six-point victory on election day.

Since the 1988 presidential campaign, during which rumors of Democratic candidate Gary Hart[4] surfaced as a result of investigative reporting (and likely derailed his candidacy), presidential candidates of both parties find their private lives open to scrutiny, both from opposing candidates and journalists covering the campaigns. In addition to sexual behavior, the media also inquire about criminal history, drug use, and academic performance in college.

One example was the candidacy (and later presidency) of Bill Clinton. Arkansas media had already investigated rumors that Clinton had numerous affairs while serving as governor of that state in the 1980s, but found few of them could be substantiated. During the 1992 presidential campaign, those rumors surfaced again, prompting interest from the national media.

Those rumors and news reports continued once Clinton was in office and intensified during his second term, as federal prosecutors looked into a failed real estate venture in which Clinton and his wife were involved a decade earlier. As a result of the investigation, more news came to light about Clinton's fling with White House intern Monica Lewinsky—an affair that eventually led to the president's impeachment and acquittal by the U.S. Senate.

When Illinois politician Jack Ryan challenged Barack Obama the U.S. Senate seat representing Illinois in 2004, reporters from the local ABC affiliate were successful in persuading a judge to unseal the records from his divorce from actress Jeri Ryan. The reporters claimed the information, customarily secret under Illinois law, was of public interest because one cause of the couple's divorce was rumored to be Jack Ryan's insistence that the couple visit sex clubs—behavior unbecoming for someone running for a federal office. Ryan's attorneys, however, claimed that the reporters' interest in the case was based more on voyeurism than true public concern.[5]

When these cases are discussed in a journalistic or ethical context, the central questions that often emerge are: (1) To what extent does the personal conduct of a president (or any other elected official) affect his or her job? (2) If it does not affect the individual's job, is it any of the public's business?

In response to those questions, some observers contend that a public official's private life has no effect on his or her performance in office. That opinion is often shared by supporters. Many Clinton supporters who voted for him in his 1996 re-election campaign told pollsters they disagreed with his personal behavior but approved of his performance in office, apparently finding no contradiction in the two opinions.

More recently, similar opinions were expressed about 2016 candidate Donald Trump, whose supporters—even evangelical Christians—said they were offended by his reputation as an alleged sexual harasser but were more interested in his political opinions and potential to be an effective president. The following year, the same supporters backed a candidate for a U.S. Senate seat representing Alabama, even after serious allegations of the man's past sexual conduct became public.[6]

Some critics suggest that once in office, a public official's reckless sexual behavior leaves him or her vulnerable to blackmail by business interests and political opponents, and in the case of presidents, by foreign governments. In addition, they believe, such behavior does reveal information about the individual's judgment and values—something that voters have a right to know about and the media has a right to investigate.

While journalists and media critics frequently debate the privacy rights of public figures, it is also common to debate the rights of their children. One factor that is often part of the debate is the age of the children who become central figures in a news story; another is the degree to which the children are part of their parents' public lives or political campaigns.

In a 2001 case, for example, the adult son of a big-city mayor was arrested and charged with sexual assault. Journalists and their editors decided to treat the story the same as it would any other—by identifying the suspect by name. The story did not reveal that his father was the mayor, based on the precedent of not identifying the parents of any other criminal suspects unless it was critical to the story. It is not known if the editors based their decision on the "veil of ignorance"—making decisions without regard of the identity of those involved (see Chapter 2)—but the result was the same.

While it's unlikely a media organization would decline to publish or broadcast a crime story because of the suspect was the son or daughter of a public figure, some might give the family relationship more emphasis, especially in cases in which irony or hypocrisy was involved. In the early 1980s, for example, the son of an assistant coach with a National Football League team was arrested and charged with drunk driving after he caused a fatal crash. Ordinarily the media would not mention the identity of the suspect's father, but they did so in this case because the coach frequently visited high schools to speak to students about the dangers of alcohol and drug abuse.

A similar case of irony occurred in 2002, when the twenty-four-year-old daughter of Florida Governor Jeb Bush (and niece of then-President George W. Bush) was arrested on a drug charge. The daughter had previously spent time in a drug rehabilitation center, a fact that many Florida journalists were aware of but did not report out of respect for her privacy and because she, unlike her father and uncle, had not become a public figure voluntarily. After her arrest, however, the media changed its attitude toward the privacy aspect and decided to cover her arrest and prosecution because of the hypocrisy involved. She had pleaded guilty to the charges and under Florida law was allowed to enter yet another rehabilitation program in order to avoid prison time. The media pointed out that as a candidate for governor and after taking office, Jeb Bush had opposed spending government money for drug treatment and other "diversion" programs and suggested that tougher criminal penalties should be the official policy for addressing the state's drug problem. The irony in this case was that the daughter was benefiting from one of the programs that her father had opposed.[7]

A similar case of adolescent behavior being inconsistent with a parent's political position occurred during the 2008 presidential election campaign, when journalists covering the Republican ticket of Senator John McCain and Alaska Governor Sarah Palin were faced with a similar predicament when it was revealed that Palin's unmarried teenage daughter was pregnant.

Palin disclosed the pregnancy shortly before the media was expected to report it. Media critics pointed out that it was fair to emphasize the daughter's unmarried and pregnant condition because, as governor, her mother had advocated abstinence as a solution to the problem of teenage pregnancy in her home state. One observer quick to point out the hypocrisy was radio talk-show host Roland Martin, who quipped that, as governor, Palin had supported abstinence-only while opposing sex education in schools, even though "abstinence-only did not work in her own household."[8]

The Private Lives of Private People

Just as the privacy rights of public figures have both legal and ethical aspects, the same is true with the rights of private persons. As far back as 1967, legal scholar Alan Westin defined privacy as "the power of individuals to determine for themselves when, how, and to what extent information about them is communicated to others."[9] Four years later, a California court determined that "privacy does not mean total secrecy, but rather the right to define one's circle of intimacy."[10]

"Privacy remains a difficult subject in part because there's no standard conception for what it is," privacy advocate Jacob Silverman wrote in his 2015 book *Terms of Service: Social Media and the Price of Constant Connection*. "In some respects, it's personally defined—we all have varying ideas of what we would like others to know about us."[11]

In their 1996 book titled *The Right to Privacy*, Caroline Kennedy and Ellen Alderman concur, adding that even though there is no right to privacy spelled out in the U.S. Constitution, most Americans will argue that they have it.[12]

When making decisions on which should and should not be included in a media story, journalists are generally reluctant to reveal potentially embarrassing information about a private figure unless it is germane to the story. Section 5 of the SPJ code, titled "Fair Play," suggests that "journalists at all times will show respect for the dignity, privacy rights, and well-being of people encountered in the course of gathering and presenting the news."

Many states have media privacy laws that provide private individuals with legal recourse if they believe their privacy has been compromised by print or broadcast journalists. Although state laws vary in both thoroughness and terminology, most provide protection in three areas, and the same concepts apply to ethical decisions:

False Light

False light is the presentation of a person in a news story or other medium in a manner that may not be inaccurate per se, but may be exaggerated or misleading. It is different from libel because instead of claiming financial loss or serious damage to reputation, individuals base their claims on embarrassment or humiliation—damage that is easier to claim but more difficult to prove. Examples of false light include the exaggeration of a person's financial condition or their inclusion in a photograph that is published in a context different from that in which it was taken.

Private Facts

These cases deal with the disclosure of truthful information that is embarrassing to the individual involved and not considered to be a matter of public interest. Examples include details of a person's mental or physical health, family relationships, sexual behavior or orientation, victimization of a violent or sexual crime, financial matters, or academic records. When accused of violating an individual's privacy in this way, media organizations often defend themselves by claiming the information was newsworthy (necessary for audience understanding of the story), the person revealed the information voluntarily, or the information was already publicly known.

In 2005, an Ohio court ruled against a college student who sued classmates for defamation after they put up posters on campus accusing him of being gay. "Publicizing that someone is a homosexual is not libel per se because being a homosexual is not a crime, nor is it a disease," the court's decision stated. "Additionally, being a homosexual would not tend to injure a person in his trade or occupation."[13]

Intrusion

The invasion of an individual's privacy by physical means (trespassing) or through unlawful video or audio recording. Examples are included in the section titled "Hidden Cameras, Deception, and Misrepresentation" in Chapter 5.

Among the most difficult decisions that newspaper editors and television news directors must make is whether or not to publish photographs or video showing private people at times of stress, usually when they or family members have been victims of a crime or other tragedy.

Here's one hypothetical often used at journalism conferences dealing with newsroom decision-making:

A young child finds an abandoned refrigerator, and attempting to hide from his playmates, crawls inside. Unable to force the door open from the inside, he suffocates. When the boy's body is discovered, his mother calls paramedics, who place the body on a stretcher and then in an ambulance. While the boy's mother watches, a newspaper photographer captures images of both the stretcher (with the boy covered by a sheet) and the distraught mother.

That night at the newspaper office, editors face a dilemma. Do they (a) publish all of the photographs, (b) publish less dramatic photos that preserve the family's privacy (such as one showing only the ambulance, but not the mother or the stretcher), or (c) publish no photos at all?

An editor aiming for maximum impact would choose "a," perhaps based on the desire to illustrate the drama of the story. An editor choosing to respect the privacy of the family would likely choose "c," even if it meant a less dramatic presentation of the story. An editor following Aristotle's Golden Mean (see Chapter 2)—the search for the mid-point between the two extremes—would likely choose "b."

When this scenario is discussed among reporters and editors from a variety of publications, their choices are often based on the sizes of the communities their publications serve.

Most serving larger communities tend to choose "a" based on their belief that publishing the most dramatic photographs would best illustrate the drama of the tragedy and perhaps save lives by alerting parents to the dangers of leaving abandoned refrigerators where children may find them. Applying a results-oriented way of thinking in this case—the "ends-justify-the-means"—the editors claim that the impact of the story might not have been as meaningful without the image of the distraught mother.

Those working in smaller communities tend to choose "c" because of the sensitivity of their readers. Applying a process-oriented way of decision-making, they believe the need to protect the family's privacy takes priority over the news value involved.

A real-world example of this issue occurred in Ohio in 1983 when a television crew filmed a husband and wife being arrested and taken out of a bar in handcuffs, along with other individuals suspected of drug trafficking. The couple was not involved in the crime, but simply "at the wrong place at the wrong time." When the video aired on the television news, the couple was outraged enough to contact their attorney, who notified the station of the error. But over his objections the station continued to air the footage during follow-up coverage of the incident. The couple sued the county sheriff for false arrest and imprisonment and the station for invasion of privacy under the "false light" concept.

On the false arrest charge, the court ruled in favor of sheriff's department because the arrest was considered an "honest mistake" and the couple was owned only an apology and not financial compensation. On the privacy claim, the court ruled in favor of the station because the arrest, even though erroneous, took place in public and was therefore of public interest.[14]

Identifying Crime Victims

One of the most common applications of privacy theory to private individuals occurs when the individual has been the victim or alleged victim of a crime. In cases of homicide, assault, robbery, or burglary, the majority of news organizations include the identities of victims in their reports. There are multiple justifications for the policy. One is credibility: a news report indicating that five unnamed individuals were robbed at gunpoint in front of a downtown office building may not be as believed as one that listed the names of those individuals. A second justification is the fact that such matters are part of the public record; since anyone visiting the police station can examine arrest records and learn of the identity of victims, there is no reason to withhold that information from news stories. This rationale is not universally accepted, however, as privacy advocates claim that identifying victims in a newspaper story exposes them much more than simply having their names listed on a police blotter.

Different policies are often applied in the cases of sexual assault victims, however. Prior to 1975, most states had laws prohibiting the media from publishing or broadcasting the names of sexual assault victims. Because of a Supreme Court ruling that year, those laws were declared unconstitutional on the grounds that it was not appropriate to punish media organizations for reporting truthful information. The ruling established a three-part test that became known as the **Cox Doctrine**; it allows the media to report names of sexual assault victims provided the information was truthful, part of a public record, and legally obtained.

Even before the Supreme Court ruling, most media organizations had voluntarily adopted ethical policies prohibiting the identification of victims of sexual assault, especially when the victims were minors. Recently, those policies have been expanded to protect victims of domestic violence. Those situations are often complicated in cases in which alleged perpetrators are identified. A policy of not naming victims of domestic violence or family sexual abuse is pointless, media critics claim, because by identifying the alleged perpetrator, the media outlet has indirectly identified the likely victim.

Most media critics and mental health experts support the current policy of not identifying rape victims, however. Mental counselors who deal with victims on a daily basis contend that sexual assault is different from other crimes in that it's more personal and traumatic than burglary or automobile theft, and that the media should recognize it as such. Media critics and counselors agree that rape victims are often traumatized twice—first time by the crime, and then by the shame of being publicly identified. They also cite statistics about the percentage of sex crimes that are not reported and predict that if publishing and broadcasting the names of victims became routine, it would discourage other victims from reporting similar crimes.

Experts also claim that withholding the name of the victim does not detract from the credibility or newsworthiness of the story. If one of the objectives of a news story is to warn the audience of a trend in crimes in a certain part of town, they content, identifying a victim as "a 29-year-old woman walking alone downtown" is sufficient for readers to get the message; they don't need to know the victim's name.

Two prominent individuals who advocate maintaining the current no-names policy are former newspaper editor and television news executive Jerry Nachman and feminist scholar Katha Pollitt.

Beginning in the 1980s and continuing until his death in 1994, Nachman spoke frequently about the issue, agreeing with both the "under-reporting of the crime" claim and the "twice a victim" claim. He illustrated the second claim with what he called the "Bloomingdale's Scenario" in which the victim in a well-publicized rape case receives unwanted attention several years later when store clerks recognize her name on her credit card.

Like many other scholars who have researched and written about this issue, Pollitt believes that rape is different from other crimes in that the victim is often considered to be partly responsible. "There are no other crimes in which the character, behavior, and past of the complainant are seen as central elements in determining whether a crime has occurred," she wrote in a 1991 op-ed piece in *The Nation*. "When my father was burglarized after forgetting to lock the cellar door, the police did not tell him that he was asking for it."[15]

There are some media practitioners and critics who believe that rape victims should be identified, but they are in the minority. Some believe that because media organizations publish and broadcast the names of victims of other crimes, they create a double standard when they do not identify sexual assault victims; if media organizations identify victims of robberies, muggings, car-jackings, and purse-snatchings, they should also do so in cases of sexual assault. They also believe that publishing and broadcasting the names of victims will prevent individuals from making false accusations of rape (even though statistics indicate that false accusations of sexual assault are rare) and, as a matter of fairness, if suspects in rape cases named, their accusers should also be named as well. Others contend that withholding the names of rape victims perpetuates misconceptions about rape, including the perception that victims are partly to blame.

Michael Gartner, former president of NBC News, supported the position of identifying rape victims because "names add credibility, round out the story, and give the viewer or reader the information he or she needs to understand the issues and make up his or her own mind about what's going on." He added that that journalists are in the business of "disseminating news, not suppressing it" and opposed media policies that state the victim's name will be used only with his or her permission. "In no other category of news do we give the newsmaker the option of being named," Gartner wrote in a 1991 column in *Columbia Journalism Review*.[16]

"In the long run, we'll never get rid of the stigma if we don't treat these like regular crimes," says Geneva Overholser, former editor of the *Des Moines Register* and professor of journalism at the University of Missouri. "It's just not ethical to make a choice about guilt or innocence, which is effectively what we do. It makes us look like we are assuming innocence on one part, guilt on another ... we should not be determining who deserves our protection."[17]

Some newspaper publishers worry that withholding the names of alleged sexual assault victims gives power to anonymous accusers. Herman Obermeyer, former publisher of the *Northern Virginia Sun*, said those who conceal the names of alleged victims but not alleged attackers are being subjective in their coverage and violating the principle of "innocent until proven guilty."[18] Adds Overholser: "There will always be difficulties, Truth-telling has victims."[19]

All of the above arguments for and against identifying alleged rape victims are based on the assumption that both the alleged victim and alleged suspect are private individuals. But what rules apply when either the victim or suspect is a public figure? Two cases of the latter scenario have drawn attention to the question.

In 1991, William Kennedy Smith was tried and acquitted on charges that he raped a female acquaintance on the beach near the family home in Palm Beach, Florida. As the nephew of Senator Edward M. Kennedy and the late President John F. Kennedy, media interest in the trial was based partly on the "bad boy" reputation of Kennedy men. The second case involved professional basketball player Kobe Bryant, who was accused of raping the employee of a Colorado hotel in 2003.

In both cases, law-enforcement personnel, court officials, and journalists followed their ethical policies and attempted to protect the privacy of the victims in the early stages of those trials (during television coverage of the Smith trial, the victim's face was covered by a computer-generated blue dot). But as national media interest intensified, the names became public as a result of sloppy reporting on the part of individual journalists. Once the names became public, other media felt that continuing to conceal their names was no longer necessary. Some media defended their decision to name the victims based on their "cat's-out-of-the-bag" rationale. Because other media (in both cases, tabloid newspapers, online news sources, and gossip-oriented television programs) had already identified the women, many mainstream media outlets decided that to continue to withhold the names was pointless. But others decided to stick with their policies of not identifying alleged victims without their consent. "We can't be driven by what the Internet or television does," said John Temple, editor of the *Rocky Mountain News*, in explaining his paper's decision to stick with its no-names policy. He cited the case of four women at the United States Air Force Academy in Colorado whom the paper identified in a story about their alleged sexual assaults, but only because they agreed to be named.[20]

Smith was eventually acquitted of the rape charges, and the case against Bryant was dropped after the victim refused to testify, even though her name had already become public.

The *Durham Herald-Sun* in North Carolina has an unusual policy that prohibits the naming of not only alleged sexual assault victims, but victims of all crimes. The newspaper staff found itself in quandary in 2006 when members of the lacrosse team at nearby Duke University were charged with raping an exotic dancer at a party. After considerable internal discussion, the editors eventually decided to stay with its long-standing policy, even though the name had already been disclosed by other media.[21]

In the 2019 case of Jeffrey Epstein, a billionaire accused of sex-trafficking teenage girls, the alleged victims were in their twenties when the case began receiving national publicity. After his suicide, they sued Epstein's estate and volunteered to have their names disclosed in the media because they placed the importance of "telling their story" as outweighing their privacy concerns.[22]

Harassment and the Paparazzi

The harassment of public figures—especially Hollywood celebrities—has been a problem ever since the media began reporting on those individuals' private lives in the late twentieth century. A few celebrities actually enjoy the spotlight, while others may not like it but accept it as an unavoidable part of the celebrity lifestyle. Still others do not appreciate the attention and actively work to maintain their privacy. Those who attempt to do so by physically confronting or threatening photographers or hiring private bodyguards often find the resulting altercations often lead to larger publicity problems. Protecting celebrities from photographers is seldom a priority for law-enforcement personnel, and the court system has little sympathy for celebrities in these cases, as they chose their careers voluntarily and therefore must accept the negatives that go with it.

One of the most famous exceptions to that general rule was the case involving former First Lady Jackie Kennedy-Onassis and a specific freelance photographer who had followed her around the world for more than a decade after she left the White House. Onassis sued the photographer for intrusion and in 1972 won a restraining order that required him to stay away from her and her children. But in the five decades that have passed since that case, political wives, Hollywood celebrities, and professional athletes have had little success in keeping tabloid reporters and photographers at a distance.

In 1997, a car carrying Princess Diana was being chased at high speeds by tabloid photographers through the streets of downtown Paris when the car crashed in a tunnel, killing Diana, her boyfriend, and the driver. Following the tragedy, worldwide attention focused on the conflict between journalists' right to photograph celebrities and those celebrities' claims that even when in public, they deserve a certain level of privacy.

The death of Princess Diana re-introduced the term *paparazzi*, which had been around for several decades but was not widely used before the Paris tragedy. While some believe the term to be an Italian word for "freelance photographer" or "photographic stalker," the term was actually derived from Paparazzo, a character in the 1960 film *La Dolce Vita*, which reminded director Federico Fellini of "a buzzing insect, hovering, darting, stinging."[23]

Sonny Bono, a former entertainer who was elected to the U.S. House of Representatives, introduced a bill in Congress that would have made harassment by news photographers a federal crime, but it was rejected on First Amendment grounds. Bono and his ex-wife, Cher, were frequent targets of tabloid photographers.

In 1999, however, California became the first state to incorporate an "anti-paparazzi" clause into its privacy law. The statute prohibits trespass onto another's property "with the intent to capture any type of visual image, sound recording, or other physical impression of the plaintiff engaging in a personal or familial activity" where it would be "offensive to a reasonable person." The measure was signed into law by then-Governor Arnold Schwarzenegger, a former television personality who was himself a target of the paparazzi, as was his wife, television newscaster Maria Shriver. The law has been tested in court several times with similar results: plaintiffs win in lower courts, only to have those decisions reversed by appeals courts on First Amendment grounds.[24]

Media Ride-Alongs

The popularity of "reality" shows on television has drawn attention to a new and controversial method of newsgathering known as the **ride-along**, in which journalists accompany law-enforcement officials and emergency medical personnel and record their work.

One of the earliest known cases involving this newsgathering tactic took place in 1979, when a man suffered a heart attack in the bedroom of his home. A film crew from a local television station, developing a story about the quality of emergency medical care in the community, recorded the event and used the highlights on the evening news. The family sued the station for invasion of privacy, and after six years of litigation, settled the matter out of court (see Case Study 6F).

In numerous legal cases in the 1990s, court rulings determined that media ride-alongs and similar newsgathering techniques violated the privacy rights of the people who were interacting with law-enforcement or emergency medical personnel. In 1992, a Federal District Court ruled against CBS News when the network was sued by a family in Brooklyn, New York. A television crew had accompanied Secret Service agents as they raided the home of a criminal suspect. The suspect was not home, and the agents and television crew were accused of terrorizing his wife and child. Both the Secret Service and network were found to have violated the family's privacy.[25]

In 1999, the U.S. Supreme Court ruled against law-enforcement agencies and media organizations in two similar cases involving television news crews accompanying those agencies when they executed search warrants on the homes of criminal suspects.[26]

Despite those court rulings, reality television programs still use similar techniques, and while the producers occasionally face lawsuits, most avoid liability by finding loopholes in state privacy laws or by including disclaimers that "suspects are innocent until proven guilty."

Your Turn

Case Study 6A: The Private Lives of Public People: Arthur Ashe Has AIDS

In early September 1991, *Sports Illustrated* senior editor Roy Johnson received a phone call from a reputable information source familiar with the world of professional tennis. "You know about Arthur Ashe," the source told Johnson. "He has AIDS."

At first, Johnson, who considered himself a friend of Ashe, dismissed it as simply a rumor. Then a similar call from a different source came in November.

Now believing that the information was valid, Johnson was faced with a dilemma. On one hand, he believed that because Ashe had retired from professional tennis many years earlier, he had regained his status as a private person and had the right to keep his illness secret. But on the other hand, Ashe was still one of the most respected African American men in America, as he had become an advocate for health and education issues in the United States and a champion for human rights around the world. As such, he remained a public figure, and if he was seriously ill, perhaps the public had a right to know about it.

Johnson noticed the contrast in decisions made by Ashe and basketball star Earvin "Magic" Johnson. A few weeks earlier, Magic announced that he had AIDS, and the public was mostly sympathetic, even though he admitted that his infection was due to a promiscuous lifestyle. Ashe, in contrast, had contracted the disease from a blood transfusion following major surgery.

Because of his friendship with Ashe and respect for his privacy, Johnson decided to keep the information secret, not telling any of his colleagues at *Sports Illustrated* nor asking Ashe about it directly, even though the two often saw each other socially.

Then in April 1992, *USA Today* tennis writer Doug Smith learned the same information and made a different decision. He called Ashe directly and confirmed the details, forcing Ashe to call a pre-emptive news conference to make the announcement himself. "Without any justifiable reason, Mr. Ashe's original decision about how to deal with a very private matter was not respected by the newspaper, nor was he respected as a person," wrote Candace Cummins Gauthier, a professor of ethics at the University of North Carolina Wilmington, in a 2002 journal article.[27]

The management of *USA Today* called Ashe's illness a "significant news story" and claimed it pursued it with the same zeal it would have if the disease had been cancer or other disease without a social stigma. When *USA Today* defended its decision by claiming that it didn't have "a special zone for AIDS," Johnson replied in his own column, "Well, it's time we created one."[28]

Johnson's condemnation of other media for breaking the story was based on his belief that, despite being public figures, active and retired professional athletes deserved the same privacy rights as anyone else. That was especially the case with AIDS, which despite being contracted through blood transfusions and accidental needle sticks, still carries a stigma related to promiscuity, homosexuality, and illegal drug use. Roy Johnson contrasted Ashe's decision with that of Magic Johnson, who chose to reveal his illness in part to warn other professional athletes as well as the general public of the dangers of unprotected sex.

In defending the newspaper's decision, *USA Today* Sports Editor Gene Policinski wrote that "one of the greatest athletes of the century has a fatal illness—by any journalist's definition, that's news."[29]

In coming to the newspaper's defense, other editors said they would have made the same decision, some of them adding two other justifications. The first was that Ashe's illness was inconsistent with the common belief that the disease affected mostly drug addicts and homosexual men. The second was the irony of Ashe sitting on the board of directors of a life insurance company involved in the national debate over insurance coverage for AIDS patients.

Johnson was not alone in his criticism of *USA Today* and other media who disregarded Ashe's privacy. "If the man dies one day earlier because of the stress caused by this story, it's not worth it," said one media critic.[30]

Media critic Howard Kurtz admonished journalists for not reporting the Ashe story once they were aware of it. In his own account of the issue, Kurtz wrote that concealing the illness of a public figure simply because that person is a friend "serves to reinforce people's worst suspicions about the press—that we sometimes get too close to the people we cover."

Ten months after the story broke, Ashe died at the age of forty-nine.

1. Evaluate the contrasting decisions made by Roy Johnson of *Sports Illustrated* and Doug Smith of *USA Today*. Which one has the stronger case?
2. Which philosophers (from Chapter 2) could you cite in supporting or opposing those decisions? Which ethical codes apply?

Case Study 6B: The Private Lives of Private People: Outing Gay, Lesbian, and Transgender Persons

Media outlets are frequently accused of "outing" gay individuals, including both public and private persons. Many times the criticism comes not from the individuals directly affected, but by advocacy groups supporting the privacy rights of gay and transgender individuals. Regardless of the status of the individuals, the media typically defends their identification of a person's sexual orientation as "newsworthy," meaning it was necessary to include that information in order for the audience to fully understand the story.

Perhaps the earliest known example of "outing" occurred in 1975 when ex-marine Oliver Sipple was in the crowd at an outdoor event when a woman attempted to assassinate President Gerald Ford. Sipple grabbed the woman's arm and kept the gun pointed up in the air until the Secret Service agents were able to take the weapon away. Sipple was portrayed in the media as a hero who saved the president's life.

The story of Sipple's homosexuality came out in a *San Francisco Chronicle* story in which columnist Herb Caen quoted local gay leaders as saying they were proud and that "maybe this will change the stereotype." *Los Angeles Times* reporter Daryl Lembke interviewed Sipple at length, and while Sipple admitted to supporting gay causes, he was ambiguous about being gay himself. In a separate column, Lembke speculated that Sipple's alleged homosexuality was the reason for Ford not publicly thanking him.[31]

Other newspapers across the country re-published the story, which eventually reached Sipple's hometown newspaper, the *Detroit News*, where his parents learned of their son's alleged homosexuality for the first time. That prompted Sipple to sue the *Chronicle* for invasion of privacy, claiming that his family, previously unaware of his sexual orientation, learned of it by reading the article. On a larger scale, Sipple claimed, the publicity exposed him to "contempt and ridicule" and caused him "mental anguish, embarrassment, and humiliation."[32]

The Chronicle claimed two defenses: newsworthiness, because of its belief that Sipple's heroics went against the stereotype of gay men being cowardly and the unconfirmed speculation that Ford refused to acknowledge his heroism because of his sexual orientation. The *Chronicle* also claimed a "public domain" defense because Sipple's sexual orientation was already publicly known (but not known to his family in

Michigan). The case was dismissed, as the court ruled that Sipple had voluntarily waived his right to privacy by publicly supporting gay causes.[33]

After Sipple died in 1989, former President Ford finally acknowledged his heroism in a condolence letter to his family. Attending his funeral were several journalists involved in the original story. Lembke wrote in a post-funeral column that "If I had to do it over again, I wouldn't."[34]

A similar case occurred in 1983 when Toni Diaz became the first female study body president at the College of Alameda in California. Sidney Jones, the education reporter for the nearby *Oakland Tribune*, read about her story in the college's student newspaper, and Diaz consented to an interview. Following the interview, Jones checked public records and not only found that Diaz had an arrest record, but that she used to be a Puerto Rican man named Antonio Diaz. Prior to enrolling at the college, Diaz had undergone several surgeries and hormone therapy to become a woman. Because the college had touted Diaz as its first female student body president, Jones and his editors at the *Tribune* believed that including that detail in the story was newsworthy. A California trial court and appeals court disagreed, siding with Diaz in her invasion of privacy law suit. Both courts ruled that her sex change was not related to her role in campus politics.[35]

In 2005, the *Spokesman-Review* in Spokane, Washington, was accused of "outing" Jim West, the city's mayor. The newspaper learned that he was a closeted homosexual who had been meeting younger men in online chat rooms for years. At first, reporters and editors decided that the man's sexual orientation was unrelated to his job performance and was therefore off-limits. But when they learned that West had been using his position to meet interns and other young men working for the city, they decided the "unrelated to job performance" factor no longer applied. Even though the newspaper was still accused of "outing," they were confident in their defense that the story was no longer about West's sexual orientation but was now about his abuse of power. Reports and editors also pointed to West's hypocrisy, as he had been an opponent of proposed local ordinances and state laws aimed at protecting the rights of gays and lesbians in employment and housing.[36]

In 2013, sports blogger Caleb Hannan spent eight months investigating a product called "Dr. V's Magical Putter," hoping only to determine whether the product was a real breakthrough in golf equipment or just another example of "over-hyped junk" being sold on television infomercials. While never learning much about the product itself, he discovered what he thought was a more interesting story: the inventor, who identified herself only as "Dr. V," was actually a transgender woman named Essay Anne Vanderbilt.

That was the story that Hannan published in the online magazine *Grantland* in January 2014. The story also alleged that Vanderbilt was a con artist and not a real doctor; she had fabricated a life history that included a Ph.D. from the Massachusetts Institute of Technology and top-secret jobs for military contractors.

She had also allegedly cheated an investor out of $60,000. Just prior to learning about the article and its contents, Vanderbilt committed suicide. Whether she was more embarrassed by the revelations about those lies or being outed as transgender was never determined, but the case became a turning point in the campaign for respect and fair treatment for transgender persons.[37]

1. In the case of Oliver Sipple, do you agree with the newspaper's claim of "news-worthiness," based on the stereotype of gay men being cowardly and suspicion about the motives of the president in not acknowledging him?
2. In the case of Anthony/Toni Diaz, do you agree with those who say that her status as a transgender person was irrelevant to her role in campus politics? Or with those who say the college inadvertently made the story newsworthy by promoting the fact that she was the first female student government president (without knowing that she was not always female)?
3. In the case of Jim West, do you agree with the newspaper's contention that it was not "outing" the mayor, but instead simply exposing his abuse of power?
4. In the case of Vanderbilt, those who believe the blogger invaded her privacy contend he should have stuck with an analysis of the product and that a person's sexual orientation or transgender status is seldom relevant to the story. The opposite view is that her being transgender is part of a larger story of deception (along with the fake degree and job history). Which side do you agree with?

Case Study 6C: The Private Lives of Private People: Should Lottery Winners Remain Anonymous?

In January 2018, a New Hampshire woman won $560 million in the multi-state Powerball Lottery, but she wanted to keep knowledge of her financial windfall within a small circle—her family, her banker, and her attorney. But under lottery rules, the names of big-jackpot winners are made public—a policy designed to protect the lottery against accusations of fraud and malfeasance. Lottery officials also like to use the cliché photographs of winners holding giant cardboard checks in their advertising and marketing materials.

Powerball is jointly run by the state's Lottery Commission and counterpart organizations representing the lotteries of other states. Attorneys for Powerball and the state of New Hampshire argued in court that the rules requiring public disclosure of winners' names, hometowns, and winning amounts were necessary to maintain the integrity of the lottery and were consistent with the state's public records laws.

But winner Jane Doe, as she became known in court documents, wanted to protect herself from the public spotlight and what she and her lawyer feared would be hordes of distant relatives (or individuals claiming to be) and scam artists wanting to claim their share of the money.

The state, however, didn't agree. "The petitioner's understandable yearning for normalcy after entering a lottery to win hundreds of millions of dollars is not a sufficient basis to shut the public out of the business of government," Assistant Attorney General John Conforti wrote in court documents.[38] Charlie McIntyre, executive director of the New Hampshire Lottery, added that the Powerball winner must abide by the disclosure law "like any other."[39]

The following month, a federal judge ruled in favor of the winner, but announced that the narrow ruling applied only to that case and wasn't meant to set a precedent for the lotteries of other states or other multi-state lottery games such as MegaMillions.[40]

In the majority of states, the names of winners is considered public information under state law, and some lottery commissions even require jackpot winners to appear at news conferences as a condition of receiving their winnings. Others do not announce the names of winners overtly, but allow them to be found using public records searches. Only a small minority of states, including Delaware, Kansas, Maryland, North Dakota, Ohio, South Dakota, and Texas, allow lottery winners to remain anonymous, but it's a matter of policy, not law.

In other states, legislatures are considering revising their public records to include "privacy exemptions" for lottery winners, claiming it would protect them from "scams, shady businesses, greedy distant family members, and violent criminals looking to shake them down."[41] Others are considering laws that would provide one year of anonymity in order to allow winners time to prepare for having their names disclosed.

1. Which side do you believe has a stronger argument—lottery winners, who claim they have a right to privacy, or the lottery officials, who claim that public disclosure is necessary to maintain the integrity of the lottery?
2. What is your opinion of the "compromise" idea that would allow winners one year of anonymity to prepare for having their identities disclosed? Would that be an effective way of serving both interests—protecting the privacy of the winners while still preserving the integrity of the lottery?
3. Which concepts or philosophies from Chapter 2 can be applied in this case? What about codes of ethics?

Case Study 6D: The Private Lives of Private People: Making a Profit from Mug Shots

After a young woman in Florida was arrested in 2009 for driving on an expired license, she thought her ordeal would quickly be over after she paid the fine and renewed her license. She was wrong. Because police "mug shots" are public records under Florida law, her photo was published in the online edition of the local daily newspaper, the *St. Petersburg Times*, along with those of accused murderers, rapists, and car thieves.

Luckily for the woman, the teasing she got from family members, friends, and co-workers lasted only a few days, but the photo remains in the newspaper archives in perpetuity. Beyond the humiliation, what bothered the woman, other low-level offenders, and media ethicists the most was the *Times* was making a profit out of their misfortune. Editors of online newspaper editions admit that mug-shot pages are among their most popular features, and each time a reader clicks on that section, advertising revenue goes up.

Following the *St. Petersburg Times'* merger with the competing *Tampa Tribune* in 2011, the new publication became *The Tampa Bay Times*. Its online edition, called *Tampa Bay Online*, now publishes only the arrest photos of felony suspects and not those of individuals suspected of traffic offenses or other misdemeanors. But the issue is still controversial at other daily newspapers, including *Newsday* (New York), the *Chicago Tribune*, the *Orlando Sentinel*, and the *Palm Beach Post*, where advertising managers admit those sections account for large numbers of page views and related advertising revenue.

In addition to criticizing the financial connection, media ethicists and even some law-enforcement officials worry about individuals being ridiculed by local radio disc jockeys and other negative consequences. Even with the disclaimers that "individuals are innocent until proven guilty," journalism ethicist Robert Steele says there is "a stench of unfairness to this kind of cyber-billboard," and Orlando public defender Robert Wesley called mug-shot pages "online Salem pillories," a reference to the public shaming of witches in seventeenth-century Massachusetts.[42]

1. Is there a privacy concern here? In most states, mug shots are public records and in most states, newspapers have the right to publish them, but should this include those accused of misdemeanors or minor traffic offenses?
2. Are you concerned about the issue of newspapers generating advertising revenue from the publication of these photos?
3. Which concepts or philosophies from Chapter 2 can be applied in this case? What about codes of ethics?

Case Study 6E: The Private Lives of Private People: The Honor Student Dies a Hooker

In 1976, a former high school honor student from Missoula, Montana earned a scholarship to Radcliffe College, a prestigious women's institution in Massachusetts. After flunking out of college, Cindy Herbig moved back to Missoula, worked at a series of dead-end jobs, had a falling out with her parents, and within a year was working as a prostitute in Washington, D.C. In 1977 she was arrested, and in January 1979 she was murdered at age twenty-one.

The local daily newspaper, the *Missoulian*, published only a brief obituary that focused on her accomplishments earlier in life and none of the details surrounding the lifestyle that likely led to her death. But then, while Hal and Lois Herbig were planning their daughter's funeral in Missoula, they learned that *The Washington Post* was planning a detailed story about her life, complete with the sordid details. Through their lawyer, the parents pleaded with the newspaper not to include that information. *Post* editors declined and went forward with their plans to publish the story.

The *Missoulian*, a paper that subscribed to *The Washington Post*'s syndicated news service, decided to reprint the story, which led to another unsuccessful plea from the family to either not publish the story, or if that was not possible, to delay it until after the funeral.

The local paper went forward with the story, justifying its decision based on the need to warn other families of the dangers of sex trafficking, believing that the men who recruited Cindy and took her to Washington were still operating in bars in Missoula. Regarding the timing of the story, they simply responded that they could not allow the precedent of allowing family members of crime victims to dictate when they published stories.

After the story ran, the community was outraged. Many local businesses cancelled their advertising with the paper, hundreds of subscribers canceled, and the town's largest law firm dropped the paper as a client. Even other newspaper staffers disagreed with the decision. Editorial page editor Sam Reynolds wrote that "It was a shame to read about Cindy Herbig … a shame for the newspaper profession, shame for once to be a part of it, shame above all for inflicting additional hurt where hurt had visited more than enough."[43]

In light of the controversy, newspaper executives contended that if they had a chance to do it again, they would still run the story but would have agreed to the family's request to delay its publication until after the funeral. "Under deadline pressure, journalists do the best they can to get the news out, even news that hurts," said one newspaper executive.[44]

Case Study 6F: Media Ride-Alongs: No One Asked You to Leave, but No One Invited You In

On a cool fall day in 1979, fifty-nine-year-old Dave Miller suffered a heart attack in his Los Angeles home. Alerted to the situation by the screams of Miller's wife, Brownie, neighbors came over and immediately called 911. Paramedics arrived within minutes, but so did a KNBC camera crew that was researching a story on the quality of emergency medical care in the community. While Brownie Miller and the neighbors waited downstairs, the camera crew recorded the drama as the paramedics worked desperately but unsuccessfully to save her husband's life.

In the days that followed, Brownie Miller was busy planning her husband's funeral and didn't give much thought to the presence of the camera crew. But when other family members saw numerous replays of the incident on the television news and commercials promoting the station's series on the training and competency of paramedics, they were outraged. They persuaded Brownie Miller to complain to the management of the station, and—when that didn't work—to sue the station for invasion of privacy, based not only on the physical intrusion by the camera crew and equipment, but also on the emotional trauma caused by watching Dave Miller die over and over again on television.

During the protracted legal battle, station management and attorneys offered the following defenses:

1. Because there had been considerable criticism of emergency medical services provided by local government, the station was functioning in its "watchdog" role and performing a public service by reporting on a matter of public interest.[45]
2. The television crew claimed to have made a special effort to not show Dave Miller's face. Miller's daughter and friends disputed that claim, reporting that they recognized Dave and Brownie Miller, as well as the interior of their home, in the news reports. In court testimony, one employee of the station also contradicted that claim by reporting they were mostly concerned with making sure they did not interfere with the paramedics' work.[46]
3. Because neither the wife nor neighbors objected to the crew's presence, the rule of "implied consent" should be applied. The family and its attorney responded that the issue was not that no one asked the station's employers to leave, but that no one had invited them in.

During the six years of litigation that followed, a lower court ruled in favor of KNBC, and an appeals court reversed and ruled in favor of the family. Before the case could be appealed yet again to the California Supreme Court, the two sides reached an undisclosed out-of-court financial settlement.

1. Which interest should take priority in this case—the family's right to privacy, or the media's right to research stories of public interest?
2. Who had the strongest argument in this case? The management of the television station, who argued that "no one asked us to leave," or the family members, who argued that "no one invited you in"?

Discussion Problem 6A: The Private Lives of Public People: The Mayor and the Missing Kid

Just one year into his term, the mayor of your city has died unexpectedly. The city's charter stipulates that in the event of the mayor's death or resignation, the city council chooses from among its own members a person to serve the balance of the mayor's term. After several days of debate, the council is hopelessly deadlocked and is unable to choose between the two council members interested in the job. Then one member suggests a compromise candidate: the newest member of the council, who is at first reluctant but eventually agrees to take the job. At twenty-eight, he is the youngest member of the council and the least experienced, but he is the only member that all of the other members can agree on to ascend to the mayor's office.

You're the city hall reporter for the local daily newspaper and have the primary responsibility for covering the activities and personalities involved in the city council and the mayor's office. As soon as the council's decision is made public, you decide to write an in-depth profile of the new mayor, who will be the youngest mayor in the country and has become a national news story almost overnight.

In your profile, you want to go beyond his political career and include some personal information, but because of his short period of time on the council, his family life is a mystery. You decide to conduct extensive background research on the man, spending several days gathering information from previously published newspaper and magazine articles, Internet sources, social media profiles, and public records. But you notice an interesting discrepancy regarding the mayor's family: In all of the articles published prior to 2015, the mayor and his wife are said to have three children, and their names and ages are listed. But in all of the articles published in 2015 and since, only the two youngest children are listed. Because the information is consistent among the two categories of news stories, there is no doubt that something must have happened to the oldest child.

1. Would you ask the mayor about the oldest child? If your answer is "yes," explain why you believe that information is of public interest, and how you would attempt to overcome the mayor's objections to having that information released. If your answer is "no," explain how you would deal with the likelihood that other reporters will notice the discrepancy and will want to ask the mayor the same question.
2. What are other possible solutions to this dilemma?
3. Which philosophers discussed in Chapter 2 might help you make this decision? Which ethical codes and provisions might apply?

Discussion Problem 6B: The Private Lives of Public People: The Senator and the Tattoo

Senator Bob Randall is a decorated war veteran running for president. One of his campaign issues is a proposed constitutional amendment to provide punishment for desecration of the American flag by burning or any other acts the courts determined to be disrespectful. At the height of the campaign, the senator's nineteen-year-old daughter, a student at Enormous State University, is taken to the hospital after complaining of dizziness and nausea. At the hospital she is diagnosed with hepatitis, and the media covering the senator's campaign soon learn the cause of the infection—the tattoo of an American flag on her left buttock.

1. Do the media have the right to report the cause of the daughter's illness?
2. Does the inconsistency between the senator's position on flag desecration and the daughter's choice of body art make the issue more newsworthy?
3. Is the daughter's age a consideration? What if she was sixteen? What if she was twenty-five?
4. Does the daughter's role (or lack of it) in the campaign affect your answer? If she plays an active role in the campaign, including supporting (or opposing) the flag desecration amendment, does that affect your answer?
5. Which of the philosophers studied in Chapter 2 might help a journalist make this decision? What about the ethical codes?

Discussion Problem 6C: The Private Lives of Private People: Who Votes and Who Doesn't

You've recently become the editor of a weekly newspaper that serves a largely African American readership in your community. After the previous presidential election (before you were hired), the paper published the names and addresses of registered voters who did not vote. The candidates or issues that individuals voted for or against remained secret, but whether or not they went to the polls is public information under your state's open records law.

The newspaper defended itself by claiming it was simply trying to encourage (its critics used the term "shame") citizens into voting in future elections. But many of those named said their privacy had been invaded.

"Sometimes when you embarrass people, they will do the right thing," said the newspaper's publisher (your new boss) in an interview with a professional journal covering the newspaper industry. The publisher added that the goal was to increase voter turnout among African Americans, which he claimed was one of the most effective ways to create social and political change in the city, state, and country.

Although many questioned the cause-and-effect claim, the newspaper's strategy may have worked. In the following mid-term election, voter turnout in the community increased by more than 20 percent. That's significant, considering mid-term elections usually see a drop-off in voter turnout compared to presidential election years.

Despite the positive results, the topic remains a controversial one among the people of your community, regardless of whether or not they subscribe to your paper and whether or not they found their names on the list. "This seems to be a stupid tactic to get someone to vote," wrote one reader responding on the paper's website. "It's no one's business who didn't vote and their reasons." Another reader wrote, "I believe that publishing the names of citizens along with their addresses is a punitive, embarrassing, and dangerous practice."

Now that another presidential election is just a few months away, it's time to decide whether or not to print the list again.

1. Do you agree with the newspaper's explanation of its motives, that it is merely attempting to increase voter turnout, or the opinion of the critics, that this is an invasion of privacy?
2. Are you in favor of printing the list again? What if you printed the names only, without addresses?
3. One reporter suggests printing the list of non-voters again, but this time giving them "fair warning" of the newspaper's intention the week before election day. Good idea or bad idea?

Discussion Questions

601. Re-read the three cases involving the son of the football coach, the daughter of the Florida governor, and the daughter of 2008 vice-presidential candidate Sarah Palin. Do you agree with the policy that children of public figures are not treated differently than the children of private persons? Do you agree with the media's decision to treat these two cases differently because of the inconsistency between the children's behavior and the parents' public comments?

602. Are there any philosophers or concepts from Chapter 2 that can be applied to the issue of privacy for either public or private persons?

Notes

1 E.J. Graff, "The Line on Sex." *Columbia Journalism Review*, September/October 2005, pp. 8–9.
2 Howard Kurtz, *The Media Circus: The Trouble with America's Newspapers*. New York: Random House (1994), p. 155.
3 Stephen Bates, *If No News, Send Rumors*. New York: St. Martin's Press (1989), p. 144.
4 In 2018, the Gary Hart–Donna Rice story became the topic for the feature film titled *The Front Runner*, with Hugh Jackman portraying Hart.
5 Graff.
6 Astead W. Herndon, "Why Evangelicals Are Again Backing a Republican Despite Allegations of Sexual Misconduct." *The Boston Globe*, November 20, 2017.
7 Ashley Parker, "Jeb Bush Drops Guard to Share Family Account of Addiction." *The New York Times*, January 5, 2016.
8 Kurtz, "From the Radio Right Comes an Amen Chorus for Palin." *The Washington Post*, September 4, 2008, p. 25-A.
9 Alan Westin, *Privacy and Freedom*. New York: Atheneum (1967), p. 7.
10 *Brisco v. Reader's Digest Association*, 4 C.3d 529 (1971).
11 Jacob Silverman, *Terms of Service: Social Media and the Price of Constant Connection*. New York: HarperCollins (2015), p. 284.
12 Ellen Alderman and Caroline Kennedy, *The Right to Privacy*. New York: Alfred A. Knopf (1995), p. xiii.
13 "Ohio Court Finds No Libel in Labeling Student as Gay." SPLC Legal Alert, December 2005.
14 Daniel J. Solove, *The Future of Reputation*. New Haven, CT: Yale University Press (2007), p. 163. See also: *Penwell v. Taft Broadcasting*, 469 N.E. 2d 1025 (1984).

15　Katha Pollitt, "Naming and Blaming: Media Goes Wilding in Palm Beach." *The Nation*, June 24, 1991, pp. 833–838.

16　Michael Gartner, "Naming the Victim." *Columbia Journalism Review*, July/August 1991, pp. 54–55.

17　Sally Dadisman, "Naming Names: Should News Organizations Identify the Accuser in the Duke Lacrosse Case?" *American Journalism Review*, August/September 2007, pp. 22–23.

18　James Burges Lake, "Of Crime and Consequence: Should Newspapers Report Rape Complainants' Names?" *Journal of Mass Media Ethics*, Vol. 6, No. 2(1991), pp. 106–118.

19　Joe Strupp, "What's in a Name?" *Editor & Publisher*, July 28, 2003, p. 25.

20　Strupp.

21　Dadisman.

22　Madeleine Carlisle, "Epstein Accusers Get Their Day in Court." *Time*, August 28, 2019.

23　Randy Bobbitt, *Exploring Communication Law*. Boston: Allyn & Bacon (2008), p. 149.

24　"An Extreme Example: The California Anti-Paparazzi Law." Position paper issued by the Reporters Committee for Freedom of the Press, August 1, 2012.

25　*Ayeni v. CBS*, 35 F. 2d 680 (1984).

26　*Hanlon v. Berger*, 27 Media L. Rep., 1716 (1999) and *Wilson v. Layne*, 119 Ct. 1692 (1999).

27　Candace Cummins Gauthier, "Privacy Invasion by the Media: Three Ethical Models." *Journal of Mass Media Ethics*, Vol. 17, No. 1 (2002), pp. 20–34.

28　Roy Johnson, "None of Our Business." *Sports Illustrated*, April 20, 1992, p. 82.

29　Gene Foreman, *The Ethical Journalist*. Malden, MA: Wiley-Blackwell Publishing (2011), p. 245.

30　Johnson.

31　*Sipple v. Chronicle Publishing*, 20 Media L. Rep. 1690 (1984). See also: Randy Bobbitt, *Exploring Communication Law*. New York: Taylor & Francis (2018), 199–200.

32　*Sipple v. Chronicle Publishing*. See also: Bobbitt, *Exploring Communication Law*, 199–200.

33　Bates, p. 143.

34　Bates, p. 143.

35　*Diaz v. Oakland Tribune*, 139 C.A. 3d 118 (1983). See also: Bobbitt, *Exploring Communication Law*, p. 199.

36　Steven A. Smith, "Stories Result of Three-Year Investigation." *Spokesman-Review* (Spokane, WA), May 5, 2005, p. 1-A. See also: Strupp, "Let's Get Ethical." *Editor & Publisher*, September 2006, pp. 45–54. Graff, "The Line on Sex."

37　Susan Wildermuth, "When Privates are Public: Ethical Issues in News Media Coverage of Transgender Persons." Chapter 13 in *Controversies in Digital Ethics*, Amber Davisson and Paul Booth, eds. New York: Bloomsbury (2016), pp. 202–215.

38　Cleve R. Wootson Jr., "Lottery Winner Asks Judge if She Can Remain Anonymous." *The Washington Post*, February 13, 2018.

39　Wootson.

40　Wootson.

41　"Should Lottery Winners be Kept Secret?" Associated Press report, January 5, 2013.

42　Tim Padgett, "Mug Shot Mania." *Time*, September 21, 2009, p. 82.

43　Jack Hart and Janis Johnson, "Fire Storm in Missoula." *Quill*, Vol. 67 (May 1979), pp. 19–24.

44　Hart and Johnson.

45　Alderman and Kennedy, pp. 176–188.

46　Alderman and Kennedy, pp. 176–188.

7 Journalism and Broadcasting
Accountability Issues

Background

The Society of Professional Journalists' Code of Ethics addresses a number of issues related to accountability.

In the section titled "Be Accountable," the code requires journalists to:

- clarify and explain news coverage and invite dialogue with the public over journalistic conduct;
- encourage the public to voice grievances against the news media;
- admit mistakes and correct them promptly;
- expose unethical practices of journalists and news organizations;
- abide by the same high standards to which they hold others.

The American Society of Newspaper.Editors' Statement of Principles explains that journalists "must be vigilant against all who would exploit the press for selfish purposes." The statement also requires that journalists provide the publicly accused the earliest opportunity to respond, exercise caution when promising confidentiality to any source, and use confidential sources only in the rarest circumstances.

The Radio Television Digital News Association Code of Broadcast News Ethics requires that broadcasters:

- promptly acknowledge and correct errors;
- recognize the need to protect confidential sources and promise confidentiality only with the intention of keeping that promise.

The RTDNA code addresses issues such as truth and accuracy, independence and transparency, and accountability for consequences. Among all of the codes established by major professional organizations, the RTDNA code is the most modern in terms of its reference to social media, stating that, "'Trending,' 'going viral,' or 'exploding on social media' may increase urgency, but these phenomena only heighten the need for strict standards of accuracy."

Issues and Controversies

Clarifications, Corrections, and Retractions

Like many businesses in American society, journalism is under public pressure to be more "accountable" to its audience, including a willingness to clarify or correct alleged erroneous information.

Despite advances in technology and more emphasis placed on the impact of journalism on its audiences, research shows that the level of accuracy over the last eighty years is largely unchanged. As far back as 1936, a study of Minneapolis-area newspapers found that nearly half the stories studied included factual or spelling errors.[1]

The methodology of the study involved sending copies of the stories to individuals named in them. Over the next eight decades, subsequent studies using the same methodology but with different audiences have produced similar results. In addition to factual errors based on information included in the articles, those studies also found that sources had numerous complaints about information that was left out.[2]

In a 1985 textbook intended for use by high school journalists, veteran reporter and educator DeWitt C. Reddick offered a list rules to help journalists—both students and professionals—avoid having to publish clarifications, corrections, or retractions:

- Check the spelling of every name, address, and title in a telephone directory or other official source.
- Be wary of estimating numbers of individuals involved in a protest, meeting, accident, or other newsworthy event. Use only numbers provided by law enforcement, emergency medical personnel, or other official sources. If verification is not possible, lean toward conservative estimates.
- Unless you are writing an opinion column, do not speculate on the motives behind anyone's behavior or public comments. If you believe his or her motives are critical to the story, ask the individual what his or her motives were and then quote him or her directly.[3]

"Journalism's dirty little secret is that many errors go uncorrected because complaints are ignored, complaints never reach the right person, or worse, victims of errors feel so helpless in the face of a monolithic media organization that they never call," stated a 2004 article in the *Journal of Mass Media Ethics*. That "give-up" attitude is to blame, the article claims, for situations like that involving Jayson Blair of *The New York Times*, who succeeded in falsifying stories for years because none of his misquoted sources picked up the phone.[4]

Having stories archived in online databases makes it theoretically easier to correct errors compared to hard-copy archives, but media researcher Craig Silverman claimed in his 2007 book *Regret the Error* that many media managers fail to make the effort. "Uncorrected errors that reside in databases influence future reporting and feed the cycle of inaccuracy," Silverman wrote. "Reporters and others return to them again and again and pass along the incorrect information. Online versions of articles that contain uncorrected errors have a dangerous level of permanence."[5]

Correcting errors is addressed by many professional organizations in their codes of ethics. The National Public Radio News Code of Ethics and Practices, for example, requires that NPR journalists who find an error in their own work should not wait until the error is pointed out to act on it. However, it also specifies that all clarifications, corrections, and retractions be approved by a supervisor as well as the network's general counsel.[6]

Some media organizations are reluctant to admit mistakes and instead refer to their corrections pages as "Updates," "For the Record," or "Setting the Record Straight." But Silverman contends that newspapers should call their columns "corrections" and that such euphemisms make them less useful. "Just call a duck a duck," he told a writer for *Editor & Publisher*.[7]

As a result of errors that are published or broadcast, print journalists and broadcasters often issue **clarifications** and **corrections**. In extreme cases, erroneous news stories are subject to **retractions**. Those three terms are often confused and used incorrectly by those outside of the profession, but it is important that professional journalists (and journalism students) do not.

Clarifications

As the term indicates, a clarification is a statement in which the media organization does not admit an error, but instead simply explains how information previously published or broadcast may have been misinterpreted.

Many clarifications follow requests by individuals or organizations that are the focus of news stories and often result not from information that was reported, but from what was left out.[8] For example, a story about a criminal suspect might refer to a previous case in which the individual was charged with a crime, but omitted the fact that the charges were later dropped, or that he or she was found not guilty at trial. Without that information, some readers or viewers might assume the individual was guilty of the previous accusation. Because the harm to the individual's reputation is usually minimal, a clarification may or may not be accompanied by an apology.

In 2018, for example, *The New York Times* published a story indicating that the penthouse residence of U.S. Ambassador to the United Nations Nikki Haley was outfitted with new curtains that cost American taxpayers $52,700. Coming shortly after several cabinet members were criticized (including one who was forced to resign) for lavish spending on office furnishings and work-related travel, the story made it appear that Haley had fallen into the same trap. What was left out of the story was that spending on the curtains (which were necessary for security reasons) had been approved two years earlier, when Barack Obama was president and Samantha Power, an Obama appointee, was the UN ambassador.

The *Times* apologized to Haley and published a clarification, but it wasn't in time to stop numerous newspaper editorials critical of Haley and a barrage of social media postings calling for her resignation.[9]

Corrections

A correction is an item published or broadcast in which the media organization admits the falsity of one or more details included in a story, but contends that the overall story is factual. For example, a newspaper story might report that an incident occurred on Oak Tree Lane when it actually occurred on Oak Tree Avenue, or that an individual in a story was a pediatrician when he or she was actually a podiatrist.

Regardless of whether such errors caused any harm, most corrections include an apology to the individuals affected. When considering requests for corrections, newspaper staffers must often distinguish between actual factual errors and information that is merely embarrassing.

Retractions

A retraction is an admission that the entire story (or a substantial majority of the details in the story) is false, and the media organization responsible is admitting that it should have never been published or broadcast. Because most potentially controversial or damaging stories are thoroughly fact-checked and in many cases reviewed by attorneys prior to being published or broadcast, retractions are rare in today's media business.

Some state laws dealing with defamation include provisions regarding corrections and retractions. In some states, a media organization's good-faith effort to correct or retract a story may prevent the case from even going to court. In other states, such efforts may not prevent the case from going to trial, but will work in favor of media organizations by either resulting in court rulings in their favor or at least reducing the size of the monetary judgment awarded to the plaintiffs.

When retractions are necessary, they often make journalism history, damage the organization's reputation for years, and in some cases cost journalists their jobs.

One of the more noteworthy cases of a media blunder leading to a retraction occurred in 1998, when Cable News Network (CNN) unveiled its new investigative series titled *Newsstand*. Producers wanted a story for the first episode that would create broadcast news history. It did —but not for the right reasons. That episode claimed that during the latter stages of the Vietnam War, U.S. aircraft intentionally sprayed nerve gas on deserting American troops in what was known as "Operation Tailwind."

The story was based largely on information provided an eighty-six-year-old former Pentagon official who was living in a nursing home. Other CNN reporters said later that they had stopped using him as a source several years earlier because of his declining mental and physical condition. Shortly after the story aired it was debunked by numerous sources, prompting the network to retract it. The network conducted an internal review into the how such a clearly erroneous story could made it on air but never released its findings. Media critics speculated that the network was so intent on "hitting a home run" with the first installment of its new program that it disregarded reporters' concerns about inconsistencies in the story.

In 2004, the CBS News magazine *60 Minutes* reported an unsubstantiated story that President George W. Bush had received preferential treatment that helped him avoid going to Vietnam during his service in the Texas Air National Guard in the 1970s. CBS based its reporting on paperwork reportedly discovered in the files of Bush's commanding officer. The documents were later proven to be forgeries, leading CBS News to retract the story and lead anchor Dan Rather to personally apologize to the president. Media critics referred to "Rathergate" as one of the biggest blunders in journalism history, and it resulted in the firing of one CBS producer and resignations of three others. Rather retired from the network the following year. The saga was the basis for *Truth*, a 2015 movie that featured Robert Redford as Rather.

The following year, *Newsweek* published a story about the alleged mistreatment of suspected terrorists being held at the American military prison at Guantanamo Bay, Cuba. The story reported that American soldiers desecrated copies of the Koran, including flushing one copy down a prison toilet. Within days, violent anti-American protests broke out in Muslim countries around the world, including one incident in Afghanistan in which fourteen people died.

Pentagon officials investigated the Koran incident and other details of the *Newsweek* story, but issued a statement indicating they had found nothing to substantiate any of the account. The incident with the Koran, it turned out, involved one of the detainees (not an American soldier) who flushed a few pages (not an entire book) down a toilet to protest conditions at the prison.

Within a week of the Pentagon's report, *Newsweek* retracted the article. In its own investigation of what went wrong, the magazine's editorial staff claimed that the information came from a confidential source that had been reliable in the past. In addition to violence it caused, the incident damaged the reputation of *Newsweek* (and American media in general) and inflamed the tensions that already existed between Islamic and non-Islamic nations.

In 2015, the news-pop culture magazine *Rolling Stone* retracted a story it had published the previous year about an alleged gang rape in a fraternity house at University of Virginia. Based largely on the account of one female student, identified only as "Jackie," the story resulted in the fraternity being suspended even before campus and off-campus law-enforcement agencies could begin an independent investigation.

The Washington Post attempted to do a follow-up story and was unable to confirm the details of the original article. *Post* reporters did learn, however, that the author of the story did not contact members of the fraternity in order to include their side of the story.

Rolling Stone publisher Jann Wenner asked the Columbia School of Journalism to investigate what went wrong and suggest changes to the magazine's editorial procedures, including fact-checking the work of its reporters and freelance contributors. A senior administrator at the university, charging that the article implied that she did not take the charges seriously, won a defamation suit against the magazine and the article's author. The fraternity mentioned in the story reached an out-of-court settlement with the magazine.

In 2017, Cable News Network (CNN) broadcast an erroneous story claiming that presidential adviser Anthony Scaramucci had met with Russian investment bankers to seek financial support for Donald Trump's 2016 presidential campaign. Other members of Trump's team admitted having met with other Russian officials and private citizens, but the one about Scaramucci was wrong. Embarrassed by the error, CNN apologized to Scaramucci, retracted the story, and accepted the resignations of three employees.

The network also claimed to have conducted an internal investigation of the incident but did not release the results. The damage to CNN's reputation was compounded when a video surfaced of a network executive talking about the coverage of Trump's alleged connection to Russia being "ratings-driven."[10] For Trump, his communications staff, and his supporters, the blunder provided more fuel for their anti-media stance. Both Trump and press secretary Sarah Sanders called the story "another example of fake news by the failing media."[11]

Errors occurring in online editions are a bit more difficult to clarify, correct, or retract. At minimum, the newspaper is obligated to correct the text of the story so that readers finding it in the future will not see the error. However, some readers may have already made a printout of the original story and may not see the corrected version. In order to increase the likelihood of readers knowing about the correction, many online newspapers include corrections on its electronic front page that remains there for several days (unlike the print version, which would run the correction only one time).

Reasons Behind the Errors

Here are some of the reasons often cited to explain the frequency of errors:

The Need for Speed

On March 30, 1981, the national media falsely reported that press secretary James Brady had been killed in an assassination attempt on President Reagan. Though seriously wounded, he was very much alive; the media corrected the information within the hour.[12]

On January 3, 2006, several broadcast news outlets erroneously reported that of thirteen miners trapped for two days in a collapsed coal mine in West Virginia, twelve had been rescued alive. National newspapers had even printed the news on their front pages that landed on front porches on the morning of January 4. It turned out the media had the numbers backward: twelve miners had died and one survived.[13]

In January 2011, Arizona Congresswoman Gabrielle Giffords was shot at a public event in Tucson. Within a few hours, National Public Radio reported on the air, on its website, and by its Twitter account that the congresswoman had died. Other media then reported Gifford's death, based on the NPR report. Although seriously wounded, Giffords was still alive, prompting all of the affected media to correct the error and apologize to both their audiences and the Giffords family. Giffords' husband, astronaut Mark Kelly, was on his way from Houston to Tucson by private plane when he was informed of his wife's "death" and did not learn for several hours that she had survived the shooting.

On December 14, 2012, the national media reported that twenty-four-year-old Ryan Lanza had gone into Sandy Hook Elementary School in Newtown, Connecticut and killed twenty students, six adults, and himself. It turned out that at the time, Ryan Lanza was seventy-six miles away in Hoboken, New Jersey. The killer was his twenty-year-old brother, Adam, who was carrying Ryan's wallet and identification cards. In the aftermath of the misidentification, media critics urged journalists to not report names of suspects unless they came from official sources. In the Sandy Hook case, the erroneous identification came from sources not authorized to disclose such information. In addition to erroneously naming the shooter's brother as the suspect, many media outlets also identified the mother, Karen Lanza, as a teacher at the school (she wasn't) and reported that the shooter was allowed into the school (he shot his way through locked doors).[14]

In April 2013, the media made numerous errors in reporting on the bombing that took place near the finish line of the Boston Marathon. Within minutes, the media reported that twelve people had been killed, but later had to correct themselves—the real number was only three. Television networks then aired surveillance camera footage showing preliminary suspects who law-enforcement agencies had already cleared of any involvement. The following day, the media erroneously reported that an arrest had been made in the case, but then corrected themselves.

Smaller Staffs and Fewer Editors

Until the 1970s, most daily newspapers employed proofreaders (in addition to editors) who pored over each paragraph of the newspaper, making spelling and typographical errors rare. Newspaper historians called them the "last line of defense" against errors, as they were the last staffers to see the paper before it went to press. As computers replaced linotype operators, copyeditors replaced proofreaders. Because they were also responsible for writing headlines and photo captions, checking abbreviations and capitalization against a stylebook, and making sure articles were not libelous, copyeditors did not pay as much attention to factual details as their predecessors. When the number of copyeditors was cut in half in the 1990s, the number of spelling and numerical errors making into final editions grew in the opposite direction.[15]

News magazines once employed fact-checkers in addition to copyeditors, but at many publications those jobs have been combined. In 1996, *Newsweek* eliminated the position entirely and switched to a system in which reporters were responsible for checking their own facts.[16]

Lack of Newsroom Diversity

One of the major advantages of having a diverse newsroom is that reporters from different backgrounds will do a better job of reporting on issues related to their backgrounds. Black reporters, for example, will be less likely (compared to their white counterparts) to make errors when reporting on issues related to black families, black-owned businesses, or histori-cally black communities, universities, or churches. Likewise, female reporters are likely to have a greater understanding and make fewer errors (compared to their male counterparts) on stories related to women's health or workplace issues.

Lack of Competence in Math, Science, and History

"Math phobia" is especially problematic in business reporting. Many young reporters often don't understand stock-market terminology and some lack the basic skills to understand a company's profit and loss statement.[17]

In the 1980s, the publisher of *Florida Trend*, the state's leading business publication, was so exasperated at the frequency of errors in the monthly publication that he ordered that all new hires be experienced financial journalists.[18]

In the area of statistics, reporters stating that Candidate A holds a slim lead over Candidate B because polls show him or her ahead 45 to 42 percent might not have looked at the poll's margin for error. If the margin for error is three points (a common margin for political polls), the race is considered a statistical tie.[19]

In science news, reporters new to the beat often confuse malaria and typhoid fever; confuse temperature scales for Fahrenheit, Celsius, and centigrade; confuse grams, milligrams, and kilograms; and confuse the accomplishments of physicist Isaac Newton and astronomer Galileo. In many such cases, the reluctance to ask clarifying questions of their sources leads to errors.[20]

Reporters unfamiliar with American history (and reluctant to check facts) often confuse or interchange the accomplishments and famous quotes of the Founding Fathers and other great Americans. For example, Thomas Jefferson was the author of the Declaration of Indepen-dence and fifteen years later James Madison authored the Bill of Rights, but those accom-plishments are often reversed. Journalists also confuse Nathan Hale (who said, "I only regret that I have but one life to give for my country") and Patrick Henry (who said, "Give me liberty or give me death"). The accomplishments of Benjamin Franklin and Alexander Hamilton are also confused. Quotes from physicist Albert Einstein are often interchanged with those of novelist Mark Twain—even though the two lived at different times and worked in different fields. The careers of newspaper publishers Joseph Pulitzer and William Randolph Hearst are often confused with each other.

Failure to Fact-Check

When songwriter Paul Van Valkenburgh died in 2006, an Associated Press reporter wrote his obituary based entirely on a telephone interview with his widow. The woman erroneously told the reporter her late husband wrote the 1960s song "Itsy Bitsy Teenie Weenie Yellow Polka Dot Bikini." After the story was published, the real author of the song complained, forcing the AP to publish a correction and apologize to the song's living author.[21]

In many cases, errors result from statistics being casually tossed out by politicians or public officials and reported in the media by journalists who don't make the effort to verify them. In 2007, for example, Attorney General Alberto Gonzalez said in a speech that at any given moment, more than 50,000 sexual predators were prowling the Internet looking for young victims. When a reporter asked where he got that number, he attributed it to a segment he saw on NBC's *Dateline*. The network, in turn, attributed the number to a retired FBI agent who called it a "Goldilocks number—not too big and not too small."[22]

Nonprofit organizations are often accused of overstating statistics in order to generate more public attention or help in fund-raising. One nonprofit study reported that more than 19 percent of all teenagers had received sexually explicit messages from strangers online, while more scientific studies carried out by university researchers found that the real number was about 3 percent and was actually declining.[23] When journalists repeat the statistics without checking with another source, and then other journalists get their statistics from old stories, errors can be repeated for years.

Carelessness (Spellcheck Won't Catch Everything)

Edward H. Tenner, professor of technology at Princeton University, blames many media errors on the "bias on convenience" or "the law of least effort," meaning that people tend to be satisfied with the answers that are the easiest to obtain.[24] Ron Nessen, a correspondent for NBC News before he become President Gerald Ford's press secretary, adds that "some stories are too good to check" and "you don't want to spend too much time checking some stories because you don't want to find out you're wrong."[25]

In the last two decades, carelessness is combined with the "need for speed" to produce repeated spelling errors. The most commonly misspelled proper names have belonged to Florida Governor Charlie Crist (sometimes spelled Charley Christ), pop artist Jackson Pollock (often spelled Pollack), comedian Dan Aykroyd (often spelled Akroid) and tobacco company Philip Morris (sometimes spelled with an extra "l"). Evangelist James Dobson and sportswriter James Dodson have both complained that their names and accomplishments are often confused.

Other common mistakes involve the first names of private individuals such as Sara and Sarah, Caroline and Carolyn, Mathew and Matthew, Caitlin and Katelyn, Debra and Deborah, John and Jon, Brian and Bryan, and Kelly and Kelli. And then there's Kristin, Kristen, Kirstin, and Kirsten; as well as Kristy, Kristie, Christy, and Christie. Last names ending in "ing," "eng," "ins," and "ens" are often wrong.

Many mistakes, especially in direct quotations, result from accidentally dropping qualifiers such as "not" from phrases such as "not connected" or the prefix "un" from words such as "unrelated." Some journalists also have problems with commonly used words that contain double letters, including *parallel* and *personnel*.

Because newspapers make so many typographical errors in phone numbers, copyeditors make it a practice to call numbers to double-check them before they are published. *The Florida Times-Union* in Jacksonville, Florida, put the policy in place after transposed digits resulted in the publication of the 1-800 number for a phone-sex service instead of one for a nonprofit organization.[26]

Some examples of carelessness are not only embarrassing but also hurtful. In 2006, the *Rocky Mountain News* in Colorado published its annual fall high school football preview. In a listing of "players to watch" that fall, it listed seventeen-year-old Devon Knight as an up-and-coming star for Horizon High School, even though he had been killed in a car crash four months earlier.[27]

Other errors were dangerous. A May 1997 issue of *Newsweek* included a recipe for homemade baby food that suggested using chunks of raw carrots as food for infants. After pediatricians pointed out the choking hazard that would result from infants eating that type of food, the magazine issued a warning in the following week's issue.[28]

Ego, Arrogance, and the Infallibility Syndrome

"Reporters and editors make mistakes," wrote media scholar Jeff Jarvis in the foreword to Silverman's book. "People are fallible, but we journalists too often believe we are not. Indeed, we are probably more likely than most to make mistakes. Just as bartenders break more glass because they handle more beer, journalists who traffic in facts are bound to drop some along the way. It is time for journalists to trade in our hubris and recapture humanity and humility. And the best way to do that is simply to admit that we make mistakes."[29]

Ariel Hart, an Atlanta-based freelance fact-checker, concurs. "I think some reporters and their editors start to believe that unless a reader or listener telephones with a correction, they've made no mistakes," Hart wrote in an article in *Columbia Journalism Review*. "Then enough time goes by and they think they've gotten beyond mistakes."[30]

The term "infallibility syndrome" was coined by University of Central Florida Professor Ron F. Smith. In his 2008 journalism ethics textbook, Smith provided the example of a sportswriter who argued with his editor over the correct spelling of the name of a high school, with the sportswriter continuing to insist that he was right even after the editor showed him a photograph of the name of the school on the front of the players' uniforms.[31]

The syndrome may be an even larger deterrence for broadcast journalists, who researchers report correcting errors far less often than their print counterparts. "Many [television] news directors believe admitting mistakes might cause viewers to lose confidence in their news," wrote Andrea Miller, a University of Missouri doctoral student in a 2002 research paper.[32]

Getting Caught Up in the Story or Wanting to Maintain the Narrative

Sometimes journalists have been following a story for so long they believe they can predict what will happen next and may not even notice when the old narrative can't be supported. In its final regular-season football game of 2013, for example, Auburn University beat its archrival, the University of Alabama, on the final play of the game. As the two teams prepared to play again the following year, sportswriters repeatedly asked the Alabama head coach, assistant coaches, and players if they looked at the event as a "revenge game." All of those interviewed provided similar answers to the repeated questions: "Last year was last year. This year is this year. It's not a revenge game. We're only thinking about this year's game." But when the day of the game came, the headline on several newspaper stories read, "Alabama Seeks Revenge Against Auburn."

Ombudsmen and Public Editors

Throughout the latter half of the 1900s, many major daily newspapers employed individuals known as **ombudsmen** or **public editors** who were assigned to play "devil's advocate" by representing the interests of the readers in newsroom discussions of content decisions and field readers' complaints submitted by mail, email, telephone, and in person. Many found the latter function to be effective in preventing lawsuits for defamation and invasion of privacy because they were able to diffuse situations before they became volatile.

In a 2004 journal article, media scholars Lisa H. Newton, Louis Hodges, and Susan Keith suggested that one role of the ombudsman would be to convene periodic meetings among editors and reporters to discuss reader concerns about accuracy, bias, and the conduct of reporters. They analogized the role of the newspaper ombudsman to the internal affairs offices within police departments and the periodic "M&M" (morbidity and mortality) conferences held among hospital administrators.[33]

At many newspapers, ombudsmen compile statistics on errors, labeling them as low, medium, or high and placing them in categories such as misspellings, misattributions, incorrect statistics, or fact errors. On their spreadsheets, ombudsmen would also list causes (reporter error, source error, editing error) as well as how errors were discovered (complaint from the source, complaint by a reader, etc.) Since newspapers went public with their websites, many have encouraged readers to point out errors by emailing the ombudsman or public editor.

While some of these individuals are criticized as performing a superficial or "public relations" function, the majority are recognized as performing an important role as liaisons between media organizations and their audiences. The position is an ideal one for a semi-retired reporter or editor wishing to work part-time and stay in touch with the newspaper business.

While many media outlets have assigned specific staff members to handle audience complaints and requests for clarifications and corrections, few have formal policies dealing with how they approach the process. The wide variety of complaints and requests they receive call for dealing with each case on its own merits. But most agree that complaints from audience members be dealt with quickly, professionally, and courteously.

Smaller newspapers, instead of employing a specific person to carry out that responsibility, spread it among all of their reporters and editors by listing their telephone numbers and email addresses either below their bylines or at the bottom of their stories. National Public Radio has both a corrections editor, who deals with specific requests to clarifications and corrections, and an ombudsman, who deals with larger quality control issues such as accusations of bias.

The *Louisville Courier-Journal* is believed to have been the first American newspaper to experiment with the idea of an ombudsman, establishing the position in 1967. Among other newspapers, the idea reached its peak of popularity in the 1980s.

At *The Washington Post*, the position of ombudsman has had a lengthy and successful history. One of the position's earliest occupants, Bill Green, was the staffer who first alerted editors to inconsistencies in a Pulitzer Prize-winning story written by reporter Janet Cooke. His work led to an investigation of the "Jimmy's World" story, which turned out to be mostly fictional and caused the *Post* to fire Cooke and return the prize (see Chapter 4).

The New York Times created the position of "reader representative" after the Jayson Blair plagiarism scandal of 2003. After the recession of 2008–09, large daily newspapers such as *The Washington Post* and *The New York Times* maintained the position, but about half of the daily newspapers in the U.S. eliminated it.[34]

When Jeff Bezos purchased the *Post* in 2013, he announced a re-organization of the newsroom and elimination of dozens of newsrooms jobs, and when ombudsman Patrick Pexton left the *Post* to work as a freelance writer and consultant, he feared the position would be eliminated. That was not the case, but in the five years since he left, the position has turned over numerous times, and the authority of the position has been weakened.

The Debate over Confidential Sources

Most reporters and editors use the term "anonymous sources," but the more correct term is "confidential sources."[35]

Early in his presidency, Donald Trump followed the tradition of his predecessors in railing against the media's use of confidential sources and his own frustration with leaks in his administration. But media scholars point out that Trump, his supporters, and many Americans not employed by media organizations misunderstand how confidential sources work. *Wilmington Star-News* Executive Editor Pam Sander pointed out in a 2017 column that her newspaper—and the majority of others—don't use confidential sources nearly as often as the public believes they do. Unlike tabloid newspapers and conspiracy-based social media pseudo-news sites, mainstream newspapers use confidential sources only as a last resort. "Reporters and editors hate confidential sources," Sander wrote. "We strive to get all the information on the record. We set the bar very high for confidential sourcing. If the person won't go on the record, the reporter uses their information as background and find others who will go on the record to substantiate it. If not, the story doesn't run."[36] Ana Walker, editor of the *Longview News-Journal* in Texas, says, "We might as well be writing fiction if you can't give our readers a source."[37]

The National Public Radio News Code of Ethics and Practices allows for the use of anonymous sources only as a last resort and only in cases in which there is a significant need for the information the individual requesting anonymity has a genuine reason for doing so. The Radio Television Digital News Association Code of Ethics states that the "anonymity of sources deprives the audience of important, relevant information."

Ken Paulson, former editor of *USA Today*, recognizes the need to occasionally use confidential sources but only in limited circumstances. "The bookkeeper who sees assets wasted or stolen would never speak up without protection," Paulson told a researcher with *American Journalism Review*. "A witness to police brutality or malfeasance is never going to come forward unless they're secure that they won't be identified." Ironically, Paulson was hired at *USA Today* to restore the newspaper's reputation after the 2003–04 Jack Kelley scandal (see Chapter 4), which was blamed in part on the use of confidential sources.[38]

The use of confidential sources has been blamed for numerous plagiarism scandals, including those involving Jayson Blair at *The New York Times* and Kelley at *USA Today*. As a result, those newspapers reduced the use of confidential sources by 75 percent.[39]

In addition, an erroneous story about the alleged mistreatment of detainees at Guantanamo Bay in Cuba, published in *Newsweek* in 2005, was also blamed on the use of confidential sources.[40]

Ironically, in 2005, the *Washington Post* media critic blasted *USA Today* for using too many anonymous sources, yet used anonymous sources in that same column.[41]

In its formative years, *USA Today* had a strict policy that forbade the use of confidential sources, a directive from founder Al Neuharth. That position has softened under subsequent publishers. Today, *USA Today* and many other mainstream newspapers have policies that "discourage but don't forbid" the practice.[42]

When deciding whether to use confidential sources, reporters and editors typically consider the following five factors.

The Importance of the Story

Nearly every discussion about confidential sources begins with the example of Bob Woodward and Carl Bernstein of the *Washington Post*. In the early 1970s, the two young reporters used confidential sources in breaking their story about Watergate, a political scandal that resulted in the resignation of President Richard Nixon and changed the nature of investigative journalism for decades. Without such sources, the reporters and their editors claim, their stories would not have been as complete, and the misconduct of the Nixon administration might not have been exposed.

In his own memoirs, however, Executive Editor Ben Bradlee expressed regret over having approved the use of confidential sources, believing the reporters could have worked harder to find on-the-record sources and worrying that the precedent it set was not good for the journalism business.[43] Bradlee remained skeptical until the end of his career, telling reporters they should be used "only as a last resort, only if the information can be verified by another source, and only when the story cannot be told any other way."[44]

Bradlee once told an academic researcher that "we shudder at the thought of withholding the name of a bank robber, a party giver, or a campaign contributor … so why do we go along so complacent withholding the identity of public officials? By doing so we shamelessly do other people's bidding. We knowingly let ourselves be used for obvious trial balloons and for personal attacks. In short, we demean our profession."[45]

The Motives of the Source

Although seldom capable of reading minds, journalists and their editors need to consider the possible motives of the sources who are willing to provide information but insist on not being identified. Is the individual performing a public service? Is the person seeking revenge against a political opponent, business competitor, or former employer? Is he or she attempting to advance his or her own interests?

But just because reporters and editors determine a negative motive does not mean the individual is disqualified as a source, but it should signal the need for additional scrutiny in order to verify the accuracy of the information. In some cases, reporters and editors may conclude that the significance of the story (along with additional verification) outweighs any concerns about the motives of a confidential source.

One danger when dealing with public officials is that a member of his or her staff may pretend to be "leaking" information but may actually be floating a "trial balloon" on behalf of the official. Using this strategy, the source provides information about a preliminary idea and describes it in a way that makes it sound like it is being considered more seriously than it actually is.

If the journalist takes the bait and publishes the "leaked" information, the staff will monitor public reaction. If the reaction is positive, the proposal moves forward; if it is negative, the official discards the proposal and claims it was never a serious idea to begin with. Reporters don't like being used in this way, but many admit that it is part of the give-and-take of covering public officials. If they don't play along, they worry, the trial balloons will be floated somewhere else, and they will miss out on valid stories.

The Reason Behind the Request for Confidentiality

Why is the promise of confidentiality important to the source? Does he or she have a legitimate reason to be concerned about his or her safety or that of his or her family? Or is he or she simply trying to accomplish one of the motives listed above while enjoying the cloak of confidentiality?

One example of the appropriate use of confidential sources is the case of "whistle-blowers" who provide information on government waste and corruption or illegal activities of businesses. In these cases, sources ask not to be identified because they fear losing their jobs or placing in danger their own lives or the lives of their families.

Track Records of the Source and Reporter

Has the source provided reliable information in the past? Has the reporter made good decisions about his or her use of confidential sources in the past?

Alternative Sources for the Same Information

Can reporters find the same information from on-the-record sources? Because of the increased level of confidence and credibility involved when sources agree to be identified, most editors will encourage reporters to exhaust all other possible sources for finding the same information before going along with a source's request for confidentiality.

Editors and media ethicists who oppose the use of confidential sources cite two reasons to support their positions.

The first consideration is the relative credibility of named and unnamed sources. Sources who agree to be quoted by name in a newspaper story or have their names and faces shown during television interviews are automatically considered more credible (by both journalists and their audiences) than those who do not. Information from sources who insist on not being identified by name in a newspaper story or not appearing on camera in a television story is treated with some degree of skepticism.

The second factor is the potential for individuals to use the media to advance personal grudges against former employers or damage the campaigns of political opponents.

In the rare cases that use of a confidential source is approved, journalists should be careful when using labels such as "a source close to the investigation" and "a person in the governor's office," as too specific a label might result in other persons being able to guess the person's identity.

Closely related to the debate over confidential sources are the concepts of "off the record," "not for attribution," "on background," and "on deep background."

Off the record means that a person provides information, but is not quoted and the information is not used unless it is confirmed by other (on the record) sources. Most reporters and editors are skeptical of any information obtained under these circumstances, but many accept such conditions because those interviews often prevent the reporter from making serious mistakes.

Not for attribution means the source's words appear within quote marks, but the attribution reads "said a source familiar with the negotiations" or "said an individual requesting his name be withheld." Most newspapers have policies of using "not for attribution" sparingly, worried that excessive use of those phrases causes readers to be skeptical about the information. Sometimes the phrases used to describe "not for attribution" sources are so detailed that they give away the person's identity, sometimes intentionally.

In another cases, sources request anonymity even though they know their quotes will recognized. In the 1920s, for example, President Calvin Coolidge was always willing to be quoted, but never directly. He told reporters to attribute his remarks to "White House sources." Reporters covering the president obliged, but added their own twists to narrow down the speculation. One reporter using Coolidge quotes attributed them to "a mythical White House source" and another described the source as "a thin, sandy-haired, small-mouthed, solemn little Vermonter."[46]

In the early 1970s, Secretary of State Henry Kissinger was famous for giving media interviews during which he asked journalists to identify him as a "high-ranking State Department official traveling on the Secretary of State's airplane."[47]

On background means the sources are providing information that will not be quoted and is not directly related to the story. For example, an employee of a chemical or technology company might provide a journalist with a "crash course" in a particular scientific or technical topic in order to help the journalist understand what he or she is reporting about.

On deep background means the source does not volunteer any information, but simply agrees to review information the reporter already has and tell him or her whether or not it is correct.

Your Turn

Case Study 7: Clarifications, Corrections, and Retractions: Socialists and Enlarged Prostitutes

While retractions such as those are quite serious (but fortunately quite rare), some minor errors requiring only corrections and apologies are actually humorous. A *Dallas Morning News* columnist once mistakenly referred to a local citizen as a "socialist." She apologized to the woman in a subsequent column, clarifying that she meant to write "socialite." The daily newspaper *The East Oregonian* published a story about an Oakland Athletics pitcher who threw equally well right- and left-handed. The headline on the story identified the pitcher as "amphibious," when it should have read, "ambidextrous."

ABC News anchor Peter Jennings once had to apologize to Federal Reserve Chairman Alan Greenspan, who he said was suffering from an "enlarged prostitute." Jennings meant he suffered from an "enlarged prostate."[48]

A 2004 article in the *Dallas Morning News* stated that songwriter John Bucchino couldn't read. It was corrected the next day to indicate that Bucchino "couldn't read music."[49]

A college newspaper story about Filipinos who immigrated to California in the 1850s indicated that the name of their boat, *Nuestra Senora de Buena Esperanza*, translated into English as "Big Ass Spanish Boat." In its next edition, the newspaper corrected its mistake and apologized to its readers and Filipino-Americans in the surrounding community who were offended. The name actually translates into "Our Lady of Good Hope." The newspaper staff admitted that it found the erroneous translation on the Internet, and with no Spanish-speaking students on the staff, it had no way of checking it.

Following the 2011 raid on the Pakistan hideout of terrorist Osama bin Laden by U.S. Navy Seals, journalists at a German television station searched Internet sources for more information on the Seals. They found what they believed to be the logo of the Navy Seals, but after the station used it as part of its coverage, viewers called the station to report that it had mistakenly used a logo from a fictional organization depicted in the television series *Star Trek: Deep Space Nine.* The erroneous logo included hi-tech weaponry, a Klingon skull, and other artifacts that exist only in the fictional world of the twenty-fourth century. Station managers apologized for the error but said they had no idea how the mix-up happened.

1. Because little harm results from some of minor errors such as these and the individuals involved usually recognize the humor in them, is there a temptation to take them less seriously?
2. Are there any philosophers or concepts from Chapter 2 that can be applied here?

Discussion Problem 7: Clarifications, Corrections, and Retractions: The Spring Break Story Too Good to Be True

You're the editor of your college newspaper. A few months ago, you received a news release from an out-of-state company offering "deep discount" spring break travel packages for college students. The release doesn't provide any contact information for media inquiries, but did include a toll-free phone number and web address for sales purposes. You give the news release to one of your lazier reporters, who then writes a story about it without any additional reporting or fact-checking—not even calling the toll-free number or looking at the company's website.

The students responding to the story paid for the trips six weeks in advance, but when they arrive at the airport for their trip, they find their airline tickets are worthless, as the flight numbers and other details printed on tickets aren't recognized by the airline's employees or computers. Some of the students then attempt to cancel their hotel reservations by phone, only to find the names and addresses of the hotel are fictional. They call the company that sold the packages and learn that it has gone out of business.

In the weeks that follow this incident, you're relieved to find out that students' credit card companies provide fraud protection and were able to refund their money. But it did raise some important questions.

1. To what extent was your student newspaper to blame for publishing the story without fact-checking it? Was it your responsibility to scrutinize the "too good to be true" news release, or is this another case of caveat emptor (let the buyer beware)?
2. What other examples of "accountability" (or lack of it) from this chapter are similar?

Discussion Questions

701. Earlier in this chapter was a description of "ombudsmen" and "reader advocates" whose job it is to field complaints and requests for clarifications and corrections. By creating full-time positions to do such work (instead of having newspaper editors and television station managers), what statement are they making? That they are seriously dedicated to addressing audience concerns? Or that they make so many mistakes that it requires a full-time person to deal with the results?

702. What philosophers or concepts from Chapter 2 can be applied to the issue of "accountability"?

Notes

1 Mitchell Charnley, "Preliminary Notes on a Study of Newspaper Accuracy." *Journalism Quarterly*, Vol. 13 (December 1936), pp. 394–401.
2 Gary Hanson and Stanley T. Wearden, "Measuring Newscast Accuracy: Applying a Newspaper Model to Television." *Journal of Mass Communication Quarterly*, Vol. 81, No. 3 (Fall 2004), pp. 546–558.

3 DeWitt C. Reddick, *The Mass Media and the Student Newspaper*. New York: Wadsworth Publishing (1985).

4 Lisa H. Newton, Louis Hodges, and Susan Keith, "Accountability in the Professions: Accountability in Journalism." *Journal of Mass Media Ethics*, Vol. 19, Nos. 3 and 4 (2004), pp. 166–190.

5 Craig Silverman, *Regret the Error*. New York: Sterling Publishing (2007), p. 78.

6 "National Public Radio News Code of Ethics and Practices." www.npr.org/about/ethics (accessed July 7, 2019).

7 Graham Webster, "He'll Make You Regret the Error, for All to See." *Editor & Publisher*, May 2005, pp. 14–15. See also: Craig Silverman, *Regret the Error*. New York: Sterling Publishing (2007), pp. 213–216.

8 Conrad Fink, *Media Ethics*. Boston: Allyn & Bacon (1995), p. 129.

9 Gardiner Harris, "State Department Spent $52,701 on Curtains for Residence of U.N. Envoy." *The New York Times*, September 13, 2018.

10 David Bauder, "Retracted CNN Story a Boon for the President." Associated Press report, June 28, 2017.

11 Bauder.

12 Dan Berkowitz and Zhengjia Liu, "'Media Errors and the Nutty Professor: Riding the Journalistic Boundaries of the Sandy Hook Shootings." *Journalism*, Vol. 17, No. 2 (2017), pp. 155–172.

13 Silverman, pp. 213–216.

14 Berkowitz and Liu.

15 Silverman, pp. 265–274.

16 Silverman, p. 286.

17 Silverman, p. 120.

18 Silverman, p. 120.

19 "Polls and Surveys." *Associated Press Stylebook and Briefing on Media Law*. New York: Associated Press (2019), pp. 351–356.

20 Hanson and Wearden.

21 Silverman, p. 143.

22 Douglas McCollam, "The Shame Game." *Columbia Journalism Review*, January/February 2007, pp. 28–33.

23 McCollam, pp. 28–33.

24 Howard Rosenberg and Charles S. Feldman, *No Time to Think: The Menace of Media Speed and the 24-Hour News Cycle*. New York: Continuum Books (2008), p. 8.

25 Rosenberg and Feldman, p. 8.

26 Silverman, p. 121.

27 Silverman, p. 252.

28 Silverman, p. 287.

29 Jeff Jarvis, "Foreword." *Regret the Error* by Craig Silverman. New York: Sterling Publishing (2007), p. ix.

30 Ariel Hart, "Delusions of Accuracy." *Columbia Journalism Review*, July/August 2003, p. 20.

31 Ron F. Smith, *Ethics in Journalism*. Malden, MA: Blackwell Publishing (2008), p. 67.

32 Silverman, p. 73.

33 Newton, Hodges, and Keith.

34 Rem Reider, "Ombudsman Still Has a Place in the Newsroom." *USA Today*, February 22, 2013, p. 3-B.

35 In social science research, "anonymous" means that no one (not even the researcher) knows the identity of research participants, while "confidential" means the researcher knows the participants' identity but is ethically prohibited from revealing it. Applying these definitions to journalism, nearly all unidentified sources are "confidential" rather than "anonymous" because no serious journalist would use sources without knowing their identity.

36 Pam Sander, "Anonymous Sourcing is Vital to Democracy." *Wilmington Star-News*, March 5, 2017, p. 1-C.

37 Joe Strupp, "Losing Confidence." *Editor & Publisher*, July 2005, pp. 32–39.

38 Rachel Smolkin, "Under Fire." *American Journalism Review*, February/March 2005, pp. 19–25.

39 Strupp.

40 Ben H. Bagdikian, "When the Post Banned Anonymous Sources." *American Journalism Review*, August/September 2005, p. 33.

41 Rachel Smolkin, "USA Tomorrow." *American Journalism Review*, August/September 2005, pp. 21–29.

42 Smolkin, "USA Tomorrow."

43 Smith, *Ethics in Journalism*, p. 175.

44 Strupp.

45 Donald McDonald, "Is Objectivity Possible?" In *Ethics and the Press*, John C. Merrill and Ralph D. Barney, ed. New York: Hastings House Publishing (1978). pp. 69-88.

46 Bill Monroe, "The Worst Job in Washington." *Columbia Journalism Review*, November/December 2000, pp. 77-79.

47 Ron F. Smith, *Groping for Ethics in Journalism*. Ames, IA: Wiley-Blackwell (2003),p. 181.

48 Silverman, p. 102.

49 Silverman, p. 15.

8 Ethical Issues in Advertising

Background

Advertising Venues and Categories

By its nature, advertising is a biased formed of communication. It either encourages audience members to take specific actions (often to purchase a product or service) or advocates a point of view, or both. Unlike journalism, it has never claimed to be a neutral or unbiased source of commercial or political information. As John Crichton, former president of the American Association of Advertising Agencies, once wrote:

> The seller sees a house he owns as it ought to be: "Brick colonial, 7 rooms, 2 baths, quiet neighborhood, old shade, gardens, brick patio." It never occurred to him that his ad might read, "Brick colonial, 7 small rooms, 2 baths of which one needs new tile, old trees but the elm is dying, gardens which require maintenance, brick patio which doesn't drain well, and a roof that will need replacement in two years."[1]

There are six major venues for advertising: print, broadcast, online, direct mail, outdoor, and transit. Those distinctions are important because those venues are subject to varying degrees of government regulation, and the ethical codes of different professional organizations apply. In addition to those labels, most advertising can be placed in one of three categories: **traditional retail advertising** (that encourages consumers to visit a retail establishment), **direct response advertising** (that encourages consumers to either call a toll-free telephone number or visit a website), and **behavioral advertising**, which matches online users to their interests based on their online activities.

Behavioral advertising is the newest and most controversial. Since the mid-1990s, programs embedded in electronic mail and social media programs (the most common is known as "cookies") have allowed marketers to develop profiles of individual Internet users, based simply on websites they visit, and sell that information to advertisers. A user visiting websites dealing with how to buy a new car would be presumed to be in the market for such a purchase, for example, and would likely be the target of pop-up ads and other unsolicited information from local car dealers. An individual who spends a lot of time reading golf news and following the results of professional golf tournaments online would likely begin receiving solicitations from local sporting goods stores highlighting their latest golf-related products.

Gmail, Google's free email program, targets advertising to computer users based on keywords that appear in outgoing email messages. Social networking sites such as Facebook, Twitter, and Instagram have employed similar techniques, and periodically make changes to their privacy policies in response to consumer complaints and threats of regulatory action by the Federal Trade Commission. Much of the technology is proprietary, and its creators are reluctant to explain how it works; they simply respond to the criticism by claiming that Internet users voluntarily give up part of their privacy when they use those email and social media platforms.

Legal and Ethical Framework

Much like other potential problem areas in mass communications, advertising is subject to both legal restrictions and ethical limitations. The Federal Trade Commission is the primary government agency in charge of regulating the advertising industry, but it prefers that advertisers voluntarily produce work that is tasteful, truthful, and in its correct context. The primary professional organizations providing ethical guidance are the American Advertising Federation (AAF) and the American Association of Advertising Agencies (AAAA).

The AAF Code is the most concise ethical code among those of the major professional organizations in the communications field, consisting of only 225 words and fitting neatly onto one page. It requires that advertising content reflect the truth, avoid misleading consumers, and be in good taste. The code also prohibits bait-and-switch advertising and false comparisons and advises members to be cautious in developing advertisements that involve testimonials, price claims, guarantees, and warranties.

The AAAA Standards of Practice, also quite concise, simply prohibits five specific actions, all related to the content of advertising: (1) false or misleading statements or exaggerations, (2) testimonials which do not reflect the real opinion of the individual(s) involved, (3) price claims which are misleading, (4) claims insufficiently supported or that distort the true meaning of statements made by a scientific authority, and (5) statements, suggestions, or pictures offensive to public decency or minority members of the community.

Many issues facing advertising agencies are not based on whether a specific activity or tactic is appropriate, but rather on billing practices. Such issues include whether the agency or the client should be responsible for cost overruns on a project and whether the client will be billed for extra work required because of a mistake made by the agency or other vendor. Most such problems can be prevented by listing those contingencies in the contract, but few contracts are that detailed. And problems that are never addressed in contracts include the client asking the agency to perform personal work (such as providing airport transportation) and billing the agency, or the agency understating the cost of a project during the bidding process in order to win the account but then submitting bills for a substantially higher cost.[2]

Government Regulation

The history of commercial advertising in the United States (and efforts to regulate it) can be divided into three time periods.

Throughout much of 1800s, American merchants promoted their products through newspaper and magazine advertisements and flyers distributed door-to-door and displayed in public gathering places. Advertisers often made exaggerated or entirely fictional claims, and with little regulation by government agencies or professional regulatory organizations, consumers who were misled or cheated had little recourse. The Latin term **caveat emptor** ("let the buyer beware") was the guiding principle.

In the early 1900s, the pendulum swung to the opposite extreme, as state governments adopted advertising regulations that were collectively known as "printer's ink statutes," named after a suggested model published in *Printer's Ink* magazine in 1911. Most of those laws resulted in fines rather than imprisonment, but enforcement was vigorous. In 1914, Congress created the Federal Trade Commission (FTC), but it did not become a major authority in advertising regulation until Congress passed a series of consumer protection laws in the 1960s and 1970s and put the FTC in charge of enforcing them. Many of those laws were introduced by Senators Philip Hart and William Proxmire, who claimed that their interest was driven by complaints from their constituents about the distortion and untruthfulness found in both print and broadcast advertising.

In addition to the FTC, numerous other federal government agencies regulate advertising to a lesser extent. Those agencies and their areas of authority include:

- The Federal Communications Commission regulates television and radio advertising.
- The Federal Elections Commission regulates political advertising.
- The Food and Drug Administration regulates the advertising of food and pharmaceuticals.
- The Department of Housing and Urban Development regulates housing and real estate advertising.
- The Environmental Protection Agency requires car manufacturers to include gas mileage figures in their advertising.
- The Civil Aeronautics Board regulates airline advertising.
- The U.S. Postal Service establishes and enforces regulations on the proportion of advertising-to-news in newspapers, magazines, and newsletters sent through the mail; the higher the percentage of advertising, the higher the mailing cost.

While the FTC, state consumer protection agencies, and the court system attempt to protect consumers from blatantly false and misleading advertising, scholars who study the advertising industry assert that consumers bear some responsibility for protecting themselves by being skeptical of questionable advertising claims. In addition, court rulings have found that some commercial speech has value far beyond the promotion of products and services; it also provides consumers with important information to assist them in their purchasing decisions. By providing this limited First Amendment protection to advertising, the courts are protecting not only the advertisers' right to disseminate that information, but also the consumers' right to receive it.

Today, in addition to the FTC's regulations on advertising in general, all fifty states have revised their consumer-protection laws (originally passed in the early and mid-1900s) and added new ones that regulate advertising at the state level. At the county and city level, advertising is regulated in the form of restrictions placed on handbills, illuminated signs, transit advertising, and outdoor advertising such as billboards and benches. The courts generally uphold such regulations after determining that they do not violate the First Amendment.

Issues and Controversies

False and Deceptive Advertising

While the Federal Trade Commission has the responsibility for enforcing "truth in advertising" laws on a national level and most states have similar mechanisms in place for regulating advertising, numerous "watchdog" groups also scrutinize the industry and apply many of the same terms as the FTC and state agencies, including "false" and "deceptive."

What is the difference between an advertisement that is "false" and one that is merely "deceptive"? The dividing line is somewhat murky, but here are some examples that may help to clarify the difference.

An advertisement is considered "false" if it makes claims that are not true, such as those related to a product's ability to produce a certain result that in reality it cannot. In order to substantiate such a claim of false advertising, however, the FTC, state agency, or watchdog group would have to prove that the advertiser knew the product's true characteristics but published or broadcast the advertisement nevertheless.

Other examples of outright false advertising include the inclusion of fictional endorsements or test results, such as "doctors recommend eating product X daily" (if no such recommendation was made) or "scientists at University X tested our product and found that…" (if no such tests were actually conducted).

Conversely, an advertisement is merely "deceptive" if it makes no false statements, yet leaves out important information or is otherwise misleading. One example is the presentation of case studies showing results of product use without mentioning the length of time required; without such information the audience might infer that results are immediate. Another example is found in the advertisement that claims that product A costs less than product B, yet omits the fact that product A is sold in 32-ounce bottles while product B is sold in 48-ounce bottles.

To determine if an advertisement is deceptive, the FTC uses the **reasonable consumer standard**, meaning that each advertisement in question would be evaluated according to the likelihood that a "reasonable consumer" would be deceived. FTC guidelines clarifies that an advertisement would not be deemed to be deceptive if "only a few gullible consumers would be deceived." The FTC admits that a company "cannot be liable for every possible reading of its claims, no matter how far-fetched," and that the law "could not help a consumer who thinks that all french fries are imported from France or that Danish pastry actually comes from Denmark."[3]

In the 1970s, the FTC won deceptive advertising cases against consumer product companies that made misleading product claims and financial services companies that made dubious claims about their products.

Some of the more egregious product claims in history—all shot down by the FTC or consumer watchdog groups—include those for baby formula that claimed it prevented children from getting allergies, a smartphone app that could prevent users from the onset of Alzheimer's disease, a fruit juice that could cure erectile dysfunction, chewing gum that could prevent bad breath, a breakfast cereal that could lower cholesterol, and pet food that could extend an animal's life by 30 percent.[4]

Today, the most common areas for regulatory scrutiny are food products and nonprescription or "over-the-counter" (OTC) drugs. The FTC shares that responsibility with the Food and Drug Administration, and in numerous cases, those agencies have required manufacturers to either withdraw or substantially revise print and broadcast advertisements. Examples of ads the FTC and FDA found problematic were those claiming certain foods or OTC products could help in weight loss or the prevention of diseases or other health problems without providing proof of those benefits. The FTC, FDA, and consumer watchdog groups uses the term "sound scientific basis" to refer to the advertisers' burden of proof in documenting such claims.

"In areas like weight loss and exercise, consumers should be suspicious of any claim that sounds fast or easy," says Mary Engle, head of the FTC's Advertising Practices Division. "The company may have a small study or rely on some science, but the claims are so greatly exaggerated beyond what the product can actually do."[5]

The FTC and FDA are also skeptical about promotional phrases used on packaging and in advertising copy such as "new and improved," vitamin-enriched," and "special formula." One of the newest phrases causing regulatory problems for the makers of OTC drugs is "prescription strength." The term implies that the dosage provided is the same as the dosage in the prescription form of the drug, but upon checking, many such OTC drugs claiming to be "prescription strength" actually include less than half the number of milligrams found in the prescription version. In a similar case, one major drug manufacturer was recently ordered by the FDA to stop using the phrase "next generation" to refer to products unless they could document significant improvements over previous versions.

Another factor that advertisers must approach with caution is the inclusion of research information derived from government tests or reports. For example, if the Department of Transportation performs crash-test studies to determine which new cars are the safest and mentions that a specific product is either at or near the top, the manufacturer can quote that report in its advertising but must be careful to present the information fairly. The ad can claim that Car X was ranked first in its category or finished in the top ten for three years in a row (if true). The ad cannot, however, state or imply that the Department of Transportation encourages consumers to buy Car X, because the DOT is a neutral government agency and does not make such endorsements.

Watchdog groups caution consumers against responding to ads that suggest that consumers must respond quickly, such as those that use terms such as "limited time offer," as those "deadlines" are often extended for years. "When people feel a sense of urgency, they don't process or scrutinize information correctly," said Brent Brien, a spokesperson for the American Consumer Protection Group.[6]

In addition to being scrutinized by the FTC, advertisements making questionable claims can also result in legal action being taken by competing companies. Early in 2005, for example, a manufacturer of dental floss filed suit against a company that claimed its mouthwash was as effective as dental floss in reducing plaque and gum disease (see Case Study 8F).

In 2009, St. Louis University Hospital in Missouri claimed in its advertising that it was the "official" hospital for the St. Louis Rams, the city's National Football League team. Other hospitals in the city contended that was false advertising, as injured players were actually treated at other local hospitals. Officials for the team and SLUH denied the charges and pointed out that nowhere in the ads did the hospital claim a role in treating Rams players or other employees. Instead, they claimed the advertisements represented a "marketing agreement," but the other hospitals contended that most readers would infer that the hospital treated Rams players. The case never went to court. After the controversy, the *St. Louis Post-Dispatch* conducted a survey of all thirty-two NFL teams, as well as teams from other major professional sports, and found that more than half maintained "marketing agreements" with hospitals in the communities in which they were located. It found no other cases in which the designated "official hospital" was one that did not also treat the team's players.

The FTC regulates usage of the phrase "manufacturer's suggested retail price" (MSRP) and admonishes retailers not to use those words casually in their advertising. The FTC requires that the MSRP must be determined by the manufacturer rather than the retailer. In some cases, however, retailers use the term with an asterisk and a disclaimer that reads, "this price is only an estimate; no actual products may have been sold at this price."

A related issue is the tendency of discount or outlet stores to use price tags that show the price of the item at that store along with a "compare with" price that suggests how much that item would sell for at traditional retail stores. In many cases, those items were never meant to be sold at those higher prices or at those other stores, as the cheaper items are of inferior quality, are made of cheaper materials, or show minor defects.[7]

The Debate over Product Placements

"Product placement" or "imbedded marketing" is a form of advertising in which a company's product appears in movies and on television programs as a prop or as part of the scenery. Products such as clothing, soft drinks or other food items, and automobiles often have their actual brand names visible because those companies have paid to have those products appear. It is a form of "indirect" or "subliminal" advertising that has become more popular in the last four decades because of home video recorders and other devices that allow viewers to bypass traditional commercials.

Advantages include the fact that viewers cannot avoid exposure to the message (unlike with traditional advertising, which viewers skip by leaving the room or fast-forwarding through a recorded program). In addition, advertisers report hearing about very few negative reactions to the subliminal messages.[8]

The history of product placement in motion pictures goes back to the early years of the twentieth century, when *Wings*, the first movie to win an Academy Award for Best Picture, featured a plug for Hershey's Chocolate, and the Marx Brothers film *Horse Feathers* featured Life Savers candy.

In 1954, Marlon Brando's wardrobe in the 1954 movie *The Wild Bunch* became part of the product-placement trend, even though it was not the result of a formal agreement. In the early 1950s, sales of blue jeans were limited because of the public perception that jeans were appropriate only for work in industrial settings. But after Brando wore jeans in a variety of non-work settings in the movie, that perception changed and blue-jean sales increased dramatically.

The modern era of paid product placement in television began in the 1970s. Prior to that decade, any time a soft drink was used in the movie, it was just a red-and-white can with no visible logo. Today, on both television programs and in the movies, audiences see actual products. More recently, the trend has spread to Broadway plays and video games.

Early examples of product placements on network television included Chevrolet automobiles on *The Rockford Files* and Nike clothing (and later Dockers) on *Cheers*.

Product placements became more popular in movies in the 1980s, when Reese's Pieces were consumed by an alien creature in *The Extraterrestrial*. Brown & Williamson Tobacco paid actor Sylvester Stallone $500,000 to smoke the company's cigarettes in his movies. Health-care organizations around the country called for a ban on product placements involving tobacco and alcohol, but lawmakers were reluctant to create such legislation because of First Amendment concerns.

The 1997 James Bond film *Tomorrow Never Dies* may have been the biggest product-placement revenue generator to date, reportedly bringing in more than $100 million from nine sponsors, including the manufacturers of alcoholic beverages, automobiles, computers, clothing, and watches seen in the film.[9]

Movie producers in Hollywood and around the world contend that revenue generated by product placement sales helps to recoup some of the cost of producing and marketing the film, compensating the talent in front of and behind the cameras, and offsetting the money lost by film piracy. From the sponsor's perspective, product placement in movies is riskier than investing in television programs, as the success of feature films is more difficult to predict.[10]

A recent example of product placement in television was seen in the CBS comedy *How I Met Your Mother*, during which a young couple discussed their future while dining at Red Lobster, one of the show's sponsors. Immediately following that scene was an actual commercial for the seafood restaurant. Another example was found on the set of *American Idol*, where judges in the singing competition were seen sipping Diet Coke (one of the program's primary advertisers) in between performances.

More recently, product placements have been seen in music videos such as those featuring Britney Spears, Jennifer Lopez, and Lady Gaga.

Although no one is referring to the trend of increasing numbers of product placements as a "controversy," some television producers have concerns about the practice. In a 2006 interview, producers for the hit programs *ER* and *Law & Order* complained that as serious dramatists, they're concerned about the interference of commercialism into what they believe are products of art. They suggested that product placements are more appropriate for situation comedies, which most viewers take much less seriously. They are also concerned about potential artistic limitations that advertising commitments might place on their work. In a hospital or crime drama, for example, will an automobile manufacturer insist that its product be shown only in a positive light, and never involved in a crash or used in the commission of a crime?

Television and film producers don't always get it right with product placements. In an episode of the television drama *The West Wing*, a flashback scene showed a character using a pay telephone with the Verizon logo. The scene was said to have taken place in 1997—three years before the company was created. And the motion picture *Demolition Man* (produced in 1992 but set in 2032) featured an Oldsmobile—a placement for which the company paid. General Motors executives claimed their objective was to send a message to film audiences that their brand would be "alive and well" in 2032, but ironically, General Motors discontinued the brand in 2004.

In other cases, product placements are unintentional. During a 2019 episode of the HBO drama *Game of Thrones*, for example, viewers were amused to see a Starbucks coffee cup, left behind by a technician, in the picture. A representative of the company told CNBC that the gaffe may have been worth billions of dollars in free publicity, as it was mentioned on social media thousands of times in the week that followed. Rather than send Starbucks a bill, however, producers of the show decided to have the image digitally removed from the scene before the episode appeared in re-runs.[11]

Advertising of Controversial Products and Services

Based on decades of Supreme Court cases, neither the federal government nor state governments can prohibit the advertising of legal products or services. If a product is legal to manufacture, sell, purchase, or own (or if a service is legal to perform), no government agency or body can declare it illegal to advertise, except in unusual circumstances. Unless an advertisement is proven to be inaccurate, deceptive, or misleading; or there is a concern for public health or safety, the responsibility for regulation falls on the profession's codes of ethics, or numerous consumer watchdog groups.

The history of advertising regulation based on a concern for public health and safety dates back to the 1970s, when officials in Virginia attempted to punish a weekly newspaper for accepting advertising for a New York-based abortion clinic. At the time, a Virginia law prohibited the performing of abortions as well as the advertising of such services, even those provided in other states, where abortion was legal at the time. When the law was challenged, the U.S. Supreme Court ruled that because abortion was legal in the state in which they were performed, the newspaper had the right to accept the advertisement.

A decade later, advertising regulation was at issue in two other Supreme Court cases. In 1980, the court ruled in favor of an electric company that challenged a state law regarding the advertising of its services. The Court determined that nothing in the advertisements was untruthful or harmful. It also established a four-part test, known as the **Central Hudson Test**, for judging future advertising cases. The test established that in order to limit or prohibit an advertisement, a government agency must (1) prove that the ad is either inaccurate or associated with illegal products or services, (2) have a substantial interest in establishing the regulation, such as a concern for public health or safety, (3) demonstrate that the regulation serves that interest, and (4) show that regulation is sufficiently narrow. In 1988, one of the few cases in which the Central Hudson Test was successfully used to regulate advertising was in a case involving casinos on the island of Puerto Rico. The Court ruled that the government of that island territory had the right to regulate casino advertising because it agreed with the government's position that its regulation was based on the potential harm of gambling and its alleged connection to organized crime.

In most other cases, however, the courts have applied the "high burden of proof" principle and ruled that governments were unable to establish a connection between their advertising regulations and the desired effect. In a 1997 case, for example, the Supreme Court over-turned a Baltimore city ordinance prohibiting alcohol and tobacco advertising on billboards because the city failed to establish the link between the advertising of those products and underage drinking and smoking.

While the courts provide media organizations great latitude in making decisions about which ads to accept and reject, many voluntarily decline to sell advertising space or time to controversial interests such adult bookstores and video stores, fortune tellers, firearm sellers, practitioners of alternative forms of medicine, or employment or investment schemes they suspect might be fraudulent.

Many newspapers refuse to accept ads for massage parlors, escort services, and other businesses that are often fronts for prostitution, but not only because of the attitudes of their publishers or the sensibilities of their readers. In many cities, police departments place the "sex personals" ads as part of sting operations aimed at arresting prospective clients. Not wishing to be affiliated with what they view as potential entrapment, the newspapers simply ban all ads of that nature.[12]

The advertising of religious viewpoints has been controversial for decades, but it takes on a legal aspect when the advertising takes place in government-related venues such as public buses, bus terminals, subway trains, and subway platforms. Secular groups as the American Civil Liberties Union and Freedom from Religion Foundation (FFRF) oppose such advertising, claiming that it violates the First Amendment's establishment clause because it creates the appearance that the government is taking sides in religious debates. Most legal challenges are unsuccessful, however.[13]

Similar controversies occur when the FFRF and similar anti-religion groups sponsor their own ads to promote their secular viewpoints. In Fort Worth, Texas, for example, a consortium of religious leaders attempted to organize a boycott of the local transit system after it began accepting ads from a local atheist group in 2010. That effort was unsuccessful.[14]

When such advertising takes place in non-governmental venues such as highway billboards, those images are often vandalized, but law-enforcement agencies report that investigating such incidents are low priorities.[15]

Advertising that Implies Discrimination

In addition to being punished for publishing or broadcasting ads deemed to be false or deceptive, media outlets can also be punished for accepting ads that imply discrimination in housing or employment.

Before and during the civil rights movement of the 1960s, it was not uncommon to find newspaper employment ads using terms such as "white applicants only" or "colored need not apply." In the 1970s, a series of employment discrimination laws and court cases put a stop to ads using phrases such as "looking for pretty-looking, cheerful gal."[16]

Such advertisements would be illegal today, but the courts have ruled that in addition to not stating the intent to discriminate, employment advertisements cannot even imply that such conditions exist.

In the 1973 case of *Pittsburgh Press v. Pittsburgh Commission on Human Relations*, for example, the Supreme Court ruled that a newspaper could not categorize job listings with headings such as "male interest" and "female interest." The court based its ruling on two factors: (1) that employment advertising was commercial speech, and therefore not subject to First Amendment protection; and (2) the job labels condoned job discrimination, an illegal activity.[17]

Real estate advertising is subject to similar scrutiny. In the 1991 case of *Ragin v. New York Times*, for example, a Circuit Court of Appeals ruled in favor of a nonprofit organization suing the newspaper for failure to include black models in real estate advertisements showing potential homeowners. By carrying ads showing only white families, the court ruled, the newspaper was allowing advertisers to imply that only similar families were welcome in the neighborhoods where the properties were located, and such discrimination violated the Fair Housing Act of 1968 as well as the Fourteenth Amendment and numerous other civil rights laws. The court further ruled that assigning newspapers the responsibility of monitoring advertisements for racially discriminatory messages did not pose an "unconstitutional burden" and did not violate their First Amendment rights.[18]

Advertising and Young Audiences

The Federal Trade Commission, Federal Communications Commission, and various watch-dog groups contend that a higher regulatory standard applies to advertising aimed at children. One example is the FCC rule regarding the total number of minutes that can be allotted to advertising during children's programming.

The FTC and watchdog groups claim that children are "unqualified by age or experience to anticipate or appreciate the possibility that representations may be exaggerated or untrue." The Children's Advertising Review Unit of the Better Business Bureau adds that "younger children have a limited capacity for evaluating the credibility of information they receive; advertisers therefore have a special responsibility to protect children from their own susceptibilities."[19]

Advertisers assert that it is the responsibility of parents—not the courts or government regulatory agencies—to help children evaluate the credibility of information they receive through the mass media (see Case Study 8G).

Biting the Hands that Feed: News Content and Advertiser Concerns

While professional codes of ethics and the policies of most daily newspapers would prohibit reporters and editors from considering how a news story might affect an advertiser (either positively or negatively), whether such pressure is effective is a matter of debate.

Car dealers and real estate developers have long been among the worst offenders, attempting to use their positions as major advertisers to pressure media outlets to publish more good news and less bad news about their interests.

The problem of advertisers exerting pressure on journalistic decision-makers is not a new one. When Colonel Robert R. McCormick, publisher of the *Chicago Tribune* from the 1920s to the 1950s, personally funded the construction of a new building, he had a special elevator designated for the advertising sales staff and had it rigged not to stop on the fourth floor, where the news and editorial side of the paper was housed.[20]

As far back as 1967, a *Wall Street Journal* survey found that 23 percent of business and financial editors claimed they had been told by upper management to "puff up" positive stories or downplay negative stories about major advertisers. In the early 1990s, a survey of television and radio reporters indicated that 29 percent had received similar instructions from station owners and managers. Two decades later, similar surveys are no longer conducted, or if they are, the results are not publicized. But anecdotal evidence indicates the problem is still there—it's just not talked about.

In the 1970s, media researchers noticed a double standard in the ethical relationships that advertisers have with print journalists as opposed to their broadcast counterparts. While they could not find any evidence of print journalists ignoring stories about the connection between tobacco use and lung cancer, broadcasters were conspicuous in their lack of attention paid to the issue. They also noticed that the more cigarette advertising they aired, the less interested they appeared to be in researching stories about the health consequences of tobacco.[21]

In the case of weekly newspapers, monthly magazines, and trade publications, advertisers are often able to influence news coverage simply by making significant long-term advertising commitments that guarantee that the publications, which often struggle financially, can remain solvent. The strategy of "buy and ad, get a story" is also common among trade publications, weekly newspapers, and monthly magazines. Instead of waiting for an advertiser to make threats or promises, editors of weekly newspapers and monthly magazines avoid awkward situations by simply publishing positive stories about advertisers without being prompted. Such influence is difficult to document and seldom discussed among staff writers, but most know without asking that writing negative stories about major advertisers is forbidden.

Larger, more reputable newspapers and television stations prevent such problems by erecting figurative "walls of separation" between their news and advertising departments. That means that reporters are instructed not to consult with or discuss stories they are working on with any employees of the advertising department, and restaurant reviewers choose which restaurants to visit without consulting anyone else at the newspaper.

While advertisers' influence on the content of daily newspapers is difficult to document, that is not the case with magazines. *TV Guide* has long been criticized for avoiding controversial stories about companies that advertise in the publication and for not criticizing the networks for avoiding negative stories about their advertisers. "When a company buys an ad in *TV Guide*, it is also buying its silence," concluded a study in the *Journal of Economic Behavior and Organization*.[22]

While most daily newspapers and broadcasting outlets adhere to strict policies separating their news and advertising functions, at smaller weekly newspapers, lifestyle magazines, and trade publications, the "wall of separation" is difficult to detect—and is sometimes non-existent. In those publications, it is often difficult for a reader to tell where the news stories stop and the advertising begins.

The narrower the focus of the publication, the more likely it is to see its news content heavily influenced by advertising dollars. Some architectural magazines, for example, have policies that overtly indicate that only advertisers will receive favorable coverage. The editor of one fashion magazine, quoted in a *Wall Street Journal* article, said that, "We write about companies that advertise with us ... that's what magazines do.[23]

One example of a journalism specialty working hard to overcome accusations of unethical conduct is restaurant reviews. The relationship between restaurant reviewers and a newspaper's advertising department is often misunderstood. Many readers unfamiliar with how the journalism business works may assume that restaurant reviewers tend to write positive reviews about establishments that advertise in their newspaper and ignore those that don't. That belief may stem from the era—journalism historians say the policy was very common in the 1970s—in which restaurant reviews were written by the advertising department. Only restaurants that were major advertisers were reviewed, and the restaurants were always positive. Because so many readers believe that policy is still in place, most restaurant reviews are accompanied by a disclaimer that explains the decisions about which restaurants are reviewed are not influenced by whether or not those restaurants advertise in the newspaper. The statement also advises readers that restaurant critics dine anonymously and pay for their own meals, to counter the incorrect assumption that reviewers get better treatment and/or free meals by identifying themselves to restaurant management.

Closely related to the issue discussed above is the advertising boycott—a sponsor's decision to cancel its advertising with a specific newspaper or television station or network in retaliation for one or more negative news stories. While such boycotts are seldom discussed publicly, case studies in journalism publications indicate that such boycotts (or threats) occur more often than the general public is aware of. Under federal law, however, if businesses work together to boycott a specific media outlet, it is a violation of anti-trust laws and may be investigated by the Federal Trade Commission and U.S. Justice Department.

Advertising boycotts come in two types: (1) those that protest news coverage, and (2) those that are designed simply to avoid association with controversial hosts or topics.

Those of the first variety are seldom effective. In the 1970s and 1980s, for example, pharmaceutical companies cancelled millions of dollars' worth of advertising in *The New York Times* after it published stories about defective product lawsuits, while tobacco companies cancelled ads in *Mother Jones* after a story about the connection between smoking cigarettes and lung cancer.[24]

Advertisers often claim that boycotts represent a "last resort" in responding to what they perceive as false or unfair news coverage. They also see advertising boycotts as easier to pursue and much less expensive than libel suits. Newspaper editors and television station owners dispute the "last resort" idea, claiming that most advertising boycotts catch them by surprise. Instead, they prefer that advertisers explore less drastic methods for resolving conflicts, such as requesting the opportunity to respond to negative news stories in the form of op-ed pieces or on-camera rebuttals.

The second category has had mixed results. In the 1990s, for example, Amtrak cancelled millions of dollars' worth of advertising on NBC after the network ignored its complaints about the monologues of *Tonight Show* host Jay Leno in which he ridiculed the company's history of fatal derailments and other accidents (see Case Study 3B).

More recently, Fox News hosts Bill O'Reilly and Glenn Beck were fired as a result of boycotts, but their co-worker Sean Hannity survived, as did syndicated radio talk-show host Rush Limbaugh. In the latter cases, advertisers that threatened to cancel either changed their minds or were replaced by other sponsors.[25]

The financial impact of an advertising boycott depends largely on the size of the community. In small towns, where a large business might account for much of the newspaper's advertising revenue, the cumulative effect of a lengthy boycott might be substantial. But in a larger community, newspapers and television stations have enough other advertisers to compensate for the loss of one or a few. In addition, a newspaper or television station that is part of a national chain or network can easily survive the loss of a major advertiser, whereas a local independent newspaper or station might not.

In both categories, many advertising boycotts are short-lived, as advertisers quickly realize that they need the newspaper or television station more than the media organization needs the advertising revenue. At worst, it is a lose–lose situation for both parties. Considering the lack of case studies to document the effectiveness of boycotts, some advertisers claim that even though they might not result in a change in news coverage, they cancel their advertising out of principle, stating they will not continue to advertise in a newspaper or on a television station that has treated them unfairly.

The most common examples of an advertising boycott are those involving car dealerships that occurred in many communities in the 1990s and early 2000s. Angry about news stories concerning defective automobiles or stories that provided consumers with information on how to negotiate lower prices for the purchase of their cars, dealerships resorted to canceling their advertising in those publications and on those television stations. In some cases, dealerships worked together to organize the boycotts.

In 2013, the Food Network cut ties with host Paula Deen when advertisers refused to sponsor her program based on news stories about her use of racial slurs years earlier. After radio talk-show host Laura Ingraham mocked one of the students who survived the 2018 school shooting in Parkland, Florida, advertisers such as Johnson & Johnson, Liberty Mutual, Expedia, Nestle, and Office Depot cancelled millions of dollars' worth of advertising on her program.[26]

Early in 2017, as a rash of sexual harassment allegations were levied against Fox News executive Roger Ailes, major advertisers such as Cars.com, Peleton, and Casper Mattresses pulled their ads from the program of Fox's superstar political commentator Sean Hannity. With O'Reilly already fired and Ailes already forced to resign, the advertisers focused on Hannity, even though there were no similar allegations against him. Instead, they said, they pulled their ads because Hannity continued to defend his former colleague and ex-boss and because Fox News as a whole promoted "a climate hostile to women."[27]

In 2010, *Village Voice* columnist Foster Kamer wrote a satirical item in a blog linked to the newspaper's website. Kamer made a joke implying that James Dolan, CEO of Cablevision, engaged in oral sex with Jake Dobkin, another blogger. Rather than suing Kamer for libel, Dolan took a more expeditious path, instructing two Cablevision subsidiaries—Independent Film Channel and Madison Square Garden Entertainment—to cancel advertising contracts with the *Village Voice* worth more than $1 million. Kamer told the media that the boycott created "a culture of fear and hostility" and claimed that his work was protected by First Amendment. Dolan said he didn't dispute the First Amendment values at stake but contended that while the law allowed Kamer to express his views, it did not prevent Dolan from retaliating by cancelling the advertising contracts.[28]

Portrayals of Women

Many critics of the advertising industry claim that the ways it portrays women are offensive and often harmful. Examples include the use of excessively thin models in fashion magazines and television advertising; critics claim that young women and teenage girls exposed to those ads often develop self-esteem problems and are more vulnerable to eating disorders and other unhealthy habits and attitudes.

One such critic is Jean Kilbourne, who has written a number of books and produced a series of videos critical of not only fashion advertising, but also of cosmetics and other products of interest to women. Kilbourne uses hundreds of examples of print and broadcast ads that show women in unnatural and offensive circumstances and stereotype women as being obsessed with their appearance.

In a book on the sociological implications of advertising, American Association of Advertising Agencies President John Crichton added that consumers should expect advertising to be not only accurate, but also realistic. "Beyond accuracy, the question is often one of perception," Crichton wrote. "It is true that the dress in the advertisement is available in the sizes, colors, and price advertised—but will the dress make the purchaser look like the slim young woman in the ad? Answer: Yes, but only if the purchaser looks like her already."[29]

The Influence of Advertising on Consumer Spending

Many critics of popular culture believe that the American advertising industry manipulates the buying habits of the audience by blurring the lines between what people want and what they need. Critics say advertising leads consumers to believe they "need" a certain car, electronic device, item of furniture, or article of clothing when actually they only "want" it. Professor Theodore Levitt, an economist at the Harvard Business School, once said that consumers do not purchase products, but rather results. "People do not buy quarter-inch drills, they buy quarter-inch holes," he said. "They do not buy soap; they buy cleanliness. They do not buy clothing, they buy appearance."[30] Charles Revlon, the founder of the cosmetics company that bears his name, once said that "in our factory we make cosmetics, in the store we sell hope."[31]

Today, economists and consumer advocates blame the advertising industry's tactics, along with easy access to retail credit cards, with the epidemic of personal debt and bankruptcy that began in the 1990s and continues in the early part of the new century. Consumer advocate Dave Ramsey, author of a number of financial-planning books and host of a nationally syndicated radio program, blames the advertising industry, as well as the credit-card industry, for contributing to the epidemic of over-spending and personal bankruptcy. Ramsey says the advertising and credit-card industries conspire to encourage Americans to "spend money they don't have to buy things they don't need to impress people they don't like."

Your Turn

Case Study 8A: Advertising Venues and Categories: The Growth of Advergaming

One of the fastest-growing advertising venues is "advergaming"—the placement of advertising in video games, which has caught the attention of brands such as Arby's, Audi, Coca-Cola, PepsiCo, Gillette, and Budweiser, who spend millions of dollars each year trying to reach the important demographic of men age twenty-one to thirty-five but find traditional advertising less effective than in the past.

One form of advergaming involves sports video games. In 2017, the esports economy was expected to account for $696 million, which included advertising, merchandise sales, sponsorship of events, and ticket sales to those events. About $155 million of that total was for advertising alone, according to a 2017 article in *Advertising Age*. The same article predicted that both numbers would more than double by 2020.[32]

The term "advergaming" was coined in 2000 to refer to the art of inserting commercial messages into video games. The technique includes product placements (discussed earlier in this chapter), short product pitches seen at the beginning of a game session, and the appearance of a company logo painted on the field or on a banner seen during an animated sports competition.

1. What are some of the advantages and disadvantages of placing advertising within video games, as opposed to other venues?
2. What are some of the possible ethical challenges, compared to other advertising venues?

Case Study 8B: Advertising of Controversial Products and Services: What Are the Odds?

Although seldom the target of legal action, the advertising of state lotteries is often criticized by consumer groups as false or deceptive. Much of the criticism is based on how state lottery agencies use their advertising campaigns to glamorize the new lifestyles of lottery jackpot winners without mentioning the nearly astronomical odds associated with winning the large prizes.

Business ethicists contend that lottery advertising is aimed the most vulnerable markets: households with the lowest income and education levels. "State lottery administrators and the advertising agencies they employ intentionally sell the lottery as a solution to financial problems, a way out of a depressing situation, and a remedy for ennui," report James M. Stearns and Shaheen Borna in an article in the *Journal of Business Ethics*.[33]

Critics of state lotteries claim that the advertising of the games detracts from the work ethic by promoting the idea that the way to get ahead in life is through luck rather than hard work. Many anti-lottery educators point out the mixed messages teenagers receive: in school, they are taught about the importance of hard work, but then they see the lottery advertising that says that all one must do to get rich is buy a lottery ticket. Some lottery critics believe, but cannot prove, that lottery advertising is timed to coincide with the delivery of welfare and social security checks, a charge that lottery agencies deny.

According to the Council on Compulsive Gambling, fewer than half of state-run lotteries disclose the odds of winning in print advertising, and only 25 percent do so in television ads. In a 1993 article in the *Boston College Law Review*, Professor Ronald J. Rychlak wrote that few lottery ads could pass the Federal Trade Commission's rules that apply to privately run sweepstakes.[34]

In addition to debates over the odds of winning, another controversy involves the problem of lottery agencies that continue to advertise certain games long after the major jackpot prize had been won. In Illinois in 1983 and New Jersey in 2008, newspaper, television, and radio advertisements touting a game's million-dollar grand prize continued to run after the only winning ticket had been purchased and redeemed. In both cases, the lottery agencies blamed the problem on "miscommunication between the agency and their advertising contractor."

Yet another ethical consideration associated with lottery advertising concerns a potential conflict of interest. As both subjects of news stories and sources of advertising revenue, state lottery agencies often enter into an uncomfortable relationship with the media. Newspapers and television stations profit greatly from lottery advertising and then either intentionally or unintentionally help promote lotteries by glamorizing the lifestyles of the winners and covering drawings and other lottery-related events as news stories, regardless of the minimal news value involved. No one has classified the relationship as quid pro quo, but media ethicists might call it incestuous—or at least an unintended consequence.

1. In general, do lottery agencies bear the responsibility of making sure potential lottery customers fully understand the odds associated with purchasing lottery tickets in hopes of winning multi-million-dollar jackpots? Or should this be an example of caveat emptor (let the buyer beware)?
2. Re-read the last paragraph if this case. Do you agree that television stations that cover lottery-related news stories (such as live drawings and stories that glamorize the lifestyles of new jackpot winners) while their advertising departments are benefiting from lottery advertising are involved in a conflict of interest? (Consider the fact that there are few other positive news stories in which there is also an advertising connection).

Case Study 8C: False and Deceptive Advertising: What Time Does the Movie Really Start?

Although few people would refer to it as a "controversy" or "ethical dilemma," movie audiences often complain that feature films typically begin twenty to thirty minutes after the scheduled time advertised in local newspapers and in other public sources of information. The reason behind the trend is the increased number of movie previews and advertisements that precede most feature films.

The criticism comes at a time when movie attendance is at an all-time low and theater income is down.[35]

Many theater operators blame the downturn on the national economy and the loss of market share to DVD vending machines, online movie streaming, and the expansion of cable and satellite movie channels. In addition to the loss of income, many theaters have closed—especially older venues that cannot be retro-fitted with today's modern projection and sound equipment.

Theater operators defend the practice by claiming that showing more commercials and previews of upcoming films provides latecomers the chance to find their seats without walking in front of other patrons or otherwise distracting from the film. Cynical observers, however, believe it is simply the theater owners' desire for the income derived from pre-movie advertising.

In 2004, the president of the National Association of Theater Owners acknowledged that audiences often complain about the commercials, but he did not offer any specific solutions, simply stating that "We get into trouble when we start to look like TV."[36]

In 2005, Connecticut State Representative Andrew Fleischmann introduced legislation requiring movie theaters to advertise the actual start of the feature film rather than the start of the previews and commercials. The legislation failed. That same year, Loews Cineplex, one of the major theater chains in the U.S., began including disclaimers in its advertising that "the feature presentation will begin 10 to 15 minutes after the posted time," but audience reactions have been mixed.

1. Should this be considered an issue subject to "truth in advertising laws," or looked at as "just one of life's inconveniences"?
2. Compared to other forms of alleged advertising deception (such as those involving food and drug products), is this really worthy of the time of the Federal Trade Commission and other advertising regulators and watchdog groups?

Case Study 8D: False and Deceptive Advertising: Worthy Causes or Bait and Switch?

While nonprofit organizations are seldom criticized for the work they do, some are scrutinized for the manner in which they conduct their fund-raising appeals through either paid advertising or telemarketing. While watchdog groups such as the Better Business Bureau Wise Giving Alliance and the American Institute of Philanthropy monitor and evaluate organizations' fund-raising tactics, the news media also raises questions about the process. Three such examples have surfaced in the last decade.

The first category of nonprofit organizations to come under media scrutiny was that of Police Benevolent Associations (PBAs). Most PBAs are organized at the city or county level, and their main purpose is to provide support for the families of law-enforcement officers killed in the line of duty. Instead of raising money using volunteers, however, many PBAs hire professional fund-raisers that do the majority of their work using telemarketers. Their fund-raising appeals suggest the money raised will be spent on providing financial support for widows of slain police officers and college scholarships for their children. While some of the money does go to that purpose, much of it goes to political activities, such as lobbying in the state legislatures regarding issues of interest to law enforcement and supporting political candidates the associations have endorsed. While some donors may agree with spending money on those other purposes, others may not; and many donors feel misled by the telemarketers' heart-warming stories about widows and children receiving financial support. In addition, many critics object to the PBAs hiring outside firms (which often keep between 25 and 75 percent of the money collected) instead of using volunteers.

Similar criticisms have been launched at AIDS-related charities, many of which are also organized at the local level. Among their chief fund-raising activities are bicycle rides, and many such events are organized by professional firms that keep more than 70 percent of the money raised, leaving less than 30 percent for AIDS-related causes. In contrast, the American Lung Association's annual bike rides, organized entirely by volunteers, raise similar totals but give 60 to 75 percent of the money raised to the organization's causes.

Another category of organizations under recent media scrutiny are those responsible for relief efforts following national disasters. Following the terrorist attacks of September 11, 2001, those organizations executed some of the most successful fund-raising efforts in history, collecting millions of dollars and funding a number of programs to support recovery efforts. Early the following year, however, media reports indicated those organizations had collected more money than they could possibly spend on September 11-related recovery efforts, but the organizations were still using that appeal in their fund-raising.

In their defense, those organizations were spending the excess money to help the victims of hurricanes, tornadoes, and floods. While critics admitted those other causes were important ones, they believed the tactic of continuing to use images of September 11 victims in the organizations' fund-raising appeals (with the money already committed to other causes) was a dishonest approach. Some even compared it to the bait-and-switch tactic used by some advertisers. In 2005–06, many of those same organizations executed successful fund-raising campaigns to generate money for victims of Hurricane Katrina, but they were later criticized for continuing to use images of hurricane victims in their television spots and other fund-raising appeals long after they had raised more money than they could possibly spend for Katrina-related relief efforts.

1. If you were a frequent donor to your local Police Benevolent Association and learned that it had turned over its fund-raising operation to a professional fund-raising firm that took 60 percent of what it collected, would that change your opinion of the group? What about the fact that much of the remaining 40 percent goes to political activities rather than helping the widows and children of police officers? Would the fact that at least *some* of the money collected goes to a worthy cause be enough to keep you as a donor?
2. What about the AIDS-related charities? Is the fact that at least *some* of the money goes to AIDS-related causes enough to justify the use of an outside fund-raising firm?
3. What about the relief agencies that used images of September 11 victims and Hurricane Katrina victims in their fund-raising appeals, but spending that money on other worthy causes? Do you agree with the critics' view that such a tactic is analogous to the bait-and-switch tactics used by some advertisers?

Case Study 8E: False and Deceptive Advertising: Academic Bait and Switch

The problem of "bait and switch" tactics has long been an ethical issue facing the advertising industry. The term is used in both Federal Trade Commission guidelines and the Code of Ethics of the American Advertising Federation (although the code simply refers to it as "bait advertising"). Although the term was initially applied mostly in cases involving consumer products such as home electronics and automobiles, more recently the term has been applied to other situations, including fund-raising (see Case Study 8E) and even the promotion of colleges and universities.

The latter problem began earning media attention in the mid-1990s when the NBC series *Dateline* produced a detailed report in which it used the term "academic bait and switch" to refer to the way that major universities boast in their recruiting literature and other promotional materials about the credentials of their senior faculty—many of them Nobel and Pulitzer Prize winners—and imply to parents that their children will be taught by those individuals. What the universities don't disclose to parents, however, is those senior faculty members typically teach only graduate students, while the bulk of undergraduate classes—especially those for freshmen and sophomores—are taught by graduate teaching assistants who have little or no teaching experience and are just few years older than their students. While student evaluations often indicate the teaching skills of teaching assistants are just as good as (and sometimes better than) those of senior faculty members, the concern is that the universities' advertising is deceptive.

While the *Dateline* segment cited cases of positive student experiences with teaching assistants, it also uncovered cases of students complaining that many teaching assistants lacked basic teaching skills, were not available for assistance outside of class, or lacked the fundamental knowledge of the material necessary to teach it. In extreme cases, *Dateline* reported, teaching assistants in the technical sciences were international students who struggled with the English language, making their lectures nearly indecipherable.

To address concerns of state legislators that too much of the responsibility for undergraduate teaching is relegated to teaching assistants, many universities list a full-time faculty member on the course schedule as the "instructor of record," but still delegate the actual teaching duties to a graduate student. The official university records do not disclose that the professor listed on the course schedule is seldom in the classroom, and in many cases is not even on campus at the time the class meets.

In 2009, *The Chronicle of Higher Education* published a lengthy article along the same lines. Also using the term "academic bait and switch," the *Chronicle* article was written by a professor at a prestigious school who claimed that when he began his career as a graduate teaching assistant, he was assigned to teach freshman English composition classes that he clearly wasn't qualified to teach. "Students attend the university to be taught by experts, not amateurs," he wrote. "Before I set foot on campus, I didn't know that teaching assistants actually taught. I assume that 'teaching assistant' meant 'assisting a teacher.'" The professor, who was quoted anonymously in order to avoid harming his career, said he received less than a day of training on how to teach his courses, along with encouraging words from his department chair: "look confident."[37]

Many professors and former professors have expressed similar opinions in their books, although most used the term "academic fraud" instead of "bait and switch." As far back as 1988, retired professor Charles J. Sykes cited a joke frequently told about the statue of Abraham Lincoln on the campus of the University of Wisconsin. Lincoln is shown seated in a chair, nearly identical to how he is portrayed at the Lincoln Memorial in Washington, D.C. According to campus lore, the statue of Lincoln rises from the chair every time a senior professor who teaches more than two classes per semester walks by. On a more serious note, Sykes wrote that, "For parents who pay college costs (especially those who chose a school because they thought their children would actually study at the feet of its highly touted faculty), it has meant one of the biggest cons in history."[38]

One of Sykes' recommendations is that universities should be held to the same truth-in-advertising standards as other advertisers and should be required to disclose in their advertising as well as promotional materials the research-to-teaching ratio of faculty employment contracts and the proportion of courses taught by teaching assistants.

In his 2006 book *Our Underachieving Colleges*, former Harvard University President Derek Bok wrote that the emphasis on research means that the professors touted in the universities' promotional literature are seldom in the classroom, and that "the real teaching is left to inexperienced graduate students … lost in the crowd, many under-graduates finish college without knowing a single faculty member well enough to ask for a letter of recommendation."[39]

1. Do you agree with Charles Sykes' suggestion that colleges and universities be held to the same truth-in-advertising standards as other advertisers? If so, would a requirement that universities disclose the research-to-teaching ratio in faculty contracts and the proportion of classes taught by teaching assistants go far enough?

2. Are there any philosophers or concepts from Chapter 2 that can be applied here?

Case Study 8F: False and Deceptive Advertising: Joseph Lister and the Product that Bears His Name

The problem of manufacturers making false or exaggerated claims about the potential benefits of using their products is nothing new. As far back as 1923, the Lambert Pharmaceutical Company began marketing a new mouthwash it called Listerine, playing on the name of Joseph Lister, an English surgeon and medical researcher known for developing surgical procedures that would limit infections. Lister had nothing to do with the company or any of its products, but many consumers were misled by the product's name.

The company also claimed at the time that Listerine could cure "halitosis"—the medical term for bad breath—when in reality it could only mask the symptoms without addressing the cause. What the advertisements did not mention was that bad breath could be attributed to a number of causes, including poor diet, smoking, gum disease, and diabetes—none of which could be cured by mouthwash.

Similar misconceptions about mouthwash continue today, prompting the American Dental Association to explain on its website that "mouthwashes are generally cosmetic in nature and do not have any long-lasting effect on bad breath."

The product has not seen the end of its legal problems, however. Throughout much of the twentieth century, the company claimed that using the product could cure sore throats and reduce the severity of colds. In 1977, it was forced by the Federal Trade Commission to spend more than $10 million on ads to clarify that "Listerine will not prevent colds or sore throats or lessen their severity."

In 2005, a manufacturer of dental floss complained when Pfizer, Listerine's new parent company, claimed that the mouthwash was as effective as dental floss in reducing plaque and gum disease. Fearing a decline in sales of its dental floss, Johnson & Johnson filed suit against Pfizer, claiming that such ads were "false and deceptive" because no tests had been conducted to determine the relative merits of the two products. A federal judge agreed with Johnson & Johnson's claim and ordered Pfizer to withdraw the ad.

1. Do you think that misleading advertising has gotten better or worse in recent years?
2. Do you think that Federal Trade Commission rules are too strict, just about right, or too loose?

Case Study 8G: Advertising and Younger Audiences: Campaign for a Commercial-Free Childhood

Advertising aimed at children is a frequent target of the Federal Trade Commission and watchdog groups that express concern over the impact that advertising has on children who have not yet learned to be skeptical of commercial messages.

In 2000, children's advocates formed the Campaign for a Commercial-Free Childhood (CCFC), a program designed to monitor the advertising industry and encourage more responsible advertising aimed at children. CCFC began by targeting food and soft-drink companies for subjecting children to what it called a culture of "rampant consumerism," and today monitors all forms of television advertising aimed at younger viewers. In response to the criticism from CFCC and other consumer watchdog groups, the advertising industry in 2003 discontinued its annual "Golden Marbles" awards program that honored achievement in print and broadcast advertising aimed at children.

In response to the criticism it receives from CCFC and other watchdog groups, the advertising industry—led by executives representing major food producers—formed the Alliance for American Advertising. The alliance claims its mission is to "help advertisers defend their First Amendment rights."

1. Should the responsibility for scrutinizing advertising content directed at children lie with the company providing the products, the advertising agency creating the advertising campaigns, the media that carry the advertisements, or the parents of potential audience members?
2. What is your reaction to the positions taken by the advocacy groups mentioned in the case?

Discussion Problem 8A: Legal and Ethical Framework: Advertising Agencies and Competing Proposals

You're running a small company, and you're considering hiring an agency to come up with a long-term advertising strategy. You contact four of the largest advertising agencies in town and provide them a request for proposals (RFP). Each agency submits a written response to your RFP and also comes into your conference room to do an in-person presentation.

Agencies A and B submit fairly weak proposals and you eliminate them early in the process. But Agency C and Agency D present an interesting scenario.

Agency C submitted an excellent written proposal and you know it's exactly what your company needs to do. The problem is that when the account executives came to do the in-person presentation, they turned out to be the most obnoxious people you've ever met. You can't picture yourself working with them for the long term because you fear there would be too many personality conflicts.

Agency D submitted a written proposal that was very ordinary, and at first glance it appeared to be only slightly better than the proposals from Agencies A and B that you had already rejected. But when you met Agency D's representatives in person, they were very enthusiastic and the chemistry between your employees and their employees was very positive.

Then one of your employees suggests taking the good proposal from Agency C and hiring Agency D to carry it out.

Without consulting an attorney, which of the following do you believe?

a. It is **already illegal** or **should be illegal** for a prospective client to do that.
b. It is **perfectly legal** to do that. Perhaps it is unfair to Agency C, but the agency developed and submitted the proposal at its own risk, and that's just one of the "downsides" associated with being in a competitive business.
c. It may be legal to do that, but it is certainly **unethical** and a lousy way to treat another business.

Discussion Problem 8B: Advertising of Controversial Products and Services: The Case of the Cable Descrambler

You're the advertising manager at a daily newspaper. One morning you are called into the office of the newspaper's publisher, who has just received a call from the manager of the local cable television company, a major advertiser. The publisher calls to your attention to an ad that another advertiser has placed in the newspaper. The ad offers a device that enables the user to descramble cable television signals and, essentially, obtain cable television service for free. The ad was placed by an out-of-state company that provided only a post office box, 1-800 telephone number, and Web address. The ad was paid for in advance, and the advertisers' check has already been cashed. The advertiser paid for 12 weeks, and the ad has already run for two.

The cable company insists that you stop carrying the ad and warns that if you don't, the company will cancel its advertising in the newspaper and may also sue for the loss of subscriber revenue. Also at the meeting are the newspaper's editor and attorney. When it's your turn to speak, which of the following recommendations would you make?

a.   Cancel the ad immediately, issue a partial refund to the advertiser, apologize to the cable company, and hope that will be enough to prevent further conflict.

b.   Allow the ad to run the remaining ten weeks, since it has already been pre-paid, but promise the cable company you will not renew the ad after that.

c.   Inform the cable company that you cannot be responsible for the content of every advertisement that runs in the student newspaper, and one advertiser will not dictate policies regarding what other ads you will accept. You will allow the advertiser to renew the ad if it wishes to.

d.   Suggest that the newspaper attempt to settle the matter without going to court, but insist that the cable company prove damages—a specific dollar amount lost due to local customers using the device to steal cable signals.

Discussion Questions

801. Earlier in this chapter you read about the work of feminist scholar Jean Kilbourne, who has produced a series of books and videos critical of how the American advertising industry portrays women in a stereotypical manner. What is the root cause of these stereotypes? Does advertising reflect our attitudes toward women, or does the advertising portrayal influence our attitudes? Should advertising be regulated by the Federal Trade Commission to avoid such negative depictions, or could advertisers claim such depictions, while offensive, are protected by the First Amendment? Could commercials that are offensive to women, or portray them in a stereotypical way, be addressed by any part of the American Advertising Federation Code of Ethics (find the code online, the web address is in the appendices)? If not, should a new paragraph be added to address this concern?

802. Do you agree with the rationale used to explain the need for product placements (that the value of traditional advertising is diminished because of viewers who skip through or past them)? Does the inclusion of product placements make television programs and movies more realistic? Are the producers of the programs justified in their concern that product placements infringe upon their "art"?

Notes

1 Lee Thayer, *Ethics, Morality and the Media: Reflections on American Culture.* New York: Hastings House Publishers (1980), p. 109.
2 Shelby D. Hunt and Lawrence B. Chonko, "Ethical Problems of Advertising Agency Executives." *Journal of Advertising*, Vol. 16, No. 4 (1987), pp. 16–24.
3 Randy Bobbitt, *Exploring Communication Law: A Socratic Approach.* Boston: Allyn & Bacon (2008), p. 246.
4 John Harrington and Grant Suneson, "Cigarettes and Supplements Are among the Most Outrageous Product Claims of All Time." *USA Today*, May 11, 2019.
5 Sienna Kossman, "The Truth about False and Deceptive Advertising." www.USNews.com, posted July 22, 2013; accessed August 3, 2019.
6 Kossman.
7 Kathleen A. O'Brien, Lisa B. Kim, and Julianna D. Milberg, "Rising Number of Class Actions Targeting Outlet Stores Based on Claims of False and Deceptive Advertising." *IP Litigator*, Vol. 20, No. 6 (November–December 2014), pp. 25+.
8 Elizabeth Cowley and Chris Barron, "When Product Placement Goes Wrong." *Journal of Advertising*, Vol. 37, No. 1 (2008), pp. 89–98.
9 Jiyoung Cha, "Product Placement in Movies: Perspectives from Motion Picture Films." *Journal of Mass Media Studies*, Vol. 13, No. 2 (2016), pp. 95–116.
10 Cha.
11 Kelly Tyko, "Can Starbucks Cup on 'Game of Thrones' Translate to Billions in Free Advertising?" *USA Today*, May 7, 2019.
12 Allan Wolper, "Sexified Classifieds." *Editor & Publisher*, November 10, 2003, p. 30.
13 David Niose, *Nonbeliever Nation: The Rise of Secular Americans.* New York: Palgrave Macmillan (2012), pp. 136–138.
14 Niose, pp. 136–138.
15 Niose, pp. 136–138.
16 Heather Boushey, *Finding Time: The Economics of Work–Life Conflict.* Cambridge, MA: Harvard University Press (2016), p. 61.
17 *Pittsburgh Press v. Pittsburgh Commission on Human Relations*, 413 U.S. 376 (1973).
18 *Ragin v. New York Times*, 923 F. 2d 995 (1991).
19 Robert B. Musburger, *An Introduction to Writing for Electronic Media.* Burlington, MA: Focal Press (2007), pp. 303.
20 James O'Shea, *The Deal From Hell: How Moguls and Wall Street Plundered Great American Newspapers.* New York: Public Affairs (2011), p. 74.
21 Donald McDonald, "Is Objectivity Possible?" In *Ethics and the Press*, John C. Merrill and Ralph D. Barney, ed. New York: Hastings House Publishing (1978), pp. 69–88.
22 Marc Poitras and Daniel Sutter, "Advertiser Pressure and the Control of News: The Decline of Muckraking Revisited." *Journal of Economic Behavior and Organization*, Vol. 72, No. 3 (December 2009), pp. 944–958.
23 Edward Spence and Brett Van Heekeren. *Advertising Ethics.* Upper Saddle River, NJ: Prentice-Hall (2004), p. 88.

24 Soontae An and Lori Bergen, "Advertiser Pressure on Daily Newspapers: A Survey of Advertising Sales Executives." *Journal of Advertising*, Vol. 36, No. 2 (Summer 2007), pp. 111–121.

25 Jeanine Poggi and Jack Neff, "CMO's Guide to Ad Boycotts." *Advertising Age*, Vol. 88, No. 13 (June 26, 2017). See also: Jack Shafer, "When Advertising Boycotts Are a Bad Idea." *New York Post*, April 6, 2017.

26 Natasha Bach, "Fox News Defends Laura Ingraham over David Hogg, Denouncing Advertising Boycott as Intimidation Efforts." Fortune.com, published April 3, 2018; accessed June 10, 2019.

27 Simon Dumenco, "Ballad of the Sad White Alpha Men." *Advertising Age*, May 29, 2017, p. 38.

28 Alex Alvarez, "James Dolan is Really Going to Make the Village Voice Pay for That Penis Joke." *Advertising Age*, May 7, 2010.

29 Thayer, p. 111.

30 Thayer, p. 110.

31 Thayer, p. 186.

32 E. J. Schultz, "Are You Game?" *Advertising Age*, April 3, 2017, pp. 12–19.

33 James M Stearns and Shaheen Borna, "The Ethics of Lottery Advertising: Issues and Evidence." *Journal of Business Ethics*, Vol. 14, No. 1 (1995), pp. 43–51.

34 Ronald J. Rychlak, "Lotteries, Revenues, and Social Costs: A Historical Examination of State-Sponsored Gambling." *Boston College Law Review*, Vol. 34, No. ½ (1992), pp. 11–81. See also: Randy Bobbitt, *Lottery Wars: Case Studies in Bible-Belt Politics*. Lanham, MD: Lexington Books (2007), p. 18.

35 Anousha Sakoui, "Hollywood Had a Terrible 2017." Bloomberg News, January 2, 2018.

36 Ben Steelman, "Is Going to the Movies a Dying Pastime?" *Wilmington Star-News*, June 2, 2005, p. C-30.

37 Henry Adams, "Academic Bait-and-Switch." *The Chronicle of Higher Education*, June 16, 2009.

38 Charles J. Sykes, *ProfScam*. Washington, D.C.: Regnery Publishing (1988), p. 8.

39 Derek Bok, *Our Under-achieving Colleges*. Princeton, NJ: Princeton University Press (2006), p. 8.

9   Ethical Issues in Public Relations

Background

Defining Public Relations

Public relations is often confused with advertising, marketing, promotion, publicity, propaganda, and other terms dealing with persuasion. But there are several significant differences. There are three characteristics typically found in legitimate public relations campaigns:

1. Much like in persuasion, decisions made as a result of being influenced by a public relations campaign must be the result of **free choice**. Members of the audience must be able to freely choose among several actions: adopt the ideas or behaviors being advocated by campaign organizers, adopt the ideas or behaviors of another party involved in the issue, remain committed to their previously held ideas or behaviors, or not take part in the issue at all. The concept of free choice also means there must be no coercion involved. Professional communicators are allowed to be assertive in their work, of course, but in an ethical public relations campaign, the final choice must be up to members of the audience.
2. Decisions made and actions taken as a result of a public relations campaign must benefit both the persuader and the audience. This concept is also known as **mutual benefit**. Both the communicator and the audience must emerge from the transaction with some benefit. A campaign in which only the communicator benefits is more accurately labeled as "manipulation" or "propaganda" rather than true public relations.
3. Public relations campaigns take a **multidisciplinary approach**. Instead of working only through the media—an approach typically used in advertising—true public relations campaigns may also apply theories and techniques from fields such as psychology, sociology, and education. For example, a company trying to sell cat litter may find success with traditional advertising and marketing techniques. However, an organization attempting to promote the importance of spaying or neutering cats will have to apply a variety of other communications techniques to be successful.

Despite the emphasis on mutual benefit, public relations professionals serve as advocates for a company, nonprofit organization, or cause. To some degree, the practice of public relations is linked to the First Amendment to the U.S. Constitution and general principles of freedom of expression. Part of a PR professional's job, some observers say, is to help his or her clients or employers exercise their First Amendment rights.

In their codes of ethics, major professional organizations state that while serving as advocates, public relations professionals also have an obligation to serve the public interest, tell the truth, and focus on the fair resolutions of conflicts rather than attempting to gloss them over.

Legal and Ethical Limitations

Unlike the advertising industry, the public relations industry is not regulated by state or government agencies. However, individuals practicing public relations, as well as their clients or employers, may still get into legal trouble if they violate laws that apply to individuals and organizations in general. These problem areas include:

Insider trading: Using confidential business information to buy or sell stock in a client's business for personal gain.

Obstruction of justice: Refusing to cooperate with a law-enforcement investigation of a client or employer, or taking any other actions that impede such an investigation.

Intellectual property: Using the creative property (copyrights and trademarks) of an organization without permission. Many public relations officers are responsible not only for monitoring the Internet for potential violations of their employers' intellectual property, but also monitoring their own department's communication to make sure it does not violate the rights of others.

Defamation and privacy: Defamation involves damaging the personal or professional reputation of an individual. While more often associated with journalistic products, defamation can also take place in public relations materials such as news releases and internal publications. Privacy violations include false light (disseminating information that is true but exaggerated or otherwise misleading), private facts (disclosure of personal information that is not newsworthy), or appropriation (the use of a person's name or image for promotional purposes without permission). Much like defamation, these offenses are more common with journalistic products but can also be found in public relations materials.

Insider trading is discussed later in this chapter. For information on the other topics listed above, consult a communication law textbook.

Some General Rules

There are two general principles regarding the legal and ethical obligations of public relations professionals:

A practitioner's obligation to the law always takes priority over his or her obligation to a client or employer. This means that public relations representatives must cooperate with law-enforcement investigations or other legal matters involving a client or employer, regardless of any confidentiality agreements between the parties.

Communication between public relations representatives and their clients or employers is confidential in a general sense, but not privileged in a legal sense. While professional communicators have an obligation to maintain the confidences and privacy rights of clients or employers, that does not mean they can claim privilege in a legal proceeding. Unlike doctors and lawyers, who are legally and ethically required to maintain confidentiality with their patients and clients, public relations professionals don't benefit from legal protection. Because they often have information dealing with controversial and potentially illegal activities of their clients and employers, they may be forced to provide that information to courts or government investigators.

Professional Codes of Ethics

The two major professional organizations serving the profession are the Public Relations Society of America (PRSA), based in New York; and the International Association of Business Communicators (IABC), based in San Francisco. Both organizations provide codes of ethics for their members, and both of those codes have their merits and their shortcomings. In addition, many states and regions of the country have smaller organizations, and most have codes that mirror those of PRSA and IABC.

On the positive side, advocates of professional codes claim that they help newcomers by educating them about professional guidelines and sensitizing them to ethical problems in their field. They also provide helpful information that individuals and agencies working in the field can cite in explaining the proper course(s) of action to employers and clients that find themselves in ethical dilemmas.

On the negative side, both codes are subject to the same criticisms:

Professional codes are "watered down" by vague and imprecise language. Both codes use terms such as "integrity," "channels of communication," and "realistic expectations," but neither code offers any definitions. One of the critics is Donald K. Wright, professor emeritus at the University of South Alabama, who wrote in a 1993 article that the codes "are more cosmetic than anything else ... They're warm and fuzzy and make practitioners feel good about themselves, but they don't accomplish much. They don't even come close to being meaningful tools for ensuring accountability. They don't achieve what they've set out to do, and most are filled with meaningless rhetoric and are not taken seriously by the majority of those who practice public relations."[1]

Violations of the code seldom lead to consequences for the offenders. Unlike the codes of other professions (such as law and medicine), adherence to public relations codes is strictly voluntary. Although there are procedures in place for enforcing the codes—the strongest punishment the organizations can apply in cases of violating ethical codes is revoking the individual's membership—both organizations are reluctant to take such action.

The codes apply only to members of professional organizations. The ethical codes apply only to those individuals who belong to the organizations. Researchers estimate that in the United States, only about 15 percent of professional communicators who describe their work as "public relations" belong to either PRSA or IABC.

Like most professional codes of ethics, the PRSA and IABC codes are ripe for discussion in the categorical imperative-situational ethics dichotomy (see Chapter 2). Are the codes written to be interpreted as inflexible, carved-in-stone documents? Or should they be viewed as flexible, make-it-up-as-you-go-along sets of guidelines?

Many traditionalists in the field argue the former—that professional codes are meant to be inflexible and not subject to exceptions. Like many other critics of situational ethics, they claim that a set of rules that is too easily subject to exceptions or multiple interpretations is not a set of "rules" but rather a set of "suggestions." The more cynical among them question the value of such "flexible rules" and contend that if the rules cannot be strictly interpreted and enforced, there's little need to have them.

Others believe the opposite and conclude that "situational ethics is the dominant moral value in the decision-making process in public relations."[2]

More informally, some public relations professionals make decisions based on which course of action is most expeditious or "doing what needs to be done" with little or no consideration of the long-term consequences. But public relations theorist and researcher John Marston contends that the "ends justify the means" rationale is inconsistent with public relations ethical principles.

Here are some of the common areas covered by the PRSA and IABC codes:

Serving the public interest. Both codes state that all communication activities must be carried out with regard to the best interests of the public. In other documents, the two organizations explain that term "public interest" refers to those rights and privileges granted to Americans by the U.S. Constitution and its amendments.

Respecting the "gifts and freebies" policies of the news media. As discussed in Chapter 5, most media outlets and professional associations have strict rules governing what journalists may and may not accept from individuals or organizations which they cover—or may find themselves covering in the future. Similarly, professional organizations such as PRSA and IABC have ethical guidelines that regulate the circumstances under which public relations representatives may provide product samples or other items or services that would assist journalists in developing their stories.

Examples of behaviors that violate these guidelines include (1) giving to media representative gifts of more than nominal value, (2) providing journalists with trips or travel opportunities that are unrelated to legitimate news interests, or (3) attempting to secure media coverage by connecting it to the organization's advertising activities. A Latin term often used in discussing this issue is *quid pro quo*, the translation of which means "something for something." In this context, the term refers to an unethical agreement to swap one product, service, or favor for another, such as the giving of a gift or bribe in exchange for positive news coverage.

Journalists who take their ethical policies seriously are reluctant to accept even the most insignificant gift. One Associated Press reporter, responding to a survey, quipped that "If it's worth more than $20, I can't accept it … If it's worth less than $20, it's crap and I don't want it." Another reporter said that marketing firms, public relations agencies, and other promotional entities should avoid the tradition of giving holiday gifts to reporters who cover their clients and should instead make equivalent donations to local charities. "That might not make headlines," the journalist wrote. "But neither does all the junk they send us."[3]

An important clarification of this provision is that it does not prohibit the reasonable giving or lending of products or services to media representatives who have a legitimate news interest. The emphasis here is on the key phrases *reasonable giving or lending* and *legitimate news interest*.

According to PRSA and IABC, examples of allowable transactions include:

• Loaning a product to a journalist who has been assigned to write a story or review about that product. Because the product is not being *given* to the journalist, but instead it is being *loaned* for a short period of time, it would be considered "reasonable." Because the writer has been assigned to write the review (most public relations representatives confirm such assignments with an editor), it is considered "legitimate news interest." In cases of consumable products such as toothpaste or mouthwash (a circumstance in which it would be impractical to ask the journalist to return what is left over), the public relations or marketing representative should provide the journalist with only enough of a sample for him or her to make a judgment.

- Allowing a theater critic to attend the performance of a play would be considered legitimate news interest, although some theater critics, like movie critics and restaurant critics, prefer to do their work anonymously in order to avoid unwanted attention.
- In limited circumstances, public relations representatives will offer—and travel and entertainment journalists will accept—free airline tickets, hotel rooms, meals, and other expenses associated with their coverage of grand openings of resorts or premieres of major motion pictures.

Of all of these examples, the last one is perhaps the most controversial among public relations professionals and journalists (see "Junkets and Freebies" in Chapter 5). In the entertainment industry, the popular term is *press junkets*, which are often weekend trips for movie and television critics. In addition to the opportunity to screen an upcoming movie or television pilot far in advance of its public release, critics often receive free hotel rooms and food for the duration of the trip, and in some cases also receive free airline tickets.

In the travel and tourism industry, such trips are called "fam tours"—short for "familiarization tour." The marketing department of the Walt Disney Corporation is a frequent target for criticism, based on the lavish press parties it hosts at Disneyland in California and Walt Disney World in Florida. (A discussion of media "fam tours" associated with the 2010 BP oil spill off the coast of Florida is discussed in Case 9D).

At most major daily newspapers, the policy regarding junkets is "absolutely not." At smaller dailies and weeklies, as well as monthly travel and entertainment magazines, policies may allow for some subsidizing of journalist travel, but only if the travel is approved by an editor and there is an understanding that the journalist is under no obligation—either stated or implied—to write a positive story.

At one time such trips were limited to full-time entertainment critics and travel journalists who had name recognition within their industry, but today, such opportunities are also offered to freelance writers and bloggers who can provide some assurance that their work will be published or posted to a legitimate website. Inexperienced public relations representatives occasionally find themselves victims of "freelance scammers" who falsify their credentials in order take subsidized trips to exotic destinations with no intention of writing or blogging about them. To avoid being scammed, experienced public relations representatives verify freelance writing assignments with editors or check the blogger's track record or other credentials.

Releasing truthful information and avoiding intentional deception. False or deceptive information can influence individuals and groups to make inappropriate decisions and place their own welfare at risk. When they discover the deception and its source, most individuals and organizations will be resentful and will likely become more negative toward the cause than they were before. Whether the deception is intentional or unintentional, public relations representatives suffer from damage to their credibility—as well as that of their employers—and typically find such damage difficult to repair.

When public relations representatives are asked questions that they cannot answer for legal or competitive reasons, they should explain the reason or reasons for the delay and indicate when they might be able to respond. Most reporters will understand and respect the legal reasons, but they will not understand or respect "no comment" or any other form of evasion or deception.

Protecting confidential information. In the agency–client relationship, agency employees cannot share information from one client with another client or with anyone else except on a "need to know" basis. In general, agency employees are expected to keep information secret until the client directs them to release it.

An important clarification of the confidentiality principle is that the obligation is in effect *before a formal relationship begins* and extends *beyond the termination of that relationship.* When a client discloses confidential information to an agency (or the agency uncovers information during its research) during preliminary discussions, that information is protected under the confidentiality rule, even if that agency is not hired. Likewise, employees of a corporate public relations department, independent contractors, or agencies representing a client are bound by the confidentiality rule even after the termination of working relationships—regardless of the circumstances under which the relationship ended.

While PRSA and IABC expect agency representatives to honor confidentiality agreements with their clients, such agreements do not prohibit professional communicators from "blowing the whistle" on a client or employer who is doing something illegal or from testifying in court about a client's or employer's illegal activity.

In terms of whistle-blowing or voluntarily providing information to law-enforcement or regulatory agencies, this clarification is significant not only for what is says, but what it does not say. While it says public relations representatives *may* report unethical behavior, it does not say that they *must* report it. If a public relations representative wanted to voluntarily provide information about a company doing something illegal, but was not sure if such action was appropriate, he or she could find justification in the professional association's concept of "serving the public interest."

Cutting ties with clients or employers if those relationships require conduct contrary to ethical guidelines. Because they have greater knowledge of the behind-the-scenes behavior of an organization, employees in the public relations department may find themselves in the uncomfortable position of deciding whether or not to be a whistle-blower. Examples might include having knowledge of a company's record of employment discrimination, insurance fraud, environmental violations, stock-market irregularities, or other problems. Although they are protected against employer retaliation by federal laws, potential whistle-blowers must decide whether or not to play that role.

Larry Johnson, author of a number of books about business ethics, claims that companies should reward whistle-blowers rather than attempt to retaliate against them. "No CEO of any honest company would want his or her people to participate in illegal or immoral activities," Johnson contended in his 2003 book *Absolute Honesty.* "If you see something going on that's not right, your first option is to go to your boss and say, 'this is going on; I can't participate because it's against my values.' If that doesn't work, take it up the chain of command." Addressing the concern that anti-retaliation laws are not fool-proof and that being a whistle-blower involves the risk of losing one's job, Johnson wrote, "There will always be risk involved. Only you can make the decision on where you draw the line on what's right and wrong."[4]

Avoiding conflicts of interest, real and perceived. Public relations agencies or individual public relations professionals are admonished to not perform work for any client or employer which causes a conflict—real or perceived—with the interests of another client or employer, unless full disclosure is made to and approval is granted by all parties involved.

In an agency setting, that means that an agency cannot represent clients that compete against each other. Some agencies hoping to retain two competing clients may attempt to skirt the issue by appointing separate account teams and forbidding them to discuss the details of their work with each other. That idea may sound good in theory, but even if the firm does have separate account executives and attempts in good faith to keep that wall of separation in place, the typical agency has only one art department, one media department, and one research department. The inner workings of a public relations agency do not lend themselves to complete confidentiality within the office.

The conflict of interest principle also prohibits the performance of work for any client or employer which causes a conflict—real or perceived—with the individual's personal interest. One example of this conflict involves an individual who works full-time in the public relations department of a company (or a public relations agency) and performs work as a freelancer in his or her free time. The individual may not accept as a freelance client any company that competes with his or her full-time employer unless both the client and the employer are aware of the situation and both agree to it.

This would also apply to the case of an independent public relations consultant or employee at a public relations agency whose personal interest—such as membership in a special-interest group—is in conflict with the interests of a current client. An example would be a consultant employed by a chemical company while also serving as an officer of an environmental watchdog group. If the watchdog group is involved in litigation against or is otherwise targeting the chemical company, the consultant must either resign his or her position in the watchdog group or cease working for the chemical company or the agency that represents it. As much as he or she may claim the ability to remain neutral, at some point he or she will be caught in the conflict between the two parties and will be forced to choose which loyalty is more important. It is best to make such a decision before the conflict arises.

Promising results that are outside of the individual's direct control. It is permissible for a public relations professional to guarantee to his or her clients conditions such as quality of service, degree of efforts, or methods utilized, because those are conditions within the control of public relations representatives or agencies. Representatives and agencies can, for example, guarantee their clients that a research project will be executed ethically and responsibly, will use the most up-to-date methods and technology, or will utilize a certain sample size. Agencies cannot, however, guarantee what the results of the research project will reveal. Likewise, an individual or agency cannot promise that the client will be profiled in an industry publication, that a client will see an increase in product sales, or that proposed government legislation will be passed or defeated. Any of those may be listed as objectives, but they cannot be guaranteed because of other intervening variables and the degree to which those results are largely outside the control of the individuals or agencies attempting to accomplish them.

The ethical rule that prohibits agencies from making promises to clients about results is one that some clients find problematic, as they are accustomed to working with other service providers who are able to guarantee their work. But most experienced agency executives know that over-promising simply to win new accounts over their competitors is a bad business practice. When clients fire their agencies, one of the most common reasons for doing so is that the agencies "over-promised and under-delivered."

Issues and Controversies

Differentiating between Public Relations and Advertising

The Federal Trade Commission and court system often use the blanket term "commercial speech" to refer to the advertising and public relations industries without drawing a distinction between the two. As a result, the FTC and courts apply rules regarding "truth in advertising" to public relations materials, even though organizations disseminating the materials consider them to be part of their public relations efforts.

Sporting goods manufacturer Nike found itself in such a conflict in 2002–03 (see Case Study 9A).

Legal and Ethical Problems in Investor Relations

Investor relations is a large and complex area of federal law that is subject to frequent change. It is often difficult to keep up with those changes—meaning that when in doubt, public relations representatives should contact their companies' legal departments for guidance. Attorney and public relations expert Frank Walsh wrote in a 1991 book on legal issues in public relations that "there is a great deal for public relations professionals to know, but perhaps the most important thing for them to know is when to talk to the company's attorney."[5]

The two most critical issues in this area are public disclosure and insider trading.

Public disclosure refers to the requirement that information about a publicly held company that may affect how its stock is evaluated (by stockbrokers, analysts, or potential investors) must be released in a manner that is timely, accurate, and in its correct context. Examples include announcements about quarterly or annual earnings, potential mergers and acquisitions, changes in leadership, new products or services, major expansion plans, employee layoffs, pending litigation (as plaintiff or defendant), or a change in credit rating.

The Securities and Exchange Commission has the authority to punish companies that fail to perform up to that expectation, and stockholders can sue companies because the information was not provided in a timely manner, was deemed to be misleading, or was not in its correct context. Analysts suggest that important news be released in the late afternoon or early evening after the stock markets have closed, as opposed to releasing it while the trading floors are open.

Accusations of **insider trading** are a potential problem for public relations professionals who work for publicly traded companies or the agencies that represent them. Owning stock in companies that your public relations agency represents may result in a number of opportunities for conflicts of interest—both real and perceived.

If employees of a company or its public relations agency use inside information to illegally trade that company's stock, they might be in violation of the Securities and Exchange Act of 1934, a law dealing with insider trading. An individual becomes an "insider" if he or she is in a position to learn of business information that affects that organization's stock before that information becomes public knowledge. SEC rules prohibit such individuals from purchasing or selling stock until after the information becomes public.

Because of the complexity of SEC rules and the possibility of "honest mistakes" resulting in charges of insider trading, many public relations agencies take the added precaution of prohibiting their employees from owning stock in the companies the agency represents. Even if an agency allows it, it is a bad idea. There are plenty of other good stocks to invest in.

In addition to adhering to the regulations of the Securities and Exchange Commission, public relations professionals involved in investor relations should also be familiar with the rules of the New York Stock Exchange, Chicago Mercantile Exchange, and other national and regional financial organizations.

The Good and Bad of Media Relations

In media relations, the difficulty of meeting media deadlines has always been a source of anxiety for public relations agencies and individual representatives. Before the advent of the Internet, media relations specialists had to be concerned with only two deadlines per day—the television deadline (usually late afternoon) and the print deadline (usually early evening for the next day's morning newspaper). Today, however, most newspapers and television stations of any size have corresponding Internet and social media sites that are updated constantly, meaning that with rapidly developing news stories, deadlines occur every hour.

The working relationship between journalists and public relations professionals is one that is interdependent, but not necessarily reciprocal. Even though each side depends on the other, at times the relationship appears to be unbalanced. Corporate public relations representatives depend heavily on the journalists—especially business reporters—to disseminate company information to their external publics. Part of the job of a public relations representative is to help the journalists do their jobs better, but it is not the responsibility of journalists to assist public relations representatives in carrying out their job duties.

While relationships between journalists and public relations representatives for nonprofit organizations can sometimes be adversarial, the problem is much more serious in the cases of business journalists and corporate public relations representatives. While they are reluctant to admit it, business reporters depend heavily on information provided by public relations representatives. Without public relations representatives to provide story ideas, publications such as *The Wall Street Journal* and *Business Week* simply could not fill all of their pages. Rebecca Madeira, the public relations director for Pepsico, describes the relationship as being similar to a game of tennis: "You're on opposite sides of the net, but it's the only way to play the game."[6] James Deacon, a former White House correspondent for the *St. Louis Dispatch*, added another sports metaphor. "The government always wants reporters on their team," Deacon wrote in his 1984 memoir. "But if journalists are on the team, who will report on the game, and who will keep score?"[7]

How the Two Sides Perceive Each Other

Historically, public relations professionals and journalists have a love–hate relationship. While both depend on each other in the execution of their job duties, the working relationship between the two professions is sometimes contentious. Journalists are probably more critical of public relations representatives than the other way around, but many of those criticisms are based not on substance but on conditioning and role expectation. Some of the more cynical journalists say, "I'm a journalist; I'm supposed to hate public relations people. It's in my job description." Adds a popular public relations textbook:

> Much of the problem stems from how (differently) each of the two professions defines news … Plants that operate safely and are not laying off employees, nonprofit organizations that operate within budget and provided needed services, companies that pay a dividend for the fifteenth consecutive quarter are all signs that things are operating smoothly and make for a story that the public should hear. To a journalist, the opposite is true. Plants only make news when they endanger the public safety. Employees are at their most newsworthy when they bring a gun to work, not when they show up every day for thirty years.[8]

A recent survey conducted by a New York-based PR firm indicated that more than 65 percent of journalists distrust public relations professionals, but that 81 percent indicated they need them.[9]

The journalism profession's dependency on public relations materials has increased dramatically in the last two decades, as newspaper, television, and radio news operations trim the size of their staffs. That is especially true in the case of local television news, where news programming has expanded from an hour a day in the 1980s to more than two hours today—but with production staffs remaining the same size or in some cases shrinking.

Here are some of the most common criticisms that journalists cite about their working relationships with public relations professionals:

- Public relations professionals flood our snail-mail boxes and email boxes with unsolicited materials sent by postal mail and electronic mail and pester us with too many follow-up calls, emails, and text messages. John Trattner, an official with the U.S. State Department in the 1970s, said that trying to sell the media a story it doesn't want to buy is like trying to "sneak sunrise past a rooster."[10]
- Many public relations professionals are unfamiliar with the style, format, or deadlines of the newspaper or television or radio program they approach.
- Public relations representatives exaggerate the importance of things that we see as trivial. They over-promote events and products and look at the news media as a source of free publicity. News releases about new drugs or treatments coming to market should provide "fair balance" about the relative benefits and risks associated with them and must also be clear about the limitations of the drug or treatment.[11]
- Public relations representatives limit our access to company officials. We want to talk to the president of the company, not the PR guy. The president of the company will tell us the truth; the PR guy will just get in the way. In the case of agency personnel providing information on behalf of clients, journalists claim that those communicators are often unable to answer follow-up questions about the products or services being promoted and are unable to connect journalists with helpful sources within the client companies.
- In crisis situations, public relations representatives will stonewall, refuse to release information, and often lie to us. We want the truth and we want it now, but the PR department tries to put off releasing the information and hopes we will go away. Some external agencies or internal public relations departments make it a practice to issue news releases based on bad news at a time when media outlets are less likely to notice. Announcements made after 10 p.m. Saturday won't make it into Sunday's paper, and by Sunday night it might be too old for Monday's edition.

The Danger of Playing Favorites

Public relations professionals should avoid playing favorites—or appear to be playing favorites —among the media representatives who cover the company or nonprofit organization. The worst example is providing one reporter advance information about an upcoming announcement, thus allowing him or her to break the story ahead of his or her competitors.

An important clarification is that this rule would not prevent a public relations representative from helping a reporter working on an "enterprise story"—one in which the reporter has developed a story idea based on his or her initiative.

In politics and government, it is common for reporters to ask for an "exclusive"—an agreement that the journalist will be the first (or sometimes only) person provided with information about a certain topic. That often happens when a reporter learns about the content of an upcoming announcement several days before it is scheduled, and someone on the staff of the politician or government agency asks the reporter to not break the story in advance. In return for "sitting on the story," the journalist is given the first interview with the politician and/or government official involved.

While this practice is common in politics, in corporate or nonprofit public relations work it should be done rarely—perhaps never. The long-term damage to the organization's relationships with other journalists outweighs any short-term benefit that might result.

Dealing with Media Errors and Perceived Negative Coverage

An important part of maintaining good relationships with the media is knowing how to deal with inaccurate media coverage or what an organization believes to be coverage that may not be inaccurate per se but is unfair or misleading. In addition to deciding the "when" and the "how," another important question is "whether or not." Experienced professional communicators know that in some cases, reacting or overreacting to negative media coverage does more harm than good.

When faced with inaccurate or misleading reporting, public relations representatives for the individuals or organizations involved in the story should carefully think through their responses. Errors in media coverage can be placed in one of four categories:

Defamation: Errors that are defamatory—seriously damaging to the reputation or financial well-being of the organization—should be taken seriously by both parties. These errors might be the grounds for legal action, but this is a decision for the organization's legal department, not the public relations staff.

Serious (but non-defamatory) factual errors: These are errors that affect the audience's understanding of a story and for which there is documentation available to prove their falsity. In these cases, the public relations staff should request the media outlet for a correction or retraction, but should do so in a professional manner and without threats of legal action.

Minor inaccuracies: These are errors that do not affect the audience's understanding of the story. An example of a minor inaccuracy is reporting that a company was founded in 1984 when it was actually founded in 1985, or reporting that the president of the company holds a degree in chemistry when the degree earned was actually in biology. Errors of this type should be ignored, or at most, corrected in a less formal way—simply asking the media organization to correct the information in its clip files or electronic archives (so the error won't be repeated), but not insisting on a published correction.

Subjective errors: An example of a subjective error is a columnist or other opinion writer stating that your company's priority for the coming year is in one area of its operation, when you know it is in a different area. In most cases, errors of this type—while annoying—should be ignored.

News Releases and Manufactured Quotes

Still another part of an effective media relations program is providing the media with documents that accompany major announcements or provide background information on organizational activities. Originally known as "press releases," today the more commonly used terms are "news releases" or "media releases." Even though the entire content of a news release is seldom used in a news story, reporters often lift quotes from the release instead of calling to obtain quotes first-hand.

A common format for most news releases includes a "four-Ws" summary of the subject: the who, what, when, and where. A fifth W is the why, and that is often explained in the form of a quote from a senior official within the organization. In some cases, the author of the news release interviews the official to obtain the quote, but in other cases he or she simply manufactures the quote, usually with the approval from the official being quoted. The issue of "manufactured" or "artificial" quotes is mildly controversial.

While some journalists have a policy of not using quotes they suspect may have been manufactured, most accept it as part of their working relationship with public relations professionals and may use them if they are not silly or libelous. When doing so, many journalists will likely use connecting phrases such as *said in a statement released by the company* to indicate that the quotes did not result from an actual interview.

In most cases, public relations representatives ask the client to provide general thoughts about the topic to be discussed, expand on those thoughts to create a more detailed and effective quote, then obtain the client's permission to use the quote in its finished form. A representative who creates a quote and includes it in a news release without the client's approval risks exposing the client to embarrassment, criticism, or a possible defamation lawsuit if the quote includes factual errors.

Professionalism and Respect

It is not uncommon for members of the media, consumer watchdog groups, and the general public to express skepticism or distrust of the public relations industry.

In the previous century much of that reputation was deserved, as practitioners of the profession were caught attempting to deceive the public or mislead the media. Much of the skepticism is based on incidents of the 1920s and 1930s, when industry publicists—the forerunner of today's corporate public relations practitioners—routinely lied to government investigators, the media, and the public while representing companies in times of crisis. Today, that practice is continued by Hollywood publicists and press agents who represent the interests of their clientele by exaggerating the importance of an entertainer's accomplishments, staging phony events, and stonewalling the media's attempts to pursue legitimate news. The image of the profession in the latter half of the previous century led the Public Relations Society of America to hire a full-time public relations officer and develop campaigns to improve the image of the profession—the so-called "PR for PR" approach.

One early critic of the public relations industry was journalism historian Daniel Boorstin, who complained that consumers were at the mercy of powerful corporations using their public relations and advertising budgets to intentionally mislead and exploit the public. Boorstin was followed in the 1980s by Jeff and Marie Blyskal, a husband-and-wife team of consumer advocates and authors of *PR: How the Public Relations Industry Writes the News*. In 1989, consumer advocate Joyce Nelson took a similar stance in her book *Sultans of Sleaze: Public Relations and the Media*. Nelson claims the primary strength of an organization's public relations function is its ability to operate "under the radar ... gliding in and out of troubling situations without being noticed" and manipulating public opinion without leaving behind any evidence of its work.[12]

The alternative political magazine *Utne Reader* also scrutinizes the public relations industry. In one 1994 article, it accused the public relations profession of "shaping public life in ways we're not supposed to notice" and commented (incorrectly) that the profession's core principle was that it is "easier to change the way people think about reality than it is to change reality."[13]

Today, among the field's most vocal critics are consumer activists Sheldon Rampton and John Stauber, who authored a 1995 book titled *Toxic Sludge Is Good for You: Lies, Damn Lies and the Public Relations Industry*, the title of which indicates its tone. Today, Rampton and Stauber continue their criticism of the field through publishing *PR Watch*, a website that its founders say "calls attention to the misleading and unethical conduct" of some public relations professionals.

The profession also continues to draw harsh words in recent decades from various consumer advocates and other critics. In her 2005 book *Bait and Switch: The Futile Pursuit of the American Dream*, author Barbara Ehrenreich tells the story of a professional woman exploring a variety of career options. The author describes public relations as "journalism's evil twin" and writes that

> whereas a journalist seeks the truth, a PR person may be called upon to disguise it or even to advance an untruth ... if your employer, a pharmaceutical company, claims its new drug cures both cancer and erectile dysfunction, your job is to promote it, not to investigate the grounds for those claims.[14]

The profession took another beating in 2008 when former White House Press Secretary Scott McClellan published his book *What Happened*, which chronicled his three years working as the top public information officer in the federal government. The book itself did not create the uproar, but media critics used anecdotes from the book as examples of how public relations professionals "manipulate" the news media and public opinion. CBS News commentator Andrew Cohen said that McClellan's revelations were just the "tip of the iceberg" and that the government's use of "spin" was just one example of how the public relations industry negatively affects society. In his on-air commentary, Cohen said, "Show me a PR person who is accurate and truthful and I'll show you a PR person who is unemployed."[15]

How the public relations profession can enhance its image and earn greater respect from employers, the media, and the general public has been a subject of industry publications and conferences for decades.

The only tangible suggestion discussed is that of a licensing program. The leaderships of PRSA and IABC have considered the potential for a formal licensing procedure for public relations professionals. The program would be analogous to those in place for other professionals, such as architects and accountants.

Public relations pioneer Edward L. Bernays was the leading advocate for licensing from the late 1950s until his death in 1995. Since his passing, however, no individual or group has stepped forward to advocate licensing with the same level of enthusiasm. If public relations professionals could be licensed, Bernays argued, the program could require more educational preparation (perhaps a specific college degree), enhance the image of the industry, and provide a mechanism for removing from the profession those individuals or agencies found to be incompetent or guilty of dishonest or unethical conduct.

Those opposing the idea counter with two arguments of their own. The first counter-argument is that before a formal licensing program could be established, there would have to be a universal definition for public relations—one that all of the major professional groups could agree upon. A second problem is that neither PRSA nor IABC (nor any other professional group) wants the responsibility for setting up the bureaucracy and due process that would be necessary to administer such a program. If the licensing process were to be modeled after those of other organizations, the subsequent increase in office staff would cause membership costs to double or triple, and the legal fees associated with court challenges could increase membership costs even further.

Unethical Working Environments

Public relations professionals are occasionally given assignments that potentially call for unethical or questionable conduct, or behavior that makes them uncomfortable. Before making hasty assumptions, the individual should first clarify the assignment or task, clear up potential misunderstandings, and then determine whether or not complying with the request would involve an ethical violation.

If the individual finds the answer is "yes," he or she has a number of options. The first is to advise the client or employer that the actions being considered are not only in violation of accepted ethical guidelines, but also not in the best interests of the organization. One way to approach this difficult situation is to provide examples of how similar conduct resulted in negative results for other organizations in the past. Public relations textbooks contain many examples that could be cited. The second strategy is to simply refuse to participate and explain the reasons for doing so. The practicality of this tactic depends on the nature of the relationship between the individual and the client or employer; professionals new to their positions may lack the confidence to do so.

A third option—to be considered only in the most serious circumstances—is to sever relationships with the client or employer in question. The justification for such a drastic step is clear, however. A public relations professional forced to act in a way that conflicts with accepted ethical standards will lose confidence in the client or employer and will therefore be unable to provide appropriate counsel or serve as a credible spokesperson. But in his 1993 book *The Credibility Factor: Putting Ethics to Work in Public Relations*, Lee W. Baker writes:

> When asked to violate ethics by a boss or client, I do not take the arbitrary position that a practitioner should immediately quit, or threaten to. First, that is a bad negotiating technique. Second, it implies that all ethical issues are black and white. Some hard-liners say that we must have the courage to stand by our principles, and if necessary, walk away from a client. But how does an individual with two children in college, a mortgage, a $3,000 orthodontist bill, and a wife thinking about divorce walk away from a high-paying job on a matter of principle?[16]

Robert L. Dilenschneider, former president of Hill & Knowlton, wrote in his book *Power and Influence: Mastering the Art of Persuasion* that the public often judges an organization's ethical performance "by comparing what it says to what it does." Another adage used in discussions of business ethics is that "what an organization DOES will shout so loudly that no one will hear what it SAYS."[17]

"Public Relations ethics is often seen as an oxymoron," wrote Margalit Toledano and Ruth Avidar in a 2016 article in *Public Relations Review*. "The industry is notorious for manipulative, deceptive, and irresponsible tactics to achieve the goals of the organization it serves. Yet PR scholars argue that ethical practice is a core challenge for the profession because of the weighty responsibilities of the function within an organization and its ability to wield influence in public policy."[18]

Unethical Practices of Some Public Relations Agencies

Relationships with clients represent an ethical minefield for public relations agencies. Practices for which agencies are sometimes criticized include:

Churning: Unscrupulous agencies often create unnecessary work or exaggerate the amount of staff time actually involved in a project in order to "pad" the client's bill. Unless the client (or someone in its accounting office) scrutinizes the monthly bill, such padding may go undetected.

Bait and switch: An experienced senior account executive or agency officer (with local or national name recognition) makes the initial presentation and lands the account, but then the detail work is assigned to younger, less experienced staffers; the senior executive is never seen again. In another variation, an agency may send one or more attractive young women to make new business proposals to male clients. Those potential clients are likely unaware that once they hire the firm, they are unlikely to ever see those women again, much less have the opportunity to date them. Not only is this an unethical way for public relations agencies to treat potential clients, but also an unethical way for them to treat their own employees.

Creating unrealistic expectations: While presenting new business proposals, agency representatives may claim there is more publicity potential in a project than there actually is. They may drop titles of publications such as *The Wall Street Journal* into the conversation in order to land a prospective account, even though the agency representative already knows that such news coverage is unlikely.

Staged news conferences and "planted" questions: An agency may have employees pose as reporters at a client's news conference and ask friendly set-up questions to influence the tone of the event, or have them attend a competitor's news conference to ask hostile questions. In cases in which employees might be recognized, the agency sends college students serving as interns.

Liese L. Hutchison, former associate professor of communication at St. Louis University, suggests that agency owners and managers should insist on high ethical standards for their employees by either adopting the code of ethics of either PRSA or IABC (or developing more specific guidelines of their own), requiring employees to sign the code, inserting the code into requests for proposals, and then setting the example by demonstrating ethical conducts themselves.[19]

Confidentiality and Privilege

Codes of ethics require public relations professionals to treat as confidential the majority of the information they exchange with clients. However, this principle does not apply in situations such as being questioned by federal or state law-enforcement investigators, testifying in court, or providing a deposition in a legal proceeding.

This is quite different from the protected status provided to lawyers and physicians, who cannot be required to testify in court against their clients and patients. Many public relations professionals believe they should have the same level of confidentiality and cite the following reasons to support their position:

- A public relations representative testifying in court against a client or employer is putting his or her career on the line. Whether the testimony is voluntary or mandated by the court, he or she cannot continue to work for the client or employer against whom the testimony was given. He or she should not be put in that awkward position.
- Professional communicators deserve the same level of legal protection as lawyers and doctors. Lawyers must have the complete trust of their clients in order to provide competent legal representation, and doctors must have the complete trust of their patients in order to provide adequate health care. Public relations is no different—clients and employers must have trusting relationships with their outside public relations agencies or employees of the PR department in order for those individuals to provide their best advice or service.

- Without privilege, public relations professionals are too vulnerable. Without legal protection, public relations representatives are easy targets for prosecutors, defense attorneys, and government officials who are simply looking for shortcuts rather than doing more thorough investigative work on their own. Shield laws protect journalists; public relations representatives should have similar protection.

The rationale for *not* providing similar legal protection for public relations representatives include the following factors:

- Lawyers and doctors and lawyers work in fields that are well defined, while public relations is not well defined. If public relations professionals are given privilege, a company in legal trouble could simply re-draw its organizational chart and claim that all of its employees work in public relations and are therefore immune to subpoenas and other court proceedings.
- Granting privilege to public relations professionals may impede important government investigations. As mentioned earlier, public relations representatives often have inside knowledge of matters such as employment discrimination, insurance fraud, stock-market irregularities, and environmental damage. They should be required to provide this information because those investigations serve the greater public interest, which the industry codes identify as the most important value.
- Compared to the work of lawyers and doctors, the work of public relations professionals is not that important. Individuals facing criminal charges have the constitutional right to legal representation, while patients have a moral right to health care. No one has the constitutional or moral right to public relations advice, however. Opponents of proposals to grant privilege to public relations professionals contend that their work is simply not as important as legal representation or health care.

Litigation PR

One of the fastest-growing trends within the profession is the phenomenon of law firms hiring public relations agencies to augment their courtroom strategy. Known as **litigation PR**, the objective is to use public relations techniques to influence public opinion both inside and outside of the courtroom. Prior to the selection of a jury in a criminal or civil trial, such tactics are often effective in presenting a favorable impression of the defendant to prospective jurors who are following media coverage of pre-trial proceedings. Once the trial is underway, public relations firms are used to measure how the public perceives the media coverage.

Although litigation PR is often said to be linked to crisis management, some experts believe that in litigation PR, strategies are actually easier to execute because litigation unfolds over weeks, months, and years, rather than days. Therefore, instead of employing crisis strategies such as news conferences and emergency statements released through both traditional and social media, public relations representatives can use more long-term strategies such as issue advertising and non-crisis media interviews.

As a result of the trend, veteran public relations executives are augmenting their experience and enhancing their career potential by earning law degrees. "We're increasingly seeing [public relations] agencies with lawyers on staff, not as legal counsel, but PR pros holding JDs [law degrees]," said Kathleen Taylor Sooy, a partner in the Washington, D.C. law firm of Crowell & Moring. "Sure, the hourly rates tend to be a bit higher, but you are paying for the legal expertise."[20] The litigation PR approach is seen as a viable alternative to the usual strategy of a client's public persona being defined by the "no comment" response to questions.[21]

Today, many defense attorneys in criminal trials as well as civil trials (such as product liability cases) use focus groups to help them with both jury selection and trial strategy. One of the reasons for their popularity and success is the similarity of the group dynamics involved in focus group discussions led by a moderator and jury deliberations led by a foreperson.

Although the technique had already been in use for more than a decade, the idea of using focus groups to help trial lawyers design their courtroom strategies came to the attention of the media and the public during the 1995 murder trial of O.J. Simpson. Forensic Technologies, a California-based research firm, conducted four surveys of Los Angeles residents—potential jurors—to gauge public attitudes toward Simpson during pre-trial proceedings. The company then used two focus groups to help defense attorneys prepare for the juror screening process and determine what qualities they should look for in prospective jurors. During the trial itself, the company conducted additional focus groups, having the participants function as "mock juries" and react to videotaped segments showing the defense lawyers so they could adjust their presentation styles.

In addition to Simpson, other clients to benefit from the litigation public relations strategies include Nike and Tommy Hilfiger (in their trademark litigation against other clothing manufacturers) and pop singer Michael Jackson (defending himself against child molestation charges).

More recently, the attorneys representing a Georgia father on trial for murder after leaving his infant son in a hot car in 2014 hired a public relations firm to assist in his defense. Because the father was also charged with molesting teenage girls in an unrelated case, the attorneys wanted the public relations firm to execute a two-part strategy: downplay the molestation case while presenting the father as the "victim of an accidental case of forgetfulness."[22]

Critics contend that public relations techniques are being used in ways that the founders of the profession never intended. The technique of leaking information to the media with the intention of influencing potential jurors is one example that the profession's founders, as well as public relations ethicists, would find troubling.

Other practitioners disagree. "This is not 'spin-doctoring' in the pejorative sense, and it doesn't require anything untoward or unethical," wrote James F. Haggerty in a 2004 article in *Business Law Today*. "Rather, it involves taking a lawyer's natural persuasive skills and adapting them for a court of a different kind (the court of public opinion)—where the rules of procedure are far more nuanced, amorphous, and difficult to enforce."[23]

Public relations educator Edward J. Lordan contends that public relations professionals working with lawyers is a natural fit because of the similarity between the fields. "Both are looking out for their clients' best interests, both are legally and ethically bound to tell the truth, and both conduct research to develop positions that present their clients favorably," Lordan wrote in his textbook *Essentials of Public Relations Management*. "Addressing issues solely from a legal perspective can be extremely dangerous in the long term … it is the job of public relations managers to remind their clients that legal action can result in irreparable damage to relationships with key constituents."[24]

In addition to free-standing public relations agencies specializing in litigation PR, many large corporations are employing the strategy for their own legal situations. "Several Fortune 500 companies have recently moved some of their in-house PR staff into their legal departments," reported a 2005 article in *PR Week*.[25]

Your Turn

Case Study 9A: Differentiating Between Public Relations and Advertising: Nike Goes to Court

In 2002–03, the sporting goods manufacturer Nike entered into a lengthy legal battle that in some ways helped draw a dividing line between the fields of advertising and public relations and in some cases make that line more difficult to detect.

The company had been accused of violating child labor standards and condoning "sweatshop" conditions in its overseas factories. The company responded to those criticisms using standard public relations techniques—news releases, letters to newspaper editors, and other forms of public communication that did not resemble advertising in any way. The company also wrote letters to university administrators on campuses where students had called for their institutions to boycott the company, which was a major provider of athletic equipment.

A California-based consumer advocacy group sued the company under the state's truth-in-advertising law. The state's unusual advertising statute not only prohibited companies from disseminating false information (a determination usually left to the Federal Trade Commission), but also allowed individuals to file charges against violators, even though they may not have been personally harmed. The case centered not on whether Nike's statements were true, but whether they were protected as free speech and whether groups not directly affected by the ads should be allowed to pursue such cases.

A California trial court sided with Nike, ruling that its messages aimed at responding to public criticism were statements of opinion rather than commercial messages, and therefore deserved First Amendment protection. The California Supreme Court reversed that decision, claiming that every message a company disseminates is to some degree a commercial message and was therefore not fully protected by the First Amendment.

Nike appealed the decision to the U.S. Supreme Court, and in doing so was publicly supported by numerous other free-speech advocates, including the Public Relations Society of America and the American Civil Liberties Union.

The Court eventually ruled on the second issue—that consumer groups had a right to file claims even if not directly affected by the case—and it sent the case back to the California trial court to be tried again. Before the trial was set to begin, the two parties reached an out-of-court settlement. What was left unsettled, however, was the issue of whether it was appropriate to view advertising and public relations materials in the same light in terms of First Amendment protection.

1. Do you agree with the tendency of the Federal Trade Commission and the court system to use the blanket term "commercial speech" and treat public relations and advertising by the same legal standards?
2. Are there any philosophers or concepts from Chapter 2 that could be applied here?

Case Study 9B: Professionalism and Respect: When a PR Firm Could Use a PR Firm

Public relations firms have often generated internal problems—as well as negative publicity—by accepting clients involved in controversial public issues. In 1991, for example, Hill & Knowlton was criticized for accepting the assignment of developing an anti-abortion campaign for one of its clients, the United States Catholic Conference. The account was worth an estimated $3 million.

Many of the firm's 1,850 employees objected to the idea, and two felt strongly enough to resign. The employees were angry not only at the concept of the campaign, but also the fact they read about it in the media before hearing it from their own employer. In addition to dealing with the employees' negative reaction, a major Hill & Knowlton client (that the firm declined to identify) canceled its working relationship with the firm.

The irony of the situation was that the firm's president, Robert Dilenschneider, had just published a book on issues management and in practice the firm violated many of the principles espoused in the book. In hindsight, Dilenschneider admitted that the firm did a "very bad job" at handling the controversy.

After months of media criticism, the agency established a policy that any employee who objected to the campaign would not be required to work on it. That was an easy situation to resolve for a large organization such as Hill & Knowlton, a worldwide firm with thousands of employees; it could easily find enough to staff the account. The situation would be far different for a small firm that may have only five or six employees and requires every staff member work on every account.

In 1992, Hill & Knowlton generated controversy again when it represented an international organization called Citizens for a Free Kuwait, the purpose of which was to generate support for the U.S. military action against Iraq after it invaded its tiny neighbor. The firm arranged for a fourteen-year-old Kuwaiti girl to testify before a congressional committee looking into human rights abuses allegedly carried out by Iraqi soldiers during the conflict. The girl claimed that she had witnessed soldiers taking Kuwaiti infants from their hospital incubators and leaving them on the floor to die.

After it was learned that the stories were exaggerated (and may have been fabricated), the firm was accused of misleading Congress while not disclosing the fact that the girl was the daughter of Kuwait's ambassador to the U.S.

1. Were these situations involving Hill & Knowlton handled fairly and ethically? What would you have done differently if you were in a leadership position in the agency?
2. What if you were the owner of a small firm (fewer than a dozen employees) with a tradition of having every employee involved in every account, and several objected to working on a specific project or for a specific client?

Case Study 9C: Professionalism and Respect: A Bad Day at the Office for FEMA

In October 2007, wildfires swept across southern California, leaving thousands of families homeless and causing billions of dollars in property damage. The Federal Emergency Management Agency (FEMA) planned a news conference at its Washington, D.C. offices to brief reporters on the agency's response to the disaster.

Due to the short notice and other miscommunications, FEMA officials found themselves talking to an empty room. Rather than cancel the briefing, FEMA officials gathered agency employees to pose as journalists and ask softball questions, such as, "Are you pleased with FEMA's response so far?" Reporters were invited to listen to the news conference by telephone but were not allowed to ask questions, and television stations were later given videotaped copies of the news conference without being told that it was staged.

Once the deception was exposed, FEMA claimed it was the idea of one senior administrator, and that the media spokesperson conducting the briefing did not recognize FEMA employees as the "reporters" asking the questions. FEMA Director David Paulison, Homeland Security Secretary Michael Chertoff, and President George W. Bush all condemned the event as "unacceptable."

The fake news conference fiasco came just two years after a much bigger FEMA failure —its response to Hurricane Katrina. The Category 5 storm was one of the most expensive and deadly to hit the mainland United States, coming ashore near New Orleans in late August 2005. The storm killed more than 1,800 people (including those killed on Caribbean islands in the storm's path) and caused $86 billion in property damage.

Communication systems were down, meaning that reporters were at a disadvantage working in damaged and dangerous areas. A series of miscommunications between FEMA, city government officials in New Orleans, and state officials in Louisiana resulted in a lack of information (or sometimes the wrong information) being provided to journalists. Although several parties shared the blame, FEMA took most of the criticism, and critics used the scenario to portray the Bush administration as callous and uncaring toward the people affected. The slow and ineffective response led to the resignation of FEMA director Michael D. Brown.

Following the Katrina and fake news conference fiascos, ongoing news coverage of FEMA highlighted a number of mistakes and oversights, many of them related to unnecessary bureaucracy created by the agency's new organizational structure. FEMA was once an independent agency, but after becoming part of Department of Homeland Security following the September 11, 2001 terrorist attacks, its new leaders were mostly political appointees with little or no previous experience in disaster recovery. Many congressional leaders called for the agency to be removed from underneath the Homeland Security umbrella and once again made an independent agency.

1. How does a federal government agency such as FEMA recover from having such an ethical misdeed publicized?

2. If you were a journalist covering FEMA and knew about these incidents, would you be skeptical of any information you received from the agency in the future?

Case Study 9D: The Good and Bad of Media Relations: The BP Oil Spill

Following the British Petroleum (BP) oil spill in the Gulf of Mexico in April 2010, tourist development organizations in northwest Florida struggled to inform potential visitors from other parts of the country that the damage caused by the spill was not as extensive as the national media portrayed it. By mid-summer, they had received multi-million-dollar grants from the oil company in order to address that challenge.

In addition to using the BP grants to purchase advertising in newspapers and magazines and on television and radio, the agencies also hosted "familiarization tours" or "fam tours" during which travel journalists from across the country visited the affected areas and interviewed year-round residents, summer visitors, and hotel and restaurant owners whose businesses depended largely on tourism.

The organizers did not directly pay for the airline fares for the journalists, but did arrange for their hotels, meals, and local transportation costs to be paid for using the BP grants. In defending the program, tourism officials insisted that in accepting the "freebies," the writers were under no obligation—either stated or implied—to write positive stories or mention the oil spill in a particular way.

All of the journalists taking part in the program represented either monthly or weekly news magazines or online news organizations or identified themselves as freelancers. None represented daily newspapers or television stations or networks, most likely because that even without a stated or implied obligation, accepting such expenses violated their ethical codes or "junket" policies.

1. As indicated in the scenario, those attending the event identified themselves as affiliated with weekly magazines, travel publications, or online news organizations, with others being independent bloggers or freelancers. If asked by your employer, how could you make attending the event more attractive to daily newspapers and broadcast journalists while still respecting their ethical policies and concerns?
2. Are there any philosophers or concepts from Chapter 2 that can be applied here?

Discussion Problem 9A: Confidentiality and Privilege: The Sexual Assault Focus Group

As part of a research project in an advanced public relations class, students organize focus group sessions to gather student perception on the problem of sexual assault on campus. Because of the sensitive nature of the discussions, students are organized into separate groups for men and women. Before the sessions begin, the moderators inform the participants that their identities and their comments would be kept confidential. Each participant fills out a registration card, but moderators assure the group that is only so the students can send them thank-you cards in the mail.

During one of the focus group sessions for female students, several of the participants tell nearly identical stories about a specific downtown bar at which they suspect employees may have spiked their drinks with date-rape drugs. Although none of the women were assaulted as a result, they did recall being nauseated and dizzy for several days.

The women's comments become part of the written record of the session. Several weeks later, when the students prepare their final report, they mention the women's experience but do not elaborate on it. At the end of the semester, the professor who supervised the project submits a copy of the final report to the dean of students' office, not thinking about the impact of the information related to the date-rape drug.

The dean of students notices it, however, and contacts the professor to ask if he will disclose the names of the students participating in the focus group sessions so he can question them, find out which bar they were referring to, and notify local law enforcement.

1. What should the professor do—turn over the names of the students (which means violating the agreement that their identities would remain confidential) or stick to the promise of confidentiality given to the participants at the beginning of the session?
2. Even though information revealed in social science research may be confidential in a general sense, it is not legally protected (such as in cases of doctor–patient privilege or lawyer-client privilege). In this case, does the interest of possibly uncovering illegal activity (such as use of a date-rape drug) take priority over the moderator's promise of confidentiality? Why or why not?
3. Which of the philosophers studied in Chapter 2 might help the professor make this decision?

Discussion Problem 9B: The Good and Bad of Media Relations: Get Your Can to the Game

You're a student at Enormous State University, and a campus organization you belong to has spent most of the fall semester planning an event to benefit the food bank that helps low-income families in your community. The event, scheduled to take place two weeks before Thanksgiving, involves chapter members working with players from a minor-league baseball team to collect cans of food outside the stadium before a home game. Fans who bring at least two cans of food may exchange them for coupons that give them a discount on tickets for the game. Fans who already have their tickets when they come to the stadium will receive discount coupons for a local restaurant. Fans will also receive one raffle ticket for each can of food they bring.

In addition to providing the discounts, the management of the baseball team allows your group to use its name in promoting the event, provides prizes for the raffle, and helps the group obtain an insurance waiver required by the company that manages the stadium. The afternoon of the game, the team gives the students part of the pre-game program to present the raffle prizes and make a brief announcement explaining the year-round needs of the food bank.

The goals for the event are to:

- generate donations for the food bank;
- create awareness of the year-round needs of the food bank;
- get some practice in event-planning and developing publicity materials;
- generate publicity and recognition for the student organization.

Your faculty advisor helps your group prepare news releases to promote the event. The afternoon of the game, your members are busy collecting cans outside the stadium. The baseball players, who were supposed to be there to help collect cans and sign autographs, are nowhere in sight. Reporters from the local daily newspaper and television station arrive and start to interview the students. Then three baseball players show up, and the reporters cut short their interviews with the students and begin to interview the players.

On the 6 o'clock news that night, the television reporter who was there provides a report that does not mention the students, your student organization, or even the name of your university. Instead, the story consists only of interviews with the baseball players and makes it appear as though they were solely responsible for the food drive. The next morning, the daily newspaper carries a story that includes some quotes from the players, but also quotes the students and gives your organization the majority of the credit for the event.

1. How should your student group respond, if at all, to the television news story that gave all the credit to the baseball players?
2. Which philosophers discussed in Chapter 2 might help you make this decision?

Discussion Problem 9C: The Good and Bad of Media Relations: Go Quietly or Else

You are the communications manager for a very visible and well-respected nonprofit organization in a small town, and part of your job is to serve as the primary spokesperson and contact for local media. You report to the executive director, a seventy-five-year-old man who has been in his job for more than twenty years. He reports to a board of directors that is elected by the membership.

You are working in your office one morning when the executive director walks in, accompanied by the chairman of the board of directors. They tell you that the executive director has decided to retire the following month and they want to you draft a news release announcing the retirement and emphasizing his many years of dedicated service and how much his leadership will be missed (this is a small town in which a story such as this would make front-page news).

You begin working on the news release, but later that day you are having lunch with two co-workers who tell you the real story: The executive director has actually been fired from his job, but the board of directors is allowing him to "retire" in order to help him retain his dignity as he makes a graceful exit. As it turns out, the man is showing the first signs of senility and is in failing health. He is loved and respected by everyone in the town, but he is no longer able to do his job and the board of directors, anxious for more vibrant leadership, has told him privately to "go quietly or else." At least that is what your co-workers are telling you.

1. Codes of conduct for the public relations profession specifically prohibit you from disseminating information you know to be false. What do you do?
2. Suppose you have reason to doubt what your co-workers are saying; you believe it may be just speculation on their part. To what extent are you obligated to investigate the accuracy of the story before releasing it to the media? Before you finalize the news release, should you confront the executive director with your suspicions?
3. Which philosophers discussed in Chapter 2 might help you make this decision?

Discussion Problem 9D: The Good and Bad of Media Relations: College Degrees for Sale

You are the public relations director at Cornerstone College, a private liberal arts college that is struggling financially. One of its most popular programs is one called Bachelor of Independent Studies (BIS), which allows non-traditional students to combine traditional college courses with those in which they get college credit for life experiences such as employment, military service, or community volunteer activities. The program requires that at least 50 percent of the credits be earned through traditional classroom courses, meaning that no more than 50 percent can come from life experience. While local companies recognize the degree for employment credentials, students have not been able to use it for entry into law school and other graduate programs, leading to the perception around the campus and in the community that it is not a "real" degree. The publicity materials you have developed, however, describe it as a legitimate college degree.

You have been called into a meeting in the college president's office. At the meeting are the president, the college's chief fund-raising officer, and several other administrators. The purpose of the meeting is to decide how to recognize a local philanthropist who is about to donate $10 million to the college. The institution is desperate for the money, and though the check has not yet been received, the money has already been earmarked for various building renovations and the expansion of existing academic programs.

The president is unsure how to recognize the donor's generosity. Then the college's fundraising director makes a suggestion: since the donor recently mentioned in a meeting with college administrators that his life-long dream was to complete the college degree program that he began but never finished forty years ago, the college should consider his life experience and award him the BIS degree at the commencement ceremonies to take place at the end of the spring semester (about a month away). The fundraising director points out that this would mean more than just the traditional "honorary degrees" the college hands out to prominent citizens and that it is warranted in this case because of the size of the gift.

The president summons the director of the BIS program to join the meeting. She resists the idea because the man in question would be unable to fulfill the requirement that 50 percent of the work be in the form of traditional classes, and that it is unlikely that his life experience would be sufficient, either.

But the president and the other administrators insist that the college find a way to justify the degree, saying that because of the size of the donation and the college's need for an infusion of cash, the rules can be bent. "Make it happen," the president says. He also rules out alternatives such as an honorary degree and naming a building after the donor.

As the public relations director for the college, you face a dilemma. You have always felt confident in your working relationship with the president, and he has always trusted and followed your advice. But now you are unsure how firm the ground is underneath your feet. Like other college employees, you are aware of the institution's desperate financial circumstances. But you are also concerned about the potential damage to the college's reputation and that of the BIS program. Even though many on campus and in the community consider the BIS as not a "real" degree, you have promoted it as such in your publicity materials and are concerned that the news coverage resulting from the financial gift and awarding of the degree will damage the college's credibility and create the public perception that it is now selling college degrees in exchange for financial contributions.

1. Do you speak up at the meeting, and if so, what do you say?
2. Which concepts or philosophers discussed in Chapter 2 might help you make this decision?

Discussion Questions

901. Professional organizations such as the Public Relations Society of America (PRSA) and the International Association of Business Communicators (IABC) have rejected suggestions that they develop a formal licensing program for public relations professionals. Should they reconsider this possibility? If you were a member of one of these organizations, would you support an effort to develop such a program, even if it meant the organization would have to expand its office staff and increase annual membership fees?

902. Public relations ethicist Robert Dilenschneider says that "the public judges an organization's ethical performance by comparing what it says to what it does." Can you think of examples from current or recent news stories?

903. The PRSA and IABC Codes of Ethics (as well as other passages in this chapter) suggest that public relations professionals "sever relationships" with any client or employer if the relationship requires unethical conduct. But author Lee W. Baker, who offers his perspective on this issue earlier in this chapter, disagrees and says that such a rule is impractical. Which side do you take on this issue, and why?

Notes

1 Donald K. Wright, "Enforcement Dilemma: The Voluntary Nature of Public Relations Codes." *Public Relations Review*, Spring 1993, pp. 13–20.
2 Richard Johannessen, *Ethics in Human Communication*. Long Grove, IL: Waveland Press (2002), p. 72.
3 Dennis L. Wilcox, *Public Relations Writing and Media Techniques*. Boston: Pearson, Allyn & Bacon (2009), p. 300.
4 Larry Johnson and Bob Philips, *Absolute Honesty*. New York: Amacom (2003), p. 176.
5 Frank Walsh, *Public Relations and the Law*. Gainesville, FL: Institute for Public Relations Research (1991), p. 60.
6 Public Relations Society of America teleconference, "Media Relations." New York: PRSA (1998).
7 Conrad Fink, *Media Ethics*. Boston: Allyn & Bacon (1995), p. 67.
8 Philip Patterson and Lee Wilkins, *Media Ethics*. New York: McGraw-Hill (2010), p. 65.
9 Dennis L. Wilcox, *Public Relations Writing and Media Techniques*. Boston: Pearson, Allyn & Bacon (2009), p. 272.
10 Barbara Crossette, "A Spokesman Comments on His Job." *The New York Times*, February 26, 1982, p. 18-A.
11 Dennis L. Wilcox, Glen T. Cameron, Bryan H. Reber, and Jae-Hwa Shin, *Think Public Relations*. Boston: Allyn & Bacon (2012), p. 198.
12 Joyce Nelson, *Sultans of Sleaze: Public Relations and the Media*. Lutsen, MN: Between the Lines Publishing (1989), p. 22.
13 Joel Bleifuss, "Flack Attack." *Utne Reader*, January/February 1994, pp. 72–77.
14 Barbara Ehrenreich, *Bait and Switch: The Futile Pursuit of the American Dream*. New York: Holt Publishing (2005), p. 2.
15 "Attacks by CBS Show the Public's Opinion of PR Pros." *PR Week*, June 5, 2008.
16 Lee W. Baker, *The Credibility Factor: Putting Ethics to Work in Public Relations*. Homewood, IL: Business One Irwin (1993), pp. 182–183.
17 Robert L. Dilenschneider, *Power and Influence: Mastering the Art of Persuasion*. New York: Prentice-Hall (1990), p. 34.

18 Margalit Toledano and Ruth Avidar, "Public Relations, Ethics, and Social Media: A Cross-National Study of PR Practitioners." *Public Relations Review*, Vol. 42, No. 1 (March 2016), pp. 161–169.
19 Liese L. Hutchison, "Agency Ethics Isn't an Oxymoron." *Public Relations Tactics*, May 2000, p. 13.
20 "Litigation PR: The Eliot Spitzer Syndrome." *PR Week*, March 21, 2005, p. 13.
21 Fraser Seitel, "Litigation Public Relations." *Jack O'Dwyer's Newsletter*, March 14, 2016, p. 4.
22 Seitel.
23 James F. Haggerty, "Putting the Best Face on It: Litigation PR in the Era of 24-Hour Cable News." *Business Law Today*, Vol. 13, No. 6 (July/August 2004).
24 Edward J. Lordan, *Essential of Public Relations Management.* Chicago: Burnham Publishers (2003), pp. 102–103.
25 "Litigation PR: The Eliot Spitzer Syndrome."

10 Ethical Issues in Political Communication

Background

Political communication is regulated to some extent by the Federal Elections Commission and the election laws of individual states, but such laws are often difficult to enforce because of the value that society and the courts place on freedom of expression. In addition, new laws and rules dealing with political communication are difficult to push through Congress and regulatory agencies. In addition to First Amendment concerns, state and federal lawmakers are reluctant to change the system under which they were elected to office in the first place. Most see no reason to change the laws that might make it easier for potential opponents to defeat them in a future election.

Other than the American Association of Political Consultants (AAPC) and the American Association for Public Opinion Research (AAPOR), there are few professional organizations for individuals involved in political communication.

The AAPC Code of Ethics deals with issues such as fair treatment of clients, colleagues, and opponents; false and misleading attacks; and unfair appeals based on race, religion, and sex. In a separate statement on push polling (described later in this chapter), the AAPC condemns the practice as a "false and misleading tactic" that corrupts and degrades the political process.

The AAPOR has a code of ethics that requires members to maintain high standards for integrity; use only accepted research methodologies for collecting data; be transparent in how they collect, process, and report research results; and reject any assignment that calls for violating any principles of the code. The latter rule specifically mentions sales, fundraising, and political communication as areas in which they may be asked to manipulate their results to fit the preferences of the individuals or organizations paying for the research.

In addition to the AAPC and AAPOR codes, numerous communication textbooks dealing with political communication offer what they call "ethical guidelines." However, these guidelines are even less binding on political communicators than the voluntary ethical codes found in the advertising and public relations industries.

In 1968, the American Association of Advertising Agencies (AAAA) adopted the "Code of Ethics for Political Campaign Advertising." In short, the code requires that agencies (1) not represent candidates who refuse to adhere to AAAA standards, (2) not knowingly misrepresent the views or stated record of any candidates nor quote them out of context, (3) not prepare any material which unfairly or prejudicially exploits the race, creed, or national origin of a candidate, and (4) not make provocative statements about opponents so late in the campaign that those opponents do not have the fair opportunity to respond.[1]

Charles Larson provided a similar list of guidelines in his 1992 book *Persuasion: Reception and Responsibility*. Among his suggestions are that political communicators avoid (1) using false, fabricated, misrepresented, distorted, or irrelevant evidence to support claims; (2) oversimplifying complex ideas; and (3) advocating something they do not believe themselves. Larson points out that few politicians are aware of such voluntary guidelines, and even fewer adhere to them.[2]

Dennis Gouran, a contributor to a 1976 book edited by Daniel Dieterich, admonishes politicians and political communicators not to (1) manipulate the media into falsely casting issues in a positive light; (2) use overly complex language or euphemisms in order to obscure the truth; or (3) unnecessarily classify government documents that would otherwise be accessible to the public.[3]

During the 1976 election season, the citizens lobbying group Common Cause proposed a set of guidelines for candidates (at the federal, state, and local levels) and their campaign staffs. Unlike the two examples above, the Common Cause guidelines were cast in positive rather than negative terms. According to the guidelines, ethical political communicators (1) provide opportunities for their candidates to engage in unrehearsed communication with voters (today, candidates do so in what they call "town hall forums"), (2) hold frequent news conferences, and (3) limit their advertising to campaign issues rather than personal attacks on the opposition.

Issues and Controversies

The Science of Political Persuasion

In their 1953 book *Communication and Persuasion*, psychologists Carl Hovland, Irving Janis, and Harold Kelley explained a number of generalizations about persuasion and opinion change that are just as valid today as they were a half century ago.[4] Among them were:

1. Individuals' opinions are more likely to change in the desired direction if conclusions are explicitly stated than if those individuals are left to draw their own conclusions. Some communicators believe that if all of the facts are laid before audience members, they will make the right decisions.
2. Audience members are more likely to make the desired choice if both sides of an argument are presented instead of only one side. Audiences tend to be skeptical of an individual or organization that tells them only one side of the story and expects them to accept it without questions. A more effective strategy is to explain both sides of an issue, but then explain why one side should be preferred over the other. When both sides of a controversial issue are presented one after another, the one presented last will generally be more effective.[5]
3. Effects of persuasive messages tend to wear off over time. Even when persuasion is effective, the results are seldom permanent. As a result, repetition is necessary for persuasive efforts to be truly effective.
4. Audience members most in need of hearing a message are least likely to hear it. Parents who attend PTA meetings are mostly those whose children are having the least difficulty in school. Persons who could benefit from social services are the least likely ones to attend public meetings at which those services are discussed. Promoters must therefore use a variety of communication tactics rather depending on a few (or one).

Communication ethicist Richard Johannesen offers his own set of guidelines. Those include (1) no public official is immune from criticism for his or her performance, (2) anyone participating in a political debate has an intellectual responsibility to prepare himself or herself by learning all of the available facts, (3) it is more appropriate to criticize a person's ideas than to criticize the person, and (4) after criticizing another person's proposal, you must follow it up by introducing your own alternatives.[6]

Persuasion and Propaganda

The term "persuasive campaign" should not be confused with its less admirable cousin, the "propaganda campaign." By definition, legitimate attempts at persuasion differ from propaganda in several important ways. **Persuasion**, practiced by public relations professionals and more reputable political communicators, is defined as "an effort to gain public support for an opinion or course of action." What is implied in the definition is that the effort is based on truthful and ethical methods. Conversely, **propaganda,** as practiced by unscrupulous political communicators, is "the attempt to have a viewpoint accepted on the basis of appeals other than the merits of the case." Propaganda often uses methods that could be labeled as unethical or manipulative. Another way of drawing a distinction between the terms is to say that persuasion is based on truth, while propaganda is based on fiction or exaggeration; persuasion is based on consensus, while propaganda tries to set up adversarial relationships or "us versus them" scenarios.

Persuasion is also sometimes confused with "coercion." The difference is that "persuasion" refers to the motivating an individual or audience to do something they were already inclined or predisposed to do, while "coercion" refers to motivating an individual or audience to do something against their will, i.e. something they were *not* already inclined or predisposed to do.

Another term sometimes paired with "propaganda" is agnotology, which refers to the "intentional creation of confusion" and was coined by Robert Proctor, a professor of history and philosophy at Stanford University. In his 2008 book *Agnotology: The Making and Unmaking of Ignorance*, Proctor cites global climate change, the alleged need for military secrecy, and the relationship between tobacco usage and health as examples of issues in which one or both sides hopes that gullible audiences will accept their arguments without questioning. Proctor points out that the difference between propaganda and agnotology is that in propaganda, the speaker actually believes what he says, but in agnotology, the speaker knows his information is false.[7]

The origins of the propaganda concept can be traced back to 1622 and the tenure of Pope Gregory XV. The Pope created the Sacred Congregation for Propagating the Faith and charged it with persuading more Catholics to accept church doctrine. The word "propaganda" was eventually applied not only to institutions seeking to propagate a doctrine, but also the doctrine itself.[8]

In their 1992 book *Propaganda and Persuasion*, theorists Garth S. Jowett and Victoria O'Donnell based their definitions of the two terms on the intent of the communicator. Persuasion, according to the authors, is intended to serve the interests of both the persuader and the audience, while propaganda generally serves only the interests of the person acting as its source. Jowett and O'Donnell's view is consistent with the long-standing philosophy of public relations and public information programs producing results that are mutually beneficial or "win–win."[9]

Jowett and O'Donnell's work followed up on that done by Columbia University Professor Clyde R. Miller, who founded the Institute for Propaganda Analysis during World War II. At first, the emphasis was to study the use of propaganda in the war in Europe, but he quickly expanded its scope to include the study of propaganda from all sources, including the Ku Klux Klan, other extremist groups, and the American advertising industry.

The institute is still in operation today and identifies—in its publications and on its website—nine common propaganda devices.

Name-Calling

Much like stereotyping (discussed later in this chapter), "name-calling" is a form of "short-hand" in which a communicator attempts to reduce complex ideas and concepts to more concise and memorable forms. Most name-calling involves the use of emotional labels that are offered in the place of logic or evidence.

Name-calling has had a long and colorful history in political communication. At the time of the nation's founding, much of the name-calling was based on a public official's or candidate's personal character, as names such as "philanderer" and "adulterer" were common. But since the last half of the twentieth century, name-calling now involves an office-holder's or candidate's attitude toward the military. Conservatives and Republicans are often called "hawks" or "war-mongers" by their critics, while liberals and Democrats are labeled "doves," "commies," or "anti-war radicals." Today, liberals and Democrats in favor of improving American health care and safety net programs are labeled as "socialists."

Recent American presidents have been the target of fervent name-calling. Bill Clinton was called a "draft-dodger," George W. Bush a "war criminal," and Barack Obama a "dictator." Opponents of President Trump, in criticizing his response to racial unrest across the country in 2018–19, labeled him as a "racist" and "white nationalist."

But name-calling involving politicians is nothing new. In the 1950 Democratic primary for the U.S. Senate seat in Florida, challenger George Smathers resorted to name-calling in his attempt to defeat popular incumbent Claude Pepper. What was unusual about his choice of words was how easily they were misconstrued—which was exactly the effect he was hoping for. In numerous public speeches, Smathers labeled Pepper as a "shameless extrovert" who "practiced nepotism" with his sister-in-law. Even worse than that, Smathers claimed, Pepper and his wife-to-be practiced "celibacy" before they were married, and Pepper's sister was a "known thespian."[10]

Glittering Generalities

A communicator resorting to glittering generalities wants the audience to accept an idea without requiring evidence. The results are generalizations so extreme that receivers disregard the lack of substance behind those appeals. Examples of glittering generalities include "family values," "wasteful spending," and "liberal bias of the press." Other examples are claims that begin with phrases such as "everyone knows that ..." and "it goes without saying that ..."

Transfer

The communicator wants the audience to take the authority, sanction, or prestige of a respected idea and apply it to a new idea that the communicator wants the audience to accept. Examples include the use of symbols such as the cross to representing the Christian church or Uncle Sam to represent patriotism and love of country. If a church publication shows the cross being used to promote helping the poor, it implies that helping the poor is something that Christians should do. If a cartoonist draws Uncle Sam in a manner in which he approves of a proposed new law, it implies that all patriotic Americans should be in favor of it. When car dealers fly enormous American flags over their lots, they are sending subtle messages to potential customers that purchasing a car is the "American thing to do." Transfer is often used as a tactic in political races. In the 2008 presidential election campaign, opponents of Senator John McCain attempted to link him with the policies of President George W. Bush, hoping voters would transfer their dislike of Bush to McCain. In the 2016 general election campaign, opponents of Hillary Clinton reminded voters of the policy decisions and scandals associated with her husband, former President Bill Clinton, hoping voters would transfer their distrust of Bill to Hillary.

Bandwagon

In this approach, audiences are encouraged to adopt a certain idea or behavior because "everyone else is doing it" and they "do not want to be left behind." The marketing profession uses a variation of the bandwagon approach called the "entitlement appeal." That appeal uses marketing messages such as "you want this," "you need this," "you have to have this," and "you deserve this."

Plain folks

This approach suggests that audiences should adopt an idea because it comes from people similar to them or reject an idea because it comes from someone unlike them.

Testimonials

Appeals from influential celebrities or other authority figures whose expertise may be irrelevant to the product being sold or idea being promoted. A common example is the use of professional athletes to endorse companies or products, including those that are unrelated to the sport for which they are known.

In many cases, advertisers arrange for paid testimonials from individuals with no knowledge of or direct connection to the issue. Professional athletes and entertainers appear in commercials pitching home security systems, identity theft protection plans, or reverse mortgages, even though they would never use those products themselves. When anti-lottery groups in North Carolina purchased television advertising to promote their position when a lottery referendum was on the ballot in 2002, they sought out a paid endorsement from Dean Smith, the legendary University of North Carolina basketball coach who had been retired for five years but was still considered one of the state's most popular opinion leaders. Newspaper editorials—even those who were not taking sides in the lottery debate—questioned the appropriateness of using as a spokesperson an individual well respected in basketball circles but not an expert in public policy.[11]

In other cases, experts have the credentials to provide helpful testimonials, but critics claim those testimonials are devalued because they are paid for. Such testimonials take the form of testimony before government agencies, authorship of position papers or scientific reports, appearances at news conferences or in news interviews or television commercials, or quotations included in news releases.

Consumer protection advocates and environmental lawyers, including Robert F. Kennedy Jr., coined the term "biostitute" to refer to scientists and other paid "experts" who lend their credibility to dubious products and disreputable companies.[12]

The phenomenon can be traced back to the early 1960s, when pseudo-scientific studies funded by tobacco companies claimed that scientists could find no credible link between tobacco usage and lung cancer.[13]

Card-Stacking

A method in which the communicator stacks the cards in favor of the desired result, often by presenting one-sided evidence or half-truths.

A more modern term for card-stacking is *spin*, which is often used in a derogatory manner to refer to communication disseminated by public relations professionals.

During the presidency of Ronald Reagan, for example, political advisors frequently arranged for the president to speak to groups of seniors in venues such as senior centers and other gathering places for older Americans. The theme of those speeches was always about Reagan's support for such programs, and that is what was reported in news coverage of the events. But what the reporters seldom mentioned in their stories was that the Reagan administration often advocated reducing or eliminating funding for those programs.

In the mid-1990s, crime statistics released by the U.S. Justice Department indicated that crime rates had dropped in most major categories in the previous decade. Democrats claimed that it was because of the newly introduced crime-fighting initiatives of President Bill Clinton, even though those initiatives had not yet had time to have any effect. Republicans, on the other hand, claimed the decrease in crime rates was due to the "get tough" policies of President Reagan (out of office for more than five years) that were now beginning to take hold. Which side was correct? Neither one. Criminologists attributed the decline in crime rates to demographic shifts: Young men between the ages of 18 and 29 had become smaller in proportion to the population as a whole, and since that demographic category is typically responsible for the majority of criminal activity, the crime rate dropped accordingly.

Scare Tactics

Devices intended to influence behavior are common in advertising and political campaigns. A communicator using this tactic typically pairs a negative result with the desired behavior required to avoid it. Examples include television commercials showing an accident scene followed by the suggestion of wearing seat belts, or the scene of a house fire followed by a pitch for smoke detectors.

Politicians and their supporters are notorious for using scare tactics. Alabama Governor George Wallace, for example, warned voters during his 1970 campaign that "blacks were trying to take over Alabama" and the only way to stop it was to elect him.[14] More recently, critics of President Donald Trump accuse him of using similar appeals when warning about the dangers of Muslims and Mexicans entering the country.

Euphemisms

Terms intended to obscure or soften the true meaning of behaviors or concepts. Examples include a company referring to employee layoffs as "early retirement opportunities" or the government referring to a tax increase as a "revenue adjustment."

Other Propaganda Techniques

Although not officially part of the IPA list, there are five other argumentative techniques used in political communication: the slippery slope, the false dichotomy, the ad hominem argument, the straw man argument, and stereotyping. All are basically extensions of the "scare tactics" method previously described in that they are based on warning decision-makers (usually voters) of the perceived negative consequences associated with choices to which the persuader is opposed. They are often used in desperation because the persuader has already found more legitimate persuasive techniques ineffective.

The Slippery Slope

Sometimes called the "thin entering wedge" or "getting the camel's nose inside the tent." This is a technique in which the party that opposes a policy change warns that even the slightest change will open the door to more drastic (and harmful) changes in the future. Examples include the debate over banning a small number of controversial books from school libraries, when opponents of such action warn that once a precedent is established, other less controversial books might be at risk in the future; and the debate over state lotteries, in which case opponents warn that the establishment of lottery games will open the door to more serious forms of gambling such as casinos.

False Dichotomy

An oversimplified or artificial division of a political issue in a way that tells voters or other decision-makers that they must choose between the two opposing ideas, with no alternatives possible. Political clichés that represent this idea include "us against them" and "you're either for us or against us." In each presidential election, the false dichotomy is reflected in constant references to "red states" and "blue states."

Many politicians use false dichotomies because they believe voters or other decision-makers can more easily understand issues that involve only two choices, but when they do so they often underestimate the audience's ability to understand and process complex ideas.

Ad Hominem

From the Latin for "argument against the person." This is an extension of both "fear" and "name-calling" and is a method of arguing against an idea by attacking the person who proposes it. Many opponents of proposed spending programs, for example, base much of their persuasive efforts on challenging the motives of the advocates of the plan and referring to them as "reckless liberals" or "tax-and-spend politicians."

Straw Man Argument

Sometimes called the "straw man fallacy." This is a technique used to persuade the audience to oppose a candidate or an idea based on a premise that is likely false or exaggerated, but also easier to understand. The metaphor is based on the fact that a straw man (a falsehood) is easier to attack and defeat than a real man (a truth). The straw man argument is also known as "reaching for the long-hanging fruit."

Stereotyping

A tactic in which a communicator describes members of racial or ethnic groups in an unflattering and often offensive manner and expects members of the audience to make decisions based on overgeneralizations or outdated perceptions. Common examples include perceptions that older Americans are "set in their ways" and reject technology, Asians always excel at math and science, Mexican Americans are limited to working in agricultural occupations, and African Americans are more likely than whites to commit welfare fraud and similar crimes.

When advocates of a proposed state lottery in South Carolina wanted to play on the rivalry between that state and Georgia, they created a southern "white trash" character named Bubba, complete with bad teeth and an exaggerated southern accent. The television commercials angered individuals and groups on both sides of the lottery debate, but the advocates refused to withdraw the ads or apologize to those claiming they were offended.

Less offensive examples of stereotypes in political communication include Republican and conservative politicians being "tough on crime" and always seeking to cut taxes while spending more money on military projects and less on social programs. Democrats and liberals are typically stereotyped as being "soft on crime" and wanting to raise taxes while spending less money on military projects and more on social programs.

Opinion Polling in the Twenty-First Century

In a column in *Columbia Journalism Review*, media ethicist Andrew Kohut complained that many reporters and editors assign too much importance to the results of polls, even though they often don't understand them. And when faced with a number of polls showing a variety of results, reporters and editors will typically choose to report only those that are consistent with their own preferences.[15]

"We have more surveys than ever, yet our understanding of the public's mind is impoverished," says Steve Farkas, senior vice president of Public Agenda, a professional polling firm. "There are too many surveys that are meaningless, and that adds to the random noise, so it's difficult to distinguish quality work from just plain silliness."[16]

Conducted much differently than marketing research, political polling is a more scientific and often more controversial form of information gathering. Political polls taken by major polling organizations such as the Gallup Organization and Pew Research, as well as those conducted by major universities, are considered to be more reliable and less subject to bias than polls conducted by individual researchers or research companies working directly for political candidates or advocacy groups.

Former Vice President Al Gore Jr. recalls that when he first ran for U.S. Congress in 1976, his campaign staff did no internal polling and paid little attention to external polls conducted by media organizations and research organizations, but he didn't feel that would put his campaign at a disadvantage because his opponents didn't either. Eight years later, when he ran for the U.S. Senate seat (Tennessee) once held by his father, Albert Gore, Sr., not having a full-time pollster on a campaign staff was unheard of.[17]

The more reputable researchers use strict protocols, and advances in sampling and polling methodologies allow those organizations to predict the outcome of elections with a high degree of accuracy. There are areas of debate, however. Those issues include the following.

Weighted Samples

In some cases, researchers concerned that some demographic or psychographic groups may have been under-represented in the survey samples chosen may adjust the numbers to provide what they believe will be more accurate results. Although results should never be deliberately "slanted" to show results favorable to a cause, in some cases it is appropriate to "weight" results to provide a more realistic picture. As an example, a company with 500 male employees and 500 female employees might expect that of the 200 employees responding to a morale survey, 100 would be male and 100 female. But what should the researcher do if 150 are male and only 50 are female? For questions in which the gender of respondents is unlikely to affect their answers (such as issues of parking or building cleanliness), the results can be reported as is. But for questions in which the gender of the respondent is likely to affect answers (such as those dealing with sexual harassment, promotion opportunities, building security, or maternity leave policies), the results might be weighted to reflect the gender breakdown of the employees. In the scenario above, women's answers would be multiplied by three, then matched against the responses from male employees and then computed as a percentage. When explaining the results, however, the researcher should provide the results both ways—raw data and based on weighted results—and allow the individual or company requesting the research to decide which data to use. The researcher should then also consider why one group or the other is over-represented or under-represented in the sample and consider it as a possible "red flag" that there may be a larger problem.

Courtesy Bias and the "Bradley Effect"

One of the factors that may skew the results of any form of opinion research is the tendency of survey respondents or focus group participants to offer answers they believe are the "right" answers, answers that will not offend the interviewer or other participants, or answers they believe will make the respondents appear more sophisticated.

In public relations and marketing research, the phenomenon is known as **courtesy bias**. Respondents to non-anonymous surveys and participants in focus groups who know which company is sponsoring the survey or focus group will tend to indicate a preference for that company's products or services, whether that is their true opinion or not. In surveys or focus groups dealing with environmental issues, respondents tend to overstate their participation in recycling programs and their purchase of "green" products because they assume those are the "right" things to say. In media research, respondents often indicate they get their news from *The Wall Street Journal* or National Public Radio in order to appear more sophisticated, even though in truth they may read only tabloid newspapers (or consume no news media at all).

In political polling, the phenomenon of stating a preference for the more popular or progressive candidate, yet voting for someone else, is known as the **Bradley Effect**. It is named for Tom Bradley, the black Democratic mayor of Los Angeles who ran for governor of California in 1982. In nearly every poll taken prior to Election Day, Bradley was well ahead of his white Republican opponent, and most pundits predicted he would win easily. He lost by less than 1 percent of the vote. The discrepancy between the polling data and Election Day results was attributed to the pollsters' belief that respondents wanted to appear to be progressive and open-minded by indicating they favored the black candidate, when in actuality they had already decided to vote for the white candidate.

In the 2008 Democratic presidential primary in New Hampshire, pollsters predicted Illinois Senator Barack Obama would win easily over the only other major candidate in the race, New York Senator Hillary Clinton. They based that prediction on Obama's substantial lead in their polls. But on primary day, Clinton scored a surprising win, and pollsters theorized that the inaccuracy of their polling data may have resulted from New Hampshire voters wanting to look "trendy" by indicating support for the black candidate, even though they had already decided to vote for Clinton. Based on that theory, Obama supporters worried (unnecessarily) that polling data indicating their candidate would win in the general election might be vulnerable to a similar error.

In the 2016 presidential election, even professional pollsters were skeptical of their own results showing Hillary Clinton would easily defeat Donald Trump, concerned that they were missing the "hidden" Trump voters, either because Trump supporters declined to participate in surveys (after being randomly chosen) or they indicated a preference for Clinton even while intending to vote for Trump. Pollster Anthony Salvanto, author of a 2018 book on survey research, called those voters "Republicans, hiding in plain sight."[18]

The Bradley Effect is not limited to just candidates; it also surfaces in campaigns based on issues. In a number of elections in Southern states in the late 1990s and early 2000s, for example, polling data indicating voter support or opposition to proposed state lotteries were found to be highly unreliable. Pollsters found that respondents indicated support or opposition to the issue in polls and focus groups because of peer pressure or other factors, then voted the opposite way on Election Day.

Push Polls

These represent a somewhat recent strategy in political persuasion. Often conducted by telephone, the push poll is designed to appear as a legitimate public opinion poll administered by a neutral source, but is actually a subliminal attempt to influence public opinion by one side or the other in a political debate. A typical push poll question is: "Would you be *more likely* or *less likely* to vote for Candidate X if you knew he was accepting illegal campaign contributions from special-interest groups?"

Of course, most respondents would say "less likely," but soliciting that answer was not the point of asking the question. If you read the question again, you notice that it never accused Candidate X of doing anything wrong. It merely planted the idea in the mind of the person responding to the question. On Election Day, the respondent may not remember where or how he or she heard about it, but will remember hearing the name of Candidate X and "illegal campaign contributions" in the same sentence.

In a formal statement separate from its Code of Ethics, the American Association of Political Consultants condemns the practice and says that "push polls are not polls at all" and urges the news media and the public to draw distinctions between push polls and legitimate opinion research.

Legitimate polling organizations such as Roper and Gallup are also critical of the method and would never allow their employees to use such a tactic. It persists, however, in every election cycle, even though no candidate will acknowledge authorizing such a tactic as part of his or her campaign.

"A so-called 'push poll' is an insidious form of negative campaigning," claimed a statement issues by the American Association for Public Opinion Research. "Push polls are not surveys at all, but rather unethical political telemarketing—telephone calls disguised as research that aim to persuade large numbers of voters and affect election outcomes rather than measure opinions."[19]

Reporting the Results of Polls

Because of the proliferation of surveys conducted or sponsored by political organizations, special-interest groups, and other parties with an interest in the outcome (and journalists' interest in survey results), the use of polling information in media stories should always be done carefully. Here are some factors to consider:

Who conducted the poll? Was it done by a professional public opinion research firm, a political candidate's staff, or another organization with an interest in the outcome? Journalists recognize the significance of research conducted by firms such as the Gallup Corporation, the Harris Poll, or Pew Research. The most credible university-based polling organizations include those at Quinnipiac University (Connecticut), Elon University (North Carolina), and Middle Tennessee State University.

Privately conducted polls are often inaccurate for three reasons: (1) the inexperience or incompetence of the poll-takers, (2) bad methodology or bad sampling, and (3) the tendency of research results to reflect the wishes of the organization or political candidate paying for the research.

Sample size and how the sample was chosen. A survey with a small sample size is not as reliable as one with a larger sample. The time and place selected to sample is also important. For example, if one were to conduct a survey to determine which sport is more popular—football or baseball—using a sample chosen from a crowd of people leaving a stadium after a football game, that would obviously not be an appropriate sample. That is obviously an exaggerated example, but some researchers draw their samples using methods and locations that are almost as questionable. At the level of absolute certainty, survey research reflects only the opinions of those in the sample; but at the level of probability, the results can be projected onto the larger audience from which the sample was drawn. Many media consumers do not understand the complexity of survey research, so care must be taken when the results are announced.

Early in a campaign, pollsters draw their samples from larger groups of "registered voters," but as the election nears (usually after Labor Day), the emphasis shifts to identifying "likely voters." To determine who is a "likely voter," professional survey companies typically ask respondents three questions: (1) Did you vote in the previous election? (2) Have you been following the campaign? (3) Do you know the location of your polling place? Those respondents who answer "yes" to all three are considered "likely voters."

Illegitimate polls often use sample sizes that are either very small, very large, or not scientifically chosen. The AAPOR reminds journalists that a large sample size does not automatically lead to more reliable results, as the demographics of the sample (accurately representing the larger audience) is more important than how many people were contacted.[20]

Methodology. Was the survey conducted by telephone, mail, electronic mail, social media, in-person, or some other method?

While many larger newspapers have their own internal professional polling operation that use scientifically chosen samples, other newspapers, as well as television and radio stations, conduct less scientific polls in which individuals respond to a website or a 1-800 number. Known as a self-selecting sample, the individuals who participate in such a poll are seldom representative of a larger population. The *Associated Press Stylebook* points out that such polls are conducted mostly for entertainment value and should not be confused with scientific polls conducted by professional polling organizations.[21]

Regardless of who sponsors them, online surveys are often ripe with sampling problems. Among those are "professional respondents" who complete online surveys simply to be entered in a sweepstakes or qualify for some other benefit. Online surveys also eliminate individuals without Internet access.

Telephone polls conducted by automated systems are problematic because many potential respondents confuse them with political or commercial "robocalls." In addition, they cannot screen for gender (if a poll is short on women respondents, a human interviewer can ask for "the lady of the house") and cannot prevent children from responding.

Sponsorship. Reporters should be skeptical of any poll that is privately sponsored, and for good reason. Reporters may mention those results of privately sponsored research in their stories, but will identify the sponsor so that readers can put the results in context.

The term **funding bias** refers to results that reflect the position of the organization paying for the research. "Sponsors (of research) typically fall into two categories: those that want to discover the truth, and those who hope to prove a case," wrote pollster George Gallup in a 1980 essay. "Needless to say, the layman should beware of all research that is undertaken to prove a point, whether this be in politics or any other field ... Ideally, a sponsor of research should have only one interest—to discover the facts regardless of how those facts conflict with his own views or interests."[22]

Polls paid for by candidates or special-interest groups have a number of problems. First, they are often released as a campaign tactic or publicity device. Second, they are often plagued by sampling errors, methodological errors, and inexperienced or incompetent employees.

The wording of questions. Reporters seldom include the precise wording of survey questions in a news story, but seeing a copy of the questions is critical to judging the quality of the research. Highly skilled yet unethical researchers can craft questions using "hot button" words or employ other terms to obtain a desired result. Also, the smallest alteration to the wording of a question (either intentional or unintentional) can greatly affect the responses to that question. In a typical survey about public attitudes toward proposed state lotteries in the Southeast in the 1980s and 1990s, a neutral question such as "Are you in favor of a state lottery" would typically result in a 50–50 yes–no result. Inserting a simple adjective to recast the question as "Are you in favor of an education lottery?" causes the results to shift to 60–40 yes–no. And when the question is recast in the form of a false dichotomy, as in "Which would you prefer, a state lottery or increase in your income taxes?" the results would shift to 70–30 yes–no.[23]

Margin for error. A poll's margin for error is determined by a mathematical formula and expressed in a percentage related to the sample size. The larger the sample size, the smaller the margin of error; the smaller the sample size, the larger the margin for error.

In order to be clearly leading in a poll, a candidate's lead must be twice the margin for error; if the margin for error is 3.5 percentage points, a candidate must be leading by 7 points. If one candidate is ahead but the lead is within the margin for error, reporters should write that Candidate X holds a slight lead but within the margin for error. The Associated Press cautions against using the term "statistical dead heat," as that is seldom the case. The AP also reminds journalist that "no matter how good a poll is, no matter how wide the margin, the poll cannot say with certainty that one candidate will win the election. Polls are often wrong, especially in close elections, as there can be sampling errors or methodological errors and some voters simply change their mind between the time they respond to the poll and the day they cast their ballots."[24]

Most professional polling organizations release results with percentages rounded to the closest decimal point, such as 52.3 percent. In reporting results, however, journalists can round off numbers to fractions: 52.3 percent can become "slightly more than half." It's confusing, however, to mix numbers and fractions, so reporters should *not* write clauses such as "60 percent said X, while almost one-third said Y."

Timing. When was the research conducted? Opinions can change overnight. A poll taken the day after a presidential speech is going to give to a different result than one taken a week later. Polls taken immediately after a political party's televised convention traditionally show a "bump" in public support, but much of that increase is lost after media coverage of the event subsides and/or his or her opponent experiences a similar bump from the opposing party's convention.

The results of a survey conducted several days or weeks before a major news event might be quite different from those of a similar survey conducted days or weeks after, even if the connection between the topic of the poll and the nature of the news event was remote. Reporters often combine this detail with margin for error, writing in a story:

"The poll was taken the week of March 3 and had a margin for error of ..."

Funding of Government Communication Activities

Because of a 1913 law known as the **Gillett Amendment**, government agencies and units cannot spend taxpayer money on promotional activities or legislative advocacy unless they are authorized to do so by law or congressional mandate. The rationale behind the law is to prevent government agencies from spending taxpayer money to implement advertising and public relations campaigns related to political issues in which they have a vested interest. The law does not apply to government agencies and branches of the military and their employment of public information officers, as those functions are authorized by law and there are no conflicts of interest.

The history of the amendment can be traced back to the early 1900s and the administration of President Theodore Roosevelt, when the Department of Agriculture used taxpayer money for a promotional campaign aimed at changing the methods it was using to manage forests. The campaign was seen by some as part of a "political agenda" and was highly criticized by congressional representatives skeptical of any laws related to environmental issues. When Massachusetts Representative Frederick H. Gillett saw a job advertisement for a "publicity expert" to help the Department of Agriculture with its public relations campaigns, he introduced the law that would be named after him.[25]

The law remains controversial today, and there are occasional calls for its repeal, based mostly on the obvious: that an important function of the government is to communicate with its citizens, and what better way to do that than hire someone with public relations experience?[26]

Recent examples of federal government agencies violating the law include the Department of Education's payment of $240,000 to broadcast commentator Armstrong Williams for promoting the No Child Left Behind Act on his syndicated television and radio programs. During the Bush administration, the Government Accounting Office (GAO)—an independent agency that reports directly to Congress —determined that other federal government agencies engaged in numerous other promotional activities that violated the law, including payments to newspaper columnist Maggie Gallagher and magazine columnist Michael McManus for their support of a federal program that promoted traditional marriage over cohabitation.

The Bush administration was not the first presidential administration to violate the Gillett Amendment. In the 1990s, for example, the administration of President Bill Clinton spent more than $128 million on a variety of promotional activities. Even after the GAO determined that many of the expenditures of both the Bush and Clinton administrations violated the law, prosecutors declined to press charges, despite the complaints of numerous government watchdog groups and members of Congress.

Although the Gillett Amendment is a federal law and does not apply to states, many state legislatures have created similar laws restricting the expenditure of state funds. One example is found in the case of state universities that use public money to campaign for increases in financial support from their state legislatures. In essence, a university involved in such an activity is using taxpayer money to generate more taxpayer money, creating an inherent conflict of interest. Universities wanting to conduct such persuasive activities must therefore do so using privately raised funds.

The Influence of Political Talk Radio

Like many aspects of American political culture, the value and impact of talk radio depends largely on who is making the assessment. Political conservatives, who make up a large percentage of the talk radio audience, view it as a sacred island in what they perceive to be a vast sea of liberally biased media. For them, talk radio is their primary free-speech outlet and their only viable alternative to network and cable television news, National Public Radio, and their favorite liberal-media villain—*The New York Times*. In contrast, many liberals view talk radio as a billion-dollar industry fueled by anger, intolerance, paranoia, and distrust of government.

Beginning in late 1989 and throughout much of the 1990s, talk was the fastest-growing format on the AM radio dial. Today, about 520 AM and FM radio stations across the country have adopted an all-talk format, with nearly all offering a combination of local and nationally syndicated programming. In addition, hundreds of local stations offer talk programming for at least part of their broadcast day, bringing the total number of talk outlets to more than 1,400 and the total audience to more than 100 million. According to Pew Research, approximately 17 percent of Americans listen to talk radio on a regular basis, giving it greater reach than any format other than country music. While trends in politics and popular culture have increased the number of listeners, the growth in the popularity of car telephones (and later hand-held cellular telephones) has increased the number of callers.

A recent study by the Center for American Progress found that more than 90 percent of political talk radio programming is based on conservative viewpoints. The study compiled samples from 257 news and talk stations owned by America's five largest media conglomerates and found that combined, they offered 2,570 hours per week of conservative programming and only 254 hours of programming considered "liberal" or "progressive." Recent polls taken immediately following recent presidential and midterm elections indicate that voters who regularly listen to talk radio voted for Republican candidates by a three-to-one margin.

In his 2004 book *The Politics of Misinformation*, political scientist Murray Edelman wrote that most political debate, including that which takes place on talk radio, is based on falsehoods and exaggerations. "All but a small minority of such discussion and claims are based on false beliefs, false information, false premises, and false logic," he wrote. "And whenever one party to a political dispute begins to indulge in misrepresentation, the incentive is strong for all others to do the same."[27] Edelman's assertions raise questions about the role of talk radio hosts—do they allow falsehoods to continue, point out the weaknesses and fallacies of their arguments, or add to them?

"Facts are not terribly key to talk radio," wrote Chris Mondiacs, a political reporter in New Jersey, in a 1992 column. "There are many instances in which talk show hosts seize on an issue without fully understanding it. They come from the perspective of accusing anyone who holds a government office of being corrupt."[28] Media critic Peter Laufer comments that "aspiring talk show hosts find it easier to get on the air if they are willing to adjust reality."[29]

In 2005, the Annenberg Public Policy Center at the University of Pennsylvania conducted an in-depth study of American media and their influence on the political process. One of the startling findings of the study was that almost as many Americans (27 percent) labeled popular host Rush Limbaugh as a "journalist" as they did *Washington Post* Associate Editor Bob Woodward (30 percent).[30]

For much of the last twenty years, conservatives have complained about an alleged "liberal bias of the media." Although academic studies typically find that no such bias exists— claiming that the liberal orientation of working journalists is counterbalanced by the conservative ownership of newspaper chains and television networks—the charge continues to be made by talk radio hosts, conservative watchdog groups, and individual authors who use dubious sampling techniques and anecdotal evidence to support their point.

Many talk radio hosts believe their programs can help remedy that (perceived) liberal bias by offering conservative or libertarian perspectives on politics and current events. Many media critics and watchdog groups, however, say that talk radio has overcompensated for a problem that doesn't exist.

Former Vice President Al Gore called talk radio the "Limbaugh–Hannity–Drudge Axis" (referring to conservative hosts Rush Limbaugh and Sean Hannity and blogger Matt Drudge) and wrote that the

> fifth column of the fourth estate is made up of propagandists pretending to be journalists ... through multiple overlapping outlets covering radio, television, and the Internet, they relentlessly force-feed the American people right-wing talking points and ultra-conservative dogma disguised as news and infotainment.[31]

Your Turn

Case Study 10A: Cindy Watson vs. the Hog Farmers

Prior to 1995, Cindy Watson was a little-known businesswoman in Rose Hill, North Carolina who never expressed any interest in politics, other than to vote in local, state, and national elections. But when an official of the Duplin County Republican Party asked her to run in a special election to fill a vacant seat in the state legislature, she reluctantly agreed.

When elected, she became the first Republican to represent the heavily Democratic Duplin County since the Civil War. Ironically, she had no idea that her work in the legislature would spark another civil war and focus national attention on her small district in southeastern North Carolina.

Shortly after taking office, Watson heard from dozens of her constituents, who complained that waste and stench from area hog farms were causing asthma in children and seniors and that waste was contaminating water wells with bacteria. Large-scale hog farming was the county's biggest business and a major part of the local economy.

By 1997, Watson had joined forces with environmental groups and other legislators to confront the corporate polluters. Watson co-sponsored legislation that would place a temporary moratorium on new pork production operations and require existing companies to phase out the lagoons that collected the waste of 9.3 million hogs. The state had previously tried to pass environmental regulations aimed at curtailing hog industry polluters, but heavy lobbying by the hog industry had always quashed those efforts.

But in 1998, after an accident resulted in the spill of 25 million gallons of hog waste into North Carolina's New River, the people of the state rallied around Watson's proposal, and the legislature passed the law. That's when the hog industry decided that Watson, as well as two other legislators who helped her pass the moratorium, had to be defeated.

Spending more than $2.9 million in the year leading up to the 1998 election, the corporate hog farms—operating under the name Farmers for Fairness (FFF)—saturated the districts of Watson and two other Republican legislators with negative ads and push polls. The ads painted the three legislators as being anti-business and exaggerated their positions on a variety of issues unrelated to the hog industry. All three lost their seats to primary challengers, and that November all three seats fell into Democratic hands.

The North Carolina Board of Elections began an investigation into the tactics of Farmers for Fairness, during which it called several of the group's political consultants to testify. Several admitted that Watson and the two other legislators had been specifically targeted for defeat, but they also claimed that their tactics were both legal and ethical.

One consultant testified in BOE hearings that FFF was so determined to see the three legislators defeated in the primary that it was willing to risk losing those seats to Democrats in the general election. Another consultant said in media interviews that the group was merely exercising its right of free speech—and that the only way it could do so was "to buy it."[32]

In the years following the conflict, Watson became nationally known as a martyr for the problems in the American political system, earning her respect and sympathy from Republicans and Democrats alike. In 2004, she was presented with the John F. Kennedy Profile in Courage Award for her tenacity in representing the interests of her constituents and standing up to the corporate interests.

1. Does reading this story make you more cynical about politics than you already were?
2. Are such cases simply a byproduct of free speech that we must tolerate in order to maintain our First Amendment freedoms?

Case Study 10B: Taking License with Free Speech

In the late 1900s and early 2000s, legislatures in several southern states dealt with proposals to offer specialty license plates dealing with controversial topics.

The first series of conflicts involved the states that offered tags bearing the slogan "Choose Life" and graphics supporting adoption as an alternative to abortion. In many of the states, abortion-rights groups such as Planned Parenthood and the National Organization for Women (NOW) challenged the plates under the principle of "equal protection," claiming that "when the state creates a forum for the expression of political views, it cannot promote one opinion and deny the forum to opposing opinions."[33]

In 2001, a court in Florida dismissed the first of those suits, claiming that NOW failed to prove the program was unconstitutional.

In October 2004, however, a court in Tennessee ruled that the state's "Choose Life" plate violated the constitution because it promoted only one side in the abortion debate and did not allow groups with opposing viewpoints to sponsor their own plates. Lawmakers in Tennessee worried that a strict interpretation of the court ruling might prompt individuals to challenge the appropriateness of the state's other specialty license plates, such as those supporting endangered species and encouraging citizens to protect environmentally sensitive lands, such as the Great Smoky Mountains National Park. In November 2004, a higher court ruled that the state of Tennessee had engaged in "viewpoint discrimination" and declared the license plates unconstitutional. Early in 2005, the U.S. Supreme Court declined to hear the appeal, leaving in place the ruling of the circuit court. While Florida maintains its program of "Choose Life" plates, other Southern states have avoided potential litigation by eliminating all potentially controversial license plates.

The "Choose Life" cases led to two appeals court rulings in 2008 and 2015. In the first case, the Seventh Circuit (serving states in the Midwest) ruled that license plates were "nonpublic forums" and that state governments were the final authority as to which groups could and could not have their own plates. In the more recent case, the Second Circuit (serving states in the Southeast) reached the same conclusion.[34]

The second area of controversy emerged in 2011 when the Sons of Confederate Veterans (as the name indicates, it consists of descendants of Civil War veterans from Southern states) established "Confederate Heritage" license plates in nine Southern states. The license plate programs were part of the group's planned commemoration for the 150th anniversary of the beginning of the Civil War. Proceeds went to restore battlegrounds and other historic sites related to the war.

From 2011 through 2015, challenges to Confederate license plate programs in Mississippi and Texas worked their way through the court system. Mississippi's five-year program calls for honoring a different Confederate leader each year, and the choice of General Nathan Bedford Forrest for the 2014 plate drew the ire of civil rights groups, who pointed out Forrest was also an early founder of the Ku Klux Klan. That case has not yet been decided. In 2015, however, the U.S. Supreme Court ruled that the state government of Texas was not required to establish a Confederate license plate program.

As of 2019, nineteen states have authorized license plates bearing the motto "In God We Trust." Despite being the nation's official motto, the plates have also generated controversy. Although cases specifically related to the motto being on license plates have not yet been argued, the U.S. Supreme Court has ruled that other applications of the motto do not violate the constitution. Legal scholars predict that if such a case reached the court system, the courts would make a similar ruling as long as the plates were optional rather than required. In Tennessee in 1917, the legislature considered a bill requiring "In God We Trust" to appear on all license plates, but the state's attorney general advised against it, worried that it might raise constitutional issues.[35]

1. If you were the governor of a state in which this issue was debated, would you (a) allow only one side in a controversial debate to sponsor license plates, depending on the preference of the legislature; (b) allow both groups to sponsor license plates provided they followed the same guidelines as non-controversial groups; or (c) decide that state license plates should stay out of politics and disallow any political or potentially controversial messages.
2. Is there a slippery slope problem in this conflict? Suppose you choose (b) and allowed both sides in the abortion debates to sponsor their own license plates. What if a white supremacist group and other controversial groups wanted their own license plates?

Case Study 10C: Mixing Entertainment with Politics

One of the fastest-growing trends in American politics is that of Hollywood celebrities taking sides in political debates and campaigns.

Critics often point out that while the celebrities themselves may be knowledgeable about the campaigns and issues, their fans may not be. Therefore, those critics believe it is inappropriate for celebrities to use their name recognition and appeal to influence the outcome of elections. In their defense, the celebrities point out that as Americans, they are simply exercising their First Amendment rights of free speech.

A large majority of these cases involve liberal celebrities endorsing liberal candidates. Actors including Martin Sheen, Sean Penn, Susan Sarandon, Woody Harrelson, Barbra Streisand, Jane Fonda, Alec Baldwin, and Ed Asner have supported Democratic candidates by speaking at campaign events, appearing in television commercials and campaign videos, and endorsing candidates in media interviews.

Sheen has drawn criticism from conservatives for his portrayal of a liberal president on the television series *The West Wing* and appearance in anti-war films such as *Apocalypse Now* and *The War at Home*. Baldwin has been an outspoken critic of Republican leaders for more than a decade, but recently has drawn extra criticism for his not-so-subtle satirical impression of President Donald Trump on *Saturday Night Live*.

In 2003, the country trio Dixie Chicks created controversy by making disparaging remarks about President George W. Bush during a concert appearance in England. Although the performers later apologized to the president, they supported his opponent, Democrat John Kerry, in the 2004 election, and in subsequent elections continued to support Democratic candidates for a variety of federal offices. That prompted political commentator Laura Ingraham to author a book titled *Shut Up and Sing* that was critical of the Dixie Chicks and other entertainers getting involved in politics.

While the majority of entertainers getting involved in politics are doing so from a liberal perspective, some conservatives do so as well. Among the most popular are country singer Toby Keith and actors Gary Sinise and James Woods.

Sinise, for example, uses his name-recognition to advocate for many causes related to health care for veterans. When Woods portrayed New York Mayor Rudy Giuliani in a made-for-television movie about the September 11 terrorist attacks, he told television critics that he accepted the role partly due to his admiration for the mayor and partly due to his desire to honor the memories of the firefighters who died in the World Trade Center and the military men and women who died at the Pentagon.

1. Do you agree with the critics who say that it is inappropriate for celebrities to use their influence in this way, or with the performers themselves, who claim they are simply exercising their First Amendment rights of free speech?
2. To what degree to these endorsements affect your voting decisions?

Case Study 10D: Stop Using Our Song!

When Alaska Governor Sarah Palin took the stage at the Republican National Convention in August 2008 to accept her party's nomination for vice-president, her theme song—"Barracuda"—played in the background. During the campaign, the song, chosen based on Palin's nickname, continued to be used as background music. One legal problem: the rock group Heart, which recorded the song in 1977, still held the copyright and had not given Palin or anyone associated with her campaign permission to use it.

"Sarah Palin's views and values in no way represent us as American women," the group's leader singers, Ann and Nancy Wilson, said in media interviews.[36] No formal legal action was taken, but the Wilsons did ask her to stop using the song. Palin's running mate, Arizona Senator John McCain, was not as lucky. After using the 1980s song "Running on Empty" as his theme music, he was sued by Jackson Browne, the recording artist who still held that copyright.

The "Barracuda" and "Running on Empty" cases are just two examples from a thirty-year history of politicians using popular songs as their theme music on the campaign trail and in television commercials.

Other famous cases of musicians rejecting the use of their work in political ads involve Bruce Springsteen, who complained when President Ronald Reagan used snippets of Springsteen's song "Born to Run" in television commercials during his 1984 re-election campaign, and Tom Johnston, who complained when Florida Governor Bob Martinez used more than a minute of Johnston's instrumental work "Long Train Running" in television commercials during his 1990 re-election bid.

David Byrne of the group Talking Heads sued Florida Governor Charlie Crist for appropriating the group's 1985 hit song "Road to Nowhere" without permission or compensation. Byrne continued to press the suit even after Crist agreed to stop using the song in his 2010 campaign for the U.S. Senate. The spot was never shown on television, but was instead on the campaign's website and YouTube videos associated with the campaign.

During the 2012 presidential campaign, Republican vice-presidential candidate Paul Ryan took the stage accompanied by Twisted Sister's 1984 hit "We're Not Going to Take It." After the band's lead singer Dee Snider complained, Ryan stopped using it.

When he kicked off his 2016 presidential campaign in June 2015, real estate mogul Donald Trump used as background music the Neil Young song "Rockin' in the Free World." Young immediately complained, prompting Trump to stop using it.

Most artists who hear their work used in political campaigns base their complaints not on the lack of compensation or even the lack of permission—just their desire not to have their fans (or anyone else) mistakenly believe they were endorsing a political candidate. Before reaching the point of litigation, many cases are typically resolved when lawyers representing the artists send "cease and desist" letters to the politicians. In nearly every case, the candidates immediately stop using the music, and in many cases also apologize to the copyright holders. Those artists often say that while the apologies are appreciated, the damage is already done because many of their fans will not see the apology.

1. Because they are considered political speech rather than commercial speech, should politicians be allowed to use copyrighted material under the same parts of copyright law that allow the use of copyright material in journalism and teaching?
2. Would your answer change if the political advertisements or campaign videos were required to include a disclaimer on the screen that clarified the artist performing the music is not endorsing the candidate?

Discussion Problem 10: All or Nothing

You're serving on the city council in your community. The local professional football team is threatening to move to another town unless the city builds a new stadium. Your state's constitution allows individual communities to adopt "local option" sales taxes of up to 1 percent, but such taxes (basically raising the sales tax from 6 to 7 percent) must be approved by the voters. The council has proposed adopting the 1 percent tax increase, with all of the proceeds going to build the new football stadium. Before the proposal can make it onto the ballot, however, two unions—one representing school teachers and the other representing law enforcement—come forward to oppose the idea. They provide polling data (that you determine is reliable) showing the proposal to earmark all of the new revenue for the football stadium losing at the polls, 58–42 percent. But when the poll described a hypothetical plan to designate 50 percent of the revenue for the stadium, 25 percent for local schools, and 25 percent for the police and fire departments and paramedic service, the proposal would win at the polls, 62–38.

When the city council approaches the owner of the football team with the idea of sharing the revenue from the tax, he rejects the idea and insists that all of the revenue go to stadium construction. "It's all or nothing" he tells the council. He says that his main concern is that once other groups in the community hear about the change in the proposal, they will come forward and demand their own share of the revenue. "Today it's the police and schools, tomorrow it will be libraries and hospitals, then next week it will be the museums and the art galleries ... it will never stop," he says.

1. Which propaganda techniques do you recognize in this scenario?
2. What concepts and philosophers from Chapter 2 can be applied to this issue?

Discussion Questions

1001. The First Amendment provides a greater degree of protection for political speech than commercial speech, and therefore the Federal Elections Commission and state governmental agencies find it difficult to regulate political ads, even those that are clearly exaggerated and sometimes false. Should this change? Is there a way to increase the truthfulness of political ads without violating the First Amendment?

1002. Of the propaganda techniques listed in this chapter, which have you seen in recent election campaigns or modern-day commercial advertising campaigns?

Notes

1 Richard L. Johannesen, *Ethics in Human Communication*. Prospect Heights, IL: Waveland Press (2002), p. 152.
2 Charles Larson, *Persuasion: Reception and Responsibility*. Belmont, CA: Wadsworth Publishing Company (1992), pp. 37-38.
3 Dennis Gouran, "Guidelines for the Analysis of Responsibility in Governmental Communication." *Teaching About Doublespeak*, ed. Daniel Dieterich. Urbana, IL: National Council of Teachers of English (1976).
4 Carl Hovland, Irving Janis, and Harold Kelley, *Communication and Persuasion*. New Haven, CT: Yale University Press (1953), p. 44.
5 Laurie J. Wilson and Joseph D. Ogden, *Strategic Communications Planning*. Dubuque, IA: Kendall/ Hunt Publishing (2010), p. 29.
6 Richard L. Johannesen, Kathleen S. Valde, and Karen E. Whedbee. *Ethics in Human Communication*, sixth edition. Long Grove, IL: Waveland Press (2008), p. 77.
7 Robert Proctor and Londa Schiebinger, *Agnotology: The Making and Unmaking of Ignorance*. Palo Alto, CA: Stanford University Press (2008).
8 Johannesen, p. 115. See also: Jay Black, "Semantics and Ethics of Propaganda. *Journal of Mass Media Ethics*, Vol. 16, Nos. 2 and 3 (2001), pp. 121–137.
9 Garth S. Jowett and Victoria O'Donnell, *Propaganda and Persuasion*. Newbury Park, CA: Sage Publications (1992), p. 99.
10 Kerwin Swint, *Mudslingers: The Twenty-Five Dirtiest Political Campaigns of All Time*. New York: Union Square Press (2006), p. 47.

11 Randy Bobbitt, *Lottery Wars: Case Studies in Bible-Belt Politics, 1986–2005*. Lanham, MD: Lexington Books (2008), p. 180.

12 Mike Papantonio, presentation at "The People's Law School," May 21, 2019.

13 Al Gore, *The Assault on Reason: Our Information Ecosystem, From the Age of Print to the Age of Trump*. New York: Penguin Books (2017), p. 289.

14 Swint, p. 228.

15 Andrew Kohut, "Polls Speed Down the Slippery Slope, But They Don't Have To." *Columbia Journalism Review*, November/December 2000, pp. 66–67.

16 Lori Robertson, "Poll Crazy." *American Journalism Review*, January/February 2003, pp. 40–45.

17 Gore, p. 8.

18 Anthony Salvanto, *Where Did You Get This Number? A Pollster's Guide to Making Sense of the World*. New York: Simon & Schuster (2018), pp. 59–62.

19 "AAPOR Statement on Push Polls." American Association for Public Opinion Research website, www.aapor.org. Posted June 2007, accessed July 23, 2019.

20 "AAPOR Statement on Push Polls."

21 "Polls and Surveys." *Associated Press Stylebook and Briefing on Media Law*. New York: Associated Press (2019), pp. 351–356.

22 George Gallup, "The Ethical Problems of Polling." *Ethics, Morality, and the Media*. New York: Hastings House Publishers (1980), pp. 207–213.

23 Bobbitt, *Lottery Wars*, p. 12.

24 "Polls and Surveys." *Associated Press Stylebook and Briefing on Media Law*. New York: Associated Press (2019), pp. 351–356.

25 Maureen Taylor and Michael L. Kent, "Towards Legitimacy and Professionalism: A Call to Repeal the Gillett Amendment." *Public Relations Review*, march 2016, pp. 1–8.

26 Taylor and Kent.

27 Murray Edelman, *The Politics of Misinformation*. New York: Cambridge University Press (2001), p. 8.

28 Mike Hoyt, "Talk Radio: Turning up the Volume." *Columbia Journalism Review*, November/December 1992, pp. 45–50.

29 Peter Laufer, *Inside Talk Radio: America's Voice or Just Hot Air?* New York: Carol Publishing Company (1995), p. 247.

30 Randy Bobbitt, *Us Against Them: The Political Culture of Talk Radio*. Lanham, MD: Lexington Books (2010), p. 13.

31 Gore, p. 66.

32 Bill Moyers, *Free Speech for Sale*. Video documentary by the Corporation for Public Broadcasting, 1999.

33 James J. Kilpatrick, "Taking License with Free Speech." Syndicated newspaper column, November 6, 2004.

34 David L. Hudson Jr. and Andrew Gargano, "License Plates." First Amendment Center website, posted January 17, 2018; accessed August 22, 2019.

35 Hudson and Gargano.

36 "Use of 'Barracuda' for Sarah Palin Nets GOP a Heart Attack." *New York Daily News*, September 6, 2008.

11 Ethical Issues in Workplace Communication

Background

Because of the number of hours that Americans spend at their jobs, and the volatility of their workplace relationships, good workplace communication skills are crucial for being successful. "For most people who work outside the home, their work group is one of the most important social groups that they are involved in," wrote Rudy Nydegger in his 2018 book *Clocking In: The Psychology of Work*. "It is frequently true that not counting time sleeping, most people spend more time with work colleagues than with any other family member or friends."[1]

There are no federal or state laws that apply specifically to workplace communication, but laws from other areas, such as those regarding defamation and privacy, may apply. In addition, labor and employment laws regarding workplace issues such as employment discrimination and sexual harassment may have implications for professional communicators. Typical problem areas in workplace communication include harassment of co-workers or subordinates, lying to cover up mistakes, lying to or misleading a superior or subordinate about the status of a project, taking credit for another individual's work, and falsifying expense reports, time sheets, or other financial documents.

There are no professional organizations that deal with all aspects of business communication, but specific aspects of business communication are subject to the ethical codes of organizations such as the Public Relations Society of America (PRSA) and the International Association of Business Communicators (IABC). These codes were discussed in detail in Chapter 9.

In addition to the PRSA and IABC codes, the two organizations serving the field of personnel administration—the American Society for Personnel Administration (ASPA) and the Society for Human Resource Management (SHRM)—have codes of ethics that cover a variety of issues. ASPA employs a code of ethics that requires its members to (1) maintain truthfulness and honesty, (2) ensure that others receive credit for their work and contributions, (3) guard against conflicts of interest or their appearance, (4) respect superiors, subordinates, colleagues, and the public, and (5) take responsibility for their own errors.

SHRM has a sweeping "code of conduct" that deals with issues such as confidentiality of personnel records, appropriate use of public funds, fairness in the employee recruiting process, and the responsibility of organizations to protect whistle-blowers.

Issues and Controversies

Sexual Harassment, #MeToo, and the "Weinstein Effect"

While sexual harassment has been a workplace problem ever since men and women began working together centuries ago, the problem became more prevalent in the 1970s and 1980s as increasing numbers of women entered the workplace. The term **sexual harassment** was coined in the mid-1970s by feminist author and journalist Lin Farley.[2]

Today, the term is used to refer to a variety of offensive behaviors, including unwelcome sexual advances, requests for sexual favors, and other verbal and physical conduct of a sexual nature. Sexual harassment is considered one of the major factors in employee turnover and loss of productivity, as well as a major legal issue for employers of any size and type.

Government figures indicating sexual harassment claims dropped 25 percent between 2000 and 2017 but have risen dramatically since, a result of widely publicized scandals involving famous individuals, major corporations, and media organizations. A social media campaign known as #MeToo has brought new awareness to the issue.

In 2018, the Equal Employment Opportunities Commission reported that sexual harassment complaints increased more than 12 percent over the previous year. EEOC officials cautioned that the results don't necessarily indicate an increase in the actual occurrences of harassment, but rather an increase in the willingness of alleged victims to come forward—a side effect, perhaps, of the #MeToo movement.[3]

Although the term had been around for more than two decades, the media paid little attention to the issue until the 1990s when they pursued three major news stories: the confirmation hearings for Supreme Court Justice Clarence Thomas, whose nomination was threatened by accusations of sexual harassment by a former co-worker; the "Tailhook" scandal involving the harassment of female naval aviators attending an annual conference; and the events leading up to the impeachment of President Bill Clinton, whose affair with a White House intern focused new light on male–female relationships in the workplace.

More recently, sexual harassment claims have damaged or ended the careers of Fox News founder Roger Ailes, political commentators Bill O'Reilly, Mark Halperin, Charlie Rose, and Matt Lauer, movie producers Harvey Weinstein and James Toback, and politician Al Franken. In addition to those individuals, the ride-sharing service Uber was also in the news in 2017 after numerous female employees complained about a "culture of sexual harassment" at the company's headquarters in San Francisco.

In 2017–18, the "dishonor roll" was expanded to include the world of professional sports. Jerry Richardson, owner of the National Football League's Carolina Panthers, was forced to sell the team after a league investigation uncovered years of alleged sexual and racial harassment claims filed by lower-level employees against front-office executives.

About the same time, a *Sports Illustrated* investigation into the front office of the Dallas Mavericks of the National Basketball Association uncovered claims of sexual harassment filed by team's female employees against a former employee. While team owner Mark Cuban was not accused of the behavior, the report did claim he failed to follow-up on the accusations when he became aware of them.

Even nonprofit organizations with otherwise stellar reputations are not immune from problems. In 2019, the Nature Conservancy asked for and received the resignation of its chief executive officer and two other top officials after a lengthy investigation that found they condoned a culture of sexual harassment and other forms of misconduct.[4]

While complaints from employees in mid-level and upper-level positions get the most media attention and generate the most lawsuits, those involving jobs at the lower end of the economic scale represent a greater portion of the total number of complaints. In 2016, the EEOC reported getting more complaints from restaurant workers (about supervisors and customers) than any other field. "Many waitresses have come to expect it," stated a 2019 *Time* cover story on minimum-wage workers.[5]

Researchers studying the issue of sexual harassment in the workplace have coined the term "Weinstein Effect" to refer to the trend of men accused of sexual misconduct enduring short-time criticism (and legal costs) but escaping any long-term consequences. In many cases, media reports claimed that men found guilty of such conduct simply paid out-of-court legal settlements, apologized for their behavior, and then continued it as though the original conduct never occurred.[6]

But the same cannot be said for guilty parties in the corporate world. "We're now at an inflection point where companies, and even entire industries, need to make a pretty basic decision," said Joelle Emerson, founder of Paradigm, a consulting firm specializing in diversity and inclusion, in a 2017 media interview. "The decision is to take this seriously, or get left behind."[7]

Long before the cases of Ailes, O'Reilly, Halperin, Rose, Lauer, Weinstein, Toback, Franken, Uber, the Carolina Panthers, Dallas Mavericks, and the Nature Conservancy became public, the landmark court case dealing with sexual harassment was argued in 1986. In *Meritor Savings Bank v. Vinson*, the U.S. Supreme Court ruled that employers bear the responsibility of protecting their employees from sexual harassment and can be found liable for not taking action, even in cases in which management was not aware of the problem. After that ruling, companies across the country developed formal sexual harassment policies and made them part of written policy manuals and new employee orientation programs.

Those policies, following the lead of court rulings and legal publications, identify two categories of sexual harassment. **Quid pro quo** (from the Latin for "something for something") is the demand by a work supervisor or other superior for sexual favors in exchange for a promotion, salary increase, or other workplace privileges; or the threat to terminate an individual for not complying with the request. **Hostile work environment** is a term used to describe offensive jokes of a sexual nature, repeated remarks regarding a person's body or clothing (even if meant to be complimentary); unwelcome hugging, kissing, or other physical contact; and pornographic images such as screensavers, posters, calendars, or photographs.

Most organizational policies include a formal process that begins with the employee bringing the matter to the attention of a supervisor. If the offending party is the supervisor, the complaint is filed with either the next supervisor on the organizational chart, or with the human resources office. The purpose of the internal procedure is to resolve the conflict without going to court or generating media attention. Because the litigation process is expensive and emotionally draining for both the plaintiff and defendant, most companies find formal policies are critical to resolving conflicts early in the process.

In extreme cases, however, employers are unable or unwilling to address sexual harassment complaints internally, leaving victims with no other choice than litigation. Once within the court system, such cases are argued in civil court based on laws regarding employment discrimination. Those laws include anti-retaliation provisions that prohibit employers from firing or otherwise retaliating against plaintiffs.

While the common perception is that sexual harassment occurs mostly between male supervisors and female subordinates, that is not always the case. The Equal Employment Opportunities Commission (EEOC) estimates that each year, 15 to 20 percent of individuals filing sexual harassment claims were male, with perpetrators in those cases being both male and female. And while sexual harassment is more often a case of an individual attempting to exercise power rather than seek sex, sometimes it is neither.[8] The EEOC points out that in addition to establishing and enforcing policies in cases involving conflicts between employees, companies must also be watchful for cases of harassment in which the perpetrators are customers, clients, or outside vendors or contractors. In those cases, company leaders should inform those perpetrators that such conduct is inappropriate, and if necessary notify the perpetrator's employer. If that fails, employers should be prepared to terminate the business relationship with the offending vendor.

Sexual harassment violates Title VII of the Civil Rights Act of 1964. In 1991, Congress amended that section of the law to provide stronger financial penalties against companies who fail to protect their employees.[9]

Employers should also be aware of a concept called "third-party harassers," which refers to the problem of vendors and customers being the alleged perpetrators. In those cases, the employers are just as liable as if the offense was committed by an employee.

A 1995 article in *Nation's Business* identified five steps that organizations take in preventing sexual harassment problems: (1) develop a company policy on the issue, (2) train both managers and employees,[10] (3) take all complaints seriously, (4) recognize that harassment is not just a crime of men against women, and (5) consider mediation as an alternative to litigation.[11]

A 2017 study conducted by researchers at the Harvard Medical School and the University of California at Los Angeles found that nearly one in five employees reported being the target of sexual harassment or bullying. Citing the national unemployment rate being at a sixteen-year low, the researchers concluded companies could to a better job of filling vacancies and retaining employees by reducing harassment. "There's a message here," the report concludes. "Working conditions really do matter."[12]

A survey of college students found that 25 percent report having been touched, grabbed, or pinched in a sexual manner, while 53 percent reported being the target of comments, jokes, or gestures.[13]

Despite the popularity of the social media hashtag #Me Too and the media attention it has generated, the concept is not without its critics. Some observers believe the issue has been overdramatized as a way to punish movie producers and newscasters for their political leanings. Others, including many women working in Hollywood, simply believe the numbers of reported cases is being exaggerated. Following the launch of the "Me Too" social media hashtag, women claiming to be unaffected by the problem mocked the movement with their own hashtag, "Me Neither."

Racial and Religious Harassment

While sexual harassment has been a well-publicized workplace issue for several decades, an increasing number of managers have reported receiving complaints of racial and religious harassment as well.

Racial harassment has been a growing problem since the introduction of the Internet into the workplace in the mid-1990s, with the worst examples being the distribution of offensive jokes and visual images via an organization's email network. The courts and employer policy manuals define racial harassment as "epithets, slurs, negative stereotyping, threats, intimidation, hostile acts, denigrating jokes, or the display or circulation of written or graphic material that denigrates or shows hostility to an individual or group."[14]

In terms of religious and political harassment, simply inquiring about a person's religious beliefs is acceptable, even though such questions might make the person being asked uncomfortable. But just as repeated requests for a date or other attention paid to a co-worker can graduate to sexual harassment if those incidents are both persistent and unwanted, repeated attempts to lure a person into a discussion of religion can also cause problems for both the individual and the employer.

Just as employees have the right to seek protection from their employers in cases of alleged racial or sexual harassment, they also have the right to complain about inappropriate inquiries about religion. Examples include repeated inquiries about church attendance or unwanted invitations to attend someone else's church, persistent inquiries about political affiliations or voting decisions, or intentionally denigrating others for their religious beliefs.

The harassment of co-workers and subordinates based on their religious beliefs has been a workplace issue for decades, but addressing it had been a low priority for organizational leaders until recently. In the decade following the terrorist attacks of September 11, 2001, the number of Muslim employees reporting cases of harassment increased exponentially.

In cases of racial or religious harassment, the courts use the term "hostile work environment" in the same way they use the term in sexual harassment cases.

Mixing Work and Politics

Because of the amount of time individuals spend at their jobs, it is inevitable that workplace conversations will eventually include political beliefs. In many cases, those discussions may lead to discrimination, ridicule, and harassment.

"As we all know, the lines between our work lives and personal lives are increasingly blurred," wrote Johnny C. Taylor, a human resources expert and columnist for *USA Today*. "And when you add camera phones and social media to the mix, the things we do on our non-work time—such as attending a rally or sharing a few choice words with an elected official at a city council meeting—are no longer exclusively private activities."[15]

To avoid potential problems, many employers prohibit their employees from wearing campaign buttons on their clothing or displaying campaign posters, literature, and other religious or political materials in their workspaces.

After several years of criticism, Google announced in 2019 that it had issued new guidelines to its employees limiting the discussion of politics and other topics not related to work. It also replaced the volunteer employees monitoring internal message boards (for offensive content) with paid staffers. The company's internal network offered thousands of message boards ranging from social issues to sports, but in recent years some of the discourse went off-course and became either offensive or threatening. In addition to the paid monitors, the company added a feature that would allow users to flag content that violated the rules, just in case a monitor missed it. Specific content the company hopes to eliminate includes name-calling or blanket statements about groups or categories of people.

Part of the impetus for the policy was a 2017 controversy in which Google fired an employee for an internal memo in which he stated that women were not as good as men in technical positions. While that was the reason given for the firing, the employee claimed he was fired for expressing conservative views in a political forum on the internal message boards.[16]

In 2017, a Virginia woman shown on social media giving the "middle finger" to the passing motorcade of President Donald Trump was fired by her employer, a government contractor.[17]

In 2019, employees at a construction site in Pennsylvania were told they were expected—but not required—to attend an on-site speech by President Trump. Many employees who objected to the president's visit indicated they would not attend and would rather stay at their jobs. But shortly before the speech began, they were told that if they did not attend the speech, they would be required to leave the property and the absence would be counted as an unpaid sick day. When employees complained, a spokesman for the company told the media that "as with most hourly positions, they would not be paid for hours they did not work." The workers were not unionized, but the leader of a union not involved in the dispute told the media the workers should not have been required to attend what appeared to be a "glorified campaign rally." The company responded that it was not a campaign event, and the policy of requiring attendance was aimed at "showing respect for the speaker." A labor lawyer, also not affiliated with the case, told the media that the company was within its rights to require attendance at the meeting and that no laws were broken in the process.[18]

Workplace Honesty

According to a recent survey by CareerBuilder.com, 19 percent of workers admit to lying in the workplace at least once a week. Among the reasons cited were appeasing a customer (26 percent), covering up a project failure or missed deadline (13 percent), to explain tardiness or absence (8 percent), or to sabotage the work of a colleague (5 percent). The same survey revealed that 24 percent of all managers had fired an employee for dishonesty. Other examples of workplace dishonesty include using sick days for reasons other than illness; falsifying time sheets, expense reports, or other internal documents; and spreading gossip about co-workers and superiors.

Another common unethical behavior is lying to potential customers about the company's ability to meet a deadline or achieve some other service-related goal, or lying about the positive qualities of a company's products or services or the negative qualities of a competitor's products or services.

In a 1991 article in *Entrepreneurial Woman*, ethicist Michael Josephson listed several rationales that employees often use to justify dishonest or unethical behavior in the workplace.[19] They include:

False necessity. Employees often believe they are behaving as they do because they feel morally or ethically required to do so. For example, an employee may intentionally sabotage the work of a colleague by telling himself or herself "that project never should have been approved" or "that's not the right direction for this company" when the actual reason behind the behavior was personal or professional jealousy.

Relative filth. Some employees believe that taking ethical shortcuts is acceptable because other employees or the company as a whole is doing something they perceive as much worse. For example, employees may list on their time sheets a few hours they did not work or add a few fictional expenses to travel reports and justify it in their own minds because they know (or suspect) that other employees falsify their time sheets or expense reports to a greater degree. In another example, an employee justifies the theft of office supplies by telling themselves "the company wastes so much time on landscaping and repainting the building, it will never miss a few dollars' worth of copier paper and paper clips."

Rationalization. Sometimes known as the "big stretch." An employee may justify unethical conduct with flimsy excuses, such as taking a slightly longer lunch hour than is allotted and claiming to make it up by working late that night (whether that actually happens or not), or telling himself or herself, "I'll print out my kid's school project at the office because that printer is nicer than what we have at home, and besides, the company doesn't pay me what I'm worth."

Self-deception. In this scenario, employees (or potential employees) tell a falsehood so many times that they no longer remember whether it is true or false. One common example is the individual who early in his or her career falsified information on a résumé, such as claiming to have been captain of the high school football team or recipient of an academic award. Each time the résumé is revised, the false information remains, and after multiple revisions the individual is so comfortable with the information that he or she forgets that it was fictional to begin with.

The ends justify the means. A supervisor may coerce employees to work overtime without compensation in order to reduce or eliminate a backlog in work by saying that if the goal is not accomplished, the department or individual employees will be treated unfavorably in the future. There is actually no substance to the threat, but the supervisor believes the goal of reducing or eliminating the backlog of work was more important than being honest with the subordinates.

In a recent National Business Ethics Survey of more than 3,000 American workers, 10 percent reported feeling pressured to compromise the organization's ethical standards, with the sources of pressure including top management (36 percent), middle management (39 percent), and co-workers (15 percent). More than 65 percent reported encountering a situation that invited ethical misconduct on their parts, while 74 percent reported observing some level of misconduct by others in the organization.

Of those claiming to have observed others' misconduct, only half reported those situations to superiors. The most common reasons given for reporting the unethical conduct were confidence that corrective action would be taken and that "it was the right thing to do." The most common reasons given for non-reporting include fear of retaliation, belief that someone else will report it instead, or skepticism that any corrective action would be taken.

Résumés

One common source of workplace dishonesty is not current employers, but potential ones. One recent survey found that 80 percent of all résumés received included some level of falsehood. Of those, 60 percent were described as "minor exaggerations that had little impact," 15 percent were described as "outright lies," and 5 percent were described as "real whoppers." Among the most outrageous claims made by candidates in résumés included (1) being a member of the Kennedy family, (2) graduating with degrees not offered by the institution they attended or graduating from universities that did not exist, (3) claiming to have owned a company when the candidate had actually worked in the mailroom or other entry-level position, and (4) claiming military experience dating back to before the individual was born. One reported incident involved an applicant for a journalism position submitting a portfolio of work samples that included an article written by the editor conducting the interview.

In other cases, employers report interviewing multiple students from the same high school graduating class claiming they were a valedictorian, captain of the football team, or class president; and college graduates claiming to have won non-existent awards or exaggerating the number of hours spent in volunteer activities. As a result of this trend, many interviewers are verifying such claims with references and asking more detailed questions during in-person interviews.

"Employers are clearly clued into the fact that some applicants are either exaggerating their experience or handing over résumés that are fiction than fact," wrote Megan Elliott in 2018 article posted on Glassdoor.com.

> But that doesn't appear to stop some people from telling a few whoppers as they attempt to weasel their way into a job. Giving into the temptation to lie when applying for a job is risky. You could miss out on a job offer, damage your reputation, or even get you fired once your fibs are revealed.[20]

Elliott identified the top ways employers detect résumé falsehoods as (1) alma maters that can't confirm that you graduated, (1) dates on a résumé that don't add up, (3) job titles that sound too good to be true, (4) references that don't back up a candidate, and (5) a simple Google search that reveals the truth.[21]

Several recent examples of falsification of résumés made national news.

In 2001, newly hired Notre Dame football coach George O'Leary was found to have falsified several critical details on his résumé and was forced to resign five days into his job (see Case Study 11C).

The following year, a journalist writing a profile of Ronald Zarrella, chief executive officer of Bausch & Lomb, found that New York University's School of Business Administration had no record of Zarrella earning an M.B.A. there, as Zarrella claimed on his résumé and on the company website. When that news became public, Zarrella submitted his resignation, but it was not accepted by the company's board of directors. Instead, Zarrella forfeited his $1.1 million annual bonus at the end of that year.[22]

In 2002, shareholders of the software company Veritas (which means truth in Latin) saw the value of their stocks drop 20 percent when it was revealed that the company's chief financial officer, Kenneth Lonchar, had lied about earning an M.B.A. at Stanford.[23]

In 2013, the chief of staff to Florida Governor Rick Scott kept his job after admitting that he lied about the date of his graduation from the University of Alabama. In materials issued by the governor's office and on the State of Florida website, Rick Hollingsworth claimed that he attended the University of Alabama and held a degree in communications. He made similar claims as an employee of the city of Jacksonville, and prior to that as an employee for a major railroad. While Hollingsworth did attend the University of Alabama in the 1990s, he did not complete the degree until 2009.

Ironically, Scott had previously signed a measure repealing a state law that made it illegal to lie about one's academic credentials, unaware that it would affect his chief of staff.[24]

In 2018, a candidate for public office in Florida admitted that she lied on her campaign website about her educational background. Republican Melissa Howard, running for a seat in the Florida Legislature's 73rd District, claimed to hold a degree from Miami University in Oxford, Ohio. The deception came to light when several online media outlets looking into Howard's background found discrepancies in her campaign materials and accused her of misstating her credentials. Howard responded on her website by publishing a photo of her holding a diploma showing she earned a bachelor's of science in marketing, which Miami does not offer.

Officials at the university confirmed that Howard spent four years at Miami, studying retailing but never earning a degree. They also confirmed that the diploma shown in the photograph was a fake.

Under Florida law, anyone misrepresenting his or her academic credentials can be charged with a misdemeanor. Howard avoided heavy fines by agreeing to drop out of the race and performing twenty-five hours of community service.[25]

Background Checks

Because verifying the information included in résumés and on application forms is time-consuming, most employers wait until the field has been narrowed to a manageable number of candidates and carry out such work only after the candidate has had a successful interview and is under serious consideration. In other cases, employers may wait until a formal offer has been made and accepted, warning the candidate that the offer is "contingent upon a background check."

The background check usually begins by with verifying the information on the résumé, and if serious discrepancies are found, most employers will offer the candidate an opportunity to clarify the discrepancies in order to allow for typographical errors or similar mistakes. While some employers may be forgiving, many others are not, especially when they find the deception to be intentional. Many employers report that intentional deception results in a withdrawal of the job offer, even in cases in which the erroneous information was not a factor in the original assessment of the candidate's qualifications.

When such deception is detected, many individuals defend themselves by claiming that "everyone lies on their résumé" and that they are at a disadvantage if they don't. But most employers and workplace ethicists disagree. "Widespread lying on résumés doesn't justify your doing the same thing," wrote business ethicist Bruce Weinstein in a 2006 newspaper column. "Even if your friends and co-workers are doing it, it is ethically irrelevant to your own behavior."[26]

Another method that employers use to get a more complete picture of job candidates is checking their "online persona" on social media sites such as Facebook and LinkedIn. Many job placement counselors advise their clients that "if you wouldn't want your grandmother to see it, remove it from your Facebook page." Lewis Maltby, founder of a nonprofit organization that studies workplace privacy issues, adds that "you can't blame HR people for looking at social networking sites because hiring the wrong person is a very expensive mistake."[27]

Employers are not legally required to inform candidates of negative hiring decisions based on what they have found on social media sites, and it is unlikely they would do so voluntarily. But even if they did, employment lawyers claim, the candidate would have no legal recourse because the hiring decision was not based on a factor prohibited by federal law, such as age, race, religion, gender, or disability.

Some employers see a scanning of a candidate's social media content as an "on the cheap" version of a background check that can screen out candidates before a more thorough (and expensive) background check can be performed by an outside investigative firm.

"An immutable law of human nature and a key to human survival—that we learn from our mistakes—seems to have been suspended online," claims a 2013 article in *USA Today*.[28]

Adds Steve Rubel of Edelman Public Relations: "You need to realize that your image is shaped by what you share."[29]

"One of the things people don't realize is that social media is the place where a lot of employers and recruiters go first to find out about people," said Candace Moody, vice president of communications for WorkSource of Jacksonville. "If you've got party photos, if you've got embarrassing posts, if you've got posts that are talking trash about your previous employers, you're in bad shape."[30]

Some interviewers take the concept a step further, asking job candidates to reveal their social media passwords during the initial interview so they can check to see if the material accessible only through the individuals' private settings matches what they found on the public side of their social media platforms. Alarmed by what they saw as an obvious privacy violation, many state legislatures have passed laws prohibiting the practice. In addition, social media platforms such as Facebook and Instagram have added such prohibitions to their terms of service.[31]

Periodic scanning of employee's social media postings may continue long after an employee is hired, as supervisors or human resources personnel may be looking for evidence the employee is criticizing co-workers, superiors, or the company itself; or is disclosing confidential business information. Members of the U.S. military are cautioned that their social media postings are often monitored to make sure their postings don't reveal secret military information or jeopardize the safety of the service member or his or her family from foreign or domestic threats.[32]

Letters of Recommendation

Another major problem area in business communication is the issue of employee evaluations and letters of recommendation. Even if they are seen by only a small number of people, documents that criticize individuals' job performances or suitability for employment can be the object of defamation lawsuits filed by the offended parties. Employers are therefore extremely cautious in the words they choose when describing a former employee's job performance or explaining to a third party the reasons for one's termination.

Human resources personnel are also cautious in giving and receiving information (either in writing, telephone, or email) about past or present employees, including letters of recommendation, the results of performance reviews, or other evaluative information. The potential cost of litigation has caused many employers to enforce policies about who can provide information about current and former employees and what kinds of evaluative information can be shared.

Even well-meaning supervisors and former supervisors find themselves in trouble after providing what they believed to be positive letters of recommendation or employment evaluations for current or former employees. Most result from simple misunderstandings, but employees who believe they were not hired by another employer as a result may sue the individual, the company, or both. Because of such legal liability, many companies require work supervisors to write letters of recommendation on personal rather than company stationery and preface them by stating they are providing their opinion and not that of the company as a whole. Other employers prohibit supervisors from writing letters of recommendation or providing employment references in their entirety. In cases in which an employee left the company under negative circumstances, many employers require all evaluative documents to be reviewed by their legal departments before being released.

While cases of being sued for information revealed in response to a reference check are worrisome, a more recent trend is that of employers being sued for what they *did not report*. Examples include not reporting that an individual is a convicted child molester when the prospective employer is an elementary school, or not reporting a former employee's tendency to act violently toward co-workers.

Job Interviews

Despite extensive training in employment recruiting procedures conducted by an organization's human relations professionals, many hiring officers ask job candidates questions that are either unrelated to the job or simply unethical attempts to obtain information that could be used to discriminate against those candidates. Examples include inquiries about national origin or ethnicity, age, marital status, or family planning.

A 2017 survey by CNBC and Associated Press found that half of all Americans who had ever applied for a job had been asked questions they believed were inappropriate and were used to discriminate against them. Thirty-five percent had been asked about their age and the same percentage had been asked about marital status, while 21 percent had been asked about their medical history or whether they had a disability. Eleven percent had been asked about whether they or a partner were pregnant or planned to become pregnant, and 9 percent were asked about their religious beliefs.[33]

"Asking a question related to these characteristics generally isn't illegal in and of itself," stated an AP article summarizing the survey's findings. "But if the person who was asked the question does not get the job, it could be used as evidence of discrimination. Even if the person is hired, the improper question could help build a case down the road of a pattern of discrimination."[34]

There are many questions that are either unethical or illegal for an employer to ask, depending on the nature of the employer's business. As a general rule, government and private industry employers cannot ask questions that might require candidates to provide information that could be used to discriminate against them. The most problematic questions are those involving age, race, nationality, religious beliefs, marital status, health, and disability. Employment law experts recommend that in order to be safe, all questions should be job-related and the same questions be asked of all candidates.

Churches and nonprofit organizations that are faith-based have more leeway to ask questions about a candidate's religious beliefs. For example, administrators of a church interviewing candidates for positions such as church secretary, day care center worker, or private school teacher can ask questions about a candidate's religious beliefs.

Here are some commonly used guidelines:

Subject	Allowed	Not allowed
Age	Are you at least 18 years old?	How old are you? Can you provide a birth certificate?
Nationality	Are you authorized to work in the U.S.?	In what country were you born? Are you an American citizen?
Criminal history[35]	Have you ever been convicted of a felony?	Have you ever been arrested?
Disability	Are you able to perform all of the tasks in the job description?	Do you have a disability?
Family and relationships	Can you work the hours listed in the job notice?	Are you married? Do you have children or plan to have children? Do you have a boyfriend/girlfriend?
Religion	Can you work Saturdays and Sundays?	Do you go to church? What is your religious affiliation?
Residence	How long have you lived at your current address?	Do you own or rent your current home? Have you lived outside of the country?

After conducting a background check on prospective employees, employers are required by law to inform candidates if information from credit checks or criminal records checks was used to disqualify them; the rationale behind the law is to allow candidates the opportunity to tell "their side of the story" or challenge potentially inaccurate information. No such law applies to information from checking out candidates on social media, but Chris Hoofnagle, a legal researcher at Berkeley Law School, believes there should be one. "A requirement that employers who conduct online searches of applicants notify them about the search will at least give applicants a chance to be heard," Hoofnagle says.[36]

Communicating with Disabled Co-Workers and Customers

When a company employs individuals who are disabled, many co-workers are unsure about how to communicate with them. Even well-meaning co-workers can offend disabled colleagues through comments and actions.

Despite their advocacy for laws such as the Americans with Disabilities Act, many persons with disabilities do not seek special treatment; they desire only to be treated on an equal basis with others. Some are offended by what they perceive as an artificially sympathetic or patronizing attitude of persons without disabilities. As one example, some object to the modifier "challenged," such as descriptions of persons as "mentally challenged" or "physically challenged." A person who uses a wheelchair, for example, might look at a set of concrete steps and say, "That's not a challenge—that's an impossibility." On a 1990s television sitcom, an adult who never grew beyond the height of four feet was complaining to another character about the patronizing attitude of some persons of standard height. "Do you mean when they bend over to talk to you?" the other character asked. The reply: "No, I mean when they *pick you up* to talk to you."

Advocacy groups for the disabled caution against using negatively charged words and phrases when speaking with or about disabled employees or writing about them in company publications. Examples of terms to avoid include "crippled" (*disabled* is the preferred term), "suffers from," "victim" (write *person with cerebral palsy*, not *cerebral palsy victim*), and "wheelchair bound" (call the person a *wheelchair user* instead; few people are truly bound to a wheelchair; they use it mainly for transportation).

Other suggestions include:

1. If a hearing-impaired individual is accompanied by an interpreter, always speak to the individual, not the interpreter.
2. If a person is missing his or her right arm or if the right arm is a prosthetic, wait for him or her to offer to shake hands. Most individuals in that situation will offer their left hand, but wait for them to make the first gesture.
3. If you offer assistance to a blind person, wait until the offer is accepted. If you offer to accompany a blind person to a location within your building, he or she will likely extend an arm and wait for you to take it.
4. Treat disabled persons with the same respect and dignity as the non-disabled. Do not speak down to them or address them by first name unless you address others the same way.
5. Do not touch a person's wheelchair or other artificial device. Most individuals using wheelchairs consider it as part of their body.

6. If a person has a speech impediment, listen carefully and resist the temptation to finish sentences for them. If you do not understand, do not pretend that you do; politely ask them to repeat what they have said.

7. If you inadvertently make a potentially insensitive remark while speaking with a disabled person, do not be embarrassed. Examples include "Gotta run," "See you later," or "Did you hear ..." Offer an apology only if the person appears to have been offended. That is unlikely, as many disabled persons are accustomed to such casual remarks.

8. To get the attention of a hearing-impaired person, tap him or her on the shoulder or wave to get his or her attention. When speaking with a hearing-impaired person, speak slowly (but not excessively so) and keep your hands away from your face so the individual can read your lips.

9. When speaking to someone in a wheelchair, find a chair to sit in so you will be at the same eye level. If no chairs are available, do not lean over to speak with them.

Employer Monitoring of Employee Email and Web Activity

While the government is unwilling or unable to regulate communication over the Internet, that is not the case with private industry. Employers often monitor incoming and outgoing email traffic on company-owned computer networks. Court rulings, in supporting their right to do so, have stated that companies own all of the information contained on those computer networks.

Not only are employers trying to prevent the unauthorized release of company information, but they are also attempting to limit other forms of communication that may result in lawsuits involving libel, privacy, or sexual or racial harassment. In a recent survey conducted by the American Management Association, more than two-thirds of companies responded that they routinely monitor the email communication of their employees as well as monitor the websites they visit—both the work-related and non-work-related.

Experts in the fields of both law and technology point out that when individuals use their employers' computer equipment and Internet access to vent in cyberspace, their bulletin board postings and electronic mail postings are not as private as they might believe.

In an effort to prevent employees from engaging in libelous speech or otherwise exposing the company to legal liability, many large employers are monitoring employee email traffic and hiring outside consultants to develop systems for determining the origin of anonymous postings to industry bulletin boards. "If you work at a Fortune 500 company, chances are good your email has been reviewed at least once," says Joan Feldman, founder of the Seattle-based Computer Forensics Inc., which helps companies track their employees' illegal or unethical use of company-owned technology.[37]

According to Bruce Barry, a professor of management at Vanderbilt University, when individuals get "called on the carpet" for information posted online, it's "less often a case of employers violating free-speech rights and more a case of employees being victims of their own bad judgment."[38]

While some free-speech and privacy advocates claim that employer monitoring of email violates the rights of employees, recent news stories provide the best evidence of the dangers that companies face by not doing so. When federal investigators looking into allegations of financial wrongdoing at Enron in 2003 gained access to archived computer files, for example, they found pornography, racial comments, offensive jokes, and other material in employee email that would have exposed the company to lawsuits if it had been detected before the company dissolved.

Despite the potential danger involved in not monitoring employee email, many companies are still reluctant to do so. One factor is the cost, which for companies with large numbers of employees may be substantial. Another factor is trust—employers simply prefer to trust their employees and respect their privacy. Many companies in this category wait until they have "probable cause" or other suspicions before snooping in email files.

One such "trust" incident occurred at the *Toledo Blade*, one of Ohio's largest daily newspapers, in 2006. Wanting to determine which staff member sent an anonymous email criticizing the newspaper's Pulitzer Prize entry to the organization administering the competition, the management hired a private investigator. Following preliminary evidence, the investigators confiscated the company-owned laptop computer of a reporter and used a computer forensics expert to analyze its hard drive. The newspaper fired the reporter, who had sent the anonymous email through his personal Yahoo! account, but using the company-owned laptop. Following the incident, however, the company reverted to its policy of not monitoring employee email except in extreme circumstances.

Court rulings have consistently found that because they are providing the technology, employers are free to conduct such monitoring, and employees do not have a legitimate claim that their privacy has been invaded. That ruling assumes, however, that employers are doing so for a legitimate purpose such as protecting company assets or preventing the transmission of material that is sexually or racially offensive, is harassing, or violates copyright law. Courts would be more sympathetic to the employee if he or she is able to prove that the monitoring is unrelated to legitimate purposes or is voyeuristic in nature.

Only two states—Connecticut and Delaware—prohibit employers from watching employees' web activity or intercepting emails unless they provide advanced notice of the monitoring. Many employers in those states have their employees sign documents acknowledging the employers' rights. In the other forty-eight states, employers may do such monitoring except in cases in which it is voyeuristic in nature or the employers' intent is to monitor or disrupt union or collective bargaining activity.[39]

A 2014 decision by the National Labor Relations Board confirmed an employer's right to monitor their employees' online activity in order to investigate or prevent the harassment of co-workers, defamation, or the disclosure of trade secrets.[40]

While they discourage their employees from using the company's online access for shopping, dating, or participation in social media networking or fantasy sports leagues, they are reluctant to do so as long as the employee is doing so during lunch breaks or after working hours. But for most employers, engaging in non-work online activities during working hours is a major drain on productivity. Even though many employees claim they would "never do that during working hours," research indicates that at least some of their peers do. One survey of Internet retailers found that two-thirds of their business takes place during business hours (9 a.m. to 5 p.m.), with a significant fall-off on the weekends.[41]

Despite the absence of state laws prohibiting them from doing so, employers should still resist the temptation, says Marc Rotenberg, executive director of the Electronic Privacy Information Center. "Having the right to do it doesn't make it the right thing to do," Rotenberg said in an interview with the *Daily Record* in Kansas City, Kansas.

If you reason that since it's the employer's equipment, they have the right to monitor, does that mean there's no expectation of privacy in the employer's restrooms as well?

I make that point only to underscore the fact that ownership alone doesn't resolve the privacy issue. I think that in personal communications, and even for use of the Internet, there should be some safeguards for employees' expectations of privacy.[42]

Two decades of court rulings generally back up employers:

- In 1993, two employees of the Nissan Motor Corp. sued the company for invading their privacy by monitoring their email communication, despite having signed a copy of the company's policy that prohibited using the system for non-work purposes. One of the employees claimed that she was humiliated when one of her sexually explicit emails was used in a training session as an example of inappropriate computer use. A California court found in favor of the company.[43]
- In 1996, a former employee was unsuccessful in a wrongful termination suit against the Pillsbury Company. The court ruled that the company's right to preventing its computer system being used for inappropriate and unprofessional comments outweighed the employee's privacy interests. The employee had been terminated for criticizing supervisors and co-workers.[44]
- In 1999, the stock brokerage firm Salomon Smith Barney fired two executives after a routine check of internal communication discovered their use of the company's internal email system for transmitting sexual explicit material.
- Also in 1999, the "zero tolerance" policy of the Edward Jones & Company resulted in nineteen employees' contracts being terminated after creating or forwarding racist and sexist jokes and sexually explicit images.[45]
- In 2011, courts in California and Georgia ruled in separate cases that employers did not violate the privacy rights of their employees by monitoring their personal email communication. In the California case, the court ruled that the employee's communication with her attorney was not protected by attorney–client privilege. In the Georgia case, the court ruled that an employer had a legitimate interest in monitoring an employee's email to determine if he was running an outside business on company time.[46]
- In 2019, employees at the McKesson Corporation, a San Francisco-based supplier of medical equipment, discovered the company had been monitoring their email activity for years; they were upset, but under California law had no legal foundation on which to complain. The company justified the monitoring by explaining that by examining the employees' communication with each other as well as with customers and suppliers, it could determine how such interactions can be improved. It also wanted to discover why certain departments had higher employee turnover rates than others.[47]

"Employers are parsing those (online) interactions to learn who is influential, which teams are most productive, and who is a flight risk," wrote *Wall Street Journal* reporter Sarah Krouse in a 2019 article.[48]

Despite companies having the law on their side, lawyers suggest that employers who choose to electronically monitor their online activity prevent problems by advising employees that monitoring may occur, requiring them to sign documents acknowledging that possibility, and issuing lists reminding employee of what forms of online activity are permissible and not permissible.

Your Turn

Case Study 11A: Mixing Work and Politics: Problems at Home Depot

In 2009, home improvement retailer Home Depot required an employee to remove a button reading "One Nation Under God" from his store-issued apron. The employee insisted that he was merely expressing his love for the country and showing support for a family member serving in the military. But the company claimed that despite his intent, the button violated the company's policy about wearing any items on their aprons or personal clothing that advocated a political or religious viewpoint. Because Home Depot is a private employer and not a government agency, the employee had no claim that his First Amendment rights were violated.[49]

1. Do you agree with the conclusion that because Home Depot is a private employer and not a government agency its employees had no First Amendment rights regarding political buttons?
2. What concepts or philosophers from Chapter 2 could be applied to this case?

Case Study 11B: Mixing Work and Politics: The Lawyer and the Congressman

In 2017, a New Jersey lawyer who was a political activist in her non-working hours was warned by her employer to cease those activities, even though she did not use any of the employer's resources nor use its name. Saily Avelenda, assistant general counsel for Lakeland Bank, was told by bank officials that her political work created a conflict of interest. Her activities came to the attention of the bank's board of directors when republican Congressman Rodney Frelinghuysen wrote a letter calling Avelenda the "ringleader" of an effort to discredit him. When pressed by the local media, bank officials stated they "could not comment on the status of current of former employees" but added that "each employee has the opportunity to support community activities or the political process in the manner she or he desires."[50]

Avelenda eventually resigned her position.

New Jersey is one of several states that does not have specific protections for employees criticized by their employers for their political activities. There are no federal protections for such activity, but the National Labor Relations Act protects employees for activities related to labor unions or collective bargaining.

Labor attorneys who represent individuals suing employers or former employers acknowledge the difficulty in pursuing such cases because the First Amendment applies to the actions of government but not to those of private employers.[51]

The only exceptions, points out human resources expert Johnny C. Taylor, would be if an employer were to terminate or discipline only employees of a certain religion, gender, or sexual orientation.[52]

1. Do you agree with the position of the company or that of the former employee?
2. Are there any philosophers or concepts from Chapter 2 that can be applied here?

Case Study 11C: Workplace Honesty: The (Bad) Luck of the Irish

On December 9, 2001, the University of Notre Dame announced it has found the perfect man to fill its football coaching vacancy. Fifty-five year old George O'Leary, the head coach at Georgia Tech, was popular and successful, and his Irish-Catholic ancestry came as a bonus. The new job looked like a good fit as well for O'Leary, a lifelong football coach who had worked his way up through the coaching ranks and had coveted the Notre Dame head coaching position for more than a decade.

Just a few days after his introductory news conference, the deal began to unravel when sports journalists looking into O'Leary's background discovered inaccuracies on his résumé, including a master's degree from a university that did not exist. O'Leary had also claimed a playing record that included earning three letters at the University of New Hampshire, when in fact he had not played in one game.His new employer initially supported O'Leary when the discrepancies became public, and O'Leary assured Notre Dame officials that there was nothing else they needed to know. When further background checks found that O'Leary had falsified other credentials as well, the school asked for and received his resignation on December 13.

"Due to a selfish and thoughtless act many years ago, I have personally embarrassed Notre Dame, its alumni and fans," O'Leary said in a statement released by Notre Dame. "The integrity and credibility of Notre Dame is impeccable and with that in mind, I will resign my position as head football coach."[53]

Notre Dame athletic director Kevin White released a statement as well, commenting:

> George has acknowledged inaccuracies in his biographical materials, including his academic background ... I understand that these inaccuracies represent a very human failing; nonetheless, they constitute a breach of trust that makes it impossible for us to go forward with our relationship.[54]

Ara Parseghian, the former Notre Dame coach who led the Fighting Irish for more than a decade, added that, "I can't understand how you could go all those years and not catch or correct it."[55]

Within days, many sports journalists reported that college football and basketball coaches around the country were "checking their bios in their schools' media guides and on the websites" to make sure they were accurate. Meanwhile, the O'Leary affair provided plenty of material for public discussion. Many callers to sports talk radio programs said the incident simply validated or increased their already negative perception of big-time college athletics. Outside of the sports world, many individuals quoted in media stories said it was "no big deal" because "everyone lies on their résumé."

After spending two seasons as an assistant coach for the Minnesota Vikings, O'Leary returned to college football in 2004 as head coach at the University of Central Florida.

- Who is responsible for the embarrassment experienced by Notre Dame—O'Leary (for providing false information on his résumé) or the university (for not verifying the details of his résumé before the hiring)?
- Do you agree with the opinion of those who said the incident validated or increased their already negative opinion of college sports?

Case Study 11D: Workplace Honesty: Riley Weston's Little White Lie

In the late 1990s, Hollywood fell in love with Riley Weston. As a writer for the WB Network's hit show *Felicity*, Weston was hailed as a "child prodigy," and *Entertainment Weekly* called her an "up-and-coming nineteen-year-old" and named her to its list of the "100 Most Creative People in Entertainment." There was only one problem: she wasn't nineteen; she was thirty-two. Several years earlier, because the best acting roles in television were for teenage girls, she began listing her birth year as 1979 on employment applications. She had also legally changed her name to conceal her previous acting roles playing teenage girls in the early 1980s—when she really was a teenager.

Weston continued the deception as she transitioned from acting to writing. Believing that no one would take her seriously as a writer of young-adult television programs and movie screenplays, she continued to present herself as a teenager.

Her real identity and age were revealed after a background check found the social security number she provided belonged to a much older woman—Weston's previous identity. Shortly thereafter, her network contract expired and was not renewed, and Disney Films withdrew its $500,000 offer to write a screenplay.

Weston admitted the deception and apologized to her fans, but railed against the double standard and Hollywood's obsession with youth. "If I were getting a job in any other industry, would anyone care how old I am?" she asked reporters.

Today, Weston is an actress (portraying women closer to her real age), singer, voice-over performer, and novelist. Her first book, *Before I Go*, was published in 2006.

1. Does the frustration of dealing with what Weston called "Hollywood's double standard and obsession with youth" justify her deception?
2. Is this a case of the ends justifying the means?
3. Is there a tendency to excuse what Weston did by saying that it's "just show business"?

Discussion Problem 11A: Letters of Recommendation: Harry, Sally, and the Professor's Dilemma

Dr. I. C. Waterboyle is an award-winning chemistry professor at Enormous State University. This morning he received an email from Harry, a former student, asking for a letter of recommendation for a job with a new chemical firm coming to town. Attached to the email is a job description for the position. Dr. Waterboyle remembers Harry as an average student who made mostly Cs and did only the minimum amount of work to get by. He does not respond to the email, but instead moves it to a folder labeled "to do later." He intends to write the letter, but is too busy to do it today.

The next day, Dr. Waterboyle is at Shoppalott Mall and runs into Sally, a former student who once worked for him as a research assistant. He remembers her as an excellent student and research assistant who made all As. They talk mainly about what is happening with the university's football team, and neither mentions anything about Sally's career or the new company.

When he arrives at his office, Dr. Waterboyle starts to write the letter for Harry, but then has a thought: Sally, who may or may not know about the new chemical company, would be a much better fit for the job (based on the job description) than Harry.

1. What should Dr. Waterboyle do?

   a. Write the letter for Harry because he asked for it, and even though he may not be the best fit, he should protect the confidential nature of the communication and reward him for his initiative in finding and pursuing the job opportunity.
   b. Contact Sally and ask if she is interested in the job. If she is, he will write the letter for her only. If she is not interested, he should write the letter for Harry.
   c. Write letters for both former students and let the company decide which one is best.
   d. He should not write the letter for Harry if he does not have confidence in him, regardless of what he does for Sally.

2. Would your answer change if Dr. Waterboyle had responded to and promised to write the letter for Harry before he ran into Sally? What if Sally had asked Dr. Waterboyle if he knew of any jobs in the area?

3. Which of the following interests should Dr. Waterboyle be most concerned with?

   a. Rewarding Harry for his initiative in locating the job opportunity.
   b. Rewarding Sally for being a much better student.
   c. Helping the chemical company hire the better candidate.
   d. Protecting his reputation and that of the university for the success or failure of its graduates.

Discussion Problem 11B: Workplace Honesty: Competing Loyalties

Your best friend is an executive with a major consumer products company. You work for the same company, but in a different department, and while you occasionally see your friend at work, you see her more often socially.

Your friend is successful in her job and well thought-of among her superiors, subordinates, and peers, but a competitor has offered her a better job that will increase her salary and benefits while requiring her to relocate to a different city. Your friend is open to the idea of a job change, but says she is leaning toward keeping her current job because she has family and friends in the area, owns a house that she likes, and believes the current employer is one that she would like to work for until retirement. The competing company has given your friend one week to decide about the job offer. You are the only person outside of your friend's family that knows about the situation.

You are one of the few employees invited to a meeting at which you are briefed on the company's secret plan for reorganization. The plan includes a number of options, with most of them including eliminating several departments, consolidating others, and terminating about a quarter of the workforce. Nothing is definite, but regardless of which parts of the plan are implemented, it appears that your friend will be one of the employees let go.

At the beginning of the meeting and again at the end, you are reminded that the content of the meeting is to remain confidential and that you are not allowed to discuss it, either with co-workers, family members, friends, or anyone else.

1. Do you tell your friend about what you know so she can factor that into her decision? Is your loyalty in this case to your friend or to your employer?
2. What philosophers or philosophies from Chapter 2 would help you make this decision?

Discussion Problem 11C: Workplace Honesty: The Reverse Reference Call

A few months ago, you changed jobs. Although you are happy in your new job and it has turned out to be better than your old one, you are still bothered by the negative circumstances under which you left your previous employer. While there were several positive aspects to the old job, they were outweighed (in your opinion) by the negatives, which included sexual harassment (affecting several of your co-workers, but not you) and a lack of advancement opportunities for women and minorities. Now that several months have gone by and you're enjoying the new job, you've decided to put the experience behind you and get on with your career.

One day at your new job you receive a phone call from a person who is a finalist, but has not yet been offered, your job at the old company. She asks you for your candid assessment of the company and the people who work there.

1. What do you say?

    a. Tell the whole story—positives and negatives.
    b. Tell the person only the positives.
    c. Tell the person only the negatives.
    d. Decline to volunteer information, but agree to answer specific questions.
    e. Decline to answer; it's not your business.

2. Which of the philosophers or concepts discussed in Chapter 2 might help you make this decision?

Discussion Questions

1101. Does "religious harassment" and "political harassment" warrant the same concern on the part of employers as cases of racial and sexual harassment? Because most expressions of religious or political beliefs are protected by the First Amendment (while sexual comments and advances are clearly not), is there a potential for this being a constitutional issue?

1102. The landmark case in the area of sexual harassment was argued in 1986. In your opinion, has the problem gotten better or worse in the three decades since that case was argued?

Notes

1 Rudy Nydegger, *Clocking In: The Psychology of Work*. Santa Barbara, CA: Greenwood Press (2018), p. 54.
2 Jessica Guynn and Marco della Cava, "The Weinstein Effect." *USA Today*, October 27, 2017, p. 1-A.
3 Jena McGregor, "Sexual Harassment Charges with EEOC Rise." *The Washington Post*, October 6, 2018.
4 "Nature Conservancy Announces Interim CEO in Wake of Resignations." *Philanthropy News*, June 12, 2019.
5 Alana Samuels and Malcolm Burnley, "Living on Tips." *Time*, September 2–9, 2019, pp. 40–48.
6 Guynn and della Cava.
7 Guynn and della Cava.
8 Sharon Nelton, "Sexual Harassment: Reducing the Risks." *Nation's Business*, March 1995, pp. 24–25.
9 Nelton.
10 Many large employers such as banks, hospitals, and universities require supervisory employees to undergo sexual harassment prevention training every year and non-supervisory employees to undergo training every three years.
11 Nelton.

12 Paul Wiseman, "One-Fifth of Americans Find Workplace Hostile or Threatening." Associated Press report, August 15, 2017.

13 Mary Beth Marklein, "Students: Sexual Harassment All Too Common on Campus." *USA Today*, January 25, 2006.

14 Wiseman.

15 Johnny C. Taylor, "Off-Work Politics May Hurt Your Job." *USA Today*, July 10, 2018, p. 5–B.

16 Sarah E. Needleman and Katherine Bindley, "Google Reins in Politics at Work." *The Wall Street Journal*, August 24–25, 2019, p. 1-A.

17 Mark Moore, "Woman Fired After Giving Trump's Motorcade the Finger." *New York Post*, October 6, 2017.

18 Charisse Jones, "Can Your Supervisor Force You to Attend Speech by Politician?" *USA Today*, August 23, 2019, p. 2-B.

19 Alison Bell, "What Price Ethics?" *Entrepreneurial Woman*, January/February 1991, p. 68. See also: Amy Joyce, "When Do Workplace Lies Cross the Line?" *The Washington Post*, April 16, 2008.

20 Megan Elliott, "Lying on Your Resume? Here's How You'll Get Caught." www.glassdoor.com (posted November 18, 2018; accessed July 31, 2019).

21 Elliott.

22 David Callahan, *The Cheating Culture*. New York: Harcourt (2002), p. 12.

23 Callahan.

24 "Top Aide to Florida Governor Admits to Lying About Degree." Associated Press report, December 10, 2013.

25 "Candidate Accused of Lying About Graduating From College, Producing Fake Diploma." Associated Press report, August 12, 2018.

26 Bruce Weinstein, "Lying on Your Resume Isn't Part of the Game." Syndicated newspaper column, November 18, 2006. See also: Mary Beth Marklein, "Is There Any Truth to Today's Resumes?" *USA Today*, February 6, 2003, p. 1-A.

27 Phyllis Korkki, "Is Your Online Identity Spoiling Your Chances?" *The New York Times*, October 10, 2010, p. 8.

28 Rick Hampson, "Age-Old Bad Judgment Lives Long in the Digital Age." *USA Today*, March 20, 2013, p. 1-A.

29 Hampson.

30 Jeff Marcu, "Website Exposes Your Online Life." *Pensacola News Journal*, July 30, 2011.

31 Manuel Valdes and Shannon McFarland, "Like it Or Not: Employers Asking Job Seekers for Facebook Login Information." Associated Press report, March 21, 2012.

32 "Social Media Postings: NCIS Advises Caution." *Gosport* (Pensacola Naval Air Station, FL), May 8, 2015, p. 1.

33 Sarah Skidmore Sell, "Poll: Job Interview Questions Often Run Afoul of the Law." Associated Press report, November 3, 2017.

34 Sell.

35 Many states have passed measures called "ban the box" laws that prohibits employers from requiring candidates to indicate on applications forms whether or not they have criminal records. Jobs where new hires will be working with money or sensitive information, such as banks, are exempts from the laws.

36 Donald J. Solove, *The Future of Reputation: Gossip, Rumor, and Privacy on the Internet*. New Haven, CT: Yale University Press (2007), p. 203.

37 "More Companies Monitor Employee E-Mail." Associated Press report, March 11, 2002.

38 Bruce Barry, *Speechless: The Erosion of Free Expression in the American Workplace*. San Francisco: Berrett-Koehler Publishers (2007), p. 167.

39 Stan Hill, "The Multilayered Minefield of Workplace E-Mail Monitoring." *Employment Relations Today*, Vol. 42, No. 1 (Spring 2015), pp. 55–62.

40 Hill.

41 Hall Adams, Suzanne M. Scheuing, and Stacey A. Feely, "E-Mail Monitoring in the Workplace: The Good, the Bad, and the Ugly." *Defense Counsel Journal*, Vol. 67, No. 1 (January 2000) (https://www.questia.com/library/journal/1G1-60021943).

42 Jane Pribek, "Employer Rights When Monitor E-Mail, Internet Use." *Daily Record* (Kansas City, MO), February 20, 2006.

43 Adams.

44 Adams.

45 Jeffrey L. Seglin, "You've Got Mail. You're Being Watched." *New York Times*, July 18, 1999.

46 Lisa Frye, "Reviewing Employee E-Mails: When You Should, When You Shouldn't." www.shrm.org, posted May 15, 2017; accessed August 10, 2019.)

47 Sarah Krouse, "The New Ways Your Boss Is Spying on You." *The Wall Street Journal*, July 20–21, 2019, p. 1-B.

48 Krouse.

49 "Home Depot Employee Fired for Wearing Button." Associated Press report, October 28, 2009.

50 Jenna McGregor, "Can Your Off-Hours Political Activism Get You in Trouble at Work?" *The Washington Post*, May 31, 2017.

51 Johnny C. Taylor, "Off-Work Politics May Hurt Your Job." *USA Today*, July 10, 2018, p. 5-B. See also: Jenna McGregor, "Can Your Off-Hours Political Activism Get You in Trouble at Work?" *The Washington Post*, May 31, 2017.

52 Taylor.

53 "Academic, Athletic Irregularities Force Resignation." ESPN News, December 14, 2001.

54 "O'Leary Admits Resume is False, Quits Irish." *New York Daily News*, December 15, 2001.

55 "O'Leary Out at Notre Dame After One Week." SportsIllustrated.com, December 14, 2001.

12 Ethical Issues in Cyberspace and Social Media

Background

Except for laws dealing with telemarketing and electronic eavesdropping, there are no federal or state laws dealing specifically with technology issues. However, some laws regarding privacy may be applied to the sharing of personal (medical, banking, credit, or academic) information by electronic means.

There are also no professional codes of ethics that deal with the uses of technology in communication in general, but many technology issues are indirectly addressed in the codes of ethics of organizations such as the Society of Professional Journalists and the Radio-Television Digital News Association.

For bloggers, who often present themselves as journalists but may lack the professional credentials, blogging expert Rebecca Blood offers a "Code of Weblog Ethics." Among her suggested rules for other bloggers are: (1) publishing as fact only that which you believe to be true; (2) if material exists online, linking to it when you reference it; (3) publicly correcting misinformation; (4) writing each entry as if it could not be changed; adding to, but not re-writing or deleting, any entry; (5) disclosing conflicts of interest; and (6) noting questionable and biased sources.

Issues and Controversies

Internet Rumors, Urban Legends, and Deep Fakes

Apart from the famous cases of Janet Cooke, Stephen Glass, and Jayson Blair discussed in Chapter 4, news stories that are completely fictional seldom appear in newsprint. They've been given new life, however, on the Internet. They begin with rumors and then expand into complicated stories that are repeated and embellished to the degree at which they become known as **urban legends**. While most are meant simply to entertain or encourage people to avoid risky behaviors, others have more dubious intent.

Some Internet rumors and urban legends are created to embarrass major corporations. Fashion designer Tommy Hilfiger has been the target of numerous Internet rumors claiming the company discriminates against African American job applicants and that Hilfiger himself "doesn't like to see African Americans wearing his products." Many of the rumors refer to comments attributed to Hilfiger during his "many appearances on the Oprah Winfrey Show," but a journalist investigating the story reported that Hilfiger has appeared on the show only one time, and during that show made no comments similar to those attributed to him. Hilfiger and journalists who cover the fashion industry eventually concluded that the original rumor was likely started by either a rival company or a disgruntled former employee.

Another well-known rumor spread on the Internet suggests that the U.S. Postal Service, concerned over the growing popularity of electronic mail, has persuaded Congress to pass a law that would levy a 5 cent tax on each email message sent. Many recipients have written angry letters to their Congressional representatives protesting the tax, likely unaware that the federal government would have no way of collecting the tax—even if it wanted to. Another popular prank is the dissemination of an email message, allegedly from Microsoft founder Bill Gates, claiming that Microsoft will pay the recipient 10 cents each time the email is forwarded.

In 1995, Mrs. Fields Cookies had to deal with Internet rumors that it had donated its products to the victory party for O. J. Simpson after he was acquitted of murder.[1] In 1997, Nike faced incorrect online news reports that employees had died in two accidents at its manufacturing plants in China.[2]

A 2016 Pew Research poll found that 23 percent of Americans admit to having shared a fake news story with friends, family, or co-workers, with half of those also admitting they were aware of its falsity.[3] A 2018 study at the Massachusetts Institute of Technology found that false information on Twitter was 70 percent more likely to be re-tweeted that factual information and that real news stories took six times longer than fake news to read a benchmark of 1,500 readers.[4]

"We don't fall for false news because just because we're dumb," states a 2018 article in *Time*. "Often it's a matter of letting the wrong impulses take over. Political conventions lead us to lazy thinking. But there's an even more fundamental impulse at play: our innate desire for an easy answer."[5]

One of the biggest perpetrators of Internet falsehoods is Alex Jones, who hosts a nationally syndicated radio program titled *InfoWars* and a website of the same name. For years, Jones has theorized that the 2012 killings at Sandy Hook Elementary School in Connecticut were a hoax carried out by the Obama Administration in order to generate support for gun control laws, stated that former Secretary of State and presidential candidate Hillary Clinton and campaign manager Jon Podesta ran a pizza parlor in Washington, D.C. that was a front for a child sex trafficking operation, and suggested a link between vaccines and childhood autism. For many observers, Jones's material is humorous and harmless, but there have been consequences. After parents of Sandy Hook victims sued him for infliction of emotional distress, Jones lost many of his advertisers and for a while was banned by several social media platforms. At the Washington pizza parlor identified in the Clinton–Podesta story, a mentally disturbed man entered the restaurant with an assault rifle and shot several rounds into the ceiling, saying he was there to "save the children."

At Florida Atlantic University in Boca Raton, professor of media history James Tracy made national headlines by expanding on Jones's "research" and spreading the "Sandy Hook" conspiracy theory. In April 2013, Tracy floated his theory that the bombing at the Boston Marathon that killed three spectators and injured hundreds of others was actually a "mass casualty drill" and that no one really died. The university distanced itself from Tracy's conspiracy theories, which were posted on his personal blog and not the FAU website. "Florida Atlantic University does not agree with Mr. Tracy's views or opinions," the university clarified on its website. "His editorialized postings do not reflect the positions of the university or its leaders. The university stands with the rest of the country in our support of the victims of these two tragedies."[6]

More recently, Tracy has used his blog to suggest the government staged news stories such as murders in San Bernardino, California; Charleston, South Carolina, and the Navy Yard in Washington, D.C. In early 2016, FAU fired Tracy, claiming his behavior was outrageous enough for his tenure to be revoked. The university claimed the dismissal was not related to his outrageous theories, but was based instead on him contacting parents of

Sandy Hook children killed in the tragedy and accusing them of taking part in the conspiracy. After the parents of Noah Pozner, a six-year-old killed at Sandy Hook, asked Tracy to remove their son's photograph from his blog, Tracy responded with a demand that the parents provide proof that Noah ever lived and that they were his biological parents.[7]

The term recently coined to refer to false new stories spread on the Internet is **deepfakes.** Some observers see them as harmless fun, Hany Farid, a computer science professor at the University of California, worries that such material, when taken seriously, could have harmful effects. One example he points to is financial markets, where gullible stockholders might make major financial decisions based on a manipulated video of a company executive speaking to shareholders. "A fake video of Jeff Bezos saying that Amazon's profits are down could lead to a massive stock manipulation," he said, citing one possible scenario.[8]

"It's a difficult problem to solve because the technology needed to manipulate images is advancing rapidly and getting easier to use," stated a 2019 article in *The Wall Street Journal.* "And the threat is spreading, as smartphones have made cameras ubiquitous and social media has turned individuals into broadcasters, leaving companies that run those platforms unsure how to handle the issue."[9]

During the 2018–19 academic year, school administrators and pediatricians across the country complained that the reluctance of parents to have their children vaccinated was causing an increase in the occurrence of measles. Many blamed the problem on rumors, mostly spread online, that the measles vaccine caused autism, a phenomenon based on what they called "Facebook science, not real science."[10]

In 2018, a member of the North Carolina Elections Board was forced to resign after she posted a rumor online that democrats planned to legalize pedophilia so they could win Catholic votes by stopping lawsuits against priests regarding child sex abuse.[11]

More recently, President Trump has fueled conspiracy theories by re-tweeting rumors from social media, including accusations that the father of presidential candidate Ted Cruz was involved in the 1963 assassination of President John F. Kennedy; Supreme Court Justice Antonin Scalia, who died in his sleep in 2016, was actually murdered; and that former President Bill Clinton orchestrated the 2019 jailhouse death of criminal suspect Jeffrey Epstein.[12]

In addition to "deepfakes," another issue is what researchers are calling "dumbfakes." As the name indicates, dumbfakes are fake news stories, usually accompanied by photographs or video clips, which are so outrageous (and of poor technical quality) that few people would be fooled. But regardless of the narrow slices of the audience that would be influenced, social media platforms such as Facebook announced in 2019 it would develop software that would "downrank" false or misleading posts, including photos and videos. Instead of simply removing the material and facing accusations of censorship or political bias, Facebook announced the downranking would also be paired with links encouraging the audience to do their own fact-checking.[13]

Product and Service Reviews in Cyberspace

Websites such as Google and Yelp provide consumers opportunities to provide other potential customers with candid reviews of products and services as well as the restaurants, retailers, and other businesses that provide them. Specific sites that are popular today include RottenTomatoes.com for movies, GoodReads.com for books, and Zomato.com and Open Table.com for restaurants.

The result has been a source of valuable information for consumers, but along with the benefit has come accusations that many of the reviews are fake—either positive ones posted by the businesses themselves or negative ones posted by competitors or disgruntled former employees.

In 2002, several Hollywood movie studios were criticized after they arranged for fictitious movie reviews to be posted on websites hosted by film critics. The deception was uncovered after the critics noticed that the number of reviews had increased dramatically in a short period of time. All of the reviews were positive, and many of them included the same phrases the studios used in their promotional materials. Several critics complained that the studios were "hijacking" their websites to promote movies without paying an advertising fee.

One studio executive defended the practice, clarifying that the anonymous posters were not studio employees, but unpaid volunteers. He called the practice "aggressive marketing but not deceptive marketing" because the "posters were not pretending to be fans—they were fans."[14]

Although not as contentious as in the movie industry, a similar phenomenon is seen in the book publishing industry, as authors, agents, and publishing houses arrange for anonymous individuals to post positive reviews of their books and/or negative reviews of competing books on Internet sites such as Amazon.com. As a result, Amazon announced in 2004 it would encourage, but not require, customers to use their real names when they offer online book reviews. The company also removes reviews that it believes are artificially positive or negative or focus on the author rather than the book. While not admitting the problem of anonymous postings is widespread, the company claims that its customers will assign a higher value to reviews in cases in which reviewers use their real names and stand behind what they have written.[15]

As long as they are not outright libelous, posting fake movie reviews and book reviews online does not violate any laws, but in most cases such conduct violates the policies or "terms of service" of the websites. If the individuals involved are advertising or public relations professionals, they are likely violating the ethical codes of the professional organizations to which they belong. The Public Relations Society of America, for example, includes a clause in its Code of Ethics that requires members to identify themselves and their clients when participating in public discussions in which they are advocating a product, service, or point of view.

One side effect of the proliferation of Internet-based critics—both real and fake—is the elimination of many opinion-based positions at traditional newspapers and magazines as well as television networks. In 2010, ABC cancelled its long-running movie review series *At the Movies*, which was created in the 1970s by famed movie critics Roger Ebert and Gene Siskel. In the newspaper industry, some of the most prominent movie critics are being let go or simply not replaced when they retire. Many are also eliminating their book review sections as well as reviews of local theater productions and concerts.

Another ethical issue develops when public relations representatives fail to identify themselves when they participate in online discussion groups. Monitoring and participating in email discussions and on organizational bulletin boards can be a valuable method of gathering information about how an organization is perceived by the public. For example, if a public relations representative simply monitors discussions without participating (the slang term is "lurking"), that person is under no legal or ethical obligation to inform participants of his or her online presence. But when public relations representatives contribute to the discussion in a manner that may pose a conflict of interest, they are obligated to identify themselves. For example, if a representative for a consumer product company participates in an online discussion group, he or she should not recommend the company's products without also disclosing the fact that he or she is employed by that company. Disclosing that fact is not only the ethical thing to do, but is also advantageous. Many participants will not consider it an intrusion, but will instead appreciate the fact that an "expert" is available to answer their questions.

The same principle of self-identification applies to the issue of corporate blogs and other opportunities to deceive others in cyberspace.

- In 2005, a major cosmetics manufacturer was embarrassed when it was revealed that a blog published under the name of "Claire"—supposedly one of its loyal customers who had nothing but good things to say about the company's products—was actually published by its public relations agency.

- In 2008, discount retailer Wal-Mart hired a married couple with experience of blogging about consumer issues to travel around the country in a recreational vehicle, shopping at various Wal-Mart locations and parking overnight in store parking lots. After several weeks of glowing accounts of their interactions with store employees in several states, readers of the blog, along with national media organizations, became suspicious. It was eventually reported by Cable News Network and several newspapers that the blogging activity was part of a campaign titled "Working Families for Wal-Mart" that was carried out by Wal-Mart's public relations firm Edelman Worldwide.

- Two years later, one of Wal-Mart's chief competitors, K-Mart, was publicly criticized for its promotion in which six prominent bloggers received $500 gift cards so they could go on shopping sprees and then blog about their experiences. A spokesman for Sears Holdings, K-Mart's parent company, defended the program by comparing it to product placements on popular television shows. The program was developed by Izea, a marketing firm specializing in social media campaigns. Izea claims to work with a network of more than 250,000 bloggers, all of whom are required to disclose financial relationships within the text of their blog postings.

- In 2006, an online company called PayPerPost was established, describing itself as a marketplace where companies with new products or services to sell can find bloggers willing to review those products and services—for a price. Much like the auction site eBay, both the companies and the bloggers are required to use PayPal to make financial transactions simpler. PayPerPost has "terms of service" that require bloggers to post a minimum number of posts per month and claims it will terminate service to any blog with no posts for 30 days or longer. It also requires bloggers to disclose the fact that blog postings are paid for (but not the price) and requires them to be honest (i.e., not accepting payment for writing a review of a product they have not tested). But like auction sites and online dating services, the extent to which the site's operators are able to monitor the traffic and enforce the rules is a matter of debate. The Federal Trade Commission and consumer watchdog groups are skeptical about the practice, believing that accepting payment for writing a review from the company providing the product or service automatically detracts from the credibility of the review. Based on that assumption, the FTC in 2009 established new rules regulating bloggers who review consumer products.

In a 2013 undercover operation, the Office of the Attorney General for the State of New York charged nineteen companies writing fake reviews on Yelp, Google Local, City Search, and other consumer-review websites that praised themselves and criticized their competitors. The companies paid freelancer writers in other countries between $1 and $10 for each fake review posted in a scam that investigators called "astroturfing," a play on words based on the more legitimate technique of generating "grassroots" support. The companies were fined a total of $350,000.[16]

In addition to helpful websites and discussion boards, the Internet is also littered with hyper-negative blogs and "rogue websites" that publicly chastise popular American companies with information that is either outright false or perhaps rooted in truth but greatly exaggerated. Many such sites are hosted by either anonymous or loosely identified groups claiming to represent consumers who have had negative experiences with a company's products or services, or in some cases former employees wanting to "blow the whistle" on their former employer. Websites and blogs with names such as "XYZCompanySucks.com" and "I-Hate-XYZ-Company.com" often have little if any following, so legal experts recommend that companies monitor the content of such sites but not respond.

While there is a temptation to "set the record straight," it may be a better strategy to avoid online back-and-forth exchanges with individuals or groups with Internet access and excess time on their hands. Legal experts do, however, recommend responding in the extreme cases in which a company sees its copyrights or trademarks are being violated or the perpetrators have crossed the line into defamation.

Consumer advocates caution customers and potential customers against making decisions based on a few extremely good or extremely bad reviews. "Sites such as Yelp, Angie's List, and TripAdvisor offer a lot of information, but there's really no way to gauge their accuracy," wrote Steven Petrow in *USA Weekend*. Petrow estimates that 15 to 25 percent of all reviews on those three sites are fake, with negative reviews likely originating with competitors or disgruntled former employees out for revenge. Positive reviews are similarly suspect. "A brand-new restaurant with just one glowing review? Odds are that the chef's mother wrote it," Petrow wrote.[17]

The Positives and Negatives of Social Media

The term **social media** was coined in 2006 to refer to the proliferation of websites for which the majority of the content is provided by individual contributors and organizations rather than traditional media outlets. The major difference between traditional media and social media is that traditional media push information out to its audience, while social media attempts to draw the audience in.

As of late 2019, the most popular social media sites include YouTube, a video sharing site; Wikipedia, an online encyclopedia for which entries can be created and revised by users; LinkedIn, a professional networking site; and social networking sites such as Facebook, Twitter, and Instagram. Facebook began as a networking program for college students, but quickly expanded its audience to include younger individuals as well as adults of all ages.

In the United States, the fastest-growing segment of the population using social media is seniors (age 60 and over), but the core group of users still remains teenagers and young adults. For them, sociologists say social networks are analogous to the "shopping malls and burger joints" frequented by their parents.[18]

In 2019, an Oxford University analysis predicted that by 2070, the number of dead Facebook members will outnumber those living. Along with other social media platforms, Facebook is urging members to leave behind their passwords along with other end-of-life documents so that profiles can be deleted after death.[19]

In addition to becoming a popular site for socialization and commercial activity, the service is becoming increasingly popular as a venue for political discussion and action. Between 2009 and 2011, when governments in Asia, Africa, and Eastern Europe attempted to control political unrest by closing television and radio stations and banning public protests, the populations of those countries turned to Facebook in order to communicate with each other and share information about what was happening in their communities.

Online Dangers

Because of its popularity among teenagers, Facebook (and its predecessor, MySpace) also attracted a more dubious category of users—sexual predators. Under pressure from law enforcement, Facebook and other social media companies have developed campaigns to protect users from sexual predators and child sex traffickers. More recently, those same companies have developed programs to address other adolescent issues, including bullying, depression, and suicide.

According to a survey by the National Center for Missing and Exploited Children (NCMEC), 14 percent of children between the ages of ten and seventeen had received sexual solicitations online, but the idea of "stranger danger" is not the biggest threat. Only about one-third of those solicitations came from strangers; the other two-thirds came from peers and family members. Researchers define "solicitations" as receiving telephone calls, offline mail, money, or gifts. What most concerned NCMEC officials was that less than half of those teens indicated they reported the offending behavior to their parents or other adults.

Chris Wilkinson, a digital forensics specialist with the Escambia County Sheriff's Office in Florida, agrees that the idea of "stranger danger"—that the biggest threat to children is the raincoat wearing pervert lurking in the shadows—is an outdated concept. That danger, while once the largest threat, is now only the fifth-most common threat. The fourth most-common is the trusted family member that turns out to be a predator. The top three dangers facing children today are all related to the Internet: (1) adult or "mainstream" pornography, for which children age twelve to seventeen make up the largest share of the audience; (2) sexting and cyberbullying; and (3) child pornography.[20]

The NCMEC advises parents to (1) counsel their teens about the danger of online predators, (2) place their teens' computers in common areas where their communication can be easily monitored, and (3) watch out for unknown telephone numbers on the child's cell phone bill (or the family's bill) and unexplained gifts the child receives.[21]

In addition to problems with sexual solicitations, social networking sites have also provided new opportunities for identity thieves who trick unsuspecting teenagers into disclosing their passwords, as well as their social security numbers, birthdates, or other personal information. Teenagers and pre-teens are especially vulnerable to identity theft because they do check their credit reports and might not know about fraudulent accounts opened in their names for several years.

At the beginning of the new school year in 2013, the Glendale school district in California paid $40,500 to a company called Geo Listening to monitor its students' social-media content and provide administrators with daily reports. The school district defended the practice by saying it was intended to provide "early warnings" for indications of bullying, depression, and suicidal tendencies, but many parents said it was an invasion of their children's privacy. The program has since been discontinued, but many critics, including privacy advocate Jacob Silverman, believed that the time and money spent on the program could be better invested in hiring and training school counselors to look for those same indications in one-on-one time with students.[22]

School officials are not the only ones allegedly invading the privacy of users. In July 2019, the Federal Trade Commission fined Facebook $5 billion for privacy violations, and a month later Google reached an agreement with the FTC to pay a $200 million fine for similar violations on its video platform, YouTube. Both fines were levied following the complaints by parents that the online platforms illegally collected personal information from their children.[23]

Critics of social media claim its addictive nature is especially problematic for children, as many grew up not knowing any other way to socialize. As a result of prioritizing online relationships over real-world ones, teenagers and pre-teens are more likely to experience harassment, bullying, depression, or self-esteem problems.

Youth suicide is another problem blamed partly on the negative effects of social media. A 2019 study published in the *Journal of Pediatrics* noted a doubling in the number of suicide attempts among Americans under the age of nineteen, with a tripling in the number affecting girls and women between the ages of ten and twenty-four. "The study's authors can't prove social media is to blame, but they strongly suspect it plays a critical role," stated Senator Josh Hawley of Missouri, who cited the study in a syndicated newspaper column.[24]

Many school districts around the country are prohibiting teachers from being "Facebook friends" with students or their parents based on their belief that such communication is unprofessional and has the potential to compromise professional boundaries. The rationale for the rules includes the risk of a teacher inadvertently sharing a student's private information with other students or parents, the appearance of inappropriate relationships between students and teachers, and accusations of favoritism. In one school district in Florida, a county teachers union was able to have the rule overturned by threatening to file a lawsuit based on state laws dealing with unfair labor practices.

For the last decade, college admissions counselors have followed the lead of employers using social media profiles to evaluate job candidates and are using Facebook, Instagram, and other platforms popular with teenagers to evaluate applicants to their institutions. Images showing underage drinking, sexually suggestive images, or other inappropriate material may cause applications to be rejected before any other aspect of the individuals' credentials are considered.[25]

In 2017, Harvard University rescinded admission offers to ten incoming freshmen because of offensive material they posted on Facebook. The Harvard Crimson, the school's student-run newspaper, said the posts included sexually and racially offensive photographs and jokes about Mexicans, other ethnic groups, the Holocaust, sexual assault, and child abuse. University officials said they could not comment on specific cases, stating only that Harvard's rules that an admissions offer can be rescinded if the applicant's subsequent behavior "brings into question their honesty, maturity, or moral character."[26]

Many universities with large athletics programs require student-athletes to attend seminars during which they are counseled on how their behavior in public—on the athletic field, in public appearances, and online—affects the image of the institution. One Midwestern university began a recent seminar by introducing three basic rules: be gracious in defeat, be humble in victory, and don't do anything that would embarrass the university on Facebook or YouTube."[27]

Scrutinizing the online behavior of athletes actually begins not after they sign their scholarship agreements, but while they are still in high school. Recruiters for many Division I college football and basketball programs monitor the online postings of high school seniors they are scouting. "You can learn a lot about a kid by what he says in a public forum," says an assistant football coach at Auburn University. "If we see something that triggers a red flag, that's something we make a note of."[28]

Once in school, athletes often find that their universities restrict how and when they may use social media to communicate with friends and the general public. Athletes are limited in the extent which they can discuss game strategy and their relationships with their teammates. The universities' concerns are that such posts may violate the privacy of other athletes, provide valuable information to an upcoming opponent, and cast the university in a negative light. To combat the problem, many university athletic departments monitor student's online presence and require athletes to either keep their profiles entirely public or provide coaches and administrators access to private parts of their profiles.

Similarly, soldiers serving in the U.S. armed forces are instructed on new policies limiting their online activities. Those rules are especially critical in war zones such as Iraq and Afghanistan, where online postings may compromise security if they reveal information related to troop movements, strategies and tactics of upcoming engagements, and the travel itineraries of military leaders.[29]

In terms of commercial activity, two of the most popular sites on the Web are eBay and Craigslist. While eBay has seen its share of problems related fraudulent activity and consumer complaints, Craigslist has earned considerable attention from law-enforcement agencies based on its alleged connection to criminal activity. In 2010, the attorneys general of forty states wrote letters to Craigslist, asking the company to do a better job of screening ads for massage parlors, escort services, and other adult businesses that functioned as fronts for prostitution. That effort followed a series of news stories in Oregon and Washington D.C. in which local law-enforcement agencies broke up prostitution rings—many of them involving minors—linked to Craigslist ads.

Positive Benefits of Social Media

Despite all of its negatives, social media has a number of benefits for both personal and business applications, and a number of success stories. In 2008, for example, a middle-aged nurse who had given up her son for adoption two decades earlier used MySpace to locate him. Two years later, she set up a Facebook page in an effort to locate the birth parents who had given her up for adoption thirty years earlier. Within twenty-four hours she had located her mother, and two weeks later found her father.

Eva Buechel, a marketing professor at the University of South Carolina, believes that social media networks such as Facebook and Instagram have made social interactions easier for people who make have struggled with them before and can help young people with social anxiety better navigate eventual in-person interactions.

But she is aware that many of her peers are not as enthusiastic. "There are people who say that because it's not face-to-face, the interactions can make people feel more lonely or depressed," she told an interviewer in 2017. "If you're sad, you may need attention or affection from other people to soothe your feelings. One possibility is people will talk about their negative emotions to gain support. That's a plus."[30]

Journalistic Uses of Social Media

"Social media presents unprecedented opportunities and challenges to journalists," claims the social media guidelines included in the Associated Press Stylebook. "But fluency in social media takes time and effort and challenges journalists to use the networks in a way that doesn't undermine their credibility."[31]

The AP Stylebook and other journalism texts recommend using social media for communicating with existing sources and finding new ones, gathering user-generated content (see Chapter 3), generating story ideas, and getting non-scientific feedback on social issues.[32]

The stylebook provides the following cautions on using social media for supplementing reporting:

- Never lift quotes, photos, or video from social networking cites without obtaining the source's permission and verifying the material's authenticity.
- If a source found through social media claims to be spokesperson for an organization, confirm it through other means before using that person's information or quoting him or her.
- Before using material from social media, make sure that by doing so you are not violating anyone's copyrights or trademarks.
- When identifying yourself as a reporter, specify that your opinions expressed are yours and do not represent the editorial position of your newspaper.
- While it is acceptable to "friend" or "follow" organizations that you cover, do not do so with political candidates, as doing so might create the appearance of bias. If you are

covering the overall campaign, it would be acceptable to "friend" or "follow" all of the candidates in a race (with your editor's permission).

* Avoid getting into confrontational exchanges with individuals, regardless of how repeatedly you are criticized or "baited."[33]

Online Harassment

In addition to the problems of sexual predators, another serious issue for parents of school-age children and school administrators is the use of social networking sites for online pranks and other acts of cruelty. Online harassment can take several forms, including **cyberbullying**, **cyberstalking**, **cyberharassment**, and **cybershaming**. "When Oscar Wilde observed that the only thing worse than being talked about is not being talked about, he could not have imagined the Internet," wrote syndicated columnist Kathleen Parker in a 2009 piece.[34]

One of the earliest known cases of cyberbullying occurred in 2006, when students at a St. Louis high school created a list titled "Who's Hot and Who's Not" that included the names of 100 classmates, along with racist and sexist comments. They posted it on Facebook and signed the name of a seventeen-year-old classmate, who discovered it only after one of the girls mentioned asked him about it. After a lengthy investigation, school officials were unable to determine who was responsible. More serious cases of cyberbullying have caused several teen suicides (see Case Study 12G).

"Unwanted sexual contact online—it's something we take seriously," said Scott Berkowitz, the founder and president of the Rape, Abuse, and Incest National Network.[35]

The U.S. Department of Justice reported in 2014 that more than 850,000 American adults —mostly women—are targets of cyberstalking each year, and approximately 40 percent of adult Internet users have experienced some form of online harassment.[36]

In 2007, a high school student in Pembroke Pines, Florida established a Facebook page to rant about her English teacher, who she labeled on the page as "the worst teacher I've ever met." She expected her peers to join in by becoming "friends" and supporting her opinion, but most defended the teacher and attacked the student who created the page. She took the page offline, but the school's principal later found out about it and suspended the student for three days and removed her from her Advanced Placement classes. He called the student's behavior "disruptive behavior" and "cyberbullying." In the surrounding community, the student became known as the "Ferris Bueller of Facebook," a reference to the 1986 movie that that focused on the exploits of an academic under-achiever who thumbed his nose at the authority of his teachers and principal.

A nearby chapter of the American Civil Liberties Union came to the student's defense, claiming that her suspension was a form of punishing speech protected by the First Amendment. A federal judge ruled in the student's favor and ordered the principal to expunge the suspension from the student's file. She also received $1 in damages and $15,000 in legal fees. In his written opinion, the judge wrote that the student's expression "fell under the wide umbrella of protected speech ... it was an opinion of a student about a teacher that was published off-campus, did not cause any disruption on-campus, and was not lewd, vulgar, threatening, or advocating illegal or dangerous behavior."[37]

In 2010, the tragedy of gay teens committing suicide after years of harassment and abuse from other teens prompted syndicated newspaper columnist Dan Savage to establish the "It Gets Better" project. Beginning with a YouTube video and then expanding to a website and book, the project is aimed at providing a support system for gay, lesbian, bisexual, and transgendered teens and young adults. The website, which claims to have more than 330,000 members, features testimonials from successful adults who survived adolescence while questioning their sexual identity.

Two of the earliest examples of individuals facing legal consequences for cyberbullying occurred in New Jersey in 2012 and Massachusetts in 2017. In the New Jersey case, a former Rutgers University student was convicted of invasion of privacy for secretly taping his roommate's homosexual encounter with another man and posting the video online. The victim of the bullying committed suicide shortly thereafter.

In the Massachusetts case, a teenager was convicted of involuntary manslaughter for telling a friend to "go ahead and kill himself" in a series of text messages.

Although it did not result in a suicide, one the most notable case of cyberbullying of a college student took place at the University of Michigan in the fall of 2010. While the victim was a student, the perpetrator was not. He was Andrew Shirvell, the thirty-year-old assistant attorney general for the state of Michigan, who engaged in a three-month vendetta against Chris Armstrong, the student assembly president at UM. Shirvell, a UM alumnus, used his personal blog to call Armstrong a "racist and liar" who was promoting a "radical homosexual agenda" at the university. In addition to his online campaign, Shirvell stalked Armstrong by showing up outside of his home, videotaping one of his parties through an open window, and showing up at campus events where Armstrong spoke carrying protest signs. Shirvell insisted his actions were protected as free speech, but his superiors in state government didn't agree. After months of attempting to talk him out of his campaign, they fired Shirvell for improper use of state resources and "conduct unbecoming a state government official."

Later that year, officials at several universities in the southeast, including Florida State, Alabama, Auburn, Tennessee, and Louisiana State, investigated numerous cases of "cyberstalking" involving female students seeking membership in various sororities. Contacting the women on Facebook, the anonymous individuals claimed to be officers or alumni of the sororities and suggested ways the women could improve their chances of being accepted, including posting nude photos and answering questions of an intimate nature. When the women refused to comply, they were verbally abused and threatened.

Also in 2010, a thirty-six-year-old woman in New York found that someone had created an artificial profile of her on a popular online dating site. The profile included a photo the woman had posted on Facebook and included some details that were correct and others that were fictional. Operators of online dating sites such as Match.com, eHarmony, and Plenty of Fish say that creating profiles using another person's photograph and information violates their terms of service and from a legal standpoint, is a form of harassment. While they claim that they have no idea why a person would go to the trouble of creating a fake profile for another person and then paying to post it, they do cooperate with law-enforcement investigations when contacted.

Opera singer Leandra Ramm and actress Jennifer Lawrence have complained about cyberstalkers for more than a decade.[38] "It is not a scandal. It is a sex crime," Lawrence told a reporter from *Vanity Fair*. "It is a sexual violation. It's disgusting. The law needs to be changed, and we need to change."[39]

"When our digital space is invaded with sexual harassment, violent messages, and threats; when our private data, information, and photographs are exposed, it feels like it should be against the law," wrote Marlisse Silver Sweeney, a professor of business law at the University of British Columbia, in a 2014 article in *The Atlantic*. "The law is notoriously slow to adapt to technology, but legal scholars say that if done right, the law can be used as a tool to stop this behavior."[40]

Adds Danielle Citron, a professor at the University of Maryland's Francis King Carey School of Law: "At its most basic legal definition, cyber-stalking is a repeated course of conduct that's aimed at a person designed to cause emotional distress and fear of physical harm."[41]

Cyberharassment can include threats of violence (often sexual), spreading lies asserted as facts (like a person has sexually transmitted disease, a criminal record, or is a sexual predator), posting sensitive information online (whether that's nude or compromising photos or social security numbers), and technological attacks (falsely shutting down a person's social-media account). "Often, it's a perfect storm of all these things," Citrin said.[42]

The term cybershaming refers to the act of taunting individuals, known or unknown, based usually on their appearance or behavior. One of the earliest known cases took place in South Korea in 2005, when a young woman riding on a subway train allowed her dog to defecate at her feet. Within hours, the photographs were all over the Internet, accompanied by criticism of the "dog-shit girl." The woman was so embarrassed by the attention that she dropped out college, and the story eventually spread around the world.[43]

In 2013, public relations executive Justine Sacco became a victim of cybershaming while on her way to visit family in South Africa. She began a series of tweets describing her experiences in airports as well as during the transatlantic flight. Prior to the last leg of her flight, from London to Cape Town, she tweeted, "Going to Africa. Hope I don't get AIDS. Just kidding, I'm white!"

Sacco recalls turning her phone off and sleeping for most of the flight, but when she awoke and got off the plane, she found her tweet had created an international social media controversy. Strangers from around the world posted critical and threatening responses, and even friends and co-workers piled on. But the toughest response came from her employer, the parent company of a number of online news and social media services. She was fired before returning to the United States.

The National Center for Education Statistics reported in 2019 that 20 percent of all teens are victims of harassment or threats, delivered either online or by text message. The study also found that girls are three times as likely as boys to be targets.[44]

The Kind Campaign, a California-based anti-bullying group, estimates that 90 percent of the bullying experienced by girls is carried out by other girls and consists mostly of hostile comments about body image or alleged sexual behavior.[45]

Bullying is especially problematic on Instagram, where a 2019 study found that 80 percent of teenagers are frequent users and more than half experience some form of bullying.[46]

Sheri Bauman, a counseling professor at the University of Arizona, has spent years studying the effects of online bullying and calls Instagram a "one-stop shop for bullying" because "it has it all—an audience, anonymity, an emphasis on appearance and channels that range from public feeds to behind-the-back group chats."[47]

In 2019, Auburn University gymnast Samantha Cerio was the victim of what some might consider a benign form of harassment, but it was hurtful to her. After the video of her dislocating both knees at a competition made the rounds on social media, she was not directly taunted or threatened, but she wanted the circulation of the video to stop. "My pain is not your entertainment," she posted in her own response to the video.[48]

A 2017 study by the Pew Research Center found that 21 percent of women under the ages of 18 and 29 report being harassed online, compared with only 9 percent of men. About half of the women who reported harassment said the unwanted attention included the receipt of explicit images.[49]

In the last decade, many states have either passed or are now considering laws to address the problem, but some of those laws are criticized as either infringements on free speech or too vague or overbroad. The laws that raise the most legal questions are those that punish students for communication that originates outside of the school, such as on their home computers.[50]

In 2019, professional golfer Lexi Thompson said she took a "break from social media" because she was harassed online after being photographed playing golf with President Trump and radio talk show host Rush Limbaugh. The previous year, Thompson complained about negative comments posted to her website after she admitted to struggling with her weight and body image. "A few drops can be brushed aside," said Bobby Kreusler, Thompson's agent. "But drop after drop over a prolonged period of time can drive a person crazy."[51]

A relatively new offense related to cyberstalking is that in which a spurned individual seeks revenge on a former romantic partner by posting intimate photographs or video on social media sites. Called **revenge porn** or "involuntary porn," the concept is seen as an unfortunate consequence of the popularity of social media and people's willingness to allow partners to record the images in the first place. A 2013 study by McAfee found that half of those responding admitted to sending or receiving sexually explicit images online, and almost one-third admitted to cyberstalking former romantic partners. The same study found that one in ten exes threatened to reveal intimate photos, and more than half of those followed through on those threats.[52]

The concept of revenge porn has spawned new websites dedicated to the practice, and at least two founders have been criminally charged—not for allowing the images to be posted, but for extortion after they contacted the victims and demanded money in exchange for removing the images. What some people perceive as a "prank" can have tragic consequences. In 2008, an eighteen-year-old Cincinnati woman killed herself after an ex-boyfriend forwarded her nude cellphone photographs to his friends.[53]

In response to the phenomenon, California and Florida became the first two states to pass laws criminalizing revenge porn, and as of 2019, more than a dozen other states were considering similar laws.[54]

Your Turn

Case Study 12A: Internet Rumors, Urban Legends, and Deep Fakes: Don't Ask the Make-A-Wish Foundation about Business Cards

One of the most persistent urban legends is that of a terminally ill child in Europe attempting to earn a place in the *Guinness Book of World Records* for having the world's largest collection of either business cards or greeting cards. Sometimes it is a boy in England; other times it is a girl in Germany. Recipients of the message are asked to send a business card to the Make-A-Wish Foundation and urge friends, family members, and co-workers to do so. The post office box provided is not one belonging to the foundation, but to unknown individuals. Postal investigators believe the deception is one used to collect mailing addresses for the compilation of direct mail lists.

The legend is believed to have originated with a real-life story that began in 1989 when a nine-year-old boy—not terminally ill—was attempting to collect a large number of greeting cards with help from a nonprofit organization not affiliated with Make-A-Wish. As of late 2018 he had received more than 16 million greeting cards and now is in his late thirties—but the greeting cards are still coming.

The original story was spread by chain letters, but more recent variations are spread by electronic mail. One involves a seven-year-old terminally ill girl and claims that each time the email is forwarded, Make-A-Wish will donate seven cents to a fund to pay her medical bills. Despite the foundation's repeated notices to the media that the story is not true, inquiries continue to pour in to the organization's public relations office from journalists around the world wanting to write stories about the girl, and from other individuals asking how they can help.

Rumors and urban legends involving terminally ill children are considered harmless by most people, but employees at the Make-A-Wish Foundation don't agree. The organization's public relations department claims to receive hundreds of inquiries per day asking for more information about fictional children they've heard and read about, and today the organization provides numerous disclaimers on its website. "The time and expense required to respond to these inquiries distracts the Foundation from its efforts on behalf of real children with life-threatening medical conditions," the organization says.[55]

1. Other than posting disclaimers on their websites and responding quickly to media inquiries, what else can organizations do when they find themselves victims of Internet rumors and urban legends?
2. Even though they cannot prove they have been specifically harmed (such as in the case of libel suits), should they have any recourse against those initiating the falsehoods?

Case Study 12B: Internet Rumors, Urban Legends, and Deep Fakes: MarryOurDaughter.com

In 2007, a prankster in New York created a website called MarryOurDaughter.com that claimed to be a service through which parents could offer their teenage daughters—for fees ranging from $30,000 to $45,000—to older men for arranged marriages. The site's creator began by purchasing stock photographs of teenage models and creating phony life stories and profiles. He received thousands of inquiries from parents wishing to add their own daughters' photographs and profiles to the site and from adult men wishing to "purchase" young brides. In order to avoid being accused of violating state laws regarding prostitution and pimping, he did not respond to either category of inquiry. When the hoax was exposed, the founder claimed his motive was to call attention to the world-wide problem of child sex trafficking.

1. Is this another case of a harmless prank, or is it more serious than that? Does it help with the cause of fighting international child sex trafficking, or does it make a joke out of a serious issue?
2. Are there any concepts or philosophers or Chapter 2 that can be applied here?

Case Study 12C: Internet Rumors, Urban Legends, and Deep Fakes: Oklahoma Quarterbacks in the News

In the summer of 2008, University of Oklahoma football players Sam Bradford and Landry Jones were competing for the starting quarterback job. Nothing about their competition was out of the ordinary, university officials said, until Jones' father began receiving phone calls from his friends, asking if it was true that the two players had been arrested on charges of selling cocaine. After his son denied the story, Kevin Jones called the university's athletic department, which began an investigation to determine the source of the rumors. They eventually found the fictitious story posted on an Internet message board and identified as being from *The Oklahoman*, the daily newspaper in Oklahoma City. A fan of the University of Nebraska, one of Oklahoma's chief rivals, created the bogus message by lifting a template off the newspaper's website. By the time the story had been debunked, it had already been reported as fact by two Texas radio stations.

After newspaper officials tracked down the offender, the man apologized to the university and the families of the two players, claiming that he "didn't intend to harm anyone." The newspaper obtained a "cease and desist" order against the man, but did not take further legal action.

1. Should incidents such as this be grounds for defamation suits, or would that constitute a "slippery slope" problem that might eventually chill free speech online?
2. If you were the parent of one of the two players, would you pursue legal action?
3. What action should be taken by the newspaper to punish the offender?
4. What can newspapers and the operators of Internet message boards do to discourage pranks such as this?

Case Study 12D: Internet Rumors, Urban Legends, and Deep Fakes: The World According to Wikipedia

Like many celebrities, professional golfer Fuzzy Zoeller is accustomed to being scrutinized by both the media and the public, often involving news stories and Internet rumors that are either exaggerated or outright false. And like many celebrities, the easy-going Zoeller brushes off most of it, including the falsehoods. But in early 2007, Zoeller decided he had enough and sued the parent company of Wikipedia, an online dictionary and biographical index. Because of a federal law that protects Internet companies from defamation lawsuits, Zoeller instead sued to force Wikipedia to identify the source of four 2006 postings that alleged Zoeller had abused drugs and alcohol as well as his wife and four children. Eventually, Wikipedia determined that at least one of the postings originated from a computer owned by a Miami-based company, and Zoeller's attorney then pressed that firm to conduct its own investigation to find the individual responsible.

"He's just standing up for what is right," Zoeller's attorney told the media. "He's drawing a line, saying he's not going to take this anymore."[56] After the company was unable to identify the offending party, Zoeller eventually dropped the case.

Other professional athletes have also had similar problems with Wikipedia, complaining that their entries either exaggerate or outright lie about their involvement with steroids and recreational drugs.

Shortly after the Zoeller case, Wikipedia made national headlines again as a result of a mystery that remains unsolved nearly a decade later. On June 25, 2007, law-enforcement investigators found the bodies of professional wrestler Chris Benoit and two family members in their home in an Atlanta suburb. They concluded that Benoit has killed his wife, son, and then himself. A few days later, officials at Wikipedia determined that Benoit's online biography had been updated to describe the deaths on the morning of June 25—several hours before the bodies were discovered.

One need not be a national celebrity for a long period of time in order to be the victim of erroneous information on Wikipedia. In some cases, newcomers to the national stage find themselves in that position. In 2010, for example, federal judge Roger Vinson found himself the subject of false Wikipedia information. Vinson became nationally famous as the judge hearing preliminary arguments in a federal lawsuit filed by state attorneys general aimed at blocking implementation of the new health-care law passed by both houses of Congress. The Wikipedia entry described the judge as an "avid hunter and amateur taxidermist" who mounted bear heads on the walls of his courtroom to intimidate defendants.

Vinson reportedly laughed off the hoax. "I've never killed a bear, and no one should confuse me with Davy Crockett," he said in a written statement.[57] The hoax came to light when talk show host Rush Limbaugh, in characterizing the judge as "tough as nails," cited the erroneous details. When told about the falsity of the description, a Limbaugh researcher at first claimed he found it in a profile of the judge published in his hometown newspaper—the *Pensacola News Journal*—but it was later learned that the information came from Wikipedia.

The Wikipedia entry did, however, cite a *News Journal* story dated June 31, 2003—a story that the newspaper never published (and a date that does not exist). Within twenty-four hours of the hoax being exposed, Wikipedia removed the erroneous information from Vinson's profile.

1. Should celebrities who find falsehoods about themselves on the Internet pursue cases such as this, or should they simply ignore them (as many celebrities do in the case of tabloids)?
2. Should the legal liability for erroneous information lie with Wikipedia, or the individuals posting the information?

Case Study 12E: The Positives and Negatives of Social Media: Online Suicide Groups

On March 23, 2003, nineteen-year-old Suzanne Gonzales cleaned her apartment, fed her cats, and then checked into a Tallahassee hotel room where she drank a lethal dose of potassium cyanide. The Florida State University student committed suicide after weeks of conversing with other suicidal individuals on a website dedicated to the issue. Gonzales was depressed over school and her social life, and spent weeks researching methods of taking her on life and seeking support and advice from anonymous posters on the site. Her family and friends learned of her death after reading time-delayed emails—something else she learned from the suicide website.

The suicide site where Gonzales learned about potassium chloride has a worldwide following, and it claims to represent individuals of various ages, from a variety of backgrounds, and with differing reasons for taking their own lives. In one bizarre case, a seventeen-year-old Austrian girl traveled to Norway to meet a twenty-year-old Norwegian man she met through the site. The man's postings indicated that he was looking for a "suicide partner." A few days after they met in person in 2000, they jumped off a 1,900-foot cliff. The following year, a California couple met through the site, then carried out a dual suicide in a hotel room near Monterey.

Gonzales' death was the fourteenth confirmed suicide associated with the site, which most news sources and college textbooks (including this one) have chosen not to identify. Today, operators of the site claim that the actual number of deaths (which it refers to as "success stories") is actually twice that number, but that cannot be verified because the individuals used anonymous screen names and the operators refuse to cooperate with investigators.

The operators of the site defend their work by claiming they do not overtly advocate suicide, but are merely providing information to people intent on killing themselves whether they came across the site or not. They also believe their work is protected by the First Amendment's free speech clause.

Mental health experts disagree, claiming the operators of the site prey on vulnerable individuals by claiming to offer a support group without the necessary background or training in mental health issues. Also criticizing the group are Gonzales' parents. Her father, a retired firefighter, compared the website to arsonists who throw gasoline on an already out-of-control fire. He contends that the site's claim that it does not overtly advocate suicide is disputed by the fact that many of his daughter's 100+ postings generated responses that supported her decision rather than offering alternatives, such as counseling. The parents were also angry that their daughter learned how to obtain the deadly and hard-to-find chemicals by following suggestions listed on the site.

The publicity surrounding the case caught the attention of California Congressman Wally Herger, whose district includes the Gonzales' hometown of Red Bluff, near San Francisco. In 2007, Herger drafted the Suzanne Gonzales Suicide Prevention Act (nicknamed "Suzy's Law"), which would make it illegal to operate websites that encourage or promote suicide. The proposed legislation, known as Suzy's Law, was rejected in 2007, 2009, and 2011, and was never passed.

1. Do you agree with the claim of the website operators that their site is protected by the First Amendment?
2. Are there any concepts or philosophers mentioned in Chapter 2 that can be applied here?

Case Study 12F: The Positives and Negatives of Social Media: Facebook Photos Cost Teacher Her Job

When twenty-four-year-old high school teacher Ashley Payne returned from her summer vacation in Europe in 2009, she thought nothing of posting photographs of the trip on her Facebook page. Her photos included shots of her drinking wine and beer in cafes in Italy, Spain, and Ireland, and one photo included the word "bitch" on a banner in one of the bars—a reference to a Irish bar trivia game called "Bitch Bingo." Her employer, the Barrow County School System in Georgia, had a rule prohibiting teachers from "unacceptable online activities." Payne believed her privacy settings would limit access to her friends and it would not be available to students or their parents.

But in late August, only a few weeks into the new school year, Payne was called into her principal's office and confronted with the visual evidence. An email that her principal said came from a "concerned anonymous parent" prompted the inquiry.[58]

Citing the school system's policy, the principal gave her two choices—suspension or resignation. Payne chose the latter, but a few months later filed a lawsuit against the school system, claiming that the principal had violated a state law dealing with the due process that must be provided to teachers before they could be dismissed. Payne and her attorney asked for reinstatement to her position, back pay for the time she spent out of the classroom, and reimbursement for her legal fees.

Payne later learned that the anonymous email did not come from a parent, but from another unidentified person. She based her legal complaint partially on that detail and partially on the fact that she had conformed with school-board policy of not communicating with her students using social networking sites. But the school board contended that regardless of the privacy settings, Payne's Facebook page "promoted alcohol use" and "contained profanity."

"Yes, I put it on the Internet, so you can make that argument," Payne told CBS News in a February 2011 interview. "But it sort of feels like the same thing as if I had put the pictures in a shoebox in my house and someone came in and took them and showed one of them to the principal."[59]

Her attorney, Richard Storrs, added, "It would be like I went to a restaurant and saw my daughter's teacher sitting there with her husband having a glass with some kind of liquid. Is that frowned upon by the school board? Is that illegal? Is that improper? Of course not. It's the same situation in this case."[60]

Frederick Lane, an attorney not involved in the case, believes that while unfair on the surface, the situation is evidence to support his contention that once individuals post something online, they surrender part or all of their privacy. "All it takes is one person making a copy of what you've posted and it's out in the wild, and you no longer have control," Lane told CBS News. "And we're not losing that control, we're giving it away. Every time we buy with credit cards, use cellphones which signal our location, or post pictures on social networks like Facebook. Just sending an email may make private information public."[61]

A Barrow County court ruled against Payne in 2011, and after earning a graduate degree she worked briefly as a school administrator, then returned to teaching, this time at a high school in Atlanta.

1. Immanuel Kant, citing his categorical imperative, would likely side with the school system in this case, saying that "rules are rules" and despite using privacy settings, Payne violated the rule concerning "inappropriate online activity." Agree or disagree?
2. Suppose the principal or school board had refused to consider an anonymous email and insisted that Payne's accuser identify himself or herself prior to investigating the charges. Would it make a difference in how you view this case?
3. The principal may have violated state law in not providing Payne with "due process" (a formal hearing, including an opportunity to respond to the charges) before forcing her to resign. But would it have been more appropriate for the principal to have given her the opportunity to simply remove the photos?

Case Study 12G: Online Harassment: The Deaths of Megan, Jeffrey, Amanda, and Kennis

Thirteen-year-old Megan Meier was a bright and happy middle school student in the St. Louis suburb of O'Fallon, Missouri—until she met a sixteen-year-old boy identifying himself as "Josh Evans" on MySpace. After several weeks of a "cyber-romance," Josh turned on her with comments like, "you're a bad person and everyone hates you" and "the world would be better off without you." Feeling jilted and humiliated, Megan hanged herself in her bedroom on October 16, 2006—three weeks before her fourteenth birthday.

Law-enforcement officials took more than eighteen months to complete an investigation of the case, but in May 2008 they indicted forty-nine-year-old Lori Drew, the mother of one of Megan's friends. Investigators believe the two girls had a falling out, and Drew created the fictional MySpace profile in order to communicate with Megan and find out if she was spreading rumors about her daughter. With no specific laws in effect for cyberbullying, officials charged her with violating the Computer Fraud and Abuse Act (CFAA), a felony under federal law, as well as criminal conspiracy, as she enlisted the help of another teen in attempting to delete the fictional account to avoid detection after the girl's death.

When the suspect's name became public, she became the target of a cyberbullying campaign herself, as bloggers posted hateful comments online and posted directions to her home.

In November 2008, Drew was convicted of violating the CFAA. Before she could be sentenced, however, the charges were reduced to misdemeanors related to "unauthorized access to computers" because Drew had received help from her own daughter as well as the other teen, and prosecutors could not prove who actually sent the messages. The lesser charges were later dropped out of concern for constitutional challenges. Free-speech advocates celebrated the ruling, claiming that if it had gone the other way, it might have "made a criminal out of anyone who lies on the Internet."

Megan's death was the second known teen suicide to result from cyberbullying. The year before, a fifteen-year-old Florida boy, Jeffrey Johnston, killed himself after being harassed on the Internet for three years.

Amanda Todd, a fifteen-year-old from British Columbia, Canada, tragically ended her life in 2012, citing two years of online extortion and cyberbullying from a sexual predator as the cause of her depression.[62]

In 2015, twelve-year-old Kennis Cady died after falling into a coma while trying to hang herself in her East Rochester, New York home. It was only after her death that her parents and school administrators learned that she had been bullied on Instagram for months.[63]

Before the deaths, thirty-six states already had laws in place dealing with school bullying, and since the deaths many of them have expanded them to include bullying that takes place online.

Bill Bond, a retired high school principal who consults with school boards and other administrators on the issue, says that "cyberbullying is more destructive than face-to-face bullying because [the victim] gets the feeling that the whole world is being exposed to what is being said to you."[64]

1. Do you agree with the opinion of Bill Bond about the relative dangers of cyberbullying and face-to-face bullying?
2. Who bears the responsibility for preventing such cases: the schools, law enforcement, parents, or operators of social networking sites? What preventive steps could those four parties take?

Case Study 12H: Online Harassment: The Nikki Catsouras Story

Perhaps one of the most unusual cases of cyberharassment was targeted at a California family following the death of their eighteen-year-old daughter in a high-speed vehicle crash on Halloween Day in 2006. Nikki Catsouras's body, with her head nearly severed, was trapped inside her vehicle for hours before emergency personnel could extract it. Law-enforcement personnel erected a perimeter to prevent news photographers and onlookers with cellphone cameras from taking photographs, but they could not stop their own official accident photographs from winding up on the Internet. Two California Highway Patrol officers were later reprimanded for releasing the photos, but there was nothing the CHP could do once they were scattered across the Internet. Within days, the family was subjected to a flood of emails sent to their workplace and home computers by strangers adding to their grief by attaching grisly photographs. One of the cruelest came in the form of an email made to look like a business-related communication and sent to the office of her father, Christos Catsouras. When he clicked on the attachment, he saw a grisly photo of his daughter's body still trapped inside the car, accompanied by a caption reading, "Woohoo Daddy, I'm still alive!"[65]

While no one could understand the motives for such behavior, law-enforcement investigators and legal experts speculated that it was based on resentment of the family's affluent lifestyle (the wrecked car was a $90,000 Porsche). A MySpace page was set up to honor the young woman, but even that dignity was compromised by tasteless postings calling her a "black bitch" and claiming "the spoiled rich girl deserved it" and "what a waste of a Porsche."[66]

Two years later, frustrated that the emails and public glorification of the tragedy had not abated, the family filed a lawsuit against the CHP for invasion of privacy and infliction of emotional distress. In 2012, the CHP reached $2.37 million out-of-court settlement with the Catsouras family. In addition to the legal action, the family also hired a private investigator and an online investigation firm called Reputation.com to track down those responsible for spreading the photographs.

Discussion Problem 12: The Positives and Negatives of Social Media: Online Auction Sites and the First Amendment

A popular online auction site allows sellers to donate all or percentages of their proceeds to nonprofit organizations and causes, but prohibits that in cases of organizations that "promote or glorify violence, hate, racial, or religious intolerance." That rule has allowed administrators of the site to remove a number of items such as Confederate flags, KKK uniforms, and other items decorated with Nazi swastikas and other hate-related symbols. When sued over the policy (by sellers claiming their First Amendment rights are being violated), the auction site has always been victorious based on its position as a private entity rather than a government agency (meaning the First Amendment doesn't apply).

The website's policy is put to the test again when a seller indicates that proceeds from his sales (involving non-controversial items) would go to a legal defense fund for a man accused of killing a doctor who performed abortions. Administrators of the auction site inform the seller that he must either delete the reference to how proceeds will be spent or close his account altogether.

1. Do you agree with court rulings regarding hate memorabilia not being protected by the First Amendment?

2. In the case of seller wanting to donated proceeds to an accused murderer's legal defense fund, is there a First Amendment claim to be made here? Even without the First Amendment aspect to the case, is the auction site overreacting in how it is applying its own rule?

Discussion Questions

1201. As a general matter, do you agree with court rulings that Facebook, Instagram, Twitter, and other social media platforms are not subject to the First Amendment? Here's one possible analogy: In the 1980s, courts ruled in a number of cases that shopping centers, although privately owned, had to recognize some level of First Amendment freedoms in terms of political protests and distribution of political literature.

The courts used the concept of "equivalent function," ruling that shopping malls were gathering places for large numbers of people and were therefore analogous to public places. Could the same thing be said about social media? Do platforms such as Facebook and Instagram represent a "public forum"?

1202. Are there any philosophers or concepts from Chapter 2 that could be applied to any of the issues discussed in this chapter?

Notes

1 Jennifer Tanaka, "Foiling the Rogues." *Newsweek*, October 27, 1997, p. 80.
2 Tanaka.
3 Katy Steinmetz, "The Real Fake News." *Time*, August 2018, pp. 28–31.
4 Gary Marcus and Annie Duke, "The Problem with Believing What We're Told." *The Wall Street Journal*, September 1, 2019, p. 5-C.
5 Steinmetz.
6 Perry Chiaramonte, "Florida Professor Who Denied Sandy Hook Shooting Now Claims Boston Bombings a Drill." Fox News.com, April 24, 2013.
7 Chiaramonte. See also: Carl Hiaasen, "Firing of FAU Professor Long Overdue." Syndicated newspaper column, January 17, 2016.
8 Abigail Summerville, "Deepfakes Trigger Hunt for Solutions." *The Wall Street Journal*, July 29, 2019, p. 4-B.
9 Summerville.
10 Ralph Massullo, "Vaccine Doubters Weaken Immunity for All Others." *Pensacola News Journal*, August 12, 2019, p. 8-A.
11 "Elections Official Resigns After Online Post About Child Sex." *Wilmington Star-News*, October 18, 2018, p. 5-A.
12 Maggie Haberman and Annie Karni, "In Epstein Tweets, Trump Revisits a Favored Conspiracy Genre: Murder." *The New York Times*, August 12, 2019. See also: Leonard Pitts, "Epstein and the Rise of Conspiracy Theories." Syndicated newspaper column, August 15, 2019.

13   Beatrice Dupuy and Barbara Ortutay, "Deepfake Videos Pose a Threat, but 'Dumbfakes' May be Worse." Associated Press report, July 20, 2019.

14   Patrick Goldstein, "Fake Movie Reviews Upset Movie Fans." *Los Angeles Times*, October 14, 2002.

15   Nick Wingfield and Jeffrey A. Trachtenberg, "Amazon Prods Reviewers to Stop Hiding Behind Fake Names." *The Wall Street Journal*, July 28, 2004, p. 1-B.

16   "A.G. Schneiderman Announces Agreement with 19 Companies to Stop Writing Fake Online Reviews and Pay More than $350,000 in Fines." News release from the Office of the Attorney General for the State of New York, September 13, 2013. See also: John R. Johnson, *Everydata: The Misinformation Hidden in the Little Data You Consume Every Day*. Brookline, MA: Bibliomotion, Inc. (2016), p. 2.

17   Steven Petrow, "Can You Trust Online Reviews?" *USA Weekend*, November 7–9, 2014, p. 12. See also: Sacha Pfeiffer, "Ratings Sites Flourish behind Veil of Anonymity." *Boston Globe*, September 20, 2006, p. A-1.

18   Michelle Andrews, "Decoding MySpace." *U.S. News & World Report*, September 17, 2007.

19   Edward C. Baig, "Death Complicates a Facebook Status." *USA Today*, April 30, 2019.

20   Chris Wilkinson, "Protecting Your Children from Online Threats." *The People's Law School*, Pensacola, Florida, May 14, 2019.

21   Wilkinson. See also: Colin Poitras, "Where Predators Gather." *The Hartford Courant*, May 22, 2007, p. 1-A.

22   "Glendale is Paying Service to Monitor Students Online." *Glendale News-Press*, August 24, 2013. See also: Jacob Silverman, *Terms of Service: Social Media and the Price of Constant Connection*. New York: HarperCollins (2015), p. 133.

23   John D. McKinnon and Rob Copeland, "YouTube Fined over Children's Privacy." *The Wall Street Journal*, August 31, 2019, p. 3-B.

24   Josh Hawley, "Imagine a Better World Without Facebook." Syndicated newspaper column, May 23, 2019.

25   Mary Beth Marklein, "Colleges Check Applicants on Facebook." *USA Today*, September 22, 2011, p. 4-A.

26   Sally Ho, "Harvard Freshmen's Ouster over Posts an Eye-Opener." Associated Press report, June 20, 2017.

27   Libby Sander, "Off the Field, Athletes Learn Lessons in Spin." *Chronicle of Higher Education*, November 16, 2007, p. 1.

28   Jay G. Tate, "Facebook Opens Door to Digital Fumbles." *Montgomery Advertiser*, August 15, 2010, p. 1-C.

29   "Social Media Postings: NCIS Advises Caution." *Gosport* (Pensacola Naval Air Station, FL), May 8, 2015, p. 1.

30   Zach Fox, "SC Professor: Social Media Can Ease In-Person Interaction." Gatehouse Media report, December 16, 2017.

31   "Social Media Guidelines." *Associated Press Stylebook and Briefing on Media Law*. New York: Associated Press (2019), pp. 365–382.

32   "Social Media Guidelines."

33   "Social Media Guidelines."

34   Kathleen Parker, "Internet Freedom Sacrifices Decency." Syndicated newspaper column, August 30, 2009.

35   Marlisse Silver Sweeney, "What the Law Can (and Can't) Do About Online Harassment." *The Atlantic*, November 2, 2014.

36   Sweeney.

37   Randy Leonard, "The Ferris Bueller of Facebook." *Florida Today*, January 20, 2008, p. 7-A.

38   Sweeney.

39   Sweeney.

40   Sweeney.

41   Sweeney.

42 Sweeney.

43 Donald J. Solove, *The Future of Reputation: Gossip, Rumor, and Privacy on the Internet.* New Haven, CT: Yale University Press (2007), pp. 1–2.

44 Sally Ho, "Cyberbullying on the Rise in U.S." Associated Press report, July 27, 2019.

45 Ho, "Cyberbullying on the Rise in U.S."

46 Katy Steinmetz, "The Instagram Challenge." *Time*, July 22, 2019, pp. 46–51.

47 Steinmetz.

48 Tom Schad, "Injured Gymnast Hopes to Walk Down the Aisle." *USA Today*, April 16, 2019, p. 1-C.

49 Clarice Silber, "Texas, Dating App Crack Down on Cyberflashing." Associated Press report, August 31, 2019.

50 Yamiche Alcindor, "States Take Aim at Digital Bullying." *USA Today*, March 19, 2012, p. 1-A.

51 Beth Ann Nichols, "Lexi Thompson's Social Media Break is Culmination of Harsh, Hurtful Commentary." *Golfweek*, May 1, 2019.

52 Amy Kristen Sanders, "Obscenity, Revenge Pornography, and Cyberbullying," Chapter 9 in *Social Media and the Law*, second edition, Daxton R. Stewart, ed. New York: Routledge (2016), pp. 190–191.

53 Janet Kornblum, "Cyberbullying Grows Bigger and Meaner." *USA Today*, July 15, 2008, p. 3-A.

54 Amy Kristen Sanders, "Obscenity, Revenge Pornography, and Cyberbullying," Chapter 9 in *Social Media and the Law*, second edition, Daxton R. Stewart, ed. New York: Routledge (2016), pp. 190–191.

55 http://www.wish.org/about/chain_letter.

56 Ryan Herrington, "Not Fit For Print." *Golf World*, February 2007, p. 17.

57 Troy Moon, "A Load of Crock, Not Davy Crockett." *Pensacola News Journal*, September 26, 2010, p. A-1.

58 "Did the Internet Kill Privacy?" *CBS Sunday Morning*, February 13, 2011.

59 "Did the Internet Kill Privacy?"

60 "Did the Internet Kill Privacy?"

61 "Did the Internet Kill Privacy?"

62 Sweeney.

63 Steinmetz.

64 Janet Kornblum, "Cyberbullying Grows Bigger and Meaner." *USA Today*, July 15, 2008, p. 1-D.

65 Jessica Bennett, "A Tragedy that Won't Fade Away." *Newsweek*, May 4, 2009, pp. 38–40.

66 Bennett.

Appendix
Professional Codes of Ethics

American Advertising Federation Code of Ethics

aaf.org/ethics

American Society of Newspaper Editors Statement of Principles

asne.org

Associated Press Sports Editors Ethical Guidelines

apsportseditors.com

College Media Advisors Code of Ethical Behavior

collegemedia.org/about

International Association of Business Communicators Code of Ethics

iabc.com

Online News Association Mission Statement

journalists.org/about/mission

Public Media Journalists Association (formerly Public Radio News Directors Inc.) Code of Ethics

prndi.org/code-ethics

Public Relations Society of America Member Code of Ethics

prsa.org/about

Radio Television Digital News Association (formerly Radio Television News Directors Association) Code of Ethics

rtdna.org/content

Rebecca Blood's Code of Weblog Ethics

rebeccablood.net/handbook

Society for Advancing Business Editing and Writing

sabe.org

Society of Professional Journalists Principles and Standards of Practice

spj.org/ethicscode

Sources/Further Reading

1 An Overview of Communication Ethics

Abernathy, Gary. "The Vital Job of Small-Town Newspapers." *The Washington Post*, July 25, 2017.

Alger, Greg, and Jessica Burnette-Lemon. "Ethics in the Real World." *Communication World*, March–April 2006, pp. 28–29.

Allen, Anita. *The New Ethics: A Tour of the 21st Century Moral Landscape*. New York: Miramax Books (2004).

Benedetto, Richard. "What Readers Don't Understand about Daily Newspapers." Syndicated newspaper column, January 5, 1993.

Bennett, William. *The Death of Outrage*. New York: Free Press (1999).

Blackburn, Simon. *Ethics: A Very Short Introduction*. Oxford: Oxford University Press (2001).

Borchers, Timothy A. *Persuasion in the Media Age*. Boston: McGraw Hill (2002).

Dickson, Sandra. "The Golden Mean in Journalism." *Journal of Mass Media Ethics*, Vol. 3, No. 1 (1988), pp. 33–37.

Elliott, Deni, ed. *Responsible Journalism*. Beverly Hills, CA: Sage Publications (1986).

Fitzgerald, Mark. "For Gay Press, 'Good Old Days' Are Here Today." *Editor & Publisher*, September 2007, p. 9.

Flint, Leon Nelson. *The Conscience of the Newspaper*. New York: D. Appleton Century Co. (1925).

Hunt, Shelby D., and Lawrence B. Chonko. "Ethical Problems of Advertising Agency Executives." *Journal of Advertising*, Vol. 16, No. 4 (1987), pp. 16–24.

Johannesen, Richard. *Ethics in Human Communication*. Long Grove, IL: Waveland Press (1996).

Johnson, John H. and Mike Gluck. *Everydata: The Misinformation Hidden in the Little Data You Read Every Day*. Brookline, MA: Bibliomotion (2016).

Johnson, Peter. "Trust in Media Keeps on Slipping." *USA Today*, May 28, 2003.

Jones, Clarence. *Winning with the News Media*. Anna Maria, FL: Winning News Media, Inc. (2005).

Kidder, Rushworth. *How Good People Make Tough Choices: Resolving the Dilemmas of Ethical Living*. New York: HarperCollins (2003).

Kohut, Andrew. "Public Support for the Watchdogs Is Fading." *Columbia Journalism Review*, May/June 2001, p. 52.

"Lines Blur as Journalism Heads Back to the Future." *USA Today*, November 10, 2010, p. 8–A.

Merrill, John C., and Ralph D. Barney, ed. *Ethics and the Press*. New York: Hastings House Publishers (1978).

Newton, Lisa H., Louis Hodges, and Susan Keith. "Accountability in the Professions: Accountability in Journalism." *Journal of Mass Media Ethics*, Vol. 19, Nos. 3 and 4 (2004), pp. 166–190.

Niose, David. *Nonbeliever Nation: The Rise of Secular Americans*. New York: Palgrave Macmillan (2012).

Oppenheimer, Mark. "Why Does the Public Hate the Media?" Syndicated newspaper column, October 29, 2017.

Parker, Kathleen. "Is Technology Killing Our Decency?" Syndicated newspaper column, October 10, 2010.

Pitts, Leonard. "Celebrities and Politicos Take the Truth Out for a Spin." Syndicated newspaper column, May 30, 2007.

Policinski, Gene. "How Do We Decide Who Is, Or Isn't a Journalist?" *USA Today*, January 3, 2012, p. 5–B.

Richardson, Brian. "Four Standards for Teaching Ethics in Journalism." *Journal of Mass Media Ethics*, Vol. 9, No. 2 (1994), pp. 109–117.

Rosenberg, Howard, and Charles S. Feldman. *No Time to Think: The Menace of Media Speed and the 24-Hour News Cycle*. New York: Continuum Books (2008).

Samuelson, Robert J. "Long Live the News Business." *Newsweek*, May 28, 2007, p. 40.

Schneider, Richard. "Newspapers Still Are the Ones Finding the News." *Pensacola News Journal*, April 11, 2010.

Schudson, Michael. *The Sociology of News*. New York: W.W. Norton and Company (2003).

Strupp, Joe. "Watchdogs Still Awake?" *Editor & Publisher*, October 2009, pp. 16–20.

"Trail of Truth-Telling." *Editor & Publisher*, June 17, 2002, p. 9.

Wallace, Mike, and Beth Knobel. *Heat and Light: Advice for the Next Generation of Journalists*. New York: Three Rivers Press (2010).

Wilson, Jason. "Doxxing, Assault, and Death Threats: New Dangers Facing U.S. Journalists." *Guardian*, June 14, 2018.

Zuckerman, Phil. *Living the Secular Life*. New York: Penguin Press (2014).

2 Philosophical and Critical Perspectives on Communication Ethics

Bagdikian, Ben. *The Media Monopoly*. Boston: Beacon Press (1992).

Bok, Sissela. *Lying: Moral Choice in Public and Private Life*. New York: Vintage (1979).

Boorstin, Daniel. *The Image: A Guide to Pseudo-Events in America*. New York: Atheneum (1961).

Bovee, Warren G. "The Can Justify the Means—But Rarely." *Journal of Mass Media Ethics*, Vol. 6, No. 3 (1991), pp. 135–145.

Brooks, David, *The Road to Character*. New York: Random House (2015).

Gore, Al. *The Assault on Reason: Our Information Ecosystem, From the Age of Print to the Age of Trump*. New York: Penguin Books (2017).

Hopkins, W. Wat. "The Supreme Court Defines the Marketplace of Ideas." *Journalism and Mass Communication Quarterly*, Vol. 73, No. 1 (Spring 1996), pp. 40–45.

Lambeth, Edmund B. *Committed Journalism: An Ethic for the Profession*. Bloomington, IN: Indiana University Press (1986).

Lippmann, Walter. *Public Opinion*. New York: Simon & Schuster (1922).

Marchand, Philip. *Marshall McLuhan: The Medium and the Messenger*. New York: Tichnor & Fields (1989).

Meiklejohn, Alexander. *Political Freedom, the Constitutional Powers of the People*. Oxford: Oxford University Press (1965).

Niose, David. *Nonbeliever Nation: The Rise of Secular Americans*. New York: Palgrave Macmillan (2012).

Rand, Ayn. "Introducing Objectivism." *The Objectivist Newsletter*, Vol. 1 No. 8 (August 1962), p. 35.

Romano, Andrew. "How Dumb Are We?" *Newsweek*, March 20, 2011.

Silverman, Jacob. *Terms of Service: Social Media and the Price of Constant Connection*. New York: HarperCollins (2015).

Stauber, John, and Sheldon Rampton, *Weapons of Mass Deception*. New York: Penguin Group (2003).

3 Journalism and Broadcasting: Content Issues

Bates, Stephen. *If No News, Send Rumors*. New York: St. Martin's Press (1989).

Bozell, Brent, and Brent H. Baker, eds. *And That's the Way It Isn't: A Reference Guide to Media Bias*. Alexandria, VA: Media Research Center (1990).

Fallows, James. *Breaking the News: How the Media Undermine American Democracy*. New York: Pantheon Books (1996).

Goldberg, Bernard. *Arrogance: Rescuing America from the Media Elite*. New York: Warner Books (2003).

Goldberg, Bernard. *Bias: How the Media Distorts the News*. New York: Harper Collins (2003).

Heilpern, Will. "How 'Deceptive' Sponsored News Articles Could be Tricking Readers—Even with a Disclosure Message." BusinessInsider.com, March 17, 2016. March/April 2007, pp. 38–43.

Jamieson, Kathleen Hall, and Paul Waldman. *The Press Effect*. New York: Oxford University Press (2003).

Lang, Thomas, and Zachary Roth, "Video News Releases—They're Everywhere." *Columbia Journalism Review*, October 13, 2004.

Lemann, Nicholas. "Amateur Hour: Journalism Without Journalists." *The New Yorker*, August 7, 2006, p. 44.

Levin, Mark R. *Unfreedom of the Press*. New York: Threshold Editions (2019).

Lieberman, Trudy. "Epidemic: Phony Medical News is on the Rise, Thanks to Dozens of Unhealthy Deals between TV Newsrooms and Hospitals." *Columbia Journalism Review*, March/April 2007, pp. 38–43.

Lipstadt, Deborah. *Beyond Belief: The American Press and the Coming of the Holocaust*. New York: Free Press (1986).

Marvin, Ginny. "Consumers Can't Tell the Difference between Sponsored Content and Editorial." MarketingLand.com, September 9, 2015.

McGowan, William. *Coloring the News: How Crusading for Diversity Has Corrupted American Journalism*. San Francisco: Encounter Books (2001).

Nah, Seungahn, Kang Namkoong, Rachael Record, and Stephanie K. Van Stee, "Citizen Journalism Practice Increases Civic Participation." *Newspaper Research Journal*, Vol. 38, No. 1 (2017), pp. 62–78.

Proffitt, Jennifer M. "An Ethical Analysis of the News Coverage of the Columbine Shootings." Association for Education in Journalism and Mass Communications Southeastern Colloquium, Spring 2001.

Rosenberg, Howard, and Charles S. Feldman, *No Time to Think: The Menace of Media Speed and the 24-Hour News Cycle*. New York: Continuum Books (2008).

Shoemaker, Pamela J., and Stephen D. Reese. *Mediating the Message: Theories of Influence of Mass Media Content*. White Plains, NY: Longman Publishing (1996).

Strupp, Joe. "New Advertorials Raise Old Ethical Questions." *Editor & Publisher*, November 17, 2003, pp. 6–7.

4 Journalism and Broadcasting: Personnel Issues

Aldrich, Leigh Stephens. *Covering the Community: A Diversity Handbook for the Media*. Thousand Oaks, CA: Pine Forge Press (1999).

Bates, Stephen. *If No News, Send Rumors*. New York: St. Martin's Press (1989).

"The Big Lie." *Columbia Journalism Review*, November/December 2001, p. 91.

Fedler, Fred. *Media Hoaxes*. Ames, IA: Iowa State University Press (1989).

Garcia, Jason. "Changing Rules." *American Journalism Review*, March 2001. https://ajrarchive.org/Article.asp?id=940

Hassen, Adeel. "Blair's Victims: That Helpless Feeling." *Columbia Journalism Review*, July/August 2003, pp. 19–21.

Hulteng, John. *Playing it Straight: A Practical Discussion of the Ethical Principles of the American Society of Newspaper Editors*. Chester, CT: The Globe Pequot Press (1981).

Klaidman, Stephen, and Tom L. Beauchamp, *The Virtuous Journalist*. New York: Oxford University Press (1987).

Kurtz, Howard. *The Media Circus: The Trouble With America's Newspapers*. New York: Random House (1994).

"Lines Blur as Journalism Heads Back to the Future." *USA Today*, November 10, 2010, pp. 8–A.

Loop, Travis. "A Boost for Minority Workforce." *Presstime*, November 2002, p. 43.

Love, Robert. "Before Jon Stewart: The Truth about Fake News." *Columbia Journalism Review*, March/April 2007, pp. 33–37.

Love, Robert. "Shakedown: The Unfortunate History of Reporters Who Trade Power for Cash." *Columbia Journalism Review*, July/August 2006, pp. 47–51.

Malcolm, Janet. *The Journalist and the Murderer*. New York: Alfred A. Knopf (1995).

McGowan, William. *Coloring the News: How Crusading for Diversity Has Corrupted American Journalism*. San Francisco: Encounter Books (2001).

Mitroff, Ian I., and Warren Bennis. *The Unreality Industry: The Deliberate Manufacturing of Falsehood and What it is Doing to Our Lives*. New York: Carol Publishing Group (1989).

Murray, Steve. "Facts Don't Make the Best Stories." *Atlanta Journal-Constitution*, February 4, 2006.

Newkirk, Pamela T. "Guess Who's Leaving the Newsroom?" *Columbia Journalism Review*, September/October 2000, pp. 36–39.

O'Shea, James. *The Deal From Hell: How Moguls and Wall Street Plundered Great American Newspapers*. New York: Public Affairs (2011).

Paterno, Susan. "Santa Barbara Smackdown." *American Journalism Review*, December 2006/January 2007, pp. 44–51.

Robertson, Lori. "Ethically Challenged." *American Journalism Review*, March 2001, pp. 21–29.

Scardino, Albert. "Ethics, Reporters, and The New Yorker." *The New York Times*, March 21, 1989.

Silverman, Craig. *Regret the Error*. New York: Sterling Publishing (2007).

Vanderkam, Laura. "When Truth Masquerades as Fiction." *USA Today*, January 17, 2006.

Wallace, Linda. "Diversity: The Operating Manual." *Columbia Journalism Review*, July/August 2003, p. 18.

White, Marie Dunne. "Plagiarism and the News Media." *Journal of Mass Media Ethics*, Vol. 4, No. 2 (1989), pp. 265–280.

Wolper, Allan. "The Credibility Gap." *Editor & Publisher*, August 12, 2002, p. 26.

Wolper, Allan. "How King Con Kelley Got Away With It." *Editor & Publisher*, May 2004, p. 30.

5 Journalism and Broadcasting: Policy Issues

Bates, Stephen. *If No News, Send Rumors*. New York: St. Martin's Press (1989).

Bauder, David. "Celebrity Deaths Force Media to Examine Suicide Reporting." Associated Press report, June 14, 2018.

Braun, Paul. "Deception in Journalism." *Journal of Mass Media Ethics*, Vol. 3, No. 1 (1988), pp. 77–83.

Durcharme, Jamie. "How Should the Media Cover Suicides?" A New Study Has Some Answers." *Time*, July 20, 2018.

Eichenwald, Kurt. "A Reporter's Essay: Making a Connection with Justin." *The New York Times*, December 19, 2005.

Fox, James Alan. "Cover Shooters But Not Their Lives: Future Copycats Don't Need Role Models." *USA Today*, June 3, 2019.

Harrison, Bridget. "Blood Money." *New York Post*, September 9, 2002.

Hodges, Louis W. "To Deceive or Not Deceive." *The Quill*, December 1981, p. 9.

Killenberg, G. Michael, and Rob Anderson, "What is a Quote? Practical, Rhetorical, and Ethical Concerns for Journalists." *Journal of Mass Media Ethics*, Vol. 8, No. 1 (1993), pp. 37–54.

Kirtley, Jane. "Testing the System." *American Journalism Review*, November 2002, p. 70.

Lehrer, Adrienne. "Between Quotation Marks." *Journalism Quarterly*, Vol. 66 (1989), pp. 902–941.

McCollam, Douglas. "The Shame Game." *Columbia Journalism Review*, January/February 2007, pp. 28–33.

Puterbaugh, John. "Why We Report Some Suicides and Not Others." *Chicago Tribune*, January 23, 2017.

Stephens, Mitchell. *Broadcast News*. New York: Holt, Rinehart and Winston (1986).

Wallace, Mike, and Beth Knobel, *Heat and Light: Advice for the Next Generation of Journalists*. New York: Three Rivers Press (2010).

Wolper, Allan. "Are Travel Writers Spoiling the Trip?" *Editor & Publisher*, July 2005, p. 28.

Wolper, Allan. "Truth to Be Found in Dirty Language?" *Editor & Publisher*, March 2006, p. 22.

Ziesenis, Elizabeth B. "Suicide Coverage in Newspapers: An Ethical Consideration." *Journal of Mass Media Ethics*, Vol. 6, No. 4 (1991), pp. 234–244.

6 Journalism and Broadcasting: Privacy Issues

Alderman, Ellen, and Caroline Kennedy, *The Right to Privacy*. New York: Alfred A. Knopf (1995).

Bates, Stephen. *If No News, Send Rumors*. New York: St. Martin's Press (1989).

Gauthier, Candace Cummins. "Privacy Invasion by the Media: Three Ethical Models." *Journal of Mass Media Ethics*, Vol. 17, No. 1 (2002), pp. 20–34.

Graff, E. J. "The Line on Sex." *Columbia Journalism Review*, September/October 2005, pp. 8–9.

Kurtz, Howard. *The Media Circus: The Trouble with America's Newspapers*. New York: Random House (1994).

Shaw, David. "Public Figures, Private Lives." Chapter 1 in *Journalism Today: A Changing Press for a Changing America*. New York: Harper's College Press (1977).

Silverman, Jacob. *Terms of Service: Social Media and the Price of Constant Connection*. New York: HarperCollins (2015).

Solove, Daniel J. *The Future of Reputation*. New Haven, CT: Yale University Press (2007).

Westin, Alan. *Privacy and Freedom*. New York: Atheneum (1967).

7 Journalism and Broadcasting: Accountability Issues

Bagdikian, Ben. "When the Post Banned Anonymous Sources." *American Journalism Review*, August/September 2005, p. 33.

Berkowitz, Dan, and Zhengjia Liu. "Media Errors and the Nutty Professor: Riding the Journalistic Boundaries of the Sandy Hook Shootings." *Journalism*, Vol. 17, No. 2 (2017), pp. 155–172.

Charnley, Mitchell. "Preliminary Notes on a Study of Newspaper Accuracy." *Journalism Quarterly*, Vol. 13 (December 1936), pp. 394–401.

Hanson, Gary, and Stanley T. Wearden. "Measuring Newscast Accuracy: Applying a Newspaper Model to Television." *Journal of Mass Communication Quarterly*, Vol. 81, No. 3 (Fall 2004), pp. 546–558.

Hart, Ariel. "Delusions of Accuracy." *Columbia Journalism Review*, July/August 2003, p. 20.

McCollam, Douglas. "The Shame Game." *Columbia Journalism Review*, January/February 2007, pp. 28–33.

Newton, Lisa H., Louis Hodges, and Susan Keith. "Accountability in the Professions: Accountability in Journalism." *Journal of Mass Media Ethics*, Vol. 19, Nos. 3 and 4 (2004), pp. 166–190.

Reider, Rem. "Ombudsman Still Has a Place in the Newsroom." *USA Today*, February 22, 2013, p. 3–B.

Rosenberg, Howard, and Charles S. Feldman. *No Time to Think: The Menace of Media Speed and the 24-Hour News Cycle*. New York: Continuum Books (2008).

Sander, Pam. "Anonymous Sourcing is Vital to Democracy." *Wilmington Star-News*, March 5, 2017, p. 1–C.

Silverman, Craig. *Regret the Error*. New York: Sterling Publishing (2007).

Smolkin, Rachel. "Under Fire." *American Journalism Review*, February/March 2005, pp. 19–25.

Smolkin, Rachel. "USA Tomorrow." *American Journalism Review*, August/September 2005, pp. 21–29.

Stone, Gerald. *Examining Newspapers: What Research Tells Us about America's Newspapers*. Newbury Park, CA: Sage Publications (1987).

Strupp, Joe. "Losing Confidence." *Editor & Publisher*, July 2005, pp. 32–39.

8 Ethical Issues in Advertising

An, Soontae, and Lori Bergen. "Advertiser Pressure on Daily Newspapers: A Survey of Advertising Sales Executives." *Journal of Advertising*, Vol. 36, No. 2 (Summer 2007), pp. 111–121.

"Are Automobile Dealers Editing Your Local Newspaper?" *Consumer Reports*, April 1992, p. 208.

Cowley, Elizabeth, and Chris Barron. "When Product Placement Goes Wrong." *Journal of Advertising*, Vol. 37, No. 1 (2008), pp. 89–98.

Hunt, Shelby D., and Lawrence B. Chonko, "Ethical Problems of Advertising Agency Executives." *Journal of Advertising*, Vol. 16, No. 4 (1987), pp. 16–24.

Kilbourne, Jean. *The Naked Truth: Advertising's Image of Women*. New York: Ballantine Books (2004).

Kossman, Sienna. "The Truth about False and Deceptive Advertising." www.USNews.com, posted July 22, 2013; accessed August 3, 2019.

Parsons, Allen. "Advertising and Editorial Are Separate for a Reason." *Wilmington Star-News*, March 5, 2005, p. 1–B.

Poitras, Marc, and Daniel Sutter. "Advertiser Pressure and the Control of News: The Decline of Muckraking Revisited." *Journal of Economic Behavior and Organization*, Vol. 72, No. 3 (December 2009), pp. 944–958.

Spence, Edward, and Brett Van Heekeren. *Advertising Ethics*. Upper Saddle River, NJ: Prentice-Hall (2004).

9 Ethical Issues in Public Relations

Baker, Lee W. *The Credibility Factor: Putting Ethics to Work in Public Relations*. Homewood, IL: Business One Irwin (1993).

Berkman, Robert I., and Christopher A. Shumway. *Digital Dilemmas: Ethical Issues for Online Media Professionals*. Ames, IO: Iowa State University Press (2003).

Bleifuss, Joel. "Flack Attack." *Utne Reader*, January/February 1994, pp. 72–77.

Botan, Carl. "Ethics in Strategic Communication Campaigns: The Case for a New Approach to Public Relations." *The Journal of Business Communication*, April 1997, pp. 188–201.

Brown, Carolyn J. "Editorial Ethics and the Public Relations Practitioner." *Northwestern University Journal of Corporate Public Relations*, Winter 1991, pp. 32–36.

Brown, David H. "A Funny Thing Happened on the Way to the Forum on Ethics." *Public Relations Quarterly*, Spring 1986, pp. 20–23.

Curtin, Patricia A., and Lois Boynton. "Ethics in Public Relations." *Handbook of Public Relations*, Ed. Robert Heath. Thousand Oaks, CA: Sage Publications, (2001), pp. 411–421.

Day, Kenneth D., Qingwen Dong, and Clark Robins, "Public Relations Ethics." *Handbook of Public Relations*, ed. Robert Heath, pp. 403–409. Thousand Oaks, CA: Sage Publications (2001).

Dilenschneider, Robert L. *Power and Influence: Mastering the Art of Persuasion*. New York: Prentice-Hall (1990).

Edelman, Daniel J. "Ethical Behavior is Key to Field's Future." *Public Relations Journal*, November 1992, p. 32.

"The Ethics of Keeping Secrets." *Communication World*, August/September 1999, pp. 31–40.

Fox, James F. "Public Relations: Some Ethical Guidelines." *Ethics, Morality and the Media*, ed. Lee Thayer. New York: Hastings House (1979).

Haggerty, James F. "Putting the Best Face on It: Litigation PR in the Era of 24-Hour Cable News." *Business Law Today*, Vol. 13, No. 6 (July/August 2004).

Hutchison, Liese. "Agency Ethics Isn't an Oxymoron." *Public Relations Tactics*, May 2000, p. 13.

Johnson, Larry, and Bob Philips, *Absolute Honesty*. New York: Amacom (2003).

Landler, Mark. "When a PR Firm Could Use a PR Firm." *Business Week*, May 14, 1990, p. 44.

Lordan, Edward J. *Essential of Public Relations Management*. Chicago: Burnham Publishers (2003).

Mallinson, Bill. *Public Lies and Private Truths: An Anatomy of Public Relations*. London: Cassell Publishing (1996).

Martinson, David L. "How Should the PR Practitioner Respond When Confronted by Unethical Behavior?" *Public Relations Quarterly*, Summer 1991, pp. 18–21.

Nelson, Joyce. *Sultans of Sleaze: Public Relations and the Media*. Lutsen, MN: Between the Lines Publishing (1989).

O'Brien, Timothy. "Spinning Frenzy: P.R.'s Bad Press." *New York Times*, February 13, 2005.

Parsons, Patricia. *Ethics in Public Relations: A Guide to Best Practice*. Philadelphia: KoganPage (2008).

Pratt, Cornelius. "Public Relations: The Empirical Research on Practitioner Ethics." *Journal of Business Ethics*, Vol. 10 (1991), pp. 229–236.

Raabe, Steve. "Public Relations Industry Tackles Image Problems." *The Denver Post*, April 12, 2008.

Seib, Philip and Kathy Fitzpatrick. *Public Relations Ethics*. Ft. Worth, TX: Harcourt Brace (1995).

Seitel, Frasier. "Litigation Public Relations." *Jack O'Dwyer's Newsletter*, March 14, 2016, p. 4.

Seligman, Mac. "Travel Writers' Expenses: Who Should Pay?" *Public Relations Journal*, May 1990, pp. 27–34.

Stacks, Don W. "A Quantitative Examination of Ethical Dilemmas in Public Relations." *Journal of Mass Media Ethics*, 1989, pp. 53–67.

Toledano, Margalit, and Ruth Avidar. "Public Relations, Ethics, and Social Media: A Cross-National Study of PR Practitioners." *Public Relations Review*, Vol. 42, No. 1 (March 2016), pp. 161–169.

Vargas, Ann. "Liar, Liar, PR on Fire." *PR Week*, May 1, 2000, pp. 18–19.

Walsh, Frank. *Public Relations and the Law*. Gainesville, FL: Institute for Public Relations Research (1991).

Wilcox, Dennis L. *Public Relations Writing and Media Techniques*. Boston: Pearson, Allyn & Bacon (2009).

Wilcox, Dennis L., Glen T. Cameron, Bryan H. Reber, and Jae-Hwa Shin. *Think Public Relations*. Boston: Allyn & Bacon (2012).

Williams, Dean. "Un-Spun: Ethical Communication Practices Serve the Public Interest." *Communication World*, April/May 2002, pp. 27–35.

Witmer, Diane F. *Spinning the Web: A Handbook for Public Relations on the Internet*. New York: Longman Publishing (2000).

Wright, Donald K. "Enforcement Dilemma: The Voluntary Nature of Public Relations Codes." *Public Relations Review*, Spring 1993, pp. 13–20.

10 Ethical Issues in Political Communication

Black, Jay. "Semantics and Ethics of Propaganda. *Journal of Mass Media Ethics*, Vol. 16, Nos. 2 and 3 (2001), pp. 121–137.

Bobbitt, Randy. *Us Against Them: The Political Culture of Talk Radio*. Lanham, MD: Lexington Books (2010).

Combs, James E., and Dan Dimmo. *The New Propaganda*. New York: Longman (1993).

Edelman, Murray. *The Politics of Misinformation*. New York: Cambridge University Press (2001).

Gallup, George. "The Ethical Problems of Polling." *Ethics, Morality, and the Media*. New York: Hastings House Publishers (1980).

Gore, Al. *The Assault on Reason: Our Information Ecosystem, From the Age of Print to the Age of Trump*. New York: Penguin Books (2017).

Gouran, Dennis. "Guidelines for the Analysis of Responsibility in Governmental Communication." *Teaching About Doublespeak*, ed. Daniel Dieterich. Urbana, IL: National Council of Teachers of English (1976).

Hovland, Carl, Irving Janis, and Harold Kelley. *Communication and Persuasion*. New Haven, CT: Yale University Press (1953).

Hoyt, Mike. "Talk Radio: Turning up the Volume." *Columbia Journalism Review*, November/December 1992, pp. 45–50.

Jackson, Brooks, and Kathleen Hall Jamieson. *UnSpun: Finding Facts in a World of Disinformation*. New York: Random House (2007).

Jamieson, Kathleen Hall. *Dirty Politics: Deception, Distraction, and Democracy*. New York: Oxford University Press (1992).

Jamieson, Kathleen Hall. *Everything You Think You Know about Politics … And Why You're Wrong*. New York: Basic Books (2000).

Johannesen, Richard L., Kathleen S. Valde, and Karen E. Whedbee. *Ethics in Human Communication*, sixth edition. Long Grove, IL: Waveland Press (2008).

Jowett, Garth S. and Victoria O'Donnell. *Propaganda and Persuasion*. Newbury Park, CA: Sage Publications (1992).

Kohut, Andrew. "Polls Speed Down the Slippery Slope, But They Don't Have To." *Columbia Journalism Review*, November/December 2000, pp. 66–67.

Larson, Charles. *Persuasion: Reception and Responsibility*. Belmont, CA: Wadsworth Publishing Company (1992).

Laufer, Peter. *Inside Talk Radio: America's Voice or Just Hot Air?* New York: Carol Publishing Company (1995).

Robertson, Lori. "Poll Crazy." *American Journalism Review*, January/February 2003, pp. 40–45.

Salvanto, Anthony. *Where Did You Get This Number? A Pollster's Guide to Making Sense of the World*. New York: Simon & Schuster (2018).

Swint, Kerwin. *Mudslingers: The Twenty-Five Dirtiest Political Campaigns of All Time*. New York: Union Square Press (2006).

11 Ethical Issues in Workplace Communication

Adams, Hall, Suzanne M. Scheuing, and Stacey A. Feely. "E-Mail Monitoring in the Workplace: The Good, the Bad, and the Ugly." *Defense Counsel Journal*, Vol. 67, No. 1 (January 2000).

Barry, Bruce. *Speechless: The Erosion of Free Expression in the American Workplace*. San Francisco: Berrett-Koehler Publishers (2007).

Bell, Alison. "What Price Ethics?" *Entrepreneurial Woman*, January/February 1991, p. 68.

Callahan, David. *The Cheating Culture*. New York: Harcourt (2002).

Guffey, Mary Ellen. *Business Communication: Process and Product*. Cincinnati: Southwestern College Publishing (2000).

Guynn, Jessica, and Marco della Cava. "The Weinstein Effect." *USA Today*, October 27, 2017, p. 1–A.

Hampson, Rick. "Age-Old Bad Judgment Lives Long in the Digital Age." *USA Today*, March 20, 2013, p. 1–A.

Hill, Stan. "The Multilayered Minefield of Workplace E-Mail Monitoring." *Employment Relations Today*, Vol. 42, No. 1 (Spring 2015).

Joyce, Amy. "When Do Workplace Lies Cross the Line?" *The Washington Post*, April 16, 2006.

Korkki, Phyllis. "Is Your Online Identity Spoiling Your Chances?" *The New York Times*, October 10, 2010, p. 8.

Krouse, Sarah. "The New Ways Your Boss Is Spying on You." *The Wall Street Journal*, July 20–21, 2019, p. 1–B.

Marklein, Mary Beth. "Is There Any Truth to Today's Resumes?" *USA Today*, February 6, 2003, p. 1–B.

McGregor, Jenna. "Can Your Off-Hours Political Activism Get You in Trouble at Work?" *The Washington Post*, May 31, 2017.

"More Companies Monitor Employee E-Mail." Associated Press report, March 11, 2002.

Nelton, Sharon. "Sexual Harassment: Reducing the Risks." *Nation's Business*, March 1995, pp. 24–25.

Nydegger, Rudy. *Clocking In: The Psychology of Work*. Santa Barbara, CA: Greenwood Press (2018).

Pribek, Jane. "Employer Rights When Monitor E-Mail, Internet Use." *Daily Record* (Kansas City, MO), February 20, 2006.

Seglin, Jeffrey. "You've Got Mail. You're Being Watched." *The New York Times*, July 18, 1999.

Sell, Sarah Skidmore. "Poll: Job Interview Questions Often Run Afoul of the Law." Associated Press report, November 3, 2017.

Singer, Gilbert. "Sexual Harassment: It Won't Go Away on Its Own." *The Magazine of Northwest Florida Business*, August 2008, pp. 20–21.

Taylor, Johnny C. "Off-Work Politics May Hurt Your Job." *USA Today*, July 10, 2018, p. 5–B.

Wessel, Harry. "Workplace Ethics Issues Take Center Stage Again." *The Orlando Sentinel*, May 21, 2003.

Wiseman, Paul. "One-Fifth of Americans Find Workplace Hostile or Threatening." Associated Press report, August 15, 2017.

12 Ethical Issues in Cyberspace and Social Media

Alcindor, Yamiche. "States Take Aim at Digital Bullying." *USA Today*, March 19, 2012, p. 1–A.

Fox, Zach. "SC Professor: Social Media an Ease In-Person Interaction." Gatehouse Media report, December 16, 2017.

Goldstein, Patrick. "Fake Movie Reviews Upset Movie Fans." *Los Angeles Times*, October 14, 2002.

Ho, Sally. "Cyberbullying on the Rise in U.S." Associated Press report, July 27, 2019.

Johnson, John R. *Everydata: The Misinformation Hidden in the Little Data You Consume Every Day*. Brookline, MA: Bibliomotion, Inc. (2016).

Kornblum, Janet. "Cyberbullying Grows Bigger and Meaner." *USA Today*, July 15, 2008, p. 3–A.

Marcus, Gary, and Annie Duke. "The Problem with Believing What We're Told." *The Wall Street Journal*, September 1, 2019, p. 5–C.

Parker, Kathleen, "Internet Freedom Sacrifices Decency." Syndicated newspaper column, August 30, 2009.

Poitras, Colin. "Where Predators Gather." *The Hartford Courant*, May 22, 2007, p. 1–A.

"Social Media Guidelines." *Associated Press Stylebook and Briefing on Media Law*. New York: Associated Press (2019), pp. 365–382.

Solove, Donald J. *The Future of Reputation: Gossip, Rumor, and Privacy on the Internet*. New Haven, CT: Yale University Press (2007).

Steinmetz, Katy. "The Instagram Challenge." *Time*, July 22, 2019, pp. 46–51.

Steinmetz, Katy. "The Real Fake News." *Time*, August 2018, pp. 28–31.

Stewart, Daxton R., ed. *Social Media and the Law*, second edition. New York: Routledge (2016).

Sweeney, Marlisse Silver. "What the Law Can (and Can't) Do About Online Harassment." *The Atlantic*, November 2, 2014.

Tanaka, Jennifer. "Foiling the Rogues." *Newsweek*, October 27, 1997, p. 80.

Index

Kennedy, Caroline 128
Kennedy, Edward M. 132
Kennedy, John F. 77, 111, 126, 132;
    assassination of 61, 262
Kennedy, Robert F. Jr. 219
Kennedy-Onassis, Jackie 133
Kerner Commission 78–9
Kerrigan, Nancy 108, 115
Kerry, John 104, 232
Keyes, Edward 88
Khmer Rouge 82
Kierkegaard, Soren 33
Kilbourne, Jean 176
Kind Campaign 271
King, Rodney 61, 108
Kissinger, Henry 159
Klaidman, Stephen 70
K-Mart 264
KNBC 141–42
Knight, Devon 154
Knight-Ridder 4
Knobel, Beth 111
Kohut, Andrew 222
Koran 150
Kreusler, Bobby 272
Kroc, Joan 14
Kroc, Ray 14
Krouse, Sarah 251
Ku Klux Klan 218
Kurtz, Howard 39, 70–1, 125, 135

La Dolce Vita 133
Lady Gaga 37, 170
Lambert Pharmaceutical Company 182
Lambeth, Edmund 35
Lang, James M. xv
Lang, Thomas 60
Lanza, Adam 152
Lanza, Ryan 152
Larson, Charles 216
Latino audiences 7
Lauer, Matt 238–39
Laufer, Peter 229
Law & Order 170
law school xv
Lawrence, Jennifer 270
lawyers, confidentiality and 203
Leahy, Patrick 103
Leavenworth, Steven 64
Lehrer, Adrienne 103
Lembke, Daryl 136
Leno, Jay 62–3, 174
lesbian students, and bullying 269–70
letters of recommendation 246
Levin, Mark R. 55
Levitt, Thomas 176
Lewinsky, Monica 108, 126

LGBT audiences 7
libel law 125
liberal bias of news media, accusations of 54–57
libertarianism 6, 31–2
Liberty Mutual 175
Liberty University 92
libraries 40
license plates, anti-abortion 230–31
license plates, Confederate Heritage 231
license plates, controversial 230–31
licensing of public relations professionals 200–201
Lichter, Robert 54
Liddy, G. Gordon 108
Life 61
Life on the Tenure Track xv
Life Savers 169
Limbaugh, Rush 56, 174, 229, 272, 275
Lincoln Memorial 182
Lincoln, Abraham 114, 182
Lindbergh, Charles 108
LinkedIn 245
Lippman, Walter 38
Lister, Joseph 182
Listerine 182–83
litigation PR 203–204
"little white lies" 26
Loews Complex 179
Lonchar, Kenneth 244
"Long Train Running" 233
Longview Daily News (Washington) 34
Looking Out For #1 36
Lopez, Jennifer 170
Lordan, Edward L. 204
Los Angeles Clippers 62
Los Angeles Herald Examiner 107
Los Angeles Kings 62
Los Angeles Police Department 61, 115
Los Angeles Times 62, 103, 136
lotteries, advertising of 177–78
lotteries, debates over 219
lottery debate, South Carolina 222
lottery winners, privacy of 138–39
Louisiana State University 270
Louisville Courier-Journal 156
Love, Dennis 83
Lowe, Herbert 79
Lying: Moral Choice in Public and Private Life 35
Lynch, Jessica 81–2

MacDonald, Jeffrey 87–8
Machiavelli, Niccolo 31, 33
Macon Telegraph (Macon, GA) 83
Madeira, Rebecca 196
Madison Square Government Entertainment 175
magic bullet theory 49
Make-a-Wish Foundation 272–73
Malcolm, Janet 88, 104

public service journalism 51–2, 62
Pulitzer Prizes 77, 81, 82, 83, 107, 156, 181, 250
Pulitzer, Joseph 6, 72, 153
push polls 224
Puterbaugh, John 98

quid pro quo 110, 191, 239
Quinnipiac University Poll 225
quotations 101–104
quotes, manufactured 198–99

racial harassment 240–41
Radcliffe College 140
radio 11
Radio Act (of 1927) 49
Radio Television Digital News Association
  5, 50, 53, 60, 260
Code of Broadcast News Ethics 10, 51, 70,
  97, 113–114, 147, 157
Ragin v. New York Times 172
Raleigh News & Observer 83
Ramm, Leandra 270
Rampton, Sheldon 39, 199
Ramsey, Dave 176
Rand, Ayn 35–36
Rape, Abuse, and Incest National
  Network 269
Rather, Dan 14, 73, 150
rational decision-making 27
Rawls, John 29–30
readbacks 101–102
Reagan, Ronald 17, 71, 78, 115, 220, 233
reasonable consumer standard 167
Rebecca Blood's Weblog Code of Ethics 260
Red Lobster 169
Reddick, DeWitt C. 148
Reddit 16
Redford, Robert 150
Reed, Alistair 82
Reed, Donna 87
Reese's Pieces 169
Regret the Error 148
Reich, Robert 73
relativism 34
religious harassment 240–41
Republican Party 54, 55
restaurant reviews 173–74
resumes, honesty in 243–44, 253–54
retractions 147–51, 160
Reuters-Ipsos 13
revenge porn 272
Revlon, Charles 176
Reynolds, Sam 141
Rice, Pat 54
Richardson, Jerry 238–39
ride-alongs 134, 141–42
Rieder, Rem 112

Riegle, Donald 126
The Right to Privacy 128
Ringer, Robert 36
Roberts, Cokie 74
The Rockford Files 169
"Rockin' in the Free World" 234
Rocky Mountain News 132, 154
Rolling Stone 151
Romano, John 37
Roose, Kevin 92
Roosevelt, Franklin D. 2, 78, 126
Roosevelt, Theodore 77, 227
Root, Robert 3
Rose, Charlie 238–39
Rosenberg, Howard 9
Rosenfield, Arnold 33
Rotary International 30
Rotenberg, Marc 250–51
Roth, Zachary 60
Rothman, Stanley 54
RottenTomatoes.com 262
Rousseau, Jean-Jacques 33
Royko, Mike 105
Rubel, Steve 245
"Running on Empty" 33
Rutgers University 270
Ryan, Jack 126
Ryan, Jeri 126
Ryan, Karen 60
Ryan, Paul 234
Rychlak, Ronald J. 177
Ryder Trucks 117–18

Sacco, Justine 271
Sacramento Bee 63, 83
Sacred Congregation for Propagating the
  Faith 217
Salomon Smith Barney 251
The Salt Lake City Tribune 90–91
Salvanto, Anthony 224
sample sizes in polling 225
San Francisco 49ers 19
San Francisco Chronicle 76, 136
Sander, Pam 156
Sanders, Sarah 151
Sandy Hook Elementary School 152, 261–62
Santa Barbara News-Press 91
Santos-Garza, Venessa 105
Sarandon, Susan 232
Sartre, Jean-Paul 35
Saturday Night Live 232
Savage, Dan 269–70
Scalia, Antonin 262
Scaramucci, Anthony 151
scare tactics 220
Schaffer, Ayal 100
Schmitz, Jonathan 58